GORDON SMITH

PRINCE OF WINGERS

TONY SMITH

BLACK & WHITE PUBLISHING

First published 2011
This edition first published 2012
by Black & White Publishing Ltd
29 Ocean Drive, Edinburgh EH6 6JL

1 3 5 7 9 10 8 6 4 2 12 13 14 15

ISBN 978 1 84502 439 0

A CIP catalogue record for this book is available from the British Library.

Typeset by RefineCatch Ltd, Bungay, Suffolk
Printed and bound by Nørhaven, Denmark

CONTENTS

ACKNOWLEDGEMENTS

My sincere thanks to everyone who gave up their time, with an extra-special mention to the following:

Lawrie Reilly for writing such a magnificent Foreword and for being there for my dad – especially in his later years; Campbell Brown, for his belief in the project, and all at Black & White Publishing for their understanding, tolerance and support; Bridget Hill for her informative tales from the 1950s; Rod Petrie and all at Hibernian FC for their great assistance and genial hospitality and Tom Wright for his photographic expertise. My Aunt Rachel and Uncle Oliver, for the many hours of informal chat, regaling precious, sentimental and complex stories detailing the 'early days' in particular and my Uncle Brian and Aunt Maureen for tales 'from the jungle'.

Brian Cunnison from Qatar, for your help in obtaining 'problematic' team listings, scores for the appendix and for the use of personal photos; Mike G, for always listening well and clarifying 'challenging arguments' so selflessly and deftly and my Cousin Francis, for providing beneficial particulars. John Gibson and David Hardie, from the *Edinburgh Evening News* for 'difficult to find' facts; Craig Nelson, library manager at *Scotsman Publications* for such sterling labours and Willie McEwan, treasurer of the Hibernian former players association for acting as a liaison on behalf of certain former players. I am also extremely indebted to James Mathews from *Sky TV News* for providing hitherto inaccessible numbers; and I would like to convey my gratitude to all the people who took time to reflect on the long and illustrious career of my late father in the accolades section and in the main story itself.

Regarding permission to reprint articles and quotes in the book, I am thankful to *The Sunday Post*, the *Scottish Daily Mail*, the *Sunday Mirror* group, the *Toronto Telegram, Northern and Shell Media Publications, The Press and Journal*, the *Detroit Free Press*, the *Daily Record/Sunday Mail* and the *Edinburgh Evening News*.

For being sympathetic to my often impulsive and protracted absences from the social scene during the writing of this book, I would like to show appreciation to all my friends, especially the vegetarian-cuisine loving chef extraordinaire Richie Duncan, Sincy, Martin A, Rod M, Andy S and Andy C, as well as the fabulously nicknamed Sleaze, Dub, Spanish Derek, Wilf and Robbie 'M & S' Jamieson.

I am exceedingly grateful to my children – Danaan, Cale, Marly and Jaiden for putting up with my obsessive behavioural patterns and frequently long drawn out disappearances in the last couple of years in order to research and complete this biography. I hope the book will remove any lingering need for solace and be a great source of knowledge and information about your grandad for you to peruse in forthcoming years.

Finally for being so accommodating, a special mention has to go to Louise, my confidante, my sweetheart and during the writing of this book; my researcher, editor, assiduous proof-reader and toughest critic when required. For this and everything you do for me, I thank you from the bottom of my heart.

Tony Smith

FOREWORD

BY LAWRIE REILLY

Gordon Smith was my boyhood hero. As a youngster, I passed him on the street in Gorgie once after a Hibs–Hearts game. I invited Gordon home for his tea but he politely declined. He was to be a regular visitor to my home in the years which followed.

When I made my first team debut for Hibs against Kilmarnock at Rugby Park, I played inside right. My right wing partner was Gordon Smith and I thought that I had died and gone to heaven. I spent the whole game plying Gordon with the ball and, as always, he made excellent use of the possession which came his way, as we won 4–3.

Gordon and I were both members of Hibs legendary Famous Five of course and, it's no secret that I scored more than my fair share of goals as we won three league titles in five years. Let me make it clear, though, that I wouldn't have scored half as many goals as I did, if it hadn't been for the immaculate service provided for me by Gordon Smith. Our championship winning side was full of good players. I dare say that some of us may even have been worthy of being termed great. There was no doubt among us, however, as to who was the best player at Easter Road. In a team of stars, Gordon Smith reigned supreme.

Gordon and I were also colleagues at international level. Gordon should have won many more caps than he did. You would have to ask the Scottish selectors why he didn't because when they chose to omit Gordon, it made no sense to anyone but them. The intermittent nature of Gordon's Scotland career gave some people in the media the excuse to question his pedigree. That was nonsense and, to the joy of everyone at Easter Road, Gordon proved it to be so on our 1955 summer tour to Austria, Yugoslavia and Hungary. Gordon captained the Scottish team in two of these games and played brilliantly in all three of them. In the process, he laid to rest the myth that he couldn't reproduce his club form in the dark blue of his country. In the game in Vienna, an Austrian fan who couldn't cope with seeing his team outplayed, ran on to the pitch and tried to attack Gordon. I got myself between Gordon and the intruder and protected my old pal until the police arrested the culprit and led him from the ground. After the number of times that Gordon had used his skills to look after me on the field, it was the least I could do.

I was proud to have Gordon Smith as a team mate and a friend. He was quite simply the best player I ever played with or against – the ultimate footballing artist. It seems incredible that it has taken seventy years since Gordon's first game in a green and white jersey for his life story to be told in print. However, it has been well worth the wait. No-one is better placed to chronicle Gordon's glittering career than his son Tony. He has undoubtedly done a superb job. Tony, your dad would have been proud of you.

I commend *Gordon Smith Prince of Wingers* to all Hibs fans and to all other football followers. Whenever he stepped onto a football field, be it at Easter Road, Tynecastle, Dens Park or the national stadium at Hampden, Gordon Smith displayed elegance and excellence in equal measure. Some players are top class. Gordon was world class and Tony's book succeeds magnificently in reminding us of that fact.

Lawrie Reilly

INTRODUCTION

THERE WERE players who did wonderful things on a pitch – and then there was Gordon Smith. Smith, Easter Road idol without a shadow of a doubt, stands out as the most revered and illustrious player in the chronicles of Hibernian Football Club. Gordon Smith – the quintessence of football artistry. Some fans say he was the most poised, balanced and cultured player that Scotland has ever produced. Certain people say that he was as good as English winger Stanley Matthews – everyone else says that he was even better.

To some, including the legendary Jim Baxter, he was the greatest player in Scottish football history, the epitome of the old-fashioned winger, hewn from Scottish oak. His skill and ball control brought him many an admirer with the non-modern-day epithet, 'the Gay Gordon', his nickname during his heyday. The most famous of the renowned Famous Five, Gordon was one of the greatest right wingers the game has ever seen, with a talent that will remain vivid for as long as most observers retain anything that might be described as a memory.

A consummate professional, he turned down an extremely lucrative offer from Matt Busby and the mighty Manchester United in 1946. A blank cheque was put on the table on many occasions by Newcastle United – with Hibernian chairman Harry Swan always scoffing at the mere idea of a transfer. Many other teams tried their best to sign him, including Aston Villa, Tottenham Hotspur, Arsenal and Italian club Fiorentina. They all tried to capture him for their own but to no avail. For eighteen years, boy and man, Gordon gave his heart to Hibs.

For Heart of Midlothian, he won the Scottish League Cup and the League Championship within *nine* months of arriving at the illustrious club in August 1959. Smith – still the only player to win the League with both Edinburgh teams – was a Hearts supporter as a boy, with the likes of Tommy Walker and Alex Massie as his heroes. Although the Gorgie supporters did not hold him in as high regard as the Hibs or Dundee fans did, they certainly warmed to his grace and panache for the two seasons he played at Tynecastle – especially in that glorious first trophy-winning season.

After signing for Dundee in 1961, Smith played in what was arguably his finest ever team – and certainly theirs: the League Championship winning side of 1962. They went on to be the European Cup semi-finalists the following year, securing Smith's god-like status in the eyes of those dark blue followers.

As for representing his country, he did so on thirty-nine occasions, from schoolboy caps to Scottish Football League caps, from Select XI matches to full internationals. But it wasn't until 1955, when made captain, that he really excelled and showed his best wearing national colours.

However, there can really be only one team that stands out for this golden boy of Scottish football – Hibernian. To Hibernian Football Club he gave his best years, from a youth of sixteen to a near veteran of thirty-five – his prime years; and what a prime it was. He is revered as much today as all those years ago, when he epitomised everything that was good about the club during and just after the war; and then especially in the championship winning trio of sides and the European Cup season where he reached the semi-final for the first time. Smith was, for want of a better word, sensational and he instigated sunshine on Leith for eighteen glorious seasons.

Gordon Smith was the first superstar of Scottish football. His dark brooding good looks and his legendary fondness for the Côte d'Azur, New Orleans jazz music and fast cars made him appear more like a movie icon, a dazzling matinée idol of the halcyon post-war era.

In total, he scored over 400 goals and played almost 1,000 games. No other Scottish player in history can point to a record like that, just as no other Scottish player in history has won three League Championship medals with three different clubs, nor followed this by playing in the European Cup the following season.

He certainly gave a great deal of pleasure to many, many people. Such personalities are no longer involved in the great game – and that is a momentous pity. Above all else, those who saw Gordon Smith play football consider him to be one of the greatest players of all time.

ACCOLADES FOR GORDON SMITH

Gordon Smith was world class. Simply the best player I ever played alongside
.
Lawrie Reilly

Along with Bobby Charlton, Gordon Smith is the most graceful footballer I have ever seen. **Sir Matt Busby**

Gordon Smith was my hero. **Jim Baxter**

I was always going to remember my home debut for Hibernian anyway, but to be on the same pitch as Gordon Smith [playing for Dundee in what would turn out to be his last appearance at Easter Road] was the icing on the cake.

My Hibs supporting family told me that under no circumstances was I to tackle or upset their hero in *any* way, shape or form – or they'd never speak to me again!

Just playing on the same pitch as Gordon for ninety minutes that October afternoon was the biggest thrill I could get. I remember he smiled at me and it sent a shiver down my spine. **Pat Stanton**

Gordon was a very skilful player with two great feet lovely balance and pace.
Eddie Turnbull

Gordon Smith was a blend of Tom Finney and Stanley Matthews. **Jimmy Greaves**

My dad wanted to call me Gordon Smith Strachan after the great man – but my mum wouldn't let him! **Gordon Strachan**

In five decades in the game I have never met anyone who was more of a gentleman than Gordon Smith. I had such a high regard for him; he would give me encouragement and assurance continually [at Dens Park]. As for his football ability – he was outstanding. **Craig Brown**

A wonderful player, absolutely terrific. **Paddy Crerand**

He should have been Brazilian! Gordon Smith was just fantastic – a world-class player. He was one of Scottish football's legends and my idol as a boy.
Alan Gilzean

A Scottish and Hibernian legend I wish I had the privilege of seeing him play at Easter Road. A player whose immense talent we can only catch a glimpse of on film footage and with skills that would easily stand up in the modern game. A rare man who should have been celebrated more internationally and who, more than anyone, takes a proud place in the history of Hibernian Football Club. **Fish**

Our father rated him the best footballer he'd ever seen and he had that in common with most folk who watched the Hibs team of the late forties early fifties. Gordon's record of five championships with three separate Scottish clubs, none of them being Rangers or Celtic, will never be equalled. **Craig & Charlie Reid (The Proclaimers)**

Old boys go starry-eyed in pubs in Edinburgh when you mention his name – those who saw him reckon that he really was one of the greatest players of all time.
Irvine Welsh

The most beautiful present anyone has ever given me, apart from my children, is the 1952 Gordon Smith Testimonial Programme. **Dougray Scott**

The most graceful winger that I've ever seen in my life. **Bernard Gallacher**

He was an absolute legend. He was really talented, but was also one of the best dressed footballers of his era. He looked great every time you saw him. Fantastic style about the man. **Frank McLintock**

He was one of the finest players of all time. The things he could do with that ball were amazing. **Tommy Preston**

I received a telegram from Gordon wishing me all the best on my debut for Hibs. Imagine that: a telegram from Gordon Smith. **Jimmy O'Rourke**

Gordon Smith was the star man in the Famous Five side that won three league titles and is still the club's record goalscorer; a phenomenal feat considering he was a winger. My granddad was fortunate enough to have seen him play for Hibs and, by all accounts, he was simply brilliant. The fact that Lawrie Reilly names him as Hibernian's greatest ever player speaks volumes about what he achieved in the game. **Ian Murray**

It was to Tynecastle I sometimes ventured to worship Gordon Smith. **Peter Marinello**

Gordon Smith was a paragon of all the football virtues. To me he was a symbol of everything that is good in football. **Ian Ure**

If any footballer could be said to have it all, then Gordon Smith is the man. **George Young**

He was the finest footballer I have ever seen. **John Grant**

Gordon was one of the most glorious players of all time and I played right behind him at right-half. **Jimmy Thomson**

I played alongside Gordon during his days at Hearts. He was a class act – a very classy player. Everything Gordon did on and off the park was quality. I don't think there will ever be another Gordon Smith. **Gordon Marshall**

In all the teams I've played for, Gordon was the best player I have ever seen. **Bert Slater**

I am proud to say that I played beside Gordon during his time at Hearts. He was an artist on the right wing, a fantastic player, with fantastic balance and two great feet. **Jimmy Murray**

I was Gordon's understudy for a time at Easter Road, and when Gordon couldn't play due to an injury, you could hear how disappointed the crown were when my name was called out! This represents simply how much the supporters thought about him. Gordon was so helpful to me, always taking time to talk to me, and he was someone I always looked up to – such a lovely gentleman. **John Fraser**

A tremendous player – his goal average is the best I have ever known for a winger. **John Ogilvy**

Unbelievable to play with – a very special talent. **Hugh Robertson**

Gordon Smith was associated with Hibs' greatest years. An immaculate player, who was the leading light in our famous attack. **Harry Swan**

If ever there was a player my father [Tom Hart, Hibernian owner/chairman from 1970-82] could have been said to idolise it would be Gordon Smith. During conversations with other football people about the pros and cons of different players my father would always maintain Gordon Smith's record of games played, goals scored, assists and sheer entertainment value were unsurpassed anywhere. **Alan Hart**

I was in the company of Alex McLeish, the manager of the club at that time, when I met Gordon Smith and the three other surviving members of the Famous Five at a function at Easter Road Stadium. Alex McLeish is no mean judge of character and he remarked that even then, Gordon Smith had a special aura about him. I have been fortunate enough to know Tony Smith in recent years and know what a labour of love this book has been. **Rod Petrie**

Gordon Smith is my favourite player of all time. **Douglas Cromb**

I was fortunate enough to see Gordon Smith play for Hibs, Hearts, Dundee and Scotland. He is in my opinion the best outside right I have ever seen in my life. It was also a great honour to be his friend. **Pilmar Smith**

Gordon was a player who commanded the respect of all football fans on and off the field. **Hugh Shaw**

Gordon Smith was the perfect gentleman of football. **Wilson Strachan**

Everyone knows my association with the club as someone who wants Hibernian to play its part in the lives of all its supporters. Many, many supporters have told me that Gordon Smith was the best player they ever saw playing for the club. I understand that he was a truly special talent and the fact that this book has been written by his son will provide a very special insight into the life of the man and the legend. **Sir Tom Farmer**

Winning championship medals with three different clubs – outside the old-firm of Rangers and Celtic – is the greatest individual accomplishment in the entire history of Scottish League Football. **Bob Crampsey**

I tried many times to get Gordon Smith to talk to *Scotsport* about his wonderful career and although always friendly and chatty, he never said 'yes.' **Arthur Montford**

A pure footballer, he was akin to Dalglish and Messi in making the game look simple. One of the greats of all time. **Archie Macpherson**

From my press pew at Easter Road, within earshot of several rows of paying spectators – the cynics, hyper-critical of today's game, would say of what they were watching: 'They couldn't lace Gordon Smith's boots.'

How very true, alas. The Prince of Wingers was the prime example, on and off the field, to aspiring footballers. Too few followed it. **John Gibson**

They should have re-turfed Easter Road on Gordon's retirement, as it will never be the same again. **Rex Kingsley**

The great misfortune for Gordon was that he had to play his football in Scotland. Had he played in Spain, for instance, he would have been every bit as spectacular and effective as Di Stéfano, Puskas and the rest, because like all our real ball artists, he was too often the victim of tough tackling.

Harry Andrew

My favourite all-time Hibs player would be Gordon Smith. Hibs have had a lot of good players, but none of them even come close to him. He could use both feet, used to score goals for fun and had great vision and skill. The biggest compliment I can give him is that I would say he was a better footballer than Pele – I really believe that.

Wattie Robb, life-long Hibernian FC fan

INVESTITURE

To all the little boys who stood in the rain and sleet and snow in green and white scarves, Gordon Smith was a weekly ticket to paradise.

Brian Meek

LEGEND

Hibs were once due to play Aberdeen at Easter Road. In the company of many thousands, we made our way through blizzard conditions and worsening snowstorms to reach the ground. Alas, the snow was about a foot deep and the game was abandoned, before the turnstiles even opened. Then, the winter sun came out and manager Willie McCartney decided to wash Gordon Smith's number 7 shirt and hang it out to dry in front of the players' tunnel. 30,000 people paid the admission fee just to watch it hang there.

Hibernian fable (source unknown)

PROLOGUE

CHARISMATIC MEN AND SMALL, BORROWED BOOTS

DAY 1

IT WAS on Sunday, 27 April 1941, with Britain in the midst of hostilities against Germany, that the sanguine fifty-three-year-old Hibernian Football Club manager, Willie McCartney, had a secret assignation with a young football player from Montrose, on the austere north-east coast of Scotland. The Dundee North End junior he was hoping to sign had absolutely no idea that travelling up from Edinburgh with McCartney was club chairman Harry Swan and director Tom Hartland. Their intention was simple – to come back to the capital with the Montrose teenager's signature.

The late April air was clear and it was a fine day in the city as the black cab sloped down to Waverley Station and into the bustling concourse, which was a hive of activity, bursting to the seams with a throng of Army and Air Force personnel. Several evacuee school children clambered to be in close proximity to the train doors with their forlorn faces unsparingly kissed through gaping carriage windows. Their collars were saturated with their mothers' tears as they hugged each other tightly, while big sisters wailed uncontrollably. Little sisters appeared distraught, as 'whistle time' neared, grasping their copies of the *Beano, Rainbow* and the *Dandy.* The desolation in their eyes was evident for all to see, as the three football men made their way to Platform 13 and the north.

The previous weekend, Willie McCartney had stood and gazed in admiration while a sensational sixteen-year-old named Gordon Smith – playing football for a local junior elite team – tore apart a Hibernian/

Heart of Midlothian select in Dundee. In particular, his own centre half, the celebrated Bobby Baxter, playing directly opposite Gordon, had been left floundering on countless occasions. The game, with the best talent from the Tayside region playing against the Edinburgh professionals, heralded the opening of Dundee team Lochee Harp's new ground, Beechwood Park.

An article in the *Sunday Express* the day after the match reported that the youngster had actually signed for Hearts. The Hibernian boss was up in arms, losing his equanimity, briefly, until it was corroborated that this was just 'press talk'. Nevertheless, he learned that the Hearts chairman, who was also the interim manager, had offered Smith a trial for Monday, 28 April. Knowing that Hearts' visitors at Tynecastle Park that evening for the rearranged New Year's Day derby were to be none other than McCartney's own Hibernian side, he had to act fast to obtain Smith's signature.

He knew after the press 'scare' that he didn't have long to get the sixteen-year-old, making it clear to his chairman that he would like to make the youngster a direct offer.

For an assortment of reasons, the day before the derby game was the only suitable time for the men to journey to the east coast. Willie McCartney was determined to travel up, unannounced, and persuade the young man to change his mind about the Hearts trial by offering him signing terms there and then, with no test for Hibernian necessary. By showing up with his chairman and a club director, the plan was to assure and illustrate to him how serious they were in their quest. All McCartney knew was that Smith lived in Montrose and he hoped that locals would direct him to where the youngster's house was once they arrived at Montrose station. This rendezvous was very ambiguous indeed. A little fraught with impending apprehension, McCartney trusted that the youngster wouldn't be out for the day or their trip would be wasted and their hopes to sign him dashed.

Accordingly, it was a pretty edgy trio that settled into their seats. Willie McCartney, Hibernian manager since 1936, wore his immaculately polished brogues and black homburg hat, dark suited with his buttonhole garlanded with a fragrant red rose. He unobtrusively smiled at his equally well-tailored covert emissaries, as the Aberdeen-bound express eased through Princes Street Gardens. Harry

Swan ordered the men three large whiskies – purely, it goes without saying, to calm their nerves!

The gents sat down to a light lunch in the dining car beneath darkening skies, surveying the scene, which included a mass of river boats, air activity and an enormous barrage balloon flapping vigorously in the breeze from an industrious Hawes pier at South Queensferry. The thundering iron horse powered across the Forth Railway Bridge prior to roaring on through Fife and onward to Dundee. As the steaming engine, pulling a dozen or so wagons, arrived growling into an austere Jute city station, slightly late as a consequence of an obstruction on the line beyond Kirkcaldy, German planes were flying across the North Sea, heading in their direction.

Fifty miles away in a quiet Montrose alley, Gordon Smith waited, impatiently as always, for his sister to come out of Sunday school so that he could then take her and his two younger brothers to the park to kick a ball about. Football was all he lived for. Although he'd scored two goals the day before in the Dundee North End game, it was more than likely his last for the Tayside club, as he'd been offered a trial for Heart of Midlothian in Edinburgh the following day as they went up against their mighty city adversaries, Hibernian. He couldn't wait to play, quietly confident of becoming a signed Hearts player.

A few of his Dundee North End team-mates had made it clear they wanted to make the trip to Edinburgh for Monday's game to offer their support and Gordon felt extremely humbled by this gesture.

He had hardly slept for days since being informed about the trial. He was desperate for Monday to arrive, daydreaming moves in his head, anticipating that he'd be able to replicate them for Hearts in the looming 'big game'.

A tad gullible, he had even thought he was registered for the illustrious club just because he had shaken hands with the Hearts chairman and manager, Mr Alex Irvine, directly after the showpiece match the previous weekend. Mr Irvine had spoken with him in the pavilion at Beechwood Park after the game.

An appraisal in a Sunday newspaper confused him even more, with a headline that read: 'HEARTS FIX THREE GOAL CENTRE'. The paper also said the sixteen-year-old Gordon was already seventeen and that Mr Alex Irvine was actually called William!

As Gordon and his siblings played in the park, suddenly the whine of the air raid warning siren rang out, forcing the youngsters to scuttle off to the nearest Anderson shelter, gas masks dangling around their necks. Hostile attacks by Junkers medium bombers were commonplace here. Montrose, and in particular its airfield, had been targeted on many occasions in the year and a half since the onset of the war. Unfortunately, there had been some civilian casualties, as well as a few downed German planes. Only the previous month, four people, including a newborn baby, had been killed as the enemy aircraft dropped bombs in an attempt to destroy the railway bridge. One wayward bomb landed on the beach close to where Gordon lived, another demolished a house owned by a local boat-builder in Thomson Terrace; Gordon's Aunt Jessie lived in the Terrace, only two doors down from the now crushed building.

After just under an hour, it was safe to venture out to the streets again. Gordon and his siblings resumed their game in the park but soon returned home, as by then a soggy acrid mist, a North Sea haar, was rolling in, displacing the sun and turning what had been a glorious spring day into a damp and miserable one.

The Aberdeen bound train at last pulled into Arbroath but it was to go no further. It came to an abrupt halt, as the haze embroiled with dark smoke suffocated the platform. The guard informed everybody that there had been some damage done by the Luftwaffe up the track near to Ferryden. Willie McCartney's first thought on hearing this news was to hope no harm had been done to Montrose itself, especially to the young lad he was planning on signing!

Immersed in choking murkiness, the rumble of distant simmering thunder preceded the 'all-clear' drone from the local air-raid station. All and sundry congregated at the platform wondering what they were going to do next. When these sirens blared, they always evoked despondent, gut-wrenching feelings for the Hibernian boss, as his only son was serving with the Royal Scots regiment in France.

It was then that Bristol-born Tom Hartland had the idea, instantly supported by McCartney and Swan, to phone the local police in Montrose. They could say who they were and ask if they knew of Gordon Smith, and if so, could they get the youngster to meet them in a local Arbroath hotel, The Seaforth, which the men were acquainted with.

As only a short time had passed since the town had been under attack, the local constabulary were otherwise engaged. After a nerve-racking period, Harry Swan finally managed to get a call through. The local Montrose police were too busy to help personally, but they gave him the number for the John Dye Lemonade Factory, as they knew this was adjacent to the well-known junior player's address in the Piccadilly area of the town.

The chances of John Dye being at his place of work on a Sunday afternoon were very slim indeed but as luck would have it, he had gone along to 'check things out' after the air raid and was minutes away from leaving for home when the telephone rang. On the other end was Willie McCartney asking him to tell Gordon that he would like to talk to him.

Gordon, who had not long arrived back at his house, was having a discussion with his parents about the alarming eventuality that the war was growing worse, when suddenly there was a knock at the door. Gordon opened it and standing there was the lemonade factory owner from next door. John Dye conveyed his news: 'There's a gentleman on the telephone wanting to speak to you. He says his name's McCartney, a Mr Willie McCartney.'

The Dundee North End junior's primary thoughts were, what could be so important as to disturb his Sunday, his day off? But he grudgingly went with John Dye to his factory and picked up the telephone. He had no idea Willie McCartney was the Hibernian boss and thought it was some kind of hoax call at first, until the stranger managed to convince him that he was who he claimed to be!

Down the line, McCartney asked the teenager if he would like to sign for Hibernian. Gordon wasn't in the least bit excited with the prospect but after some deliberation, reluctantly he agreed to go to Arbroath to hear more of what he had to say. McCartney was relieved he'd got him to agree to meet, as his negotiating skills weren't as dependable on the phone as they were in the flesh.

Gordon was astounded by the news – completely taken aback at first. This was the opposing team to Heart of Midlothian, the team he was due to play a trial for tomorrow night, the team he thought he'd signed for just a few days ago! Although not an inveterate Hearts fan, he did have reasonably strong feelings for them and this man represented their greatest foes.

Back at his house, he asked his parents what he should do. His father, a more fervent Hearts fan, weighed up the situation and said it wouldn't do any harm to go along to the hotel to see what they had to say.

So Gordon drove to the Arbroath hotel, right at the edge of the North Sea, taking up the offer from John Dye to borrow his 1938 Austin Seven. He sported a navy blue trench coat loaned from his cousin Jimmy, as he didn't possess a coat befitting such a grand meeting, according to his unassuming mother.

The discussions at the hotel were short and sweet. McCartney introduced himself, as did Swan and Hartland. At first, Gordon thought these men were a bit of a nuisance. The Germans with their bombs to begin with and now a delegation from Hibernian FC, of all teams, disturbing his Sunday!

Quite unexpectedly, he was bewildered and captivated by the flamboyant McCartney. He listened with intrigue, greatly impressed by Harry Swan and Tom Hartland's aspirations for the club. Most importantly, they told him that, unlike Heart of Midlothian, Hibernian Football Club had no need for a trial after seeing him in action last week.

'It would be nonsensical, we know what you can do. I've assessed you already and don't want to procrastinate here. We would like you to sign these documents and we'll also offer a £10 signing on fee,' were McCartney's words to the youngster.

In 1941, £2. 8 shillings and 5 pence was the basic minimum wage, so, in the youngster's eyes, this was a vast amount of money to be offered, although by all accounts, there were transactions of much higher sums being paid elsewhere at the time. The comparative amount today would be about £1,000.

He listened intently as the deferential Willie McCartney assured him that the football club would look after his interests. There was no time to waste; they wanted the astounding Dundee North End centre forward to make his debut in tomorrow night's Edinburgh derby, the very match in which he was supposed to be playing a trial for his prized Heart of Midlothian against Hibernian!

McCartney needed an answer, and fast.

Although Gordon was extremely keen, with his world being transformed in a matter of minutes by this most enigmatic of men, he hesitated in signing anything as he thought he ought to be a little more incredulous. Knocked for six by the news, he was becoming increasingly conscious of the fact that he would be a Hibernian player as opposed to a Heart of Midlothian player.

Even if in his heart he obviously still favoured the maroon to the green as a distant fan, Gordon was swayed towards Hibernian for a number of reasons, not least the fact that these men had travelled all the way up to see him on a Sunday, of all days. It was not normal practice in 1940s Britain to do any kind of business on the Sabbath.

What proved to be the deciding factor was that Hibernian wanted to sign him there and then without the need for a trial. Nonetheless, he wasn't going to sign a thing yet. He gave his word that he would be signing for Hibernian but out of respect, would at first like to convey the news to his father and would like him there when he signed. After some reluctance, McCartney agreed on meeting up again in Edinburgh before tomorrow's game, imploring the young man not to mention this engagement to anyone but his family, for fear of Heart of Midlothian being made aware of the imminent sensational deal. He had hoped Smith's signature would be safely tucked away in his pocket today but, instead, the men hastily made arrangements for Gordon to be accompanied by his father down to Edinburgh to meet the next afternoon in the North British Hotel (now the Balmoral) a mere two hours before kick-off.

As an excited Gordon drove John Dye's car back to Montrose, McCartney, Swan and Hartland left the hotel in a local taxi heading for Dundee to catch a train south. They were delighted with their afternoon's acquisition – in all but signature. McCartney had his misgivings but was also of the opinion that Gordon would be true to his word and sign tomorrow in Edinburgh. McCartney would later convey to Gordon that all three men, whilst musing upon the eventful day, offered an appreciative prayer to John Dye and his lemonade factory!

Gordon's exhilaration was tinged with a little melancholy – he found it quite challenging to come to terms with the reality that he was going to be a 'turncoat' to his heroes; but after swiftly reminding himself of the Hibernian manager's words, his ambivalence soon diminished, as he had been so impressed by Willie McCartney's warmth and charismatic fervour.

On arriving back at his home, he informed his father, mother and his siblings of the events, where, understandably to begin with, everyone was completely taken aback by the news. Hibernian Football Club was not too highly thought of in the Heart of Midlothian supporting Smith household!

Once Gordon had explained in great detail how Willie McCartney had influenced him right from the beginning with his impeccably delivered speech, and that he felt this football club was right for him, everyone was completely supportive. The family talked excitedly of nothing else until very late that evening.

DAY 2

Early the next morning, Gordon and his father got a bus to Arbroath and then a train to Edinburgh's Waverley Station, making their way to the North British Hotel through an entrance directly from the station. Gordon had never seen such an amazing place before, with crystal chandeliers and hanging baskets adorned with oriental looking flowers. The opulent hotel lobby was packed with all ranks of the services and a multitude of foreign voices echoed in the considerable foyer. A gathering of delightful looking young ladies, impeccably dressed and with perhaps a courtesan or two amongst them, headed into the tea-room and caught the teenager's eye.

Not long after the Smiths arrival, the Hibernian party arrived, a glowing Willie McCartney almost bounding up to Gordon, shaking his hand, knowing the most audacious piece of business he'd ever done was about to come to fruition. Present were Gordon and his father, Willie McCartney, Harry Swan and the unpretentious Tom Hartland.

Without delay, they adjourned to a first floor room reserved by the club where tea and sandwiches were already on the table. At precisely four o'clock, Gordon, watched over by an ecstatic yet tearful father, signed on the dotted line to applauding and shaking of hands. With his £10 signing on fee, Gordon Smith felt like a millionaire.

Hibernian had not only offered Smith a fee of £2 per week, which was the wartime standard (though notably below the basic wage of the time), but also a fillip of a hefty bonus package. Another assurance thrown in the deal was that he would get a job as a riveter at the Henry Robb shipyard in Leith, where both trainer Hugh Shaw and his assistant Jimmy McColl were already working in a part-time capacity. Once business, tea and sandwiches had been dealt with, a lively Gordon sprang up the staircase for the briefest of visits to the twin room reserved by the football club for him and his father, to drop off a couple of overnight bags and safely place the £10 cheque into the drawer of a mahogany writing desk.

As kick-off time was fast approaching, the original Famous Five headed across town to the Gorgie district of Edinburgh to prepare for the early evening match. Already congregating at the corner of McLeod Street was an assortment of players and officials from the Leith team. McCartney introduced Gordon to Hugh Shaw, Jimmy McColl and club directors – the legendary seventy-nine-year-old Owen Brannigan, James Drummond Shiels and Sean Martin. Once inside the Tynecastle Park ground, the young man was quickly ushered to the away dressing room and introduced to his new team-mates, shaking their hands one by one as they arrived. He listened intently as Willie McCartney, Hugh Shaw and Jimmy McColl told him what they wanted of him.

The next player to appear in the Hibernian dressing room was another youngster making his debut – seventeen-year-old Inveresk Thistle player Bobby Combe, who had played with Gordon in two Scottish schoolboy international matches. Willie McCartney had incredibly signed him that same day as well as Gordon, just a couple of hours before at his house in Lorne Street before driving to the North British Hotel! Combe had been regularly training at Tynecastle, with Hearts also very keen on signing him. This was another cloak and dagger raid by the Hibernian manager.

The two teenagers, already reasonably acquainted, were to become great friends in the years that followed and the emergence in the dressing room of an additional debutant, seventeen-year-old Jock Weir, brought the average age down even further. Jock had been a Leith Renton player and was the only one of the trio who hadn't been expected to sign for Hearts.

Before leaving for Edinburgh earlier in the day, Gordon's father had contacted Dundee North End Football Club and asked if someone from the faction who was coming to support Gordon could bring down his son's boots; with all the hectic goings-on in the last couple of days, Gordon had forgotten to pick them up from his locker at the club.

Twenty minutes before the Edinburgh derby kick-off, word had circulated the inner sanctum of Tynecastle Park that Hibernian had signed 'that lad from Dundee North End', along with 'young Bobby

Combe'. As a consequence, the Hearts chairman and acting manager wasn't best pleased, to say the least. He had been looking out for the arrival of Gordon and had presumed the youngster had lost his nerve and decided not to turn up.

Alex Irvine had been all set to welcome the Dundee junior to the home dressing room and had the paperwork ready for him to sign after the match had finished, having an intuitive feeling that he would give a virtuoso performance. How right he was, but he was too late. The virtuoso performance would be *against* his team! The Hearts supremo angrily confronted the gleeful McCartney, words were exchanged and the air turned blue with profanities, with Willie McCartney exclaiming that Gordon was a signed up Hibernian player now and there was nothing Hearts could do about it.

McCartney had been the Heart of Midlothian manager from 1919 until 1935, until the arrival of Irvine, who had sacked him. Irvine's reasons have never been revealed. Some said he wanted to bring in a 'track-suited' manager, others suggested there was a religious clash. Willie's father, John, had also been the Hearts manager before him so, unquestionably, you could be sure there was no love lost between the now Hibernian boss and Irvine.

Chairman Irvine along with his fellow Heart of Midlothian directors had been picking the team since the departure of Frank Moss the previous July, and although they'd advertised for a new coach, nothing had come to fruition as yet. Moss, renowned former Arsenal and England goalkeeper and youngest-ever Hearts manager had resigned due to reasons attributed to the war and returned to England after leading the team to second place the previous season.

Unbelievably, to add to the already electric atmosphere and with kick-off only minutes away, there was no sign of the Dundee North End party or Gordon's boots! A very embarrassed Gordon explained the situation to Jimmy McColl and the assistant coach brought three pairs out of the kit-bag for the youngster to try on. Although he struggled with them, they were all too small. When it was made clear to Gordon that was all the spares they had with them, he winced as he had to squeeze his size nine feet into size sevens! With the small, borrowed boots, he jumped up and down in the dressing room, trying to mould his feet into them, and stamped the ground to get used to them. Gordon kept on jumping and stamping but his feet were compressed and painful as the youngster ran out onto Tynecastle Park and the somewhat sparse crowd cheered.

Monday, 28 April 1941, Tynecastle Park, Edinburgh
Attendance: 3,004
Heart of Midlothian 3, Hibernian 5
Heart of Midlothian: Willie Waugh, Duncan McClure, Archie Miller, Jimmy Phillip, Jimmy Dykes, Tommy Brown, Tommy Dougan, Tommy Walker, Alec Massie, George Hamilton, Robert Christie.
Chairman & Acting Manager: Alex Irvine
Hibernian: Jimmy Kerr, Davie Shaw, Alex Hall, Sammy Kean, Bobby Baxter, Willie Rice, Jock Weir, Trialist (Bobby Combe), Junior (Gordon Smith), Willie Finnegan, Tommy Adams.
Chairman: Harry Swan, Manager: Willie McCartney

With the score at 2–1 to the home side at the half-time interval, Hibernian came out all guns blazing at the start of the second period. The list below shows the sequence in which the eight goals were scored that evening.

1–0 (Hearts) Tommy Walker
1–1 (Hibs) Gordon Smith
2–1 (Hearts) Tommy Walker
2–2 (Hibs) Bobby Combe
2–3 (Hibs) Tommy Adams
2–4 (Hibs) Gordon Smith
2–5 (Hibs) Gordon Smith, penalty
3–5 (Hearts) Tommy Walker, penalty

As the players left Tynecastle Park, the 'Junior' was surrounded by well-wishers and team-mates alike, including the Dundee North End contingent, size nine boots in hand; they had arrived just in time to see the final twenty minutes, their unpunctuality attributed to a delayed train. Smith, an instant hero with the fans, had scored a hat-trick on his debut for the Leith side and was being lauded as 'something special' after producing such an outstanding performance. To this day, he is still the only player for either team to have scored three or more goals on their debut in an Edinburgh derby match.

Hibernian's new number 9, along with his father, were applauded as they jubilantly walked away from Tynecastle Park, heading for a bus to take them to the east end of Princes Street, close to their hotel, on this alluring spring night.

Harry Swan and Willie McCartney beamed with joy, so exuberant that they almost sang their goodnights to the youngster, teasing that their new star centre forward should wear those small, borrowed boots for every game! As the teenage sensation walked off into the distance, the two venerable gents were seen wryly smirking, west-end bound, to quietly celebrate not only a famous victory but a day they signed an awe-inspiring footballer right under the noses of their great antagonists Heart of Midlothian. This was to be a very memorable wartime bank holiday indeed!

As Gordon and his father strode along Ardmillan Terrace, a young boy aged about twelve came up to Gordon and, after congratulating him on the evening's success, graciously asked him if he'd like to go back to his parents house for something to eat. Gordon, slightly taken aback, listened, intrigued by the invitation and was conscious of the youngster's slightly dejected appearance after he courteously turned down the offer. It would later transpire that the boy was none other than future Hibernian and Scotland legend, Lawrie Reilly, who signed for the club five years later and, like Gordon, scored on his debut. Whilst Gordon turned down young Lawrie Reilly on this occasion, he was to visit the Reilly family's home on many occasions in the years ahead and the two's friendship was to last a lifetime.

A regrettable fact from the game was that the meagre crowd of 3,004 was the lowest ever recorded in the twentieth century between the Edinburgh teams in any first-team match, be it a cup-tie, league game, friendly or otherwise, with many future reserve and youth team games attracting a lot more through the turnstiles. The reason was thought to be because it was played on a Monday night, postponed from the originally intended date of New Year's Day 1941, when undoubtedly a much larger crowd in the region of 30,000 would have attended and seen history in the making. As the years rolled by, the fortunate 3,004 paying punters would no doubt bask in the glory of saying: 'I was there when Gordon Smith made his debut!'

On arrival at the hotel, Gordon and his father had a light supper before heading up to their fourth floor accommodation. Gordon peered out from behind the blackened shutters, seeing no lights shining in a wartime Princes Street, although it was still a hive of activity under a setting sun that illuminated the guarded skyline. It was after his exhausted forty-nine-year-old father wished him goodnight that the enormity of what had happened became clearer to the new Edinburgh football hero. Yesterday, he was playing in a public park with his siblings, looking forward with a little trepidation to the trial for Hearts against Hibernian – now he was in a lavish five-star hotel in Edinburgh after scoring three goals against the team he was due to have a trial for! It seemed like a dream because it had all happened in a mere thirty hours – from the beginning, with the meeting in Arbroath, until now, eleven o'clock at night on the following day. Monday, 28 April 1941, he thought to himself, was a day he would never forget!

As he lay in bed, the realisation dawned on him that his feet ached and suddenly felt very raw. This was the first time since removing the small boots after the game that he was conscious just how uncomfortable and swollen his feet were. It was only now, as the jubilation had ebbed, that the pain came to his attention.

Aware that his father had fallen asleep almost instantly, Gordon had one inflamed foot already out of bed and, with muted movements, yet hurriedly, he proceeded across the room to the writing desk where he had earlier placed the £10 cheque for safe-keeping. He cautiously opened the drawer. It was still there, alongside headed hotel notepaper and envelopes, and it still said to pay Mr Gordon Smith £10. After staring at it intently for a while, he carefully picked the cheque up and held it in his hands, then briefly smelt it – still finding it difficult to believe that this enormous amount of money was all his! After a few minutes contemplation, he eventually returned it to the drawer, creeping back to his bed, where he too fell into a deep sleep almost as soon as his head touched the pillow.

DAY 3

Father and son were half way through breakfast early the next morning when they were delighted to catch sight of the smiling Hibernian manager making his way into the grand hall. McCartney acknowledged them from a distance, waving a left arm high in the air. His bonhomie was evident for all to see as, apologising profusely, he edged, bumped and nudged the ornate dining-room furniture in order to reach their table.

'Look at this!' he roared, as he prised a newspaper from his inside jacket pocket, waving it vigorously while still a few tables away from the Smiths. 'Look at this paper!' his voice resonating even louder, as he progressed ever closer.

Together, they looked. So did most of the other guests, too. The bemused diners couldn't help but notice this sizeable man, smiling like a Cheshire cat. Gordon looked at the paper; his name appeared not only on the back page but also on the front!

'Absolutely wonderful,' McCartney excitedly bellowed through the dreary Tuesday morning dining room.

Before their trip home, arrangements were made by the deliriously high-spirited manager for Gordon to return to Edinburgh at the end of the week, to train and get acquainted with his new team-mates. Although this had been the last game of the 1940/41 wartime Southern Football League season, with Hibernian finishing third, the Summer Cup (a creation of the visionary chairman, Harry Swan) was impending and the Leith side wanted to be the inaugural victors. Both Gordon and his father, who were still a little stunned by the recent events, sat for most of the train journey back to Montrose in an emotionally exhausted but contented silence.

It was still under forty-eight hours since this incredible story had begun when they arrived back at the costal railway station, which had not long re-opened. Desperate to return home, they took a short cut through the old coal yard, passing spruce and pine trees just beginning to bloom. With a skip in their steps, they strode purposefully down the sunny vanilla-scented cobbled backstreets to 13 Piccadilly, next to the lemonade factory, where a euphoric gathering of friends and family had assembled. Gordon Smith had experienced an incredible forty-eight hours, but it was just the start of an even more astonishing journey.

1

THE EARLY YEARS

CHRISTINA SMITH (née Sutherland) gave birth to a baby boy at 7.20am on Monday, 26 May 1924, at 4 Spring Valley Terrace in the Morningside district of Edinburgh. Proud husband Robert was ushered in from an adjacent room and the parents announced to the world that the newborn baby was to be called Gordon – so named because of his father's exploits in the Gordon Highlanders during the Great War. According to the midwife who delivered him, he had strong legs – like those of the Heart of Midlothian hero, Bobby Walker. Maybe it was true or maybe she was just making conversation. Nevertheless, those legs, strong looking when born or not, were to bring joy to millions of football fans in years to come. While some babies' demeanour could be described as slightly pallid, Gordon exuded a hale and hearty gleam when he was pushed in his pram and shown off to the genteel but somewhat prying ladies of the locality.

There were no trappings of grandeur, however, and just because he was born in the leafy suburb of Morningside didn't mean that his family was rich and well to do; unfortunately, that couldn't have been further from the truth. They lived in rented accommodation and his father was in and out of work on a recurring basis as a grocer – taking on any odd jobs when they became available.

Gordon was the third child born in the family, after Robert Junior and William, and he was to stay in Edinburgh until a couple of months short of his second birthday when, in March 1926, the family decided to move to Montrose in Angus. The reason behind the move was primarily because his father was in search of regular employment, but also because they had relatives in the Montrose area.

They briefly moved to a small house in the coastal town's Blackfriars Street but this only lasted until June when, one sunny morning, the roof caved in. Broken wood and stone crashed down within touching distance of the two-year-old Gordon and his siblings but, amazingly, no one was injured. After this bolt from the blue, the family were then housed at 7 Mill Lane, a short distance away, and it was here another sibling for Gordon (yet another boy, Stanley) was born in early July 1926.

This new house was structurally sound, with no roofs falling in, and Gordon was to spend seven years there, until he was nine years old. He grew very fond of Mill Lane and had many happy memories there.

His earliest football moments involved kicking an orange, a stone or a tennis ball (almost any small object that could be kicked) around the house and neighbouring streets, emulating his two elder brothers. The January of 1929 saw the arrival of a sister for Gordon, Rachel, to complement the ever-increasing number of children in the Smith family, and that August, aged five, he started school at the local Southesk Primary.

Within months of attending school, his teachers, Miss Nairn and Miss Smith, had mentioned to Gordon's mother that he was a 'very deep' child – always very thoughtful. Miss Nairn went further and perceptively continued: 'I think he's going to be something – I think one day he'll possess his own personal motor car.'

By 1930, Gordon's incessant kicking of a tennis ball against the corrugated shed at Mill Lane became legendary to the locals, who would comment on the amazing dexterity and control for one so young. By kicking the ball at the shed, he never knew which direction it was going to come back at him and this he loved, as it kept him guessing. The ball would ricochet right, left and centre at random, and the young Gordon enjoyed the challenge. The more he practised the better his control got.

For the next couple of years, as he settled into primary school life, football started to become an obsession. Although no formal games were played, he would join in the customary school playground rituals of twenty- and thirty-a-side kick-about matches. Jumpers for goalposts were the norm, with Gordon eager each day for the break-time and lunch-time bells so he could participate with fellow class-mates in this free-for-all.

He would watch with envy as the older boys played for the school team on Saturday mornings, returning, naturally, to the corrugated shed for more personal training, hour after hour after hour. At the school sports day in 1931, he deviated from his beloved football to win the three-legged race with class-mate Edith Crowe – and all the other races he took part in! His speed and general athleticism were becoming almost as renowned as his football ability.

Because of this speed and, as his mother put it, 'his canniness', he was sent on some covert family errands. With the aid of his two elder brothers, Gordon would skulk along to the coal yard at the docks, under the cover of darkness, and 'retrieve' some coal, expertly place it on a porter's trolley and wheel it back to Mill Lane. Times were hard and those winter nights could be raw!

After the Easter school holidays in 1932, he began playing organised football for the school team. He was the smallest and youngest, but without doubt the fastest and the most skilful, even at the tender age of eight. His proficiency with a ball was noticeable by everyone who witnessed him play. He only had matches on Saturday mornings for the school team and so every other week, he was able to go and watch his local heroes, Montrose, in action at Links Park.

The end of January 1933 saw Adolf Hitler sworn in as *Reichskanzler* (Chancellor) of Germany; little did eight-year-old Gordon and his peers realise the huge impact that this man would have on their lives.

In the summer of 1933, Gordon's grandmother died suddenly and the family were bequeathed a bigger house in the town's Market Street – or so they believed. They moved lock, stock and barrel to number 28 but this was to be a short tenure, as there was much acrimony between Gordon's father and Uncle Walter, who thought the house should be rightfully his. Walter contested the will and, for reasons never quite revealed, he managed to uproot the family of six after an almighty fracas. The young Gordon, feeling a sense of injustice and at an impressionable age, decided he would never speak to his uncle again. So the Smiths were on the move once more, this time to 13 Piccadilly, and this was to be Gordon's last home in the seaside town of Montrose.

A new school year got underway in August, with Gordon beginning primary five and eagerly awaiting the new football season. Along with surprisingly large crowds, he and his older brothers would go and watch the local cricket team in action – often it was nearly dark before everyone headed home. Gordon enjoyed the spectacle of cricket and was fascinated by the complexity of the game – which could be pretty pedestrian one minute, yet turn to blood and thunder within seconds. Quite often some 'victims', who possibly were not paying as much attention as they ought to have been, were hit by the ball clearing the boundary ropes! It was a game that would in time become Gordon's third favourite sport, ranking just behind golf.

On radio and picture house broadcasts that summer were Bing Crosby and Guy Lombardo, but the nine-year-old was more interested in the jazz of Duke Ellington and Louis Armstrong, amongst others. It was solely African-American acts, particularly those from the New Orleans camp, who were to be influential in shaping and inspiring his musical tastes in the years that followed. Gordon and his siblings would often go to the Saturday matinée at the Playhouse Cinema in the town's John Street with *King Kong* being the current draw. The movie *I'm No Angel* ran for months at the King's Picture House in Hume Street, with its star Mae West delivering the iniquitous line, 'When I'm good, I'm very, very good, but when I'm bad, I'm better' – an expression Gordon felt summed himself up as well.

One evening, near the outskirts of town, as darkness was fast approaching, Gordon continued to play football with a gathering of local children. As he retrieved a ball from a field, he stumbled whilst climbing over a fence, catching his upper lip on a barbed wire spike. In excruciating pain, Gordon made it home with the help of his friend Bruce Geddes. Immediately, with a blood-soaked pillow pressed against the gaping wound, his mother walked him the short distance to the local infirmary. Once there, a screaming Gordon was treated by a sadistic nurse who refused any pleas to anaesthetise the affected area. She insisted on stitching the gaping wound there and then! It was only after Gordon's furious mother threatened to take things further with her GP, Doctor Hoyle, who luckily was on duty that evening, that the nurse succumbed to pressure and gave the howling child chloroform to numb the pain. He had six stitches put in that would leave a scar for the remainder of his life.

The winter brought more misery for the family, as Gordon's father was mainly unemployed again, only occasionally working as a chauffeur with the aid of his brother Jim. With this being the height of the Great Depression, there were few jobs to be had with a lot of people in the same position as the Smiths. Twice annually, philanthropist and local business man Noel Johnston would give less fortunate families in the Montrose area a ton of coal – a lovely gesture much appreciated by those in need. Not related, but another Johnston, a district nurse, would also be a help to the Smiths by donating clothes, food and towelling handed out by a local support group in the town. On these occasions, Gordon was always very excited by the gifts – likening them to Christmas day.

The early spring brought some much needed good news, as Louis North, who ran a grocer's shop near the infirmary, gave Gordon's father a job. He also indicated that when he went on holiday or on business trips, Gordon's father was to run the place for him, which would bring a much-needed boost in income for the struggling family.

The Los Angeles, the Washington and Pucci's on North Esk Road were the three ice cream parlours in Montrose that Gordon and his siblings would, on the rare occasion, be allowed to visit. As money was always tight, these treats were savoured. Pucci's was Gordon's particular favourite, as the Italians who owned and ran the shop were very generous with their portions and especially favoured the 'pint-sized footballer' whom they admired when they watched him play alongside their son for the school team.

That summer of 1934 and subsequent summers saw the Smith siblings picking berries at Balgove and Balwylie farms on Brechin Road. This was four miles from their home and Gordon used to cycle to the farms and give his brother a 'backy', leave him there, then cycle back to get his sister and take her. After a long day in the fields, he would repeat the same ritual to get everyone back to the house. The income generated was much appreciated by his parents, and Gordon would often cajole and sweet-talk the younger two in a bid to motivate them; especially troublesome was his little brother, Stanley, an unruly and slightly indolent helper, who was at times more interested in watching the trains go by and was easily distracted.

The *Pathé* newsreels at the Playhouse Picture house that summer were full of news about German Chancellor Adolf Hitler's Nazi party; on 2 August, he became the Führer of the country, although Gordon and his friends again did not appreciate the importance of these political advancements at the time. Less disconcerting, and certainly more entertaining, was the rise of the world famous comedy duo, Stan

Laurel and Oliver Hardy. Gordon would often crease up with laughter at these two fatuous gentlemen as he watched them week in, week out over the winter of 1934. Down the years, he never tired of the silliness and absurdity of their act and would fondly recall many of the storylines.

By this point, although Gordon was improving his football awareness, dexterity and certainly his fitness – with his right foot becoming known for 'blasters'– he knew that his left foot was practically just there for standing on and he wasn't happy with this at all. One evening, after another marathon twenty-a-side match, as the boys were returning to their respective homes, a much older boy from Ferryden came up to Gordon and said he noticed he was hardly using his left foot. The boy offered some much needed advice – to use a sandshoe on the stronger right foot and a football boot on the weaker left foot. He explained that due to the muddy pitches and heavy balls hurting the better right foot, Gordon would be forced to use his left and, in time, it would become stronger and more accurate. Daily, for the next three to four months, Gordon did just that and his control, power and accuracy slowly developed in his 'appalling' left foot, as he had called it.

A few months later, Gordon felt like a king when he scored his first ever goal with his left foot – in his own words, 'a rocket' from twenty yards! In August 1935, he started playing for his first juvenile football club, Bromford Boys Club, an Arbroath youth team. Local businessman Bert Stewart, who ran the Plough Inn public house, would take the youngster to games in his car. He had heard of this rising talent through the community grapevine and had watched Gordon the previous season playing for his primary school team, being impressed enough to orchestrate the signing of the youth to his local Arbroath team. Gordon's sister remembers the publican's car always had an Alsatian dog in it, too – and he would buy ice creams for all the siblings when returning Gordon back to Piccadilly after games.

During this time, the eleven-year-old Gordon also enjoyed going to the Follies theatre in the town's Dorward Road. It was an especially busy summer season with chorus girls, variety acts and comedians becoming ever more popular. *Mutiny on the Bounty* was the smash hit for the matinée crowd and Shirley Temple's 'On the Good Ship Lollipop' infuriated Gordon, whose musical preference was now a certain Thomas 'Fats' Waller.

Gordon's father was at this time working as a part-time postman, as well as doing the odd shift for Louis North, so things were looking up – both at home and on the pitch. In the spring of 1936, whilst still playing Saturday mornings for the Southesk school team and for Bromford on Saturday afternoons, the young Gordon was selected to play for the Montrose Schools Football Association team, alongside future fellow schoolboy internationalist and Preston North End great, Willie Robertson, and Ernie Copland, who was to play for Raith Rovers. A local fruit shop owner in Montrose, Stan Henderson, who was another great admirer of Gordon's ability, broke the news to the young boy one mid-morning. He went to the gates of the primary school and, as the kids were out for break-time and their usual mass-numbered football game, he beckoned some youngsters over to tell them he had something to tell Gordon Smith. When a bemused Gordon was finally prised away from the mêlée, Henderson informed him he had been chosen to play for the select team and gave the eleven-year-old half a crown as a reward for reaching this level. Gordon was ecstatic and couldn't wait until the finish of that school day to run home and proudly tell his parents his news – and, of course, hand over the money to help with domestic costs.

With the growing recognition of Gordon's talent, football was quickly becoming the main fixture in his life. For most primary school children in Montrose, every time it rained and they were sent home – probably due to lack of rain jackets – it meant a trip to the local King's Picture House, which would open to accommodate the masses; at two old pence entry fee, this remained a penny cheaper than its rival, the Playhouse. However, Gordon would predominantly spend the time getting soaking wet with a football in the rain. But despite his increasing dedication to football, Gordon remained an avid follower of the music scene. Fats Waller continued to impress the young Gordon and his current favourite, 'It's a Sin to Tell a Lie', far outweighed the lacklustre Bing Crosby, Benny Goodman, Tommy Dorsey and the like in the youngster's eyes.

2

GAS MASKS, SCHOOLBOY CAPS AND MONTROSE ROSELEA

IN AUGUST 1936, Gordon started high school, not at the state run Townhead High School, but the fee-paying Montrose Academy, after being granted a bursary for his educational and sporting achievements at the Southesk. In his first few months at his new school, his athleticism did not go unnoticed and he was picked to play for the rugby team on a Saturday morning. Although Gordon was extremely fast and nimble and very good at rugby, he didn't particularly like the sport and it took the intervention of football-loving teacher Mr Edward to alleviate the burden, helping Gordon to continue on his road to football glory. Gordon was committed to playing for Bromford on Saturday afternoons, but was also now able to play for the school football team in the morning instead of the dreaded rugby.

There were other hurdles to overcome in the transition to high school. The young Gordon had tried a sneaky cigarette like all the boys were doing but became violently sick; when he was ashen faced after lunch, he admitted to his now favourite teacher Mr Edward that he'd had some draws on a cigarette in the playground. Mr Edward advised him that smoking would be very bad for an aspiring footballer, so Gordon, largely in admiration of his teacher, was never to put another cigarette near his mouth again.

James Edward, along with Peter Clark, Ian Russell and Major Lawrie Kerr, were the four men Gordon later attributed to guiding and nurturing his fledgling football career in Montrose. Ian Russell was headmaster at St Columba's Episcopal Church school in Crieff and would visit Montrose to coach the schoolboys in the afternoons and evenings during the holidays, whilst teacher James Edward would think nothing of paying Gordon's and the other boys' bus fares to away games in the likes of Johnshaven, Stonehaven and Brechin. Peter Clark and Major Lawrie Kerr were also teachers, Clark in Montrose and Kerr in Laurencekirk. Clark, alongside Russell and Edward, ran the school team in Montrose and Kerr was a local selector on the Scottish Schools football selection committee and very involved in the scene.

After his first full year at Montrose Academy, Gordon achieved a certificate of merit from the county of Angus education committee, stating he'd achieved satisfactory progress in the technical course, and gained distinction in Mathematics and Gymnastics.

On younger brother Stanley's eleventh birthday, 2 July, *Pathé* news brought reports of continuing unrest in Germany, as well as the disappearance of famous American aviator Amelia Earhart, known as 'the queen of the air'. Her small Lockheed Electra plane had gone missing whilst flying across the Pacific Ocean as she attempted to circumnavigate the globe. Last contact had been made in Papua New Guinea. Gordon was fascinated by the whole story and had been aware of this 'female pilot adventurer' for quite some time, but became even more preoccupied with her after this ill-fated attempt, perhaps explaining his future love of air travel.

August 1937 saw Gordon continue to play for the school on Saturday mornings but he also started with a new juvenile team in the afternoons, Kirriemuir Harp, located twenty miles southwest of Montrose. Gordon would rush home and grab a jam sandwich for lunch after playing for the Academy team in the morning before cycling inland for the afternoon's match. Kirriemuir Harp played all over the county, so Gordon would simply cycle to wherever they had a match. After cycling back home to Montrose from wherever it was, having played two football games and not getting back until well after teatime, he was quite understandably exhausted!

This training obviously stood him in good stead for the future and all the miles would build up his fitness and powerful leg muscles. Gordon's career was taking off, his skill improving on an almost daily basis, but one thing that was still glaringly noticeable was that he was extremely small for his age. He was aware that his lack of height impeded him slightly in the rough and tumble of a Saturday afternoon, at a time when brawn still counted for a lot.

It was while he was playing for Kirriemuir that Gordon, now nicknamed 'the pocket McGrory' after the sensational Celtic player Jimmy McGrory, realised he had the potential to be a success in football. One day, he walked to the top of Kirrie Hill from which he could see the 'window in Thrums' made famous by J.M. Barrie, the Kirriemuir boy whose *Peter Pan* has earned enduring fame. When he reached the cricket pavilion, the gardener was weeding and Gordon stopped to chat to him, learning how Barrie had returned rich and famous to present the pavilion to his village. The young Gordon was deeply impressed by Barrie's story and went to the local library to borrow books about the famous writer, reading a little each night with a growing determination that he, too, would earn fame.

He worked hard at his football over the winter months, studying methods of the 'stars' of Links Park, mastering dribbling with the ball and toughening up his feet by devising his own tricks. He would place a stone or two into one boot so his foot would hurt and sometimes bleed, but the other foot, pain free, would grow stronger. He would alternate this until satisfying himself he was comfortable with the progress made.

The early spring of 1938 was perishing cold, although when Gordon was informed he'd been selected to represent Scotland at schoolboy level, he was so elated he felt like jumping into the town's local pond, The Curly, and leaping for joy. He would later recall this day to be one of the most pivotal in his long and illustrious football career.

The first international took place at Starks Park in Kirkcaldy, home of Raith Rovers, on 30 April, and it pitted the Scots against the Irish Schools FA. The attendance that day was 9,471 for a 5.30pm kick-off, with the Scottish boys triumphing 5–2 and Gordon scoring a brace – a shot from just inside the box and a header from close range. Lining up alongside Gordon was a young Robert Combe, who became better known as Bobby and would become one of Gordon's best friends. Gordon and Bobby's second schoolboy caps came two weeks later on 14 May, this time in England at Sunderland's Roker Park, with a 1–0 scoreline, again in the Scots favour, cheered on by a massive crowd of 33,897. Gordon's father accompanied him to these games alongside his long-time coach and selector friend, Major Lawrie Kerr from Laurencekirk.

These trips were groundbreaking for the thirteen-year-old. He had never even been to Kirkcaldy before and if he thought that was an experience, two weeks later was an even bigger one! Gordon had been all of two years old the last time he set foot in Scotland's capital and had no recollections of it whatsoever, so when the locomotive puffed into Haymarket and then tunnelled its way through the city to the enormous Waverley Station, he was giddy with anticipation. Upon arrival, as a treat, the group were marched up the famous steps and they thoroughly enjoyed their time waiting for the departure of the train south.

As they enjoyed ice cream wafers, the infrequent Edinburgh sun did its best to shine in their honour. Once they embarked on their second journey of the day, the venture over the border from Scotland into England at Berwick-upon-Tweed resulted in whistling, cheering and great exhilaration. It was quite feasible that none of the youngsters had crossed to England before – certainly, this was Gordon's first experience 'abroad'! His poor mother, although to some extent consoled knowing her husband was travelling with the party, missed her son tremendously and was very anxious until he returned to Montrose. This was the very first time he had spent the night away from the family home, so her concern was understandable.

The enormous Victorian neoclassical station at Newcastle-upon-Tyne captivated the adolescents, as the deputation changed trains for a third time that day, this time to Sunderland. The anticipation was palpable as the boys' minds were filled with the roar of a massive Roker Park attendance the following day, slightly unnerving them. In future years, Gordon would travel to England on countless occasions, as well as Europe and the Americas, but this 'taster' was spoken about for years to come and was never forgotten.

With all hopes of peace being shattered in Europe, Prime Minister Chamberlain ordered that gas masks be provided to all children in Britain. After the Great War, the threat of gas attacks was very strong and the government, fearing that the Germans would use the same tactics, took a firm stance on the matter. Once people were fitted and instructed how to use the masks, they were to be kept close at all times. Gordon's youngest brother Brian, who was two and a half years old at the time, was given a bizarre and quite scary-looking Mickey Mouse mask, as were all children under three. Pupils and even teachers wore masks for lessons if there was a drill on, which made teaching quite difficult but cut out any mischievous chatting at the back of the class.

The boxes with masks inside were despatched throughout the long hot summer and church bells were to toll if the threat of a gas attack was imminent. Whilst waiting for the Führer to release his gasses, the teenage boys of Montrose found a diverse, if not slightly inappropriate use for the masks; possibly not quite what they were designed for but they made great goalposts! For all the millions of masks despatched and the constant requirement of having masks at hand, there were to be no gas attacks in Britain during the course of the war.

In late October 1938, Orson Welles' infamous radio broadcast of H.G. Wells' *War of the Worlds,* signalling the invasion of Martians, moved the war-talk to second place, albeit briefly, when almost everyone who heard it was convinced the planet was under attack from beings from outer space. Gordon and his friends, at a gullible age, found this to be as hilarious as it was terrifying.

The season of 1938/39 was to be Gordon's last for his two teams – the Academy and Kirriemuir Harp – and what a season it was. Gordon outshone everything he'd ever done on the football field before, scoring an abundance of goals at his favoured centre forward position – frequently more than six in a game! On 25 June 1939, with war a mere two months away, fifteen-year-old Gordon Smith left Montrose Academy, a little sad, but mainly with superb memories. He also left with a 'higher education day school certificate', signed by headmaster Mr Cameron, which, though it ought to have secured him a slightly more skilled job, led to his first foray in the workplace – a tomato nursery plant labourer on the dusty edge of town.

On 31 August, the civilian evacuation began, though Chamberlain's announcement at 11.15am on Sunday, 3 September, that Britain was now at war with Germany, was not looked upon as a huge setback by most people, including Gordon. It was thought that 'the war' would be well over by Christmas; little did he or anyone know at the time that a monumental forty-seven million people were to die before peace was declared six years later.

The highlight of this last peacetime summer for a number of years was not the wages Gordon was receiving to help support the family, but the prospect of joining his new football team, Montrose Roselea – a junior team, no less! Furthermore, the smallish Gordon had now grown a few inches in quite a short space of time and his physique had developed greatly, too. On top of that, he was even paid to play football, receiving half a crown signing-on fee and a small weekly wage to augment his labourer's pay. The fifteen-year-old Smith had now left school and was a semi-professional footballer. War or no war, Gordon was having the time of his life!

3

DUNDEE NORTH END

THE RINGING of church bells had ceased, with the intention that they would only be rung should the enemy invade. Furthermore, the war was a mere six days old when France, Australia, New Zealand and Canada joined the Allies, and when Montrose and Gordon Smith had their first German visitor in the form of an aeroplane. The bomber, a Heinkel 111, must have breached the radar and other early warning systems, flying in undetected, as it 'appeared out of nowhere' in the sky near Gordon's Piccadilly home, which was in quite close proximity to Montrose Aerodrome. The aerodrome was obviously the main target for the enemy to attack and disable, and because the war was in its infancy, security measures were possibly a bit inefficient at this point.

The German plane was in fact so low to the ground, seeming to hover directly above the cobbled streets, that Gordon and his younger sister Rachel, who was ten, could clearly see the bristling moustache of the young pilot. Peering out from the side, the even younger gunner was completely visible and could quite easily have machine-gunned the pair if he'd wanted. Scottish football, and in particular the history of Hibernian Football Club, would've turned out quite differently had he been trigger-happy.

Whatever the reason, as luck would have it, the plane kept going, with the gunner giving a slight nod as the plane spun around, as if to say, 'I could've killed you – but you're just a couple of kids in some backstreet,' and onward they flew in search of the aerodrome. Obviously, Gordon and his sister were extremely alarmed by this sighting and quickly ran back home to tell their parents, partly exhilarated, partly trembling.

With its reconnaissance job done, the probable outcome for the pilot and gunner was that they flew back across the North Sea to German soil, as there were no reports of any planes shot down that day. Unfortunately, it was only the beginning. This was just the first of the many enemy planes to visit Montrose as the aerodrome was attacked on multiple occasions with numerous RAF personnel being killed in the sorties, and unfortunately some civilians dying too, as a result of stray bombs.

A few weeks later in October, days after the HMS *Royal Oak* was torpedoed and sunk by a German U-boat at Scapa Flow, the first German aircraft was shot down over Britain after being attacked by fighters over the River Forth.

Towards the end of the year, Gordon visited Dens Park in Dundee with older brother Robert and, along with nearly 5,000 in the crowd, they witnessed Dundee defeat their Tannadice Street rivals, Dundee United, 4–2. The attendance could have been a lot higher but police had turned away many people for not carrying their gasmasks. Gordon didn't have his but had somehow managed to get past them!

As 1939 ended and 1940 emerged from the mist, the realisation slowly dawned on Britain that the war was going to last longer than had first been expected, with rationing beginning on 8 January. Montrose, with its aerodrome, was now continually under attack from German bombers, Junkers 88s, the marauding Heinkel 111s and Dornier flying boats. They would emerge from the North Sea, sweeping down in search of bridges to destroy and enemy aircraft to disable. A detachment from 269 Squadron (General Reconnaissance) would enable an Anson or a Spitfire to retaliate and pursue them until they had been felled or were out of British air space.

The winter of 1940 was the coldest since 1890, so cold in fact that the water at Montrose dock was frozen over for weeks on end. Football parks were unplayable and Gordon grew increasingly frustrated by the week, but still managed to practise by continually kicking tennis balls back and forth against a wall. Any wall! When the thaw arrived and football started again, he was eager and ready to continue battle for Montrose Roselea and scored a record number of goals that spring.

On 10 June 1940, as Italy declared war on Great Britain and her Allies, Sir Winston Churchill's famous 'collar the lot' proclamation created trepidation and concern throughout the Italian community in Britain.

There were stories of innocent families being woken up by police in the dead of night and all the males aged over sixteen being led away. Mercifully, the Montrose Italian community, including the Puccis and the Fortunatos, were treated more civilly, yet interned nonetheless. Whilst most Italians from the Scottish community spent the war in large camps at Glenbranter in Argyll, Patterton in Renfrewshire, and Doonfoot in Ayr, the smaller Fife camps at Aunsmuir in Ladybank and the Bonnytown working camp near St Andrews became home for the Montrose Italians.

Gordon was quite vociferous in showing his annoyance with Churchill's decision, as he had become quite friendly with the families over the years and he was well liked by them, not only for his footballing prowess. Once the males had been interned, it was left to the grandmothers, mothers and daughters of the families to continue to run the family businesses as best they could.

Once again, Gordon's younger brother Stanley's birthday, 2 July, was important. Yet another global event took place on this date in 1940 – but it was to be much worse than Earhart's disappearance three years earlier. A Blue Star Line ocean cruiser, the SS *Arandora Star,* carrying many German and especially Italian internees and POWs, en route to Canada, was torpedoed and sunk by a German U-boat just off the coast of Ireland with 486 of the 734 Italians on board dying by injury from the blast, drowning, or as surviving eye-witness accounts recall – the worst death of the lot – being burned alive by the scummy hot oil which gathered on top of the icy water after gushing from the fallen liner. This news reverberated around the country, with much hatred and disgust aimed at Churchill and his government from all the Italians (and many British) remaining in Britain; the fact that some relations and close friends of the Montrose Italians had perished on the cursed liner brought even more misery to the women whose husbands, sons and fathers had only recently been apprehended for no other reason than being Italian. Gordon got caught up in the whole business and whilst understanding Churchill's reasons, he definitely had a soft spot for the immigrants and was very much against their arrests, internment and deportation in principle.

As the summer progressed, however, more and more attacks by German Heinkel bombers took place in and around Montrose, and Gordon slowly began to accept that maybe Churchill was right to a degree. Perhaps he had been looking at the bigger picture when he made his decision on the internment – but Gordon still felt ill at ease over the decision.

As the Italians moved out, the Poles moved in. The Polish troops were stationed at Montrose and with their suave good looks, honest hard-working demeanour and affable charm, they soon became well liked by the locals – especially the ladies! Gordon befriended some of the men, who were very good footballers and some of them even helped out with coaching at Roselea.

The Playhouse and King's Picture House remained open and were busier than ever. When air raid sirens sounded, most people would scurry off to the nearest shelter, but some avid movie-goers took their chances – not wanting to miss a crucial part of the film – and stayed seated in the dark, smoky arena. Gordon watched films with stars such as Betty Grable, Lana Turner and Rita Hayworth, as well as his perennial favourites, Laurel and Hardy, but *Rebecca* was Gordon's favourite at the time. Alfred Hitchcock's first American film starring one of Gordon's favourite actors, Laurence Olivier, and admirably supported by Joan Fontaine, had Gordon captivated by its psychological, gothic presence. The thriller fascinated him so much that he went to see it on a number of occasions.

Musically, the summer of 1940 would once again be dominated by Glenn Miller and his band – but Gordon would have none of it. He really didn't enjoy Miller's music. 'When the Swallows Come Back to Capistrano' by the Ink Spots was his then favourite and he was listening more and more to African-American acts, such as Louis Armstrong, Fats Waller and the Mills Brothers.

Bob Miller was the man instrumental in the Dundee North End signing of Gordon in the close season of 1940. The then secretary of the Dokens was made aware of the youngster's ability while he was still playing on Saturday mornings for Montrose Academy and cycling the twenty plus miles to play in the afternoon for Kirriemuir Harp. By the time Dundee North End had authorised the procurement of new players, Gordon was plying his trade for Montrose Roselea and had left school. Miller had a journalist friend who broached the idea of signing for Dundee North End to Gordon and he seemed interested. Gordon had already played in a challenge match for North End's great rivals,

Hillside United, impressing greatly and scoring an astonishing nine goals, but Miller hoped to pip them and Forfar Celtic, who were also on his trail, for his signature.

Dundee North End had been scheduled to play Forfar East End in a Scottish Junior cup-tie at Forfar's Station Park. Miller and his friend arranged for the sixteen-year-old to have a trial and when his contingent arrived at the ground, Gordon was already there, standing on the terracing wearing short trousers and his old Montrose Academy blazer.

Miller told Dundee North End chairman Jock Davie that he was looking at this diminutive youngster as a possible new striker and the North End chief was slightly incredulous. But what a debut the striker had, scoring five goals in a famous win, and the look on the chairman's face had turned from astonishment to bewilderment! He and Miller, along with the coaches and backroom staff, were on cloud nine.

Gordon was ushered to an office at Station Park and offered both professional and amateur forms – however, he was told he wouldn't get a signing-on fee if he signed the professional form, as the club had little money. Without hesitation, Gordon signed the professional form and everyone left Station Park a little delirious that late summer afternoon.

Dundee North End had signed Gordon Smith for the start of the 1940/41 season and he was delighted to play for the well-respected and renowned junior team, earning 6s. 6d per game. His day job was changing, too. He had now left the tomato plant nursery on the edge of Montrose and was working as an agent at the Liver Insurance Company in the town's Castle Street. His boss, Donald Bain, was also teaching the youngster to drive so he could do his 'insurance scamming' more proficiently! Gordon found the driving lessons to be quite straightforward and in a matter of weeks he was driving his boss's car on his own. Since June 1935, driving tests had become compulsory in Britain, but in the hot summer of 1940, with no tests available and all the examiners assigned to working for the government in a fuel rationing capacity, Gordon never actually passed an official practical test. Like many others during the course of the war, a loophole existed, so if you were proficient enough and reasonably adept behind the wheel, you were able to receive a valid driving licence. Lucky Gordon didn't even have to pay the ten shillings for the licence documentation, as this and his insurance were covered by the generous Mr Bain.

Right in the middle of the Battle of Britain, in October 1940, Montrose suffered severe aerial attacks with bombs being dropped daily – this was to be the worst month for casualties during the war. Five bombs struck Sunnyside Royal Hospital, a requisitioned naval vessel was sunk in the harbour and the Chivers jam factory was severely damaged, creating an overwhelming odour of mixed fruit jams that would linger in the air for days. In great numbers, Junkers 88s flew in very low along the high street and a few civilian casualties were reported. It was a mentally demanding time to play football – an extremely testing period to concentrate on anything for that matter – but Gordon continued to sparkle week in and week out on the football pitch.

As the season progressed, Miller and Davie asked the Dundee FC chairman, Mr Galloway, to put Gordon on provisional forms to secure his services when peacetime resumed. Whilst junior football carried on, Dundee FC had withdrawn from the North Eastern League due to incurring severe financial losses, thus enabling Dens Park to be requisitioned by the Decontamination (Food) Service, but the chairman and his fellow directors still had their offices and attended to business at the club. Incredibly, when they searched the offices and stock rooms at Dens Park, they couldn't find any forms. Obviously, they hadn't deemed it a necessity to order any more whilst the war was on. It would be another twenty-two years before Dundee FC finally managed to entice Gordon to the club – and it took three further attempts.

4

SIGNING FOR HIBERNIAN

GORDON PLAYED for Dundee North End throughout the cold winter of 1940 and into 1941, scoring goals by the dozen and creating just as many chances for his team-mates. After a junior select game on the evening of 19 April, a 3–2 win against a Hibernian/Heart of Midlothian select when Gordon scored all three goals against the renowned internationalist Bobby Baxter, Heart of Midlothian were on to him. Gordon had shot up several inches in the last year and while he had been recognised previously as a very fast, talented but smallish youngster, he was now very fast, talented and well above the average height for his age. North End gave the west Edinburgh side permission for him to play in a trial against rivals Hibernian on Monday, 28 April – the Edinburgh Spring holiday. This was to be the last league game of the 1940/41 campaign, which had been originally arranged for 1 January but was postponed due to adverse weather conditions.

The very next morning, Sunday, 20 April, a report appeared in a national newspaper saying Gordon Smith had 'so impressed' the Hearts' chairman that he had signed him at Beechwood Park's pavilion directly after the match had ended, and the young Gordon actually believed he had! In his naivety, he thought it was possible that by agreeing a trial and shaking hands with the Heart of Midlothian chairman, Alex Irvine, the deal was done. It must have been true if it was written in the papers, he thought. Perhaps Dundee North End organised it? Mind you, the paper also stated that he was seventeen when he was in fact a mere sixteen years and 328 days!

He was so deliriously excited with the prospect of turning out in the trial for Hearts against Hibernian at Tynecastle that he could barely sleep. He was a fan of Hearts, with the likes of Alex Massie, Tommy Walker and previously Barney Battles, Jr, as his heroes. He had, in particular, vivid recollections of Battles, the Musselburgh-born Scot who extraordinarily was capped by both Scotland and the USA.

The quite incredible story of what happened next has already been documented – the sensational move by Willie McCartney of travelling up to Angus on the Sunday, then securing Gordon's signature for Hibernian with a £10 signing-on fee the following day. Gordon drove a borrowed car to meet with Hibernian FC officials, wearing his cousin's borrowed coat, and scored three goals on his debut with borrowed boots!

After the two days that changed his life, Gordon still couldn't quite believe what had happened and that he was a Hibernian player. Nevertheless, the first thing he did was offer the £10 signing-on fee he received to his parents. They were deeply grateful but declined this most generous offer, telling him it was his and to save it for a 'rainy day'. Instead of depositing the cheque into a bank, he decided to invest it with a gilt-edged National Savings Certificate. He grew particularly fond of National Saving Certificates and would continue to use this form of investment throughout his life.

For the time being, he continued to work part-time as an insurance agent whilst travelling down to Easter Road a couple of times a week for training. Sensationally, amidst Gordon's itinerancies between Montrose and Edinburgh in early May, the German deputy Führer, Rudolph Hess, an expert pilot, flew a Messerschmitt plane solo from Norway to Scotland and navigated to within thirty miles of his intended destination, parachuting to a field near Glasgow. He was hoping to meet with his 'friend', the Duke of Hamilton, whom he'd met previously at the 1936 Berlin Olympics. He was intent on informing him he had a very generous 'peace offer' in his pocket but was ascertained to be mad and carted off to prison, much to the embarrassment of Hitler.

Gordon had some compassion for Hess and had hoped, possibly still with his youthful angst raging, that he would be listened to at the very least and given a fair hearing. Gordon believed that Hess was genuinely trying to make peace and deep in his heart, he also hoped this would put an end to the hostilities, so life in Britain could return to normal again.

Glasgow's shipyards on the Clyde and principally Clydebank had been decimated by the bombs of the Luftwaffe just weeks prior to Hess' landing, killing 528 people in Scotland's worst-ever civilian disaster. The news was censored at the time, but when leaked reports of the enormous death toll and further hundreds seriously wounded emerged, this severely weakened the German's bargaining powers in the eyes of the majority of the Scottish (and the rest of the British) people. The timing of Hess' 'flying visit' could have been better.

Football continued in earnest and in May 1941, the famous Stanley Matthews arrived in Glasgow – with his boots – as a 'guest player' for Rangers at the Charity Cup Final, helping them win 3–0 at Hampden Park against Partick Thistle. Matthews was to be the first of a number of famous English players who would turn out for Scottish teams during World War Two, with Matt Busby and Jimmy Caskie following shortly after to play for Hibernian. Frank Swift played in goal for Hamilton, Stan Mortensen for Aberdeen, Bill Shankly for Partick Thistle, and Tommy Lawton played one match for Morton whilst on his honeymoon!

Gordon knew it would be only a matter of time before he would have to live full time in Edinburgh but he didn't know when this would be, so he made sure that his last months in Montrose were as buoyant as ever. Now a regular local hero, he would continue to practise his physical mantra – keeping the ball up for hours and hours without it touching the ground in the pursuit of perfection – and would regale his new Hibernian team-mates with many happy reminiscences about Montrose life. For instance, his hilarious tale of local saddler Willie Praine and Gordon's neighbour, the lemonade factory owner, John Dye: 'Why was Willie Praine?' he would ask. 'Because he saw John Dye!' And at this he would fall about almost crying with laughter! His team-mates didn't find it as funny until he told them that Mr Praine and Mr Dye were real people, they really did exist, as did another local luminary, 'Hug the coast', aptly named because he would continuously walk the ten-mile circuit around Montrose basin and surrounding countryside until dropping to the ground in utter exhaustion!

During May at Easter Road, with the introductory Summer Cup a matter of weeks away, all the talk at training focused on the legendary Liverpool FC player, Matt Busby. Rumour had it he would be signing for the Leith side in June, as he was to be billeted to the Borders town of Kelso by the Army. But this excitement quickly gave way to disappointment for Gordon as, despite his sensational debut, after training with his new side for six weeks, he was dropped for the initial Summer Cup game at Parkhead against Celtic on Saturday, 7 June, as Hibernian ran out 5–3 victors. In the next two matches, the young Smith still couldn't force his way back into the team, but after suffering two narrow defeats, he was brought back in for the away tie at Shawfield in Glasgow against Clyde. Trailing 2–1 from the first leg, three Hibernian goals in a mere eight minutes helped bring the aggregate score level to 5–5. Gordon scored one of the goals, whilst the rumours were correct and Matt Busby made his debut supplying Smith with the pass for his goal.

At the play-off at neutral Ibrox Park, Gordon was on the scoresheet again as Hibs ran out 2–1 winners and the semi-final at Tynecastle Park now beckoned. A solid Hibernian performance saw Smith suffer a mild concussion in a narrow 1–0 win against Dumbarton with the solitary goal scored by Arthur Milne.

The fixture at Hampden Park was the concluding game in all competitions for the 1940/41 season. It was the Summer Cup final and it saw Hibs pitted against Rangers. Bob Hardistry from Wolverhampton Wanderers had joined Hibernian and Jimmy Caskie, who had just signed from Everton, got picked ahead of Gordon for the final. Hibs went on to defeat Rangers 3–2 and hold the cup aloft. The eleven men chosen to play received ten war savings certificates each for their efforts.

Only the day before, Friday, 11 July, Hibernian's left half Sammy Kean had got married and his young wife Maisie wasn't too happy about her new husband playing football in Glasgow the following day. After Hibernian FC won the battle, she reluctantly accepted her fate of being a football widow – a mere twenty-four hours into her marriage! Sammy Kean would, in due course, become one of Gordon's best friends in and out of football – a friendship that lasted for both men's lifetimes.

Missing out on a place in the final was a huge disappointment for Gordon and irked him throughout his career. Even though he knew Caskie was a star player for Everton, he still felt it was unjustified that he was dropped after playing in three wins in a row in which he scored twice. Smith, alongside fellow disappointed squad members Gallacher,

Anderson, Cummings, Gilmartin, Flemming, Cuthbertson and Adams, sat in the Hampden Park stand, although none of the others was quite as miserable as the seventeen-year-old.

Gordon's first short season at Hibernian ended with him sitting watching the final, wallowing in self-pity and utterly dejected. The statistics prove he may have been justified in venting his youthful anger, as he'd certainly not had too bad a start to his Hibernian career by any means!

Played:	4
Won:	4
Hibernian Goals scored:	12
Goals conceded:	7
Goals scored by Gordon Smith:	5

Gordon felt physically sick and although he wanted to head back to Montrose, he had to endure the final from the side-lines with the rest of the non-playing Hibernian squad. He had seriously contemplated walking out and heading back to the North East, as he was so utterly dejected, but calmed down a little after he'd telephoned home. Once again, John Dye and his lemonade factory would be the catalyst and the saving grace. Gordon spoke with John Dye to see if his father was in. Luckily, he was, and following an emotional chat, Gordon decided to stay, for the time being anyway. It is interesting to note that in the next eighteen seasons plying his trade for the Leith club, he was never dropped again. Gordon never really recovered from, by no means accepted, certainly didn't understand and under no circumstances approved of the reasoning for this very early career knock-back and would continue to cast up this day as the 'most horrendously upsetting day' of his entire life. This was to be, at seventeen, the lowest point of his football career.

5

SUNSHINE IN WARTIME LEITH

AS THE hot summer of 1941 reached its peak and the new season was about to begin, Gordon was still coming to terms with the Summer Cup final exclusion. He had spent the previous four weeks continually fighting with his conscience – his father intervening every now and again to keep him from 'throwing in the towel'. Since the age of eight, he had been the first choice in any team he had played, always the top name on a team-sheet, with the teams structured around him, and then suddenly he was dropped for the biggest game of his life – for no apparent reason other than Caskie being a famous player for Everton. He knew he had not let Hibs down whatsoever with his play during the previous matches. The opposite, he thought, if he was honest. He'd scored five goals in only four matches and was very proud of his contribution as a whole – which included assists for team-mates to score. Although it still rankled him and he just couldn't get it out of his head, he had decided to battle his demons and was going to fight for a starting place. He knew he needed to make a fresh start with the new season looming.

Just prior to the opening match of the 1941/42 wartime season against Greenock Morton at Cappielow, after a chance meeting with Bob Miller at Edinburgh's Haymarket Station, Gordon received some news that did nothing to help the situation. Apparently, over the summer of 1941, the press had become aware of other clubs' interest in the eye-catching young footballer, and after noting this to Hibernian, the club had responded with a claim that they wouldn't part with Gordon for £15,000. However, not even four months earlier, they had only given Dundee North End a miserly £40 for his release. North End appealed to the Scottish Football Association but to no avail; they never received a penny more for their celebrated player. So for a grand total of £50, Hibernian got their luminary – without question, the bargain of the twentieth century, certainly in Scottish football terms.

Subsequently, as he started his first full season in Edinburgh with Hibernian, certainly not in the best frame of mind, he must have been thinking about where he might have been if fate had shown him a different hand. Either Dundee or Heart of Midlothian – the two clubs he did play for many years later – could so easily have been his first professional club. If there had been even one provisional form in the Dens Park cupboard, or had Mr Irvine taken a chance like Mr McCartney and not insisted on a trial, Gordon Smith might never have played for the green and whites and become one of the greatest players in the history of the club. Fate is a strange thing.

At the beginning of the season, Hearts hosted the first Edinburgh Charities Match, a match that would become an annual event, with an Edinburgh select being chosen thereafter, mixed with players from Hearts and Hibernian. The games would alternate between Tynecastle and Easter Road. Arsenal became the first English team to visit in this wartime challenge match.

After suffering three successive defeats to Morton, Hearts and Clyde (with Gordon scoring his first goal of the season in a 1–4 loss), Hibernian finally won a game. The 8–3 away victory against Albion Rovers at Coatbridge was the first of six wins in a row and the first of two eight-goal tallies.

The second team to lose by such a huge amount were slightly larger and more famous than the lowly Albion Rovers. On Saturday, 27 September 1941, Hibernian defeated the mighty Glasgow Rangers 8–1 at Easter Road – one of the heaviest defeats that Rangers have ever suffered. This was a game that 'shook the football world' according to one newspaper headline. Official attendance was given as 14,800 but a more realistic number was reckoned to be nearer 22,000. Part of the report from the Glasgow newspaper, the *Evening Citizen*, by Harry Young read:

> Rangers got one of the severest drubbings in their football history at Easter Road this afternoon, when Hibs completely outplayed the champions. Venters, Rangers inside left, was

> ordered off the field near the end. Combe, the young Hibs inside left, was the star of the afternoon. He got four of Hibs' goals. Woodburn was injured in the first half and had to go off during the second half. Hibernian were disappointed by the non-appearance of Matt Busby, but Milne was at centre forward and Caskie at outside-left bringing the Edinburgh attack up to full strength. Baxter won the toss for Hibs and elected to play downhill. Milne scored the opener with great assurance {1–0}, giving Dawson no chance to stop a lightning drive from ten yards. Combe whipped in the second {2–0} with tremendous force from about eight yards.
>
> Rangers got a lucky respite in the twenty-eighth minute. Baxter impeded [Jimmy] Smith near the Hibernian goal and the referee awarded a penalty. Hibs protested against the decision, but the award stood and Venters, with a powerful drive, scored from the spot {2–1}.
>
> Bolt fouled Caskie near the touchline and the winger, taking the kick himself, smashed the ball across the goal for [Gordon] Smith, a former Dundee junior, to drive home from a difficult angle {3–1}.
>
> Gillick, just on half-time, was warned by the referee for a dangerous tackle on Hall.
>
> Half-time: 3–1.
>
> The pressure continued in the second half and the harassed Rangers defence had to admit a fourth and fifth defeat in quick succession. In sixty-two minutes, Milne scored from close range from a cross by Combe {4–1}. Two minutes later, Combe beat Dawson again with a fierce drive just inside the penalty area {5–1}. Twelve minutes from the end, Combe completed his hat trick {6–1} and a minute later he had his fourth {7–1} and his side's seventh goal.
>
> [Gordon] Smith beat two men and scored Hibs' eighth goal one minute from the end {8–1}.

This account is absolutely astonishing, but true.

In 1941, an era before footballers were really famous, it was standard for all players to catch a bus or train following a game; there were no private limos or fancy cars for this generation of stars, with some thinking nothing of walking for miles before and after games! So, as usual, Gordon made his way from Easter Road Park to Waverley Station, probably well over an hour and a half after the end of the contest, with the atmosphere in the dressing room so electric and joyous that nobody wanted to leave. Gordon was delirious as he said his farewells and headed out to the street:

> I remember that after the game I walked out of the ground over the bridge and down Bothwell Street and round to the nearest bus stop on Easter Road. There was a soldier reading the 'pink' sports paper and he said to me:
>
> 'It says here that Hibs beat Rangers 8–1, what nonsense, it must be a misprint?'
>
> When an eight is poorly printed, it can look like a zero, so I knew what he meant, but I was able to say: 'No, it isn't a misprint, it's true enough, and it was 8–1. I know because I was there. In fact, I scored twice – the third and the eighth!'

Following this game, Gordon was on top of the world once more. After the despondency of the Summer Cup debacle, he was now a lot more focused for Hibs and determined to show Willie McCartney and Jimmy McColl that they'd been wrong to drop him. However, after this incredible result, the following Saturday, Hibernian lost 2–4 against Arbroath and Gordon felt absolutely humiliated as he made the short journey back to Montrose. Many of his friends and family had travelled to see him especially and his majestic team. His majestic team who could score eight against a very good Rangers side, the champions of Scotland, but only two against the minnows of Gayfield Park! Hat-tricks from Willie Finnegan and, of all people, Bobby Baxter, were highlights of the next few games, which included a couple of narrow defeats, but an eight-game unbeaten run toward Christmas kept Hibs near the top of the table.

As the season progressed, Gordon was quickly bonding with his team-mates. As well as going on his own or with his brother Stanley to the cinema, he would now go with Bobby Combe and Willie Finnegan and on occasion Matt Busby, who was like a father figure to Combe and

Gordon. Matt's preferred picture house was the St Andrew's Square Cinema on Clyde Street, alongside the Bus Station. They went to see John Ford's *How Green Was My Valley*, which had beaten other classics such as *Citizen Kane* and *The Maltese Falcon* to win the coveted 'best picture' at the Oscar Ceremony in Hollywood. Although Gordon enjoyed the film starring would-be Scot and 'best supporting actor' Oscar winner Donald Crisp, he and the others much preferred *The Maltese Falcon* and *Citizen Kane*.

With 'Stardust' by Artie Shaw and the likes of Harry James, Jimmy and Tommy Dorsey and, of course, the evergreen Glenn Miller dominating the music scene, once again Fats Waller, the Mills Brothers and the Ink Spots would be streets ahead for Gordon. He played the Ink Spots' 'We Three (My Echo, My Shadow and Me)' over and over again on his newly bought radiogram.

Gordon still had his job in Montrose with Liver Insurance and would travel back and forth for training and for matches (often severely late due to blackouts and air raids), but the situation wasn't ideal. Nearing December, with its bitter weather and snowfall, the monotonous travelling was beginning to take its toll. A beleaguered Gordon sat down with Willie McCartney and Harry Swan asking if at all possible they could 'hurry up' the promised job offered on his signing in April and, more importantly, he asked the men if they could help him find suitable accommodation.

A few days after scoring for Hibs in the 2–2 draw against Hearts at Easter Road on New Year's Day 1942, Gordon and his brother Stanley moved down to Edinburgh, staying in 'digs' with a friend of their Aunt Katy in a house in the Restalrig area of the city. Mrs Barron lived at 85 Sleigh Drive and was thrilled to have this talented young footballer and his brother come to live with her, as her husband had died some time ago and her two sons were in France with the King's Own Scottish Borderers. Although this was only to be a temporary arrangement, she was pleased to have company and to be of assistance. Gordon celebrated his first game as a player resident in Edinburgh by scoring two goals in a 6–0 home win against Third Lanark. In a letter to his oldest brother, Robert, who was in the Royal Air Force and stationed at Loth in Sutherland, Gordon wrote:

C/o Mrs Barron, 85 Sleigh Drive Edinburgh
January 15th 1942
Dear Rob,

Thanks for your letter. We are both [Gordon and younger brother Stanley] in Edinburgh and I start work on Monday. I will be changing my address but write to the above for a fortnight. I will write you tomorrow. Hope you're still alive among the snow.
Love Gordon.

Gordon started his job as a driller for the Leith shipbuilding company Henry Robb on 20 January 1942. Five days later, the USA entered World War Two, six weeks after Japan's attack on Pearl Harbour.

February saw Gordon and brother Stanley's short-term residency in Restalrig end as they, along with the rest of the Smith family, moved to a house in Edinburgh's city centre – 63 South Bridge – above a branch of the Clydesdale Bank.

Following the discussions of the previous year, Harry Swan had kept his promise – firstly with arranging the Henry Robb job and now with securing the rented property for the Smith family. Not only were Gordon and Stanley to be housed there, but also Gordon's parents, sister Rachel and youngest brother, Brian. His two eldest brothers, Robert and William, were serving in the Royal Air Force and the Army.

And so, sixteen years after taking the family away from Edinburgh, Robert and Christina were back, relocating en masse and moving in with their seventeen-year-old, third-born son. The house, unlike many in the country at this time, had an inside toilet but no bath, so the family bathed at the local Infirmary Street public baths. The local wash-houses of St Mary's Street and Niddry Street were only a short distance away, too. As well as a job for Gordon and a house for him and his family, the Hibernian chairman also arranged for fifteen-year-old Stanley to obtain work as a slater, while Gordon's father worked at Littlejohn & Co., Swan's bakery and tea-room business at the top of Leith Street. Rent for the house was paid at an office in the West End, a weekly trek that Gordon's thirteen-year-old sister Rachel would frequently have to endure.

Aside from his beloved football, music continued to be Gordon's other love. He found that listening to his jazz heroes before matches would relax him and assist his game. Since moving down to the big city, Gordon would browse all the record stores. In nearby Portobello he would visit Meg Moir's record shop, when he was uptown he went to the ever-popular Rae Macintosh at the West End – but his favourite and nearest was at the North Bridge arcade, a two-minute walk from his house.

As the league season drew to a close, Hibernian finished runners-up behind Rangers, with four wins and a draw in their final five games, Gordon scoring in each game. On 18 April, the ex-Dundee junior travelled through to Hampden with a Hibs contingent to join a crowd of 77,779 watching Scotland play England in the unofficial wartime international. Gordon cheered on Hibs team-mate and now valued friend Matt Busby, who played alongside Scottish greats Bill Shankly, Billy Liddell and Jerry Dawson in the dramatic 5–4 win over England, with another impending close friend, Willie Waddell, making his debut.

As Gordon's eighteenth birthday approached, everyone expected the youngster to receive call-up papers for one of the services, but some people say Harry Swan had other ideas, unbeknown to Gordon, and in fact many people, at that time. Whatever the reason, the papers never materialised. Was Gordon Smith too good a player to risk losing? Did Harry Swan have the power to dissuade the Crown from taking his star player? Or was Gordon just lucky to have a wartime reserved occupation?

On a 'special day out', Smith journeyed through to Glasgow with Bobby Combe to behold the arrival of the first US troops in Europe disembarking at the Clyde in Glasgow on 9 June. The ocean liner, the RMS *Queen Mary*, had sailed from New York bringing more than 15,000 men to war. Huge crowds, some say in the region of 200,000, saw the arrival of the giant ship and the Americans on the River Clyde.

In mid July 1942, Hibernian played Rangers in the Summer Cup final once again. There were only two changes from the previous season's final – goalkeeper Crozier replaced Jimmy Kerr and Smith replaced Nutley. Unfortunately, Hibs lost the game on the toss of a coin after the score had ended 0–0. This loss, with the lingering bitter memories from the previous year and, in his own words, the 'pathetic' way in which a Cup victory was decided, didn't help Gordon's mood that sunny afternoon in Glasgow. When he eventually turned up at his South Bridge home, he locked himself away in his room for the night!

The final game of the 1941/42 season was played on Saturday, 18 July, with Hibs losing an evenly matched game 2–3 against a United Military Services XI, once again played at Hampden Park, Glasgow. The attendance was 30,000 and the Services XI included Bill Shankly, Frank Swift and Stanley Matthews. Gordon and a trialist called Wallace hit the target for Hibs. The season ended with Gordon having played forty games in total and having scored twenty-five goals; third on the list of Hibernian scorers for the season – four goals fewer than equal top-scorers Bobby Combe and Jimmy Caskie.

6

FLAVOUR OF CELEBRITY LIFE

SAMMY KEAN scored Hibernian's first goal of the new 1942/43 season, the consolation goal in a 1–3 defeat to an RAF International XI at Easter Road on Saturday, 1 August, in the Edinburgh Charity Match. The following Saturday saw a better result as Hibs gained a 3–1 victory over Albion Rovers. This started a fourteen-game unbeaten run in which Gordon scored eight goals.

Gordon was frequently played at centre forward for Hibs and would not make the right wing his own for a couple of seasons yet. This helped him to become Hibs' top scorer in the 1942/43 season, with thirty-one goals in forty matches – a great achievement that he would repeat in future seasons as well.

In the evenings, he was venturing more and more to his beloved cinema, whether on his own or with his pals, Matt Busby and Willie Finnegan, to a film of their choice. More frequently, he would go with best friend, Bobby Combe, to the Picture Dome at the top of Easter Road, as they could walk there just after training. Amongst an assortment of films seen, *Mrs Miniver* was unsurpassed as Gordon's favourite at this time.

The Mills Brothers' 'Paper Doll' was a new 78 record for Gordon to get his hands on, although he did (like millions of others) have a soft spot for Bing Crosby's 'White Christmas' taken from the film *Holiday Inn*. The mix of melancholy and comforting images of home in Irving Berlin's lyrics made this a particular favourite worldwide – especially with the armed forces. Gordon took a mystery girl to see *Holiday Inn* and the relationship apparently lasted a few weeks but her fondness for wanting to go dancing at the Palais de Danse in Fountainbridge was to be the downfall of the wartime relationship – he loathed dancing!

On the 23 and 30 January, Gordon scored two hat-tricks in a row – the first against Airdrie at Easter Road and the second in Glasgow against Partick Thistle, with Hibs winning these games 7–1 and 5–1. These were his first trebles since his opening game for Hibs back in April 1941.

In early February, Gordon – still only eighteen – took delivery not of the call-up papers that most men of his age received, but a letter informing him that he was to become a 'Report Centre' worker:

The City and Royal Burgh of Edinburgh: Air Raid Precautions.
This is to certify that Gordon Smith, 63 South Bridge, has been appointed as a Report Centre Worker.
This is his authority to carry out the duties laid upon such workers by the town council.

The Report Centre in Edinburgh was part of the civil defence and the home guard; they were called upon to deal with a number of duties, some of which were top secret. They were also to be on hand to aid people to and from the Anderson shelters during air raids and would be a vital part of the city's defences should the enemy invade.

When the 1942/43 season drew to a close, the east Edinburgh team had finished in third place, with Arthur Milne and Johnny 'Cubby' Cuthbertson Hibs' other leading scorers alongside Gordon. Despite the slightly disappointing finish, they did have a trophy; they won the Edinburgh Press Charities Committee five-a-side tournament at Tynecastle on Wednesday, 7 July, by disposing of Edinburgh City, Hearts and an Army Select side in the final. The 1943 Summer Cup again saw Rangers bring a halt to Hibs' run, beating the Edinburgh side 3–1, this time in the semi-final.

The next season was to start badly for Hibs as they lost 0–4 to Rangers at Ibrox. Although starting terribly, the loss was duly followed by five straight victories, including Gordon Smith's fourth hat-trick for the greens, this time against Dumbarton in a 4–3 home win. The league season was played out with ups and downs but in early December, Gordon scored another three, this time against Albion Rovers at Coatbridge.

Gordon's favoured pastime other than his records was still the cinema and obviously you would have thought his number one of the year had to be a film starring his hero, Fats Waller. *Stormy Weather* featured a notable recording of Waller's 'Ain't Misbehavin'' and a line-up that included Cab Calloway, Lena Horne and the movie's star, Bill 'Bojangles' Robinson. During an era where African-American actors and singers didn't frequently appear in leading roles in mainstream Hollywood productions – particularly in the musical genre – this was a rarity, indeed, to be savoured. But showing at his current preferred picture house, the Victory (previously the Bungalow in Portobello's Bath Street), was the film that topped it – *Casablanca*. Starring Humphrey Bogart and including the iconic 'As Time Goes By', it was to become an all-time favourite of Gordon's, seeing it on numerous occasions along with Sammy Kean and Bobby Combe.

In mid October 1943, Gordon was a travelling reserve for Scotland in a crushing 0–8 defeat to England at Maine Road, Manchester, with an astonishing 63,000 wartime crowd witnessing this 'Mancunian massacre'. This was Gordon's first trip to England since representing Scotland at schoolboy level in the spring of 1938 in Sunderland, different in that he didn't kick a ball in anger, as travelling reserves weren't allowed to play once the team had been selected. He was perhaps more than a little glad that he didn't play as Scotland capitulated to their old rivals. The English football team were in the midst of a magnificent twenty-three-goal rampage in three internationals – sixteen against the Scots and seven against Wales. After the game, the nineteen-year-old socialised with some of his heroes, such as Stanley Matthews, Denis Compton, Tommy Lawton, Joe Mercer, Raich Carter and Stan Cullis – famous players he'd only seen on *Pathé* newsreels before but were now sharing a dinner table with him! Matthews, whom he'd met briefly a couple of times previously, gave him an especially warm welcome, saying he'd been hearing 'great things' about him from his 'Scottish spies'. Gordon was also in awe of Arsenal footballer and Middlesex cricketer, Denis Compton, who not only represented England at football, but remarkably also at cricket. Gordon had been interested in cricket since his youth in Montrose; he loved watching the sport (in later years, almost as much as football) and was full of admiration for Compton. The thrill of speaking with two of the biggest names in British sport at the time alleviated his disappointment in not playing.

Whilst still waiting to make his full international debut, he did, however, play on the wing for a Scottish Select XI a month after the Manchester debacle. Gordon and his Hibs team-mate, centre half Bobby Baxter, were selected to play against an RAF International XI at Glasgow's Hampden Park on 6 November 1943. Ecstatically proud and eager to show his skills on the international scene at last, Gordon got a train from Leith Central to Mount Florida with Baxter, where they met up with the rest of the players, including Gordon's schoolboy heroes Tommy Walker, Alex Massie and Liverpool's Willie Fagan. In front of over 50,000 fans, the Select XI lost 1–2 to a team that was basically an England XI, which included Matthews, Carter and Arsenal's Ted Drake in its line-up. Although this was Gordon's first game representing Scotland since his schoolboy caps, he would have to wait almost another year before making his full international debut for his country.

The year of 1943 ended on a very low point for Gordon. Watching from the stalls in Princes Street's Monseigneur News Theatre, the day before Christmas Eve, he learned of devastating news. His hero, thirty-nine-year-old Thomas 'Fats' Waller, had been found dead on a train that had been taking him from California to New York City to perform in his home town. His body had been removed from the train at Kansas City and his funeral, a few days later in New York's Harlem, drew around 5,000 mourners. Gordon rushed back from the cinema upon hearing the news and shut himself away for hours, playing his favourite Waller hits: 'It's a Sin to Tell a Lie', 'Two Sleepy People', 'My Very Good Friend the Milkman', 'I'm Gonna Sit Right Down and Write Myself a Letter' and 'Ain't Misbehavin''.

Although Fats Waller was the son of a lay preacher and very much revered in the jazz and blues world of 1930s and early 1940s America, he also amazingly recorded the Scottish ballads 'Annie Laurie', 'Loch Lomond' and 'When You and I Were Young, Maggie'. In the next edition of a well-known music magazine, of which Gordon was an avid reader, a moving poem written on the passing of Waller consoled Gordon a little. He cut it out and kept it in his wallet until, unfortunately, it was stolen many years later – then luckily returned out of the blue, minus some cash but with the integral elegy still tucked in a partition. It read:

Silent you lie, remote from all life's risks,
Leaving us comfort in these treasured discs.
Gone the wide grin, the wisecracks, shining face;
The sweeping, broad, incomparable bass;
The husky voice – Swift fingers, hands, now stilled.
Yet at a needle's touch the room is filled –
With a glittering sound. There ever you remain,
And sing and talk and laugh and live again.

7

1944 DIARY

UNABRIDGED EXTRACTS from nineteen-year-old Gordon's 1944 *Collins Gentleman's Diary* offer a unique insight into the young footballer's day-to-day life. His entries were precise and to the point; short and sweet, recording key contact details and match results, but not really giving too much away.

Easter Road Park 75325
Mr McCartney 78223
Mr Swan
Mr Shaw 42471 & 53536
Radford (Dentist) 35331
Mr Dutt 26105

Note that Mr Shaw had the luxury of two telephone numbers. Mr Dutt was Gordon's boss at either the Henry Robb shipyard or at the report centre, and he either didn't know Harry Swan's number or the chairman refused to give it to him. When referring to his goals scored, he at times wrote 'Me', now and then 'Gordon Smith', from time to time he must've felt he deserved 'GORDON SMITH', but more than often, it was just plain 'Smith'.

Saturday 1st January: Hibs 0–1 Hearts
Terrible game.
Monday 3rd January: Hibs 1–2 Airdrie
Bogan.

Saturday 8th January: Hibs 3–2 Clyde
Bogan, Cuthbertson 2.
Saturday 15th January: Morton 3–1 Hibs
Baxter.
Saturday 22nd January: Hibs 4–3 Falkirk
Woodburn 2, Baxter, Me.
Saturday 29th January: St Mirren 1–2 Hibs
Caskie, Cowan.
Saturday 5th February: Hibs 6–0 Third Lanark
Nelson, Marshallsay, Colvan 2, Me another 2 goals!
Saturday 12th February: Celtic 2–2 Hibs
Colvan, Caskie.
Saturday 19th February: Hibs 2–2 Partick
Kean, Nelson.
England 6–2 Scotland
Travelling Reserve at Wembley. Bitterly disappointed in not playing again but thoroughly enjoyable experience.
Saturday 26th February: Motherwell v Hibs
Match off.
Saturday 4th March: League Cup: Third Lanark 0–4 Hibs
Colvan, Nelson, Me 2.
Saturday 11th March: League Cup: Hibs 2–1 Albion Rovers
Nelson 2
Saturday 18th March: League Cup: Morton 2–2 Hibs
Nelson, Bogan.
Saturday 25th March: League Cup: Hibs 4–0 Third Lanark
Cuthbertson, Bogan, Devlin, Caskie.
Saturday 1st April: League Cup: Albion Rovers 0–2 Hibs
Marshallsay 1, Gordon Smith 1.
Saturday 8th April: League Cup: Hibs 6–3 Morton
Nelson 3, Caskie, Kean, Me.
Saturday 15th April: Motherwell 1–1 hibs
Nelson.
Monday 17th April: Hearts 1–1 Hibs
Nelson.
Saturday 22nd April: Scotland 2–3 England
Travelling Reserve AGAIN at Hampden.

With Scotland losing by six goals to two in February's international to a far superior England side, containing the likes of Stan Cullis, Joe Mercer, Stanley Matthews and Tommy Lawton, Gordon was left sitting amongst the 82,500 fans, feeling extremely disappointed that he was in the reserves again, as his diary quite clearly states. He had been desperate to play for Scotland and felt it would've been a great honour to play alongside his great friend Matt Busby and also the 'culpable' Jimmy Caskie, with whom he had developed a great understanding and had almost forgiven for 'stealing his 1941 Summer Cup final spot'.

Unfortunately for Gordon, the selectors had made their choice and he was overlooked for the right wing role in favour of Airdrie's Bobby Flavell, who would make his first and last international appearance for Scotland that day. Although Gordon didn't play, he again met up with English players and chatted about the game with his 'new best friend' Stanley Matthews following the contest, as the teams and Football Associations of both countries ate dinner.

In April's return match at Hampden, for the third successive international against England, Gordon was a travelling reserve and had to sit in the stand for the duration of the game yet again, this time amidst a colossal crowd of 133,386 – the biggest to date Gordon had seen at any ground. This time, it was Celtic's Jimmy Delaney who was victorious in winning the coveted number 7 jersey, following on from Bobby Flavell and Rangers' Willie Waddell. Scotland lost by the odd goal in five with England's Tommy Lawton scoring a hat-trick.

A handwritten note by William McCartney, placed in Gordon's diary on this date, says it all:

It's a scandal Gordon; even the selectors must know that. — Willie

Gordon continued to document the season with his sparse notes – though he did appear to celebrate the winning of the Scottish Southern League Cup in style!

Saturday 29th April: Injured
Hibs 6–1 Edinburgh City
Baxter, McIntyre, Bogan 3, Cowan.
Saturday 6th May: Clyde 2–5 Hibs
Combe, Baxter, Nelson, Woodburn 2

Saturday 13th May: Injured
East of Scotland Shield: Hearts 2–1 Hibs
Saturday 20th May: League Cup Final: Rangers 0–0 Hibs
Rangers 5 Corners; Hibs 6 Corners
We won the Cup. Very proud. Pictures with Evelyn at night.

Hibs won the Southern League Cup Final 6–5 on penalties after a no goals draw against a strong Rangers team at Hampden Park. It was a pulsating cup-tie, which included the quite astonishing sight of a Rangers player who was a newly qualified doctor, Adam Little, attending to his own goalkeeper (who broke his leg after colliding with Hibs' Bogan), a 'stonewall' penalty not given to the Edinburgh side, and a superb performance from the likes of Gordon Smith, Sammy Kean and Willie Finnegan. However, in the end, no goals had been scored.

Bill Struth's men led 5–4 on corner kicks with ten minutes to go and after Hibs drew level, both sets of players were warned by the referee for 'disorderly behaviour' as tension mounted. Corner kicks were the usual way to settle a drawn game before extra-time and penalty kicks became the modern-day norm. This was a much fairer and more exciting option than its predecessor – the winner being determined by the toss of a coin. The 'winning' corner in this match was won by Caskie, three minutes from the end of the game, and was understandably acclaimed by the whole Hibs team as if he'd scored a goal! Gordon was deliriously happy and celebrated that night by enjoying a romantic evening with the mysterious Evelyn, who would never be mentioned again. A week later, by winning 4–1 against Hearts, Hibs had won two cups in eight days.

Saturday 27th May: Roseberry Charity Cup: Hearts 1–4 Hibs
McIntyre, Bogan, Cuthbertson, (Back: own goal). Another Cup win!
Saturday 3rd June: Summer Cup: Airdrie 2–4 Hibs
Bogan 2, Smith 1, (Back: own goal).
Saturday 10th June: Summer Cup: Hibs 3–0 Airdrie
Bogan 2, GORDON SMITH 1.
Saturday 17th June: Summer Cup: Morton 1–1 Hibs
Smith.
Saturday 24th June: Summer Cup: Hibs 0–2 Morton

As Tuesday, 6 June 1944, dawned, D-Day's first phase had been launched – an airborne assault, under cover of darkness, which landed 30,000 allied troops on the coast of France. The second phase was massive. An incredible 160,000 men, the largest amphibious invasion of all time, landed on the beaches of Normandy. An outstandingly well-planned decoy operation, distracting the Germans, enabled this invasion to be a huge success and played an integral part in securing victory for Britain and her Allies the following year. The general consensus amidst the talk in the Leith shipyards was: 'If they succeed, it'll only be a matter of time before we win the war.'

For all Gordon's early scoring, including two hat-tricks, in the 1943/44 season, he only finished second top scorer for Hibs – two goals behind Tommy Bogan who scored an amazing twenty-two goals in a mere twenty-four appearances. Hibernian's run in the Summer Cup, and their season, came to a close on 24 June after a 0–2 defeat to Morton at Easter Road.

During the now quite buoyant summer of 1944, whilst collecting more and more Fats Waller rarities, Gordon grew increasingly obsessed with listening to southern African-American roots and New Orleans jazz music. He was quite definitely what you would call an ardent fan of the genre, whilst starting to enjoy the likes of Jack Teagarden, Ted Lewis, the Louisiana Sugar Babes and, especially, the trumpet player 'Bunk' Johnson, in whom he found another hero who would stand the test of time.

Johnson would be ranked up there with Waller and the Ink Spots as his perennial favourites. 'Bunk' had been born William G Johnson and, together with his New Orleans band, comprising of George Lewis on clarinet, Jim Robinson on trombone, Alton Purnell on piano, Lawrence Marrero on banjo, Alcide 'Slow Drag' Pavageau on bass and 'Baby' Dodds on drums, became another mainstay on Gordon's turntable. Gordon wasn't the trumpeter's only fan. In the eyes of the world-famous trumpet player Louis Armstrong, he was 'the man'. 'Bunk is the man they ought to talk about, just to hear him play, sends me!' Armstrong would be heard saying in *Pathé* newsreels.

Just prior to the opening match in the 1944/45 season, Hibernian travelled to Glasgow to take part in the annual Ibrox five-a-side football tournament, better known simply as the 'Ibrox fives', where massive crowds of up to 80,000 would gather to watch the likes of Celtic, Hearts,

Hibs, Partick Thistle, Third Lanark, Falkirk, Queen of the South and Greenock Morton battle it out, eagerly anticipating a Rangers win. This was not always the case, with the Easter Road men having their fair share of success. Though good fun, victorious or not, fives wasn't proper football, so Gordon didn't deem it worthy of a mention in his diary, which was sidelined in a drawer until the opening match of the new season – his first entry since 24 June.

Saturday 5th August: Edinburgh Select 3–4 Aston Villa
The Allison Challenge Cup. Match played at Tynecastle.
Walker 2, Delaney
Saturday 12th August: Hibs 0–4 Clyde
Saturday 19th August: Morton 3–2 Hibs
Bogan 2.
Saturday 26th August: Hibs 3–1 Hamilton
Colvan, Bogan, Devlin.
Saturday 2nd September: Dumbarton 0–3 Hibs
Bogan, Colvan, Smith.
Saturday 9th September: Hibs 3–1 Hearts
Devlin, Nutley, Smith.
My 100th goal for Hibs!
Saturday 16th September: Queen's Park 0–2 Hibs
Devlin 2.
Saturday 23rd September: Hibs 4–1 Rangers
Milne 2, Caskie, Smith.
Saturday 30th September: Albion Rovers 0–5 Hibs
Bogan 2, Milne 1, me 2.
Saturday 7th October: Falkirk 1–3 Hibs
Devlin, Caskie, GORDON SMITH.
Saturday 14th October: Celtic 1–1 Hibs
McIntyre.
England 6–2 Scotland
My first full international for Scotland. Extremely proud and played reasonably well. Bought 78s before trip home. A great adventure. Sad for Bobby.

Though it was Gordon's second trip to London, this was the first time he'd played at Wembley Stadium, having been a travelling reserve for the same fixture in February past. This, as he wrote so ingenuously in his diary, was an adventure from start to finish for the twenty-year-old. Knowing that he wasn't a travelling reserve but was actually going to play at Wembley made Gordon delirious with excitement. Incredibly, Hugh Shaw, the Hibernian trainer, was also Scotland's for the international, so the Hibs quintet had met at Leith Central station to take a tram uptown, where they met up with their now team-mates from Heart of Midlothian. They then took a train from Princes Street's Caledonian Station to Glasgow Central, where the rest of the squad were already congregating, before taking the train to London.

The players stayed in a hotel in north London near the Mecca of English football, with Gordon quite worried by all accounts. Even though 'the blitz' had long finished, in a letter to home he wrote that he had concerns that both he and London would be 'bombed to bits by the Germans'! The following day, after no bombing had taken place, the players were introduced to King Haakon of Norway prior to the match and twenty-year-old Gordon made his full Scotland debut at long last. Sadly, on the morning of the match, Bobby Baxter was informed his mother had died and the players touchingly presented him with a wreath preceding the contest.

England defeated Scotland 6–2, with an all-Edinburgh forward line – Gordon Smith, Tommy Walker, Arthur Milne, Andy Black and Jimmy Caskie – unable to do the city proud. Amazingly, six players from Edinburgh (four representing Hibernian and two Heart of Midlothian) played in the game – quite simply inconceivable in the modern game. Also making their debuts alongside Gordon were RB Thyne, Archie Macaulay and goal-scorer Milne, whilst Tommy Walker was the senior member of the team, earning his thirty-fifth cap.

The game, which Scotland led at half-time through a Tommy Walker goal, was dominated by a stunning second-half hat-trick scored by Everton's Tommy Lawton. Although debutant Arthur Milne managed to score a second for Scotland, further goals from England's Leonard Goulden, Raich Carter and Leslie Smith clinched what turned out to be a rout for the English. Incredibly, the 6–2 score line imitated the previous international that had been played at Wembley Stadium between the two countries a mere eight months prior, when Gordon was watching from the touchline! Only Macaulay and Caskie had survived that mauling. Huge defeat or not, there was a fleeting mention in the newspapers the following morning that praised Gordon in writing: 'Hardwick was definitely worried by young Gordon Smith.'

Saturday 21st October: Hibs 8–0 Partick Thistle
Devlin 3, Bogan 2, Milne 2, Smith.
We tore them apart.
Saturday 28th October: Third Lanark 3–6 Hibs
Milne 2, Bogan, Caskie, Smith, Devlin.
Saturday 4th November: Hibs 6–2 St Mirren
Devlin, Peat 2, Baxter, Caskie, Gordon Smith.
Saturday 11th November: Hibs 3–2 Airdrie
Smith 3.
My 10th goal in 7 games and Hibs' 35th in seven games!

Gordon obviously didn't include the Celtic game on 14 October in the Hibs goal tally, as he was playing for Scotland at Wembley that day. It should've read thirty-six goals in eight games – still a marvellous period of form.

Saturday 18th November: Hibs 0–1 Motherwell
Saturday 25th November: Clyde 2–3 Hibs
Bogan 1, Milne 1, Shaw 1.
Saturday 2nd December: Hibs 0–1 Morton
Saturday 9th December: Hamilton 1–1 Hibs
Me.
Saturday 16th December: Hibs 0–0 Dumbarton
Saturday 23rd December: Rangers 5–0 Hibs
Saturday 30th December: Hibs 2–0 Queen's Park
Finnegan, Rice.

'Rice' was the last word written in his 1944 diary – a diary that didn't give too much information away!

Just before the end of the year and the evening before he started work in the newspaper business, Gordon received the quite devastating news that his friend Bobby Combe had been taken prisoner by the Germans and was being held in a POW camp. Gordon and Bobby had grown very close in the eight years they'd known each other, especially the last three at Hibernian, and he was extremely concerned for his welfare.

At this point in his life, as well as still working in Leith at Henry Robb, Gordon launched a part-time career in journalism that was to last over twenty years, working firstly at the Edinburgh office of the *Daily Record*, followed by the *Scottish Daily Mail* and the *Sunday Mirror*, amongst others. A sideline that started with weekly columns soon became twice weekly and even daily at one point. He thoroughly enjoyed and, perhaps a little unpredictably, thrived in the hustle and bustle atmosphere of newspaper offices during the 1940s and 1950s. The first big news story he encountered at the office was the 'missing in action' status of bandleader Glenn Miller. Whilst travelling to entertain US troops in France, his plane disappeared in bad weather over the English Channel – with his body, plane and fellow crew members never recovered, conspiracy theorists had a field day. Gordon was pretty bewildered by the events in one sense, but at least he wouldn't have to listen to any new tedious 'big band' tunes.

8

FIRST TASTE OF CONTINENTAL TRAVEL AND FAST CARS

THE YEAR of 1945 was off to a bad start as Hibs lost the opening game on New Year's Day to Heart of Midlothian, and then the following day's game to Motherwell, both losses 0–3. Hibernian and Gordon then found some semblance of form with victories over Albion Rovers and Falkirk, with five goals scored by Gordon out of the total seven, including his seventh hat-trick for the club. But these were to be the final victories in a pretty disappointing league season, where Hibs finished fifth after a 1–5 mauling against a team that were also to beat them in a cup final, Partick Thistle.

On 5 May, Hibernian were chosen to host the exalted end of league season match in aid of the Soldiers, Sailors, Airmen and Families Association charity. The match against the Scottish Services Select team ended in a 2–2 draw, with most of the 20,000 plus crowd in attendance bestowing a euphoric 'welcome home' to Matt Busby. Busby, a member of the Scottish Services team, had been away from Easter Road for a couple of seasons and had returned to his own club, Liverpool, after being a 'wartime guest' in the east of Edinburgh. Following the match, Gordon showed Matt Busby around his home and then, after a hearty tea cooked by his mother, the two footballers went to the cinema – to Matt's favourite picture house, the St Andrew's Square Cinema on Clyde Street.

Gordon's mother later told him she was 'mortified' that he had brought the famous Matt Busby up those 'horrible stairs' – the common stairwell that was quite often used as a toilet by revellers and the like. 'I just hope to God he wasn't aware of the smell,' she declared. Perhaps that's the real reason why Gordon would later turn down a move to Manchester United – worried that Matt would bring up the topic of the smelly stairs!

Although World War Two wasn't to be officially won until the Japanese surrender in September, the whole of Britain celebrated on Tuesday, 8 May. This was Victory in Europe Day, with Hitler defeated and deceased. Gordon and other members of the Hibs team were in a packed Littlejohn's when in walked none other than Bobby Combe, who had just arrived back in Scotland. Only hours earlier, Combe had flown in from Germany, where he'd been held prisoner at the notorious Sandbostel POW camp close to Bremen. The ecstatic players were delighted to be reunited with him and after he'd had some food and a cup of 'Scottish tea', they fought their way through the thousands of jubilant Leith Street faces celebrating the end of the war. With Combe leading, they walked down to Easter Road Park where he 'reported back for duty' to Willie McCartney, who luckily was still in his office. Amazingly, Combe was duly picked to play in the Roseberry Cup Final team the following afternoon!

The next day, back at a slightly busier Easter Road, Jock Weir's two goals and a corner flag did just enough to seal victory against Hearts in the final – with this game also ending up 2–2 at full time. The corner flag had thwarted Hearts' hopes of a corner equaliser in the last minute after the ball ricocheted to safety and was kicked up the park. The match was over and the cup was won 7–6 on corners! Gaelic tenor, Kenny McCrae, provided the entertainment in the boardroom after the final, singing a selection of mournful solos, which was just what the players needed the day after VE Day!

The RMS *Queen Mary* was once again berthed on the Clyde. This time she was ready to take 15,000 American Servicemen back home. Once again, Gordon was enthralled and wanted to be there as the giant ship sailed out, and along with older brother William, he made a repeat of his 1941 trip to the west coast to see the majestic liner. This time, he was driven through by wealthy businessman, Willie Murphy, of Murphy's Football Pools, who was to become a confidant and close friend of Gordon's. Murphy's Pools and Thomas Strang's Pools were the two main rivals in Edinburgh at the time, before being taken over by the giant Littlewoods Pools Company years later. This form of betting, although still reasonably popular today, was massive in an age when wages were low and where even a small win could make a huge difference to people's lives.

Gordon scored five goals in six Summer Cup matches that were played between 26 May (Gordon's twenty-first birthday) and 30 June. Unfortunately, the Leith side lost the final to Partick Thistle after beating St Mirren, Falkirk and Celtic en route to Hampden Park. Although Finnegan and Howie both hit the post during the Glasgow showpiece final, Partick Thistle, who featured the legendary guest player Bill Shankly, were superior on the day. Shankly was stationed in the RAF at nearby Bishopbriggs and made sixty-nine appearances for the Glasgow side. He scored a respectable twelve goals in his time back in Scotland, whilst also defending resolutely and with great passion.

Once again, Gordon was bitterly disappointed at not winning 'Harry Swan's Cup', as he called it (the Summer Cup being the brainchild of Harry Swan back in 1941), and when it dawned on him after his second final loss in two attempts that he would maybe never win it, he got quite agitated. It evoked bitter memories of his 1941 omission from the winning Hampden Hibs team, a team that he still believed he should have played in – Caskie or no Caskie!

In early July, well over 10,000 attended the Annual Press Charities Sports Gala, this year held at Tynecastle, where the crowd was entertained by such delights as athletic events, weightlifting and, believe it or not, sheep dog displays! The star attraction, ever popular and always very keenly contested, was the five-a-side football tournament. This was what the public had waited so patiently for, this is what they'd come to see – even surpassing the sheep and the dogs! The Hibs team was comprised of Smith, Weir, Baxter, Finnegan and, a surprise choice, sixteen-year-old Lawrie Reilly, who had just signed for Hibs in April. Four years on and the same twelve-year-old boy who had asked Gordon to come to his home for his tea was now playing alongside him at Tynecastle – albeit in a five-a-side tournament. With Lawrie Reilly making his first appearance for the Easter Road team, Hibs played well in defeating Falkirk, Leith Athletic and Hearts. Rangers, who had beaten an Army XI, a Fife composite select and another Hearts team, would be victorious in the final, winning 3–2 against an unlucky Hibs side.

Lawrie, although a little disappointed and a touch crestfallen in losing his first tournament with Hibs, was still overjoyed and on cloud nine, having played alongside his hero, Gordon Smith! It took a little longer for Lawrie to establish himself in the first team starting line up for Hibs, but a friendship between himself and his idol would start that summer's afternoon – fittingly at Tynecastle, where the two had previously met. A friendship had begun that would last a lifetime.

'GORDON SMITH THE STAR IN A SPARKLING COMBINE' read the *Sunday Mail* back page following a 4–0 win for an Edinburgh Select side against Huddersfield Town in early August 1945. The game played at Tynecastle was the prelude to the league season. The select were captained by guest player Aston Villa's Alex Massie, with their goals scored by Smith, twice, Finnegan and Queen's Park's John Robert Harris. Rex Kingsley wrote in the *Sunday Mail* article:

> So far as Edinburgh is concerned, Gordon Smith has jockey Gordon Richards whacked for popularity. If I say he had a personal triumph, it's like saying Monty is quite a fair soldier. Definitely an understatement! The young right winger pulverised the visitors left defence – then paralysed it! I don't know what his pre-match transfer fee might have been and I shudder to think what it would be now! No, I don't shudder, for it would mean he's a Hibs fixture. No club could look at him! His immediate opponent was Barker of Aston Villa, a guest player in the Huddersfield side. Never was a guest treated so scurvily!

In the final season of the Wartime Southern League, where Hibernian finished runners-up to the usual suspects, Rangers, the Greens started badly by losing 0–3 against Queen of the South at Dumfries. This was followed by a Milne double in a 2–1 home victory over the mighty Rangers – the start of a seven-game unbeaten run with Smith, Combe, Bogan and Milne all prolific in front of the opposition goal.

A week following Lawrie Reilly's reserve team debut, World War Two was finally at an end. After the early August annihilation by the US atomic bombs dropped on Japanese cities Hiroshima and Nagasaki, Japan surrendered and the world was now at peace – just over six years after fighting had begun. It would be another eleven months before officially recognised football would resume, at the start of the 1946/47 season.

Defeating a Scottish Command XI 2–1, with Gordon and John Devlin the scorers, then losing to Falkirk a week later, 13 October saw Lawrie Reilly, aged sixteen years and 350 days (Gordon had been thirteen days younger on his debut!), make his first team debut for Hibernian against Kilmarnock at Rugby Park. A closely fought match ended with a 4–3 victory to the Edinburgh side with a Milne double, Bogan and a spectacular fifty-five-yard 'wonder-goal' from Sammy Kean. For his debut, Reilly played at number 8 in a forward line that read: Smith, Reilly, Milne, Bogan and Caskie.

After drawing the following week at home to Motherwell, Gordon's display against Third Lanark did enough for the watching selectors to include him in the forthcoming international against Wales – an international notable for being the only time both legendary suitors for the right wing position, Smith and Waddell, appeared for Scotland together. A crowd of nearly 100,000 attended Hampden Park and everybody was talking about two players: twenty-one-year-old Hibs star, Gordon Smith, and twenty-four-year-old Rangers legend, Willie Waddell. Waddell was played as his normal position on the right wing whilst Gordon was tried out at inside right, to accommodate both players. The selection of the pair was a success to a degree, as Waddell scored one of Scotland's goals from a pass by Smith in a 2–0 victory.

The following week, Gordon had a thrilling experience, as part of a Scottish Select team who were whisked off to Germany, playing two matches in two days. They departed from Prestwick in an RAF Douglas Dakota and this was twenty-one-year-old Gordon's first trip on an aeroplane – all the more alluring as the plane was normally used for armed service personnel only. Over the next nineteen years as a professional footballer, Gordon was to travel on many planes of all shapes and sizes but he had particularly fond memories of this first flight, which flew directly to where the team were to play their first match, landing on an airstrip within 'spitting distance' of the pitch.

Obviously, some of the Scotland squad were quite used to this mode of travel, having only recently been de-mobbed from overseas action during World War Two – but not Gordon. Aberdeen's Archie Baird sat with Gordon on the flight and detailed his war story. He'd been taken prisoner at Tobruk in Libya, spent two years at a POW camp in Italy before escaping, then went into hiding with an Italian family, posing as their son and learning the language fluently and living on meagre rations. Gordon was captivated and felt very privileged to be sitting next to a war hero!

The Scots team ran out 4–2 winners in front of around 12,000 fans – mainly servicemen – with Dennis Westcott and Reg Lewis scoring for the Combined Military Services XI and Delaney, Jimmy Garth and a brace from Walker for the Scottish XI. This exciting game was the first of two so-called 'internationals' in twenty-four hours, arranged to entertain the troops still based in Germany. Most were from the 51st Division, based in Celle, a medieval town in the lower Saxony region of Germany, and they thoroughly enjoyed the spectacle.

Gordon's performance once again made the headlines. 'GORDON SMITH'S WONDER EFFORT LED TO SECOND GOAL', written in large bold lettering, headlined the front page of the *Sunday Mail*, once again followed by a rave commentary from Rex Kingsley:

> Air-Vice-Marshal Huddleston shook hands with the players before the start and a wonderful Scottish atmosphere was created by the Dagenham girl pipers who played on the field – they are with the E.N.S.A in Celle. In the 18th minute, a second goal came from one of the most brilliantly perfect moves any football ground has ever known. A clearance was sent to Gordon Smith on the line. Facing the fans – many of whom had rushed to sit along the touch-line, he seemed to be hopelessly baulked.
>
> Most wingers would have let the ball run over. But Gordon whipped it up with one foot, hooked it over his head with the other to Baird and wheeled round along the line to get the return. From man to man that ball sped: Smith-Garth-Walker-Garth-Smith and then a low one at goal which cracked off the upright for Delaney to smack home. The crowd roared. Scots troops threw their Balmorals in the air. The Dagenham girl pipers squealed with delight, although there wasn't a Scots lassie amongst them!

Following the game, both teams dined together at the Trenchard Barracks before going to the Garrison Theatre. The Scots then flew to Hamburg in their 'private' Dakota, eager for their second match a mere few hours away, with an exuberant Gordon running to the aircraft, making sure he was first on!

The very next afternoon, in front of a massive crowd of 35,000, the Scottish select side drew 1–1 with a very different Combined Military Services XI. The CMS XI replaced six players following the previous day's defeat, while the injured Sammy Cox of Dundee was the only change by the Scots, calling in Celtic's Malcolm MacDonald.

'YOUNG SCOTS DESERVED A SECOND VICTORY', wrote Mr Kingsley in the *Daily Record* on Monday, 19 November:

> Despite the fact that the services made six team changes to wipe out Saturday's unexpected smacking at Celle, they were actually made to look poorer than that defeated eleven. At no time did they show the skill and team-sense of this surprisingly clever bunch of young Scots. 'Take him on the outside, Gordon,' was among the shouts. Gordon Smith, knocking the ball past Westwood, lofted it into the goalmouth for Delaney to crash home. But the shouts of the fans were choked as the referee gave offside against the Celt. If the decision was correct, it was tighter than a Victorian corset!

As the Scottish team flew home, the trial of Rudolph Hess, amongst others, was starting in Nuremberg. Gordon still had a 'soft spot' for the one-time German Deputy Führer – who brought back those bitter-sweet memories of his early days at Easter Road when he travelled back and forth to Montrose in the spring of 1941. Although accepting the eventual outcome of lifetime imprisonment, Gordon was pleased nonetheless that Hess didn't receive the death penalty, which could so easily have been the case.

Back home in Scotland, now early December, Hibernian defeated Rangers 3–2 at Easter Road with another scintillating display from the Hibs number 7. Jimmy Caskie had left Hibs to join Rangers and this was his first match, ironically back in Leith. Without a doubt, Smith detested Rangers in his early years in Edinburgh, although he was to mellow subsequently. The hatred was mainly due to the 'hostile Ibrox crowd' as he called them, and the often rash treatment he received from the Rangers defenders, Jock 'Tiger' Shaw, Sammy Cox and George Young, and especially the future manager Scott Symon, who had kicked Gordon in an off-the-ball incident a couple of years previously, telling him, 'There'll be more of that to come, son.' While Smith was very friendly with some Rangers players, notably the two WWs, Willie Waddell and Willie Woodburn, he definitely appeared to up his game for Rangers matches and treated them all like cup finals.

A couple of days later, Harry Young's article in the *Evening Citizen* pronounced:

> Against Hibernian on Saturday, Rangers were chiefly troubled by the individual greatness of one player – Gordon Smith. The young outside right has never shown up in a more picturesque light.
>
> I prefer to see footballers less mechanical than the Russians [Moscow Dynamo had recently played Rangers]. Players like Gordon Smith, who can weave a spell over a game, are to me at least a tonic and I wish there were more personalities of his type. Gordon's Ibrox display made it quite clear that the Scottish selectors were foolish to try to make him an inside forward. His greatness is as a winger, and I believe that the boy will eventually become even more famous than Stanley Matthews. In one respect at least, he is already streets ahead – he has a scoring shot which Matthews has not.

Just after the turn of the year, one of the many New Year greetings received by Gordon Smith was a letter from a German POW, due to return soon to his native Hamburg. In his note, Hans asked Gordon to convey to the Hibs players his appreciation of their skill and said his visits to Easter Road would always be outstanding memories of his 'stay' in Scotland.

At the end of January, Gordon was back at Hampden Park, this time to face Belgium for a national side that included Jimmy Delaney and Tommy Walker. Some people may argue this was Gordon's first 'peace-time' international game and technically his first 'official' non-wartime cap, but most record books state otherwise; even though the war had ended months ago, it wasn't until the start of season 1946/47 that 'official' caps resumed. Delaney scored twice for Scotland whilst Lemberechts and D'Aguilar were the Belgian scorers, ending the game at 2–2. Archie Baird, Jimmy Campbell and Hearts' Jimmy Walker made their international debuts for Scotland but were never to receive a full cap for their country again. John Deakin from St Mirren, making his third appearance for his country, was also never to play again at this level. After the debilitating war years, and in an ever-changing team, Partick Thistle's Jimmy McGowan and Celtic's George Paterson only played one more time in the dark blue of Scotland. Like all countries, Scotland was going through a transitional period following the war and experimented with various players and formations in order to find 'the perfect blend'.

Willie Peat's goal had been enough to seal victory for Hibs in the New Year's Day clash with Hearts and, since the season had started well, including a seven-game unbeaten run, Hibs' chances of winning the title had increased. However, an 'up and down' end of the season resulted in another second place finish behind rivals Rangers for the second year in a row.

Gordon finished the 1945/46 season as top-scorer with fourteen goals, alongside Arthur Milne. Stan Seymour, the Newcastle United manager, was a regular visitor to Easter Road to check on Gordon. Yet despite the mesmeric skills Gordon displayed week after week, Seymour himself was quite baffled by the bizarre omission of Gordon from the Scotland side that faced England in the 13 April international match at Hampden Park.

The celebrated match was billed as the 'Victory International', with the game at Hampden Park resulting in a 1–0 victory for the Scots, due to a goal scored by recent Manchester United signing Jimmy Delaney. Gordon, a travelling reserve once again, alongside Sammy Kean, had been replaced by his rival and friend, Willie Waddell. His Hibernian team-mate, Davie Shaw, partnered his brother, Rangers' Jock 'Tiger' Shaw, in defence, with Gordon and Sammy cheering particularly loudly for Davie.

The aptly named 'Victory Cup' on 20 April 1946 took the place of that year's Summer Cup, in recognition of the defeat of Germany. It got underway with a stunning hat-trick scored by Gordon in the 3–0 defeat of Dundee at Easter Road. This was followed by a 0–2 loss the following week but Gordon's three goals had done just enough to see Hibs through to the next round.

But before that next game, on May Day 1946, Hibernian travelled abroad – for the first time since Gordon had joined the club over five years earlier – to take on a British Army on the Rhine side that included Morton's Billy Steel. The match took place at the same Highbury venue in Celle, where Gordon had played the previous year for the Scottish Select XI. Gordon scored one of Hibs' goals, whilst Jock Weir scored two in a comfortable 3–0 victory. Hugh Howie had taken over from Bobby Combe as Gordon's room-mate for this trip, which ended up lasting the whole week since it included buses, trains, ferries, trams and cars – a lot slower than the Scotland Select XI's trusted Dakota!

With the team returning back to Edinburgh just hours before, the Victory Cup resumed with exhausted players, but a resounding 3–1 victory over Hearts at Easter Road was followed by a draw against Partick Thistle in Glasgow and a winning replay back in Leith, where Gordon and his team-mates were introduced to the recently elected Labour Prime Minister, Clement Attlee. The semi-final took place at neutral Tynecastle Park against a strong Clyde side, with Hibs scraping through 2–1 before regrettably losing the final 1–3 to Rangers in the middle of June at Hampden Park.

The massed bands of the 51st and 52nd Divisions had set the standard that preceded this match, which was presided over by a referee from Gordon's old Angus stomping ground. Mr Martin had been fortunate to have witnessed the rise of the young Gordon Smith many years prior in an official capacity, before the teenager signed for Hibernian and found fame. Unfortunately, he was to be of no help to the former Dundee junior in a game pretty much dominated by Rangers.

A Torry Gillick shot put into his own net by the hapless Finnegan opened the scoring for Rangers but Hibs drew level just on half-time with a strike by Aitkenhead after a brilliant move with Milne. Two second-half goals from Duncanson finished Hibs off – the first soon after the interval, and the second and clinching goal near the end of the contest.

After the disappointment of losing the cup, the gloom at the end of the 1945/46 season was to be lifted with Hibernian undertaking a tour to Czechoslovakia, predominately staying in Prague. Prague had been devastated but was already slowly recovering from the war, with the Russians still regarded as liberators. During the third flight of the trip from Amsterdam to the Czech capital, Gordon remembered being petrified, as there appeared to be a detonation on board the plane and it lost altitude dramatically before righting itself. Although he managed to convince himself otherwise, this was probably simply due to turbulence or a slight mechanical problem. Gordon had flown before but this was the first flight for many of the players, including manager Willie McCartney, and Gordon's first commercial flight. Understandably, they were all delighted to get off and set foot on solid ground.

The team played four matches, winning two and losing two. A 43,000 crowd at the opening game against AC Sparta Praha saw Gordon score in a 3–1 victory. This game was followed by a defeat to Brno but then a 7–1 conquest over Vitkovice, with Gordon scoring two goals, which lifted the Edinburgh side. The fourth and final match, like the second, ended in defeat to Slavia Praha, by the odd goal in five. A radio broadcast offered supporters in Edinburgh the novelty of listening to commentary on the two games Hibs played in Prague, presented by the roaring voice of team manager Willie McCartney.

During their stay in the Eastern European capital, Gordon, along with room-mate Hugh Howie, were awoken early one morning with water coming through the ceiling, dripping onto their heads. Sammy Kean and some other players had turned on the taps for their baths the previous afternoon but unknown to them, the water was turned off at the main for repairs. They subsequently forgot to turn the taps back round again and the water had come back on hours earlier – hence the soaking, and hence a flooded hotel with shoes and clothes floating through corridors!

Also while there, Smith and some of his other team-mates attended the trial of a suspected wartime collaborator at Prague's town hall. Gordon was fascinated with the trial, as he was with a lot of aspects of World War Two. At night, they would be invited to local banquets held in their honour and would visit theatres and go to shows, and then the next day back to the trial. Whilst in Prague, Smith also visited what he called 'a disgusting barbaric' circus and disliked it immensely because of the horrific cruelty – the only thing he was to have an aversion to on an otherwise fantastic trip. At the end of the Slavia Praha game, some young Czechoslovakians mistook the Hibernian manager for Winston Churchill and Gordon remembered Sammy Kean especially found this hilarious – as the two effervescent gentlemen did look a little similar!

The players' flight home was to be less of an adventure than the outbound one had been and the Hibs team was soon safely back in Edinburgh. Yet just hours after returning to his home, Gordon was repacking and heading out of the country again – this time with his friends Willie Murphy and Willie's wife Helen, who introduced Gordon to what would become one of his great loves – the French Riviera, especially Cannes.

After two weeks in the sun, the Hibernian footballer was back in Edinburgh again, resplendent and beautifully tanned from, in Gordon's own words, 'an absolutely marvellous holiday' – his first ever holiday, as such. The twenty-two-year-old hadn't benefited enough though, it would seem, and was presented with the keys of a new dark red MG sports car – a gift from the gregarious and very generous Mr Murphy, as a token of their friendship. A gesture, as you can imagine, that Gordon would never forget.

9

THE OFFERS START ROLLING IN

BEFORE THE start of the new season, twenty-two-year-old Gordon received a letter from new Manchester United manager, Matt Busby, saying that the Old Trafford side would 'very much like him' to sign for them. They would be offering Hibs somewhere in the region of £40,000 for his signature, if he accepted, which was a record amount at the time with Gordon's wage and bonuses increasing five-fold. The lure of playing for Matt Busby was almost too much to turn down. His magnetism, his great friendship – more than the attraction of Manchester United – had unsettled him and he told no one except his father about the offer.

Gordon thought very long and hard over this and agonised whilst making his decision. The main reason he didn't want to go was primarily because he was very happy and content at Easter Road, he loved every minute of it and he (rightly) predicted success in Leith. He also didn't really want to be away from Edinburgh and his family. Matt Busby was extremely disappointed when Gordon wrote back and turned him down, but he understood his reasons for the refusal to move to England.

Just prior to the new football campaign, Gordon, who that very morning had collected his new prized possession from the garage, took the Hibernian manager outside the players' entrance on Albion Road to show him his new MG sports car – the very first car that he could call his own. McCartney was horrified by the colour, which was a shade of dark red!

'What sort of colour do you think this is, Gordon?' he yelled. 'You'll be out on your bahookie if I see it again,' he teased.

McCartney continued his diatribe, as a large gathering of players and staff now assembled to look at the 'Hearts car' – with more hilarity than Albion Road had seen in a long time. An embarrassed Gordon, with his face now as red as his new car, was further goaded by the Hibernian boss: 'You've been here five years now – I sincerely hope you're not still harbouring a secret passion for your boyhood team!'

In the early August of 1946, at a sun-drenched Easter Road, John Cuthbertson scored what was to be the first of a massive ten goals on the day and the first post-war goal for the Leith side. Hibs demolished a Queen of the South side 9–1 as 35,000 fans cheered, with Jock Weir scoring four, Cuthbertson two, and Archie Buchanan, Johnny Aitkenhead and Gordon himself on the scoresheet. Four days later and the exhilaration of winning 2–1 at Ibrox Park was crushed with the news of the death of eighty-nine-year-old Paddy Canon, who had been with the Leith club since 1896 – first as trainer and latterly as a groundsman. Gordon had a close bond with the distinguished gentleman and was deeply upset on hearing the news.

More distress came as Smith suffered a foot injury at Pittodrie in a defeat against Aberdeen and he was replaced in the next game by young Lawrie Reilly. However, Gordon returned for the friendly against Sparta Praha and was back to full fitness for the end of October 'new-style' League Cup meeting against Third Lanark at Hampden Park. He scored a goal on his return in the 2–1 win with debutant Eddie Turnbull scoring the other.

The fourth signing of what would become the Famous Five was that of Willie Ormond from Stenhousemuir in mid November, and a week later the set was complete when Willie McCartney drove to Selkirk to snatch Bobby Johnstone away from an almighty debacle involving local team, Selkirk, and Midlothian's Newtongrange Bluebell – who were controversially wrangling over who owned the rights to his registration. Although the Famous Five were now all signed for Hibernian Football Club, it would be nearly two and a half years before the five played together in the same side.

Two nights later, Gordon won his first official cap against Northern Ireland for Scotland at Hampden Park. The 0–0 draw also featured his team-mate Davie Shaw at full back. Although this was his 'first' cap, it was the ninth time he'd represented his country since his first schoolboy international eight years earlier.

Wins at Dumfries and Tynecastle in the New Year's Day derby game, with draws against Rangers and Morton, kept Hibernian in contention for their first League Championship in forty-four years.

The 8–0 thrashing of Alloa Athletic in a cup-tie was followed by the sale of Jock Weir to Blackburn Rovers – one of the clubs also on Gordon's trail. Gordon had built up a bond with Weir off the pitch, and a good understanding on it, in their years together at the club. The £10,000 fee equalled the record amount between English and Scottish clubs. That historical fact would, no doubt, have been dwarfed had Gordon (and Harry Swan) accepted Manchester United's offer.

Heavy snow in February 1947 decimated the league programme but a Scottish Cup tie went ahead as 101,500 fans kept each other warm at Ibrox, with Hibs and Rangers fighting out a 0–0 draw. As the replay was scheduled for Easter Road, with its much smaller capacity, the Rangers Chairman asked Harry Swan to instead hold the game back at Ibrox again so both teams could benefit from another 100,000 plus pay-day at the turnstiles, but this was dismissed completely by Swan.

Before the Scottish Cup replay, Smith was to score another hat-trick for Hibs against Airdrie in the League Cup and Bobby Flavell did likewise for the Lanarkshire team in a 3–3 draw. Long before the so-called modern invention of 'the golden goal' to end a cup-tie, Hibernian won the League Cup replay against Airdrie with a goal scored in the 125th minute of the match by Willie Finnegan. The life of the golden goal was to be short lived at this juncture, with most clubs not in favour.

The largest ever crowd seen at Easter Road to date was the 50,000 who went to see Rangers in the Scottish Cup replay, which was won 2–0 by Hibs with the second goal scored in the last minute of the match. Unfortunately for Hibs, they lost the next time they played Rangers – this time in the League Cup semi-final at the end of March at Hampden Park, where 126,000 saw the Glasgow side win 3–1.

Hugh Howie scored at both ends in the Scottish Cup semi-final against Motherwell and his goal for the Leith side in the 142nd minute meant that Hibs were in their first Scottish Cup final in twenty-three years. Howie's goal, along with Hibernian goal-scorer extraordinaire Eddie Turnbull's first goal of the game, made the final score 2–1.

On the eve of Gordon travelling down to London with the Scotland team to face England at Wembley, both Aston Villa and Arsenal tabled bids for the right winger.

Gordon's tour card itinerary for the Wembley Spring International read:

Time Table for the Team.

Scotland v England at Wembley 12th April 1947

Wednesday, April 9th

9.00am Party will assemble at Central Station, Glasgow.

10.00am Train leaves for London – Lunch and tea, en route.

6.15pm Arrive Euston Station, London.

(Players of English clubs will join Party on arrival)

Party will proceed by Motor Coach to

Headquarters – White Hart Hotel, Sonning

Thursday, April 10th

Arrangements will be announced at breakfast at 9am

Friday, April 11th

Arrangements will be announced at breakfast at 9am

Saturday, April 12th

9am Breakfast

11am Leave Hotel by Motor Coach

12.15pm Lunch at the Hop Bine Hotel, North Wembley

1.30pm Leave for Stadium

After the Match proceed according to Council Time Table

Signed G.G. Graham, Secretary

Following the 1–1 draw, Gordon sat with Stanley Matthews and the English legend questioned him on why Hibs wouldn't sell him to a big English club. He mentioned in conversation to Gordon that he was leaving Stoke City, his club of fifteen years, for another club but would not elaborate further. Matthews self-effacingly told Gordon that 'you would be as successful as me down here – if not more', and before leaving with the rest of the English party, he signed the Hibernian winger's time-table card: 'To Gordon, best wishes, Stanley Matthews.'

Hibernian played Aberdeen in the Scottish Cup final in April 1947, losing 1–2. The 83,000 in attendance had paid between 2/- and

£1. 3s. 0d for the privilege of watching the final. Gordon, along with his Hibs team-mates, was heartbroken at the end of the match, with the Hibs winger saying the game had been there for the taking before storming out of Hampden in a terrible mood. Eager autograph hunters would have to put up with an empty smile from the Hibs winger.

Hibernian's last game of the 1946/47 season fell on Saturday, 10 May – the same day as the Great Britain v Rest of Europe match, which celebrated the readmission of England, Scotland, Wales and Northern Ireland to FIFA. Hampden Park was packed as 137,610 fans excitedly watched as the Great Britain side, coached by Hibernian trainer Hugh Shaw and including Swift, Matthews, Mannion and Lawton from England and Liddell and Steel from Scotland, easily won 6–1.

Following the game, Matthews and Smith had a very brief chat before Gordon joined the rest of the Hibs players heading to the Hampden pitch to face Third Lanark for a 6pm kick-off, with a crowd that was considerably smaller than it was for the earlier one at 3pm. As Matthews was just leaving Hampden and heading to the Great Britain team coach, he shouted to Gordon, 'Blackpool, here I come!' The thirty-two-year-old winger had been sold, as he rightly forecast, for £11,500 to the 'Seasiders', Blackpool, in what proved to be a great move for the English winger.

Hibs finished second in the Scottish Cup and second in the league. Their five matches against Rangers during the course of the season attracted the enormous total of 382,000 fans. Just before the Hibernian party made their way to the airport for a trip to Norway, Newcastle United made what was a 'very substantial' offer for Gordon, which was once again immediately turned down by Hibs Chairman Harry Swan.

A few days later, the club embarked on a short tour in Norway.

HIBS TOUR OF NORWAY

S.I.F. Stavanger 0–5 Hibernian (Smith 3, Turnbull 2)

Djero Bergen 0–11 Hibernian
(Smith 4, Ormond 4, Turnbull 2, Johnston)

Gjoes (Oslo) 0–7 Hibernian (Smith 2, Reilly 4, Ormond)

Sparsborg 2–5 Hibernian (Johnston 2, Buchanan, Ormond, Turnbull)

Norkopping 3–1 Hibernian (Johnston)

Incredibly, it would appear at first glance that the Famous Five were already playing and scoring goals galore. However, the Johnston without an 'e' scoring four tour goals was Leslie Johnston; although Bobby was signed for the club, it would be nearly two more years before the famous Nithsdale match and the first appearance of the five all together. With the imminent arrival of Alec Linwood from Middlesbrough, Hibs were to have another reputed forward line prior to the Famous Five gracing the pitch.

Gordon decided, in the early summer of 1947, to purchase a grocery business on Willowbrae Road. It hadn't been doing particularly well but a house was attached and he saw this as the ideal opportunity for his family to move with him from 63 South Bridge, where they'd lived for five years. With his own savings plus a loan from the bank, Smith took over the reins, making many alterations to the premises. He had considered buying the Kilspindie Hotel in Aberlady but after serious talks with his friend Willie Murphy and other local prominent businessmen, he opted for the Edinburgh venture.

With five-a-side competitions, cricket matches and training at Gullane sands keeping the Hibs players on their toes throughout the summer, Lancashire club Blackburn Rovers enquired about the Hibs winger and Newcastle United appealed to Harry Swan for the fourth time. Although deeply flattered by these offers, Gordon remained content in Leith and could sense success was just around the corner. Hibernian was the only club for him.

10

GLORY, GLORY TO THE HIBEES

> Mr McCartney was a big man, but he was always prepared to listen. At other times he could shatter us without saying a word, just by his personality and presence. If things were not going well with us, he would come down from the Directors Box and stand in the middle of the tunnel, where he knew we would see him. I would say to myself, 'Oh my God! We'll have to do something,' and we generally did.
>
> – Gordon Smith

THE NEW season of 1947/48 was about to commence – a season that would have a terrible tragedy in it, yet bestow glorious ecstasy before it had ended. Before the league season started though, Gordon played in his sixth Edinburgh Charities game against English FA Cup holders, Derby County. The Edinburgh Select lost 4–5 in an enthralling game, with English cap Raich Carter the star of the show.

As Hibs' new player Alec Linwood was photographed and interviewed by the press following his £10,000 move from the Teesside club, Hibernian played with numbers on their strips for the very first time. They regrettably lost to Hearts but the press christened the new Hibs attack as the '£50,000 Forward Line' – Gordon Smith, Leslie Johnston, Alec Linwood, Eddie Turnbull and Willie Ormond.

During this period, if Gordon had a day off that corresponded with a Blackpool home game, he would drive down to meet with Stanley Matthews. Following the match, the pair would discuss football and cars over fish and chips in one of the many coastal tea-rooms situated within a stone's throw of the Irish Sea.

In mid August, Gordon scored a prolific five goals in three days – two against Aberdeen and a hat-trick against Clyde. This was followed in the next nine games with five victories, two draws and two defeats – both by rivals Hearts, making it three defeats by their Edinburgh rivals and it was still only October!

Hibs, though, were top of the table at Halloween and the following day at Fir Park, Gordon scored in a 2–1 victory. Having collected the ball in midfield, Smith proceeded to bear down on the Motherwell goal at speed, beating man after man before splitting the full backs to prod the ball past the goalkeeper as he fell. The goal was acknowledged with thunderous applause from both sets of supporters. Gordon would later say: 'That was the best goal I have ever scored. I just couldn't do anything wrong that day. I was told afterwards that I had beaten seven men before scoring.'

On the train journey back to Edinburgh, there were a few players in the compartment along with Willie McCartney and Harry Swan. The manager was silent for a while, and then he broke from his reverie to say, 'I'd love to win this league Championship. If we could win this league, I would give every player £100.' Such a sum was a lot of money at the time and Harry Swan quickly disassociated himself from such reckless enthusiasm.

The following week, Third Lanark's players were stunned into submission by the sustained brilliance of two of the Easter Road front men, who scored all eight goals between them. In a devastating and quite magnificent performance, Gordon scored an epic five goals at Easter Road against the Glasgow side in an 8–0 win. Although matched twice in England, the five goals scored by a winger in a Scottish professional football match is a record that stands to this day. Gordon Smith was certainly at his peak as 'uncrowned king of Easter Road'.

Lawrie Reilly remembers Gordon running up the wing with the ball on his head, keeping it in the air for what seemed like an age, before crossing an inch-perfect cross for Linwood to score his hat-trick. Poor Alec Linwood – imagine scoring a hat-trick and hardly getting a mention in the press!

Four days later, alongside team-mate Jock Govan and other star players, such as Willie Woodburn, Billy Steel and Jimmy Delaney, Gordon played in an international match at Hampden, defeated at home by a Wales team for the first time in a decade.

Then, finally, Hibernian defeated rivals Hearts at the fourth attempt of the season on the first day of 1948. A 3–1 derby-day win at Easter Road secured the points for high-flying Hibs, leaving Hearts perilously close to the foot of the table.

A few days later, the Hibs team sang 'Happy Birthday' and there were fifty-two candles on club chairman Harry Swan's birthday cake. Willie McCartney then addressed the players at the Leith team's annual dinner dance at the North British Hotel for what would be the very last time before his untimely death.

Alongside Willie Ormond, Gordon played in his first Scottish Football League match at Parkhead, as the home team defeated their Irish counterparts 3–0 in front of 40,000 fans. Then it was back with Hibs for a league victory over Queen of the South, after which the Scottish Cup took precedence. The following week, on Saturday, 24 January, Hibernian defeated Albion Rovers 2–0 at Coatbridge but their manager Willie McCartney, the catalyst of all things successful at the club, passed away.

He died at his home in Hillpark Avenue, Edinburgh, after taking ill during the game. He was driven home from the match by director Wilson Terris, accompanied by an injured Eddie Turnbull. None of the Hibs players were aware of his illness as they battled through the second half at Cliftonhill. It was noticed when he entered the dressing room at half-time that he looked a bit unwell, but was still his usual cheery self. A few minutes into the second half, whilst in the boardroom, he collapsed and a doctor was summoned immediately, reporting McCartney had suffered a heart attack. Once home, he was put to bed and soon appeared to be almost his normal jovial self.

When the victorious team reached Edinburgh, their bus stopped at Mr McCartney's home and trainer Hugh Shaw went in to express the players' wishes for a speedy recovery. However, shortly after, with his wife, two of his three daughters and his son at his bedside, he had a relapse and passed away. Eddie Turnbull, after seeing McCartney to his home with Wilson Terris, had gone out for a typical Saturday night and only realised the demise of his manager as he read the news that night on newspaper billboards.

The news completely devastated Gordon. He had looked upon McCartney as a friend, a confidant and very much a father figure, and his demise completely floored him. This man whom Gordon had known for almost seven years of his life, seven years in which he had progressed from a youth to a man, was gone. Gordon freely admitted that part of him died along with McCartney that day, too.

The day before the funeral, Gordon became a freemason. The timing could be construed as a little odd but then again, feeling so down and so low, Gordon felt the security of such an organisation alleviated his mood. Like so many of his team-mates and other professional football players in Scotland at the time, the twenty-three-year-old Gordon was welcomed to the 'Grand Lodge of Ancient Free and Accepted Masons of Scotland' at Lodge St Clair, Edinburgh, No. 349.

The funeral on 27 January was a sombre affair, with McCartney's coffin carried into the main chapel by senior players: Finnegan, Govan, Kerr, Kean, Combe and captain Davie Shaw. Amongst the many mourners were former Hearts stars, Barney Battles and Alex Massie. Almost immediately following the funeral, Hugh Shaw was appointed as the new Hibernian manager, after talk of Matt Busby being McCartney's successor was quashed.

Shaw's first game in charge for the Edinburgh team also produced his first victory – a 1–0 defeat of Rangers in a game that possibly determined where the League Championship flag would fly in August.

A new record home crowd of 57,755 watched as the Hibs team, playing in honour of their late manager, defeated their deadliest foes with a Cuthbertson goal scored with only seconds remaining. Rangers still led Hibs by one point at the top of the table but the Greens had two games in hand.

Willie Ormond broke his leg against Aberdeen but Hibs' season continued on the right track as victories over the Dons, Arbroath and Morton kept Hibs on Rangers' tail. In the Scottish Cup, after beating Arbroath, Aberdeen and St Mirren, they lost in the semi-final of the Scottish Cup at Hampden Park to their main competitors Rangers, in a game that would attract 143,570 – the biggest crowd outwith a final or international match in British football history. The gate receipts totalled £9,300, which was an enormous sum for the time. Hibs' reserve goalkeeper George Farm's unfortunate mistake allowed for the only goal of the game.

Hibs' defeat of Celtic on the same afternoon Queen's Park had beaten Rangers, followed by a draw against Partick Thistle in front of 30,000 at Easter Road, meant that Hibs needed only three points from the last two games to secure the title. (Until as recently as 1994, only two points were awarded for a win.)

On the cool Monday evening of 19 April, Hibernian slaughtered Motherwell 5–0, thus needing only one more point to win the league. Rangers now had to win all three remaining games and score twenty-six goals – a highly unlikely proposition.

Five days later, on Saturday, 24 April 1948, Hibernian Football Club, with fifty-six points, were crowned champions of Scotland – without kicking a ball. After Rangers had drawn their match at Fir Park against Motherwell, Hibs had won the league for the first time since 1903. Although they lost four league games away, including the inconsequential final match ten days later at Dens Park to Dundee, they remained unbeaten at home during the whole of the campaign.

Gordon Smith played twenty-nine league games netting nineteen goals – top scorer for the fifth time in eight seasons. Both Newcastle United and Aston Villa offered £25,000 for Smith but he was beginning to be known as the £40,000 footballer. Little did anyone know that Matt Busby had priced him at that figure nearly two seasons earlier.

Hibernian had won the title after all and fulfilled Willie McCartney's dream 'to win this League Championship'. It was a tragedy he never lived to see the glorious day. Gordon was ecstatic. His feelings had gone through a total metamorphosis, from being devastated as Hibs came second the previous year, to this feeling of sheer delight.

The day the championship was won, there were celebrations the likes of which public houses in Leith had never seen before. Hibernian won the Scottish League in 1947/48 for Willie McCartney and for all Hibs fans, and Gordon was in seventh heaven – he was apparently seen singing when leaving the Dominion Cinema later that evening!

Smith next represented the SFL in Dublin alongside Davie Shaw and Jock Govan as the visitors secured a 2–0 win. And four days later, back at Hampden in a full international against Belgium, he was on the winning team once more, playing alongside four other Hibernian players. Along with Smith, Govan and Shaw fresh from the Irish victory, they were joined by clubmates Eddie Turnbull and Bobby Combe, who scored one of Scotland's goals in another 2–0 score-line. Six Hibernian players had been in the squad, with Hugh Howie a travelling reserve.

Scotland then flew to Switzerland and France for two further international matches. In an unchanged side from the one that defeated

Belgium nineteen days previously, Scotland had a goal by Gordon Smith disallowed in the first half, but at least in true Swiss style, the players each received an inscribed Zenith watch after losing 1–2 with their only goal scored by former Hibs player Leslie Johnston. Whilst in Switzerland, as well as loving 'the clean crisp air', Gordon ransacked the local Krompholz & Co. record store in Berne's Spitalgasse 28, buying a large quantity of Fats Waller records to add to his ever-growing collection.

Bobby Combe was omitted from the France game, with Eddie Turnbull dropping back and playing at half back. Incredibly, Gordon was played at centre forward, but the Scots were soundly beaten 3–0 by a strong French side at the Olympic Stadium in Paris. This was to be Gordon's last 'full' cap for four years until playing against England in April 1952. He was chosen for a couple of international matches in this period but pulled out due to injury on both occasions. Quite unbelievably, the next time he represented Scotland, apart from playing in league matches, Hibernian would be back-to-back champions of Scotland!

Hibs' tour of Belgium via London started without the 'Scotland Six' so Gordon missed a visit to London's Hippodrome Theatre to see Vic Oliver. Alec Linwood scored in a 1–2 defeat by Standard Liege and following a 2–2 drawn match against a Liege select, the Scotland players joined the touring party to defeat Diables Rouges 5–2 and Charleroi Olympia 4–0, with Gordon scoring a screamer and Lawrie Reilly scoring two.

The final match of the tour was against Antwerp where Hibernian played under floodlights for the very first time, losing 1–2. This was also the first time the players had used a white ball in a game, as opposed to the normal brown or orange ball.

As Gordon celebrated his twenty-fourth birthday during the tour, the Belgian officials had kind-heartedly baked a cake to honour the Scotland star, but there was much consternation and indignation when the sponge appeared with a miniature footballer wearing a maroon jumper!

Gordon didn't venture abroad for his holiday in 1948, but instead he journeyed to Manchester with his brothers to see the touring Australian cricket side play England at Old Trafford. Much to his pleasure, his friend and former Arsenal player, Denis Compton, scored 145 not out, and in the next Test at Leeds, the Aussies were invincible, with cricketing superstar Don Bradman's 173 not-out securing victory. Cricket attendance at the time, like those of football, was huge and the two Test matches that Gordon saw were to become record attendances of 133,740 at Manchester and, still a record today, 158,000 at Leeds.

Gordon went to see another two cricket matches involving the great Australian touring side, as they played in Aberdeen as well as Edinburgh, finishing their tour in Britain with an impressive set of figures. They had remained undefeated in thirty-four matches, winning twenty-five and drawing nine. Gordon loved cricket at this point but in years to come, golf would move in to demote the sport into third place.

11

THE EMERGENCE OF THE FAMOUS FIVE

> The blend and the interchanging of the five – we nearly achieved perfection. One-footed Ormond, who didn't need a right; Reilly, who couldn't do more than ten yards, but needed only five; Johnstone, who pictured the advantage he needed before he gained it; Turnbull, who fired 'rockets' his colleagues came to take for granted; and then there was me.
>
> – Gordon Smith

RUMOURS THAT Stanley Matthews and Stan Mortenson had been seen in Gordon Smith's grocery store proved correct, with the English legends popping in to see Gordon prior to the annual Edinburgh Select Match. Blackpool FC was in town and the game played at Tynecastle that first Saturday in August 1948 ended 1–1 with Bobby Combe scoring for the hosts. Smith was on great form and as well as showing them around his shop earlier, he showed the legends how the game should be played by offering a breathtaking performance.

The unfurling of the 1947/48 League Championship flag was witnessed by 35,000 Hibs fans on a humid August day. Hibs played East Fife and the 5–2 victory was fitting for the occasion.

'And now, Mr Chairman, will you leave us?' – the immortal and awe-inspiring words that were often used by the bounding Willie McCartney to Harry Swan in the dressing room prior to a match, at a time when it was not common to bar directors from dressing rooms. Unfortunately, it was McCartney who had left and Hibs' next match was a testimonial in his honour against Manchester United. A white ball was used by Hibs for the first time in Scotland, as they had been impressed with the clarity of it in Belgium, and a 2/- entry-fee greeted the 36,000 fans who turned up to honour their late great manager, on 22 September. Ted Buckle of Manchester United scored the only goal of the game. Following the match, at the North British Hotel, the United manager Matt Busby recalled his time at Hibs as the best of his playing career.

A new record attendance was set in October of 1948 when 52,974 fans showed up at Easter Road as the Leith side entertained Celtic in a League Cup match. This stunning turn-out was followed by the defending champions beating Rangers at Ibrox 4–2 with a Smith rocket from all of forty-two yards catching goalkeeper Bobby Brown unawares. A drawn match on Christmas Day against Queen of the South meant Hibs were top of the league but unfortunately, in the New Year's Day derby at Tynecastle, they lost 2–3.

A report from the *Evening Citizen* two days after the Hearts defeat and following a 3–0 victory over Clyde at Easter Road read:

> Gordon Smith, I am sure, could retain complete mastery over a football even on an ice-rink. On an Easter Road surface of uncertain reaction, he was the graceful, gliding creator of football in the first half, which gave Hibs a firm hold on the game. But when, in the second half, Smith was neglected by his supports, the game relapsed to plebeian levels and Hibs lost their poise, if not a goal.

At the end of the month, Gordon was highlighted in the press again. This time, the account is taken from *The People's Journal and Angus Herald*.

> When Mr James F. Edward, Kinnettles School, Montrose, was a teacher in Southesk School, Montrose, he trained the football team. He was sure his star nine-year-old centre forward would go far in the game.
>
> Tomorrow, Mr Edward is going to Station Park, Forfar, to see his 'laddie' play. He is internationalist Gordon Smith of Hibs.
>
> 'Gordon was a grand wee chappie,' enthuses Mr Edward.
>
> 'He scored a lot of goals. I used to stand on the line and shout, "Come on, Gordon!" I once told him that he would be

an international and that I hoped he wouldn't forget I was the first to cry, "Come on, Gordon!"'

The International winger didn't forget. In a broadcast when he became famous, he said that Mr Edward had been the inspiration behind his football career.

Mr Edward laughs at memories of his early association with Gordon Smith.

'Gordon and his pals used to come along to my home in Montrose and ask my wife if I was coming out to play football. Gordon's brother played outside left in the Southesk team, and the right winger was Willie Robertson, now of Preston North End.

'Later I transferred to Parkhouse School in Arbroath, where the headmaster was Mr Keir, a director of Arbroath FC. I told him about Gordon Smith and, as there were no juvenile teams in Montrose then, we arranged for him to play for one of the Arbroath teams (Bromford). Mr Keir wanted to keep an eye on him.

'Later Gordon played for a Kirriemuir team, then went into Dundee junior football before signing for Hibs.

'He used to send me notes from the Continent and elsewhere when he travelled to play various teams.'

Mr Edward has never seen his former pupil play in senior football. Once, when Gordon was playing in Dundee, his old teacher arranged to travel from Aberlemno where he was headmaster.

'But,' he smiles ruefully, 'the children took whooping cough and I was tied to the house. But I'll be at Station Park on Saturday,' he vowed.

James Edward did see his old protégé Gordon Smith deliver two inch-perfect crosses for the visitors' first goals – headers by Ormond and Turnbull – and along with 5,346 other hardy souls, he braved torrential rain as Hibernian won 4–0 to progress further in the cup. An Angus Plumb header and another Willie Ormond left-foot drive completed the scoring.

In early March, after struggling to beat Raith Rovers, Hibs lost in the next round of the Scottish Cup against East Fife 0–2 at Easter Road.

Smith played at centre forward and Reilly wore Gordon's number 7, but the formation change didn't work out.

The same month, Gordon started golf lessons at Longniddry with Bill Morris. Smith was indifferent about it at first. A lot of the Hibernian players were golfers and Gordon had told them that he wouldn't play on their outings until he knew more about the game. He also started playing in the city at the Braid Hills Golf Club, aided by professional Dave Houston, then later at Gullane by Hugh Watt, before showing his fellow team-mates just how proficient he had become at hitting the wee white ball.

As Sammy Kean announced his retirement from the playing side of things at Easter Road, one era had ended but another would begin two days later following Kean's last game for the club; a forward line that would eventually become known as the Famous Five – Smith, Johnstone, Reilly, Turnbull and Ormond – played together for the very first time. At Sanquhar on 21 April, a Hibernian 8–1 defeat of Nithsdale Wanderers was no great shock, in fact, it was quite expected; the game is famous not for the scoreline, but for the fact that it was the first time, albeit in a friendly match, that the Famous Five played together in a game. Ormond with two, Reilly with two, Turnbull with two, Smith and Mick Gallagher, the Eire internationalist half back, were the scorers for Hibs on that now famous day.

Four days later, Hibernian travelled to London for a Challenge Match against north London side Tottenham Hotspur, winning 5–2 in front of over 40,000 fans. A John Ogilvie double, along with goals from Smith, Johnstone and Turnbull, sealed the win.

The next morning at breakfast in the team hotel, two incidents occurred that showed the high esteem in which Smith was held in the capital. Firstly, in a morning newspaper, Gordon read a very complimentary article:

> As a Scottish journalist domiciled in London, I saw Hibs give a grand display against Spurs at White Hart Lane to win 5–2.
>
> What a pity Gordon Smith cannot produce internationally the form he displayed in this game. He had the 40,000 crowd roaring in the last half hour with a display of wing play I've never seen as good before.
>
> He danced around three defenders before crashing a goal

past Ditchburn, his style of play, that Stanley Matthews could not have bettered.

Gordon Smith, I am certain, is the equal of Matthews and Finney as a ball player.

Gordon Smith will go down into history as the man who preferred to walk alone. I've seen him do things that neither Finney, nor Matthews have ever attempted. I've seen him do things with a ball that no other player in my life-time has attempted, let alone achieved. In many ways, he is probably the most naturally gifted footballer the game has ever known. Yet while the Scottish national team has a trip to the USA, he still continues to sell groceries in his shop in Edinburgh, and seems quite happy, thank you.

Secondly, just ahead of the Edinburgh team's departure back to Scotland the morning following the game, a deputation from Arsenal FC arrived at their central London hotel, seeking out Harry Swan. The Arsenal manager, Tom Whittaker, came straight to the point. 'We'd like to have Gordon Smith at Highbury.'

Harry Swan did a lightning bit of calculation, then came back with Hibernian's figure for Smith's transfer. 'We'd like to have the Highbury stands and offices at Easter Road – if a swap could be arranged.'

It's a good job Swan didn't give Stan Seymour the same reply when Newcastle United had recently made their umpteenth inquiry about Gordon – because Mr Seymour's immediate reaction would have been to get the wrecking ball and a team of removal men on the job at St James' Park as quick as possible!

An inconsiderable disparity occurred on 30 April as Hibernian were 'humbled in the highlands' by a Highland League Select, who beat them 1–0 at Inverness. Dave Siegel's twenty-eighth minute goal for the Select was the difference between the teams, although Hibs had fielded five internationalists. Three minutes from time, Hibernian attacked with Gordon Smith as the spearhead, trying hard for the equalizer, but Alex, known as Eck, MacDougall brilliantly saved from the centre at point-blank range.

The Famous Five forward line was recalled for the second time in its short life in a 4–0 victory in Belfast on 4 May, with goals from Johnstone with two, Smith and Turnbull sealing the victory over an Irish FA XI.

The match was played at Windsor Park in Belfast and was in aid of the Ulster War Memorial Building Fund. Wartime Hibee Hugh Colvin played in the Irish side and was given a warm welcome in the Hibs changing room ahead of the game.

News reached the Hibs party the following morning of a terrible tragedy. On returning from a match in Lisbon against Benfica, the entire playing squad of illustrious Italian champions, FC Torino, perished in a plane crash. The Italian Airlines Fiat jet was on approach to Turin airport, amidst a severe thunderstorm with poor visibility, when it crashed into the Basilica in the nearby town of Superga. Gordon and his fellow Hibs team-mates were horrified by this disaster. On top of the tragic loss of life, air travel was becoming a very important and regular part of their lives and they were deeply affected by this horror story. Gordon would be even more devastated in just under a decade's time when another football air tragedy occurred, this time involving friends that he knew well.

In the meantime, Tottenham Hotspur tabled a £35,000 bid for Gordon Smith, who had been the 'talk of London' since his recent majestic performance at White Hart Lane. Hibernian refused point blank to sell their star player to them, Arsenal, Newcastle United or anyone else for that matter!

A group of Scottish internationalists, including Gordon's team-mate Lawrie Reilly and Rangers friends Willie Woodburn and Willie Waddell, sailed on the RMS *Queen Mary* to play a series of challenge matches on the east coast of the USA and Canada at the end of May. The players' cabins were in economy class with the officials obviously in first class! The majestic liner took a week to reach New York City and during the sail, the SFA could visit the players but the players could not visit the SFA in their more elite cabins. However, the players had been given a 'substantial sum' of US dollars to spend whilst in New York, with Lawrie telling the story that he bought 'about a dozen pairs of nylons' for his soon-to-be wife. How decadent!

During this halcyon period, Hibernian Football Club were the best team in Scotland, arguably in Britain, and had there been a European competition, undoubtedly Hibs would have either won it or been knocking at the door.

12

ANOTHER SPORT WINS GORDON'S HEART

IN JULY 1949, Gordon met the golfer Bobby Locke for the first time, just prior to the tournament at Royal St George's Golf Club in Sandwich, Kent. Mutual friend Stanley Matthews introduced the pair. Locke and Gordon instantly clicked and became firm friends, with Gordon amending his booking and staying in his central London hotel for a week instead of the pre-planned three days. The pair was to remain in close contact until Locke's death in 1987.

The thirty-two-year-old South African golf phenomenon, Arthur D'Arcy 'Bobby' Locke, would go on to win the British Open Golf Championship on four occasions – winning the tournament three times in four years. He won the 1949 Open Championship by two shots over Ireland's Harry Bradshaw, following a play-off when they had been level on 5 under par after four rounds completed. Argentinean Roberto De Vicenzo, finishing two shots behind, came third. He was a big football fan and Gordon had great delight in recounting stories to him as the trio dined together at a nearby restaurant the night before Locke's play-off victory over the Irishman.

Locke's relationship with most of the players on the circuit was good, but there was an underlying and growing resentment from some. 'Locke was simply too good, they had to ban him,' quoted 1948 US Masters winner Claude Harmon; but Locke was great friends with American golfing genius, Ben Hogan, whom Gordon had been reading about and would become another of his heroes and achieve an even greater feat than Locke. By winning the US Open Golf Championship, four times in total, as well as the US Masters twice, the PGA twice and the British Open Championship in 1953, Hogan's haul of nine 'majors' in a seven-year period (1946–1953) has never been equalled – even the sublime Eldrick 'Tiger' Woods only managed a mere eight major wins in the same period of time!

Hogan and Locke had a mutual respect and enormous admiration for each other. The South African, known for his famous quotation 'You drive for show, but putt for dough,' marvelled at the graceful Hogan and would tell Gordon: 'He's the one you should be watching, not me!' The similarities between Locke, Hogan and Smith were there for all to see. Although Smith was a footballer, all three aspired to be the best and aimed for greatness, and over the next few years, they all reached their goal.

In the subsequent twenty-five years, Smith would follow Locke to every Open Championship in July and to many other tournaments around the UK and Europe as well. Any chance he got, he would be off to watch the great South African player. It would be fair to say that Gordon was becoming obsessive about golf – only months after essentially rejecting it!

Just before the new season of 1949/50 began, Hibs had taken part in a football 'head-tennis' tournament against Hearts. They played in the centre of Edinburgh at Princes Street Gardens with Hibs heading in style and winning 3–2.

The pre-season runs in the King's Park (now known as Holyrood Park) and to Seafield and Portobello were gruelling and legendary. Hibs also continued to travel down the coast to run up and down the sand dunes of Gullane beach, twenty-five years before Rangers manager Jock Wallace received the credit for introducing this form of stamina-building training.

Gordon Smith was made captain of Hibernian for the season and he would write articles for the *Scottish Daily Mail* every Wednesday and Friday. Yet again, Newcastle United offered a vast, undisclosed sum for Smith – the highest yet, apparently. Gordon had been seen entering the chairman's office along with Newcastle United's George Martin and Stan Seymour; discussions lasted for a 'lengthy' period but nothing came of it.

Gordon's run in the Edinburgh Charity Matches continued and this year, his sixth in a row, the Select entertained Wolverhampton Wanderers at Easter Road with a large 46,077 crowd in attendance. The

Edinburgh Select, with Alfie Conn scoring both goals, weren't a match for a Midlands side who scored three and included Bert Williams and Billy Wright in their line-up.

Gordon, effervescent with 'the Bobby Locke effect', now started playing alongside his Hibs colleagues on their golf outings and his practice had unquestionably paid off. Without a doubt, he was right up there with the best of the Hibs golfers and was, as he put it, 'going to master this royal and ancient pastime'. Jimmy Kerr and Bobby Combe were Hibs' champion golfers but newcomer Smith, alongside new trainer Sammy Kean, were hot on their heels. As golf frenzy gripped the club, it was talked about continuously at training and even on match days by the players – a lot more than any talk of famous forward lines, for now at least.

On 15 October, the Famous Five played together in a league game for the first time. Smith and Turnbull were the Hibs' scorers on the day and, appropriately for the occasion, Gordon had written in the Match Day programme:

> Try everything to get that extra yard. A winger who can take the ball forward on the turn can leave a defender well behind and get into position for a cross before he has recovered. The cross is vital. Vary your crosses with a hard low effort at times – it only needs the touch of a boot or a bounce of an unwary defender to beat the 'keeper. When shooting, make the far-post your objective – try a run in occasionally and change direction with a left foot shot to the near corner.

In mid October, Gordon was recalled for an SFL international match after a year and five months in the wilderness, but it was to be another two and a half years until he played his next full international for Scotland. Smith returned to Dublin to play against the League of Ireland with team-mate Lawrie Reilly playing on the left wing, scoring the only goal of the game.

The following week's home game against Rangers was memorable for Gordon more for the music than the football! It was Smith's turn to choose a song to be played over the PA system preceding the game and his choice of Fats Waller's 'My Very Good Friend the Milkman' was surprisingly sung along to by a large number of the crowd.

On 9 November, Gordon travelled to Glasgow to watch Lawrie Reilly in action for the national side against Wales, with Billy Liddell playing on the right wing. This was Scotland's first ever World Cup qualifying game for the 1950 World Cup in Brazil. Even though UEFA had sanctioned that the top two from the 'Home International Championships' of England, Scotland, Wales and Northern Ireland could qualify, for some absurd reason known only to them, the SFA took a dim view of this and decided that they would only send a team over to Rio de Janeiro if they finished top of the group. In other words, they had to finish ahead of England, which required beating them at Hampden; unfortunately, they lost 0–1 and therefore missed out on a tournament and an adventure of a lifetime.

The Hibernian team's love of golf was to feature in their trip to Birmingham toward the end of the year for a friendly against Aston Villa. The 2–5 loss at Villa Park was overshadowed by a heated contest at Sandhills Golf and Country Club in the Warwickshire countryside. Second-team captain Willie Clark's concentration was interrupted when an unknown player shouted he'd seen a ferret run up his trousers – just as he was about to swing his seven iron! Upon their return to Edinburgh, the golfing exploits continued at Longniddry in East Lothian, as Gordon had carded only 68 with a hole to play before the weather closed in and the round had to be abandoned.

Just ahead of Christmas, Gordon scored four goals in a league game against Falkirk as Hibs won 5–1. And on Christmas Eve, as club captain, he presented an onyx clock to the directors from all the players before their home win over Raith Rovers.

Every Hogmanay for the previous two or three years, Gordon had driven down to his friend Willie Murphy's Dalrymple Hotel in North Berwick, where he would stay the night and get a good rest before the usual New Year's day derby. Before he started doing this, he had been woken by drunken revellers meaning well but disturbing him with shouts of, 'Hope you play well tomorrow, Gordon,' and singing 'A Gordon for Me' at the top of their voices outside his bedroom, which was situated at the front of his house on Willowbrae Road. So this year, after getting a good night's sleep in North Berwick, he travelled straight to the match with Murphy his guest for the largest attendance ever recorded at Easter Road – 65,840. However, the game ended in a defeat to rival Hearts, which upset Gordon even though he'd scored in the first half.

In a surprise move, three and a half years after Matt Busby's private letter, and this time openly, Manchester United again asked Hibernian if they would be interested in letting Gordon go. This offer was joined by that of Italian club Fiorentina, who also wrote to ask for the winger. Had Gordon joined the team from Florence, he would have been one of the first British footballers to play in Italy.

Following the Hibs training runs to Seafield and Portobello in the afternoons, Gordon was often seen back at Portobello beach with his friend Bobby Combe, where they would treat their swollen ankles in the healing salt water. Most of the players scoffed at this but trainer Jimmy McColl had said he'd heard it done in Ireland with racehorses. Harry Swan and Hugh Shaw ridiculed the players for believing it was helpful but Gordon thought if it could make a horse run fast, it was good enough for him!

Gordon scored another hat-trick in mid-February as Hibernian defeated Motherwell 6–1. On 11 March, a special cheer was reserved for long-sidelined Hugh Howie as he made his comeback in a game that saw Hibs win 4–2 against Dundee.

At the end of March, Gordon played in another SFL match – this time at Ayresome Park in Middlesbrough. The Scottish team lost 1–3 with Lawrie Reilly again played out of position at number 11!

On Saturday, 8 April, the new Easter Road Rail Halt was officially opened as Hibernian defeated Clyde 6–3 in front of 25,000 people. Gordon Smith and directors had met the Clyde players and fans from the train before the game. This new halt on the Waverley to Granton line was situated just behind the main terracing and became very beneficial to travelling football fans, as it enabled them to come straight to the ground. Unfortunately, following the game, they still had to walk to the nearest station – Abbeyhill – as there was only one platform. The halt couldn't accommodate trains travelling in the opposite direction! During the game, all of the – soon to be officially coined – Famous Five had scored, with Willie Ormond bagging two.

On Thursday, 13 April, for the ECATRA (Edinburgh Cab Trade Football Club) charity match against their London taxi driver counterparts, Hibernian's Gordon Smith and Heart of Midlothian legend Tommy Walker were linesmen for the duration of a game. Willie Smith, Gordon's elder brother, played at half back for the Scots team who won the match 4–3.

At the end of April, as the Hibernian squad flew to London to play Tottenham Hotspur, they heard that Rangers had won the League. At White Hart Lane, Hibs defeated the new English second division champions Tottenham Hotspur 1–0 courtesy of an Alf Ramsay own goal. Despite this achievement, the 1949/50 season ended with Hibs finishing in second place behind champions and treble winners Rangers. For the third season in a row, Gordon Smith was Hibs' top goal-scorer with twenty-five. The Famous Five scored seventy-nine out of Hibernian's record eighty-six league goals between them but their team still finished second to Rangers in the League.

Gordon wasn't the best time keeper at Easter Road for training or matches, often arriving in the changing room with a mere twenty minutes to go until kick-off, but he was always early at the airport or train station for tour matches. Hibs' next tour was a three-week continental trip through Austria, Germany and Switzerland, which they left for immediately after their game with Tottenham Hotspur.

The tour itinerary read:

May 2nd London Airport to the Austrian capital, Vienna.

<u>Austria</u>
May 4th Sportsklub Rapid Wien 3–2 Hibernian
(Turnbull, Ormond)
May 6th Linzer AC 1–3 Hibernian
(Smith, Turnbull, Ormond)

<u>Germany</u>
May 10th FC Augsburg (Bavaria) 2–4 Hibernian
(Turnbull, Reilly, Smith, Ormond)
May 14th FC Bayern München 1–6 Hibernian
(Smith 2, Reilly, Ormond, Souness, Johnstone)
May 18th VFB Mühlburg (Karlsruhe) 0–3 Hibernian
(Smith, Aird, Johnstone)

<u>Switzerland</u>
May 20th Berne 0–1 Hibernian (Johnstone) (Floodlit game)

May 22nd Return to Edinburgh

Whilst in Vienna, the team met distinguished English actor John Mills, who was staying in the Hibernian team's hotel, and they ventured down the tunnels made famous in the film *The Third Man*. Dagmar Rom, the glamorous world champion skier, escorted Gordon down sewers.

As soon as the team returned home, Harry Swan made enquiries about installing a floodlighting system, or drench-lighting system as it was sometimes called, at Easter Road.

With Scotland finishing runners-up to England in the Home International Championships, they were selected to travel to Brazil for the fourth World Cup Finals held in the South American country between 24 June and 16 July, with the massive 200,000 capacity Estádio do Maracanã the reward for the finalists. However, the SFA had said Scotland would only travel should they win the Home International Championship, and even though captain George Young pleaded with SFA secretary George Graham, they did not back down and stuck to their ruling, so Scotland stayed at home.

During the summer break from football, Gordon visited Troon and met up with British Open Golf champion Bobby Locke again. Locke won the tournament for the second year in a row and the night following his victory, he celebrated with Gordon at the Braid Hills Hotel in Edinburgh.

Gordon Smith's official wages since joining Hibernian, season by season up until the end of the season 1949/50 were as follows:

1941/42	£109 HFC	£72 Driller Wage	£100 Benefit	
1942/43	£109 HFC	£72 Driller Wage	£100 Benefit	
1943/44	£174 HFC	£88 Driller Wage	£100 Benefit	
1944/45	£126 HFC	£109 Driller Wage	£100 Benefit	
1945/46	£327 HFC	£145 Driller Wage	£100 Benefit	
1946/47	£1,340 HFC	£126 Driller Wage	£24 *Daily Record* Wage	£30 Fees
1947/48	£2,874 HFC		£169 *Daily Record* Wage	£40 Fees
1948/49	£2,078 HFC	£70 Fees		
1949/50	£2,000 HFC			

Alongside the bid by Manchester United, Blackburn Rovers and Arsenal had also wished to secure the services of the Scottish winger.

Tottenham Hotspur had offered the huge sum at the time of £35,000, Aston Villa on three occasions were snubbed, and Newcastle United had tabled at least eight bids, including the laying down of a blank cheque by Stan Seymour.

Smith could have earned a fortune by signing for any one of these clubs but was happy and content in Edinburgh, and especially with Hibernian. Hibs wages improved drastically after the war and ended with more money readily available, especially during the title-winning season of 1947/48, as a £2,874 salary was a vast amount for the time. The bonus scheme at Easter Road may also have been a mitigating favour, as vast amounts of cash would change hands in brown envelopes at the discretion of the chairman.

13

CHAMPIONS AGAIN

AHEAD OF the 1950/51 season, Hibs won eight five-a-side tournaments including contests in Belfast, Glasgow, Tillicoultry and Troon. Their bounty for these victories included an array of prizes such as card tables, electric razors, cigarette lighters, canteens of cutlery and cash prizes of £5 and £10. However, the biggest one was held at Meadowbank Stadium, watched by a huge 15,000 crowd, with Hibs winning this as well – by a corner!

At Leith Links, assembled crowds topped 6,000 as fans clambered to view the annual match between cricket club Leith Franklin and the Hibs team, who thoroughly enjoyed the contests – with some of them loving the willow and ball game as much as Gordon.

Things at Hibs had changed slightly for the new season, with Willie Finnegan joining Dunfermline and Davie Shaw joining Aberdeen, though they still trained at Easter Road for the time being. New boys included John Grant and Willie MacFarlane, who Gordon made friends with almost immediately and were promptly put through their paces by coach Sammy Kean.

This was the beginning of arguably the best two seasons in the history of the club. Retaining the captaincy for the forthcoming campaign, Gordon wore his 'lucky' number 13 on his training jersey, with deadly partner Lawrie Reilly donning a number 16 for his.

The standard training week would consist of a run up Arthur's Seat or to Portobello on Mondays, a day off and golf on a Tuesday, on Wednesdays and Thursdays there would be hard training on 'hill 60', leaving Friday for sprinting – lap after lap – then the players would have a meeting and voice suggestions to the manager and his coaches.

Incredibly, those meetings really meant nothing to the players, who would just go out and play their own game. Sometimes there would be games of 'head tennis', a medicine ball exercise routine and, on some mornings, badminton games.

Hibs, like all British teams of the era, were NEVER allowed to practise with a ball during official training! The reason for not allowing a ball was that it was felt it would make the players 'hungrier' for it the following Saturday. As the years went on, the club did relent somewhat but if there had been a bad result the previous week, the ball would not come out of the locker at all. Although not all the players did, Gordon practised with a ball on his own in the afternoons almost every day – even on his golf days of Tuesdays and Sundays.

Luckily for Gordon, a couple of seasons before, he had broken a finger when 'exercising' using a medicine ball; he had thought this method of training for a football player was absurd, so was happy to be excused evermore from the medicine ball classes!

As usual, the season kicked off with the Edinburgh Charities Select match; this year the game was held at Tynecastle with Newcastle United the visitors in a 1–1 encounter. In the League Cup, Hibs disposed of Dundee, St Mirren and Falkirk with ease, scoring a barrow-load of goals with Gordon scoring six in his first four appearances of the season, including a hat-trick in a scintillating 5–4 victory at Brockville – but this was just a taste of what was to follow in the quarter-final clash with Aberdeen.

Gordon had attended a private party in early September to celebrate the seventieth birthday of club director Tom Hartland, but a few days later, he was devastated to miss the Hibernian outing to Ayr to go to the races and play in a testimonial match for Ayr United centre-half, Norrie McNeil. Instead, he had to attend the Western General to receive treatment on his damaged shoulder and was told quite brusquely that there was to be no football or no golf until further notice – Gordon's world had come crashing down!

After eighty-six appearances for Hibs without troubling the scorers once, Davie Shaw was now the Aberdeen left back – in direct opposition to Gordon. Like Gordon, Davie was also a keep-fit fanatic. He still lived in Edinburgh at Portobello's Wakefield Avenue, where he was often seen out early in the morning, ushering his wife and son to their back garden to join him for some PE exercises! Both players' fitness was crucial to an unprecedented quartet of games to decide the outcome of the League Cup quarter-final. Gordon would later recall that the four cup games against Aberdeen, which were watched by an incredible 158,000 fans with eighteen goals scored in 420 minutes of cup action, were possibly his all-time favourite matches as a player.

Gordon missed the first-leg of the quarter-final at Pittodrie and the opening league match of the season against Falkirk, as he continued to struggle with the shoulder injury. The Pittodrie game was a disaster for Hibs, as they lost 1–4, and it appeared Gordon would also miss the return back in Edinburgh four days later. The absence of Gordon Smith, reported the papers, made a tremendous difference to Hibs.

Although not altogether at fault, they said that Souness had lacked the experience of Smith with the deputy winger having at least two clean cut chances – which Smith probably would have scored – and they also implied that Smith would have had the vision to create more chances. Talking to the press following the defeat, Gordon said: 'I'm going to the pictures next time, I just couldn't stand it!' Goals from Don Emery, Harry Yorston, George Hamilton and Jack Hather, with a solitary reply from Johnstone, had probably done enough for Aberdeen to progress to the semi-finals of the competition. Or had they?

The day of Wednesday, 20 September, would always remain a special one for Smith. It had begun with Gordon deciding that he was fit to play in the evening return cup-tie against Aberdeen. He hadn't informed anybody other than Sammy Kean and Hugh Shaw of his decision – not his family, his friends or the players. He had asked Kean and Shaw what they thought of the idea and they were all in favour of him playing but had said he would need to check with Dr John Bruce, the Hibs team doctor, who was based at the Western General hospital. Gordon drove to the hospital but was told Dr Bruce was in Glasgow and wasn't due back until later that afternoon. Hours went by and Gordon returned to the hospital after pacing up and down all day in his house – but to no avail. Dr Bruce had returned but had been sent out on an emergency somewhere. Gordon pleaded with the nurse to tell him where and although she should not have, she did, and Gordon rushed to eventually track Bruce down at the scene of an accident. A shocked Bruce at first thought that Smith couldn't play but eventually relented with under an hour to go until the 5.30pm kick-off!

When Gordon arrived at Easter Road, the players had no idea he was going to play; the famous Hibs winger had taken the liberty to put on his Hibs strip underneath his long coat and when he removed this in the changing room, the players cheered as though they'd won the game! The cheering, which could be heard in the Aberdeen changing room, was nothing in comparison to the 42,000 fans' roar when Smith's name was announced as a late change – the announcer had relayed: 'Smith will play at number 7 instead of Jim Souness, Gordon Smith is back.'

When Hibernian captain Gordon Smith shook hands with newly installed Aberdeen skipper Davie Shaw, Smith said Shaw had a 'look of defeat' in his eyes. Gordon and the Hibs team had run out to tumultuous applause. Although Gordon did not appear to be too fit, the psychological effect on his team-mates, not to mention the supporters, was well worth the risk. Gordon would later describe this game as one of his most memorable ever in a green shirt. This time it was Hibs' turn to win 4–1, with goals from Johnstone, Reilly, Ormond and an own goal by Chris Anderson, with the reds' only reply coming from Gordon's Scotland comrade, Archie Baird.

Before the two teams met again in a replay at neutral Ibrox Park, Hibernian played Hearts at home in the second league match of the season, losing 0–1 and, extraordinarily, played Aberdeen again in the league at Pittodrie, going down 1–2. For a team who would win the League Championship in April, two defeats from their first three matches was not the best way to go about it!

The Ibrox match on 2 October ended 1–1 and it was decided that the tie had to be settled as soon as possible – the following night at Hampden Park was agreed, as heavy rain had made the Ibrox pitch a mud bath. The Aberdeen players stayed another night in their team base, the Central Hotel in Glasgow, whilst the Hibernian players returned to their homes. During the Ibrox clash, Smith admitted he had his worst ever miss. 'The ball came over from Willie [Ormond], and I side-footed it onto the crossbar. It was 1–1 at the time and I'll never forget it. After that, I learned never to criticise. Anyone can miss.'

The referee, Mr Jackson, knew all the players pretty well by now, as he had officiated in the trio of the matches between the two teams in the League Cup thus far, but the following night was to be his and their last – for the game had to be settled, as the winner would play Queen of the South in the semi-final in just three days' time. With goals from Smith with two, Johnstone, Reilly and Turnbull, the Hibernian team demolished a tired Aberdeen side 5–1 and Hibs were into the semi-finals – at last. Hibs had played six games in eighteen days watched by 198,678 people; five of those games had been against Aberdeen!

Hibs took care of Queen of the South 3–1 at Tynecastle, with an Eddie Turnbull hat-trick ensuring they would meet Motherwell in the final. Before that game, Hibs played Motherwell again in league action winning 6–2 at Fir Park, with Smith injured mid-way through the first period. His injury forced him to withdraw from the Scottish international team facing Wales at Cardiff's Ninian Park the following week – his place taken by Celtic's Bobby Collins. Smith's team-mate Lawrie Reilly did play for Scotland, scoring two for his country in a 3–1 victory.

The week of the League Cup final, the team enjoyed a mini-break at the Marine Hotel in North Berwick, where they played table tennis, held card competitions and, naturally, golfed. Turnbull and Howie were the victors on this occasion. When Bobby Combe informed the squad his wife had gone away for a while to see her mother, Gordon paradoxically remarked that generally Bobby's game improved when she wasn't around – much to the hilarity of the other players!

On Saturday, 28 October, Hibernian lost the League Cup final 0–3 to Motherwell and Gordon blamed Hugh Shaw for putting Jimmy Bradley in the team in place of the injured Eddie Turnbull. This was Bradley's first team debut – at a Hampden Park final! Gordon, still not 100 per cent fit after his recent injury, was livid after the game, storming out of the changing room after crumpling up and tossing aside his runners-up prize of £5. He ignored the other players' pleas for him to pick it up, so a small number of the players enjoyed a night out in the public houses of Portobello with his 'losers' money!

Hibs' concentration was now back on league action and following a 1–1 draw in front of 70,000 at Ibrox in early November, they won three games in a row, scoring nine goals. Alongside Eddie Turnbull and Willie Ormond, Gordon represented the Scottish Football League on 29 November at Ibrox, as they defeated their English counterparts 1–0 with a John McPhail goal.

Gordon would still enjoy driving down to England to meet up with Stanley Matthews, with the two acclaimed gents of soccer discussing the pros and cons of floodlighting on more than one occasion. Mathews thoroughly disapproved of the 'new invention', saying it changed the pace of the ball completely. Also during this time, Gordon's grocery business was booming and he decided to open a post office inside the shop at his Willowbrae Road address, putting his father in charge of running it. This was now Gordon's second commercial interest alongside his grocery and would be joined by a third in five years' time.

In early December, Eddie Turnbull was sent off for 'defending' Gordon from horrendous tackling by a Third Lanark player during another victory for the Edinburgh side in Glasgow. On the train journey back home, Smith not only thanked Eddie profusely, but also defeated his coach Sammy Kean with his new skill – playing cards.

On 13 December, Eddie Turnbull represented Hibs for Scotland while Smith still couldn't get back into the team after being out for injury, with Celtic's Bobby Collins holding his number 7 place. By losing 0–1 to Austria at Hampden Park, the Scots suffered the indignity of becoming the first of the four British associations to lose at home to a foreign country.

There was good news in the league title race, though, as by the end of the year, Hibs had gone ten matches undefeated with nine of those victories. Goalkeeper Tommy Younger and Smith tried out new 'baseball style' boots for the hard pitches in the recent wins over St Mirren, Falkirk and Clyde.

However, the New Year of 1951 started shoddily for the Leith side as they were defeated by rivals Heart of Midlothian at Tynecastle. Gordon scored Hibs' only goal in the 1–2 loss but was on target again the next day at Easter Road as Hibs, re-finding their form, slaughtered Aberdeen, who included newly signed Jimmy Delaney from Manchester United, 6–2.

Four days later, Smith scored twice in a 3–1 victory at Kirkcaldy against Raith Rovers and continued his fine form with another double against Motherwell. Sadly, though, Hibs' run of victories was stopped by Partick Thistle in a 1–1 draw at Easter Road on 20 January.

People, as usual, took offence at Gordon not staying very long at Hibernian's annual dance at the North British Hotel the following evening. He would stay this year for just five minutes at the start and arrive back at the end for the last fifteen minutes or so. This was a new record – even by his escapist standards. A garrulous guest had put him off, so he made a well-planned and well-practised discreet exit!

He went back and forth between the Western General hospital and the Turkish baths at Portobello in order to finally fix his lingering shoulder problem. A 5–0 victory in the Scottish Cup against St Mirren following a 1–1 draw, and a further 1–0 league win – this time in Glasgow against Celtic–put Hibernian one point ahead of Rangers in the table.

The second round of the Scottish Cup against Rangers at Ibrox on 10 February, watched by 102,342 people, was another of Smith's favourite games that he played in. Hibernian defeated the Glasgow giants 3–2 after scoring two goals in two second-half minutes, silencing the supporters in the Copland Road end.

Following the victory, Harry Swan treated the Hibernian team to a few days' break at the Westerdunes Hotel in North Berwick. This luxurious setting was where Smith would first set eyes on what would be his future home.

Upon Gordon's return to Edinburgh, waiting for him was a virulent letter with no return address from a Rangers supporter embittered that Smith had stopped the Glasgow team on their run for the Scottish Cup. The letter was so venomous and foreboding that the Hibs winger took the letter to his local police station but thankfully no further developments followed.

Against Airdrie in the Scottish Cup, in front of 24,000 fans, Hibs secured a 3–0 victory thanks to a hat-trick by Lawrie Reilly, who was duly carried off the pitch by fans shoulder-high. More league victories followed but on Tuesday, 20 March, Gordon's car was written off as he travelled back to Edinburgh from a golf game in Gullane. Luckily, he walked away from the wreckage. A report in the following day's *Scottish Daily Mail* read:

> Gordon Smith, the Hibernian and Scotland International footballer, escaped with a knee bruise when his car was in collision with another at a junction at Prestonpans, East Lothian yesterday. His car was badly smashed and had to be towed back to Edinburgh. The other car in which there were four men, bounced 70 feet on to the road bank after the impact and overturned.

The four men in the other car, William Shedden, N.C.B official, John McCree, John Reid and William Sandilands – all of Prestonpans – were 'badly shaken'.

Smith said last night: 'I am perfectly fit. The knee bruise is very slight. It will not interfere in any way with my football.'

On the last Saturday in March, Hibs exited the Scottish Cup at the hands of the same Motherwell team who had beaten them in the League Cup final. The Fir Park men won the semi-final 3–2 at neutral Tynecastle in a disastrous day for Hibernian with Ormond carried off with ruptured ligaments, Ogilvie carried off with his leg broken in two places and Smith having a goal disallowed near the end, which would have earned Hibs a replay. An angry Gordon remarked: 'Hearts had put down moss on the pitch, and no type of boot could provide a grip. The park was disgraceful, probably the worst I've played on in Scotland.'

Smith's leg had also been put in plaster, as he had damaged a tendon, so he missed the drawn game against Dundee, but Hibs had done enough. Even with injuries to so many top players, Hibernian secured the League title with fifty-seven points on Saturday, 14 April 1951, at Shawfield, winning 4–0 against Clyde with half a reserve team of Younger, Govan, Cairns, Howie, Paterson, Buchanan, Souness, Combe, Mulkerrin, Turnbull and Higgins. Jimmy Mulkerrin, playing at centre forward, made his debut for the first team – and what a day to do it! In front of 36,879 fans, and with still four league games to play, the Leith side were, for the second time in four years, champions.

Gordon also missed the next two games but made it back in time for the final two league matches of the season against Celtic and Rangers. In ten years, he had never missed a match against Rangers and didn't want to start a trend now. It was just as well, as he had an immaculate performance, scoring two of Hibs' goals in a 4–1 victory and two days later, the league champions disposed of Celtic 3–1, with both games played at a joyous Easter Road.

The Hibernian number 7, along with all the players, would benefit from win bonuses and away draws at the likes of Ibrox Park, Celtic Park, Pittodrie or Tynecastle. However, from time to time, he and selected other Hibernian players would find possibly somewhat 'extravagant' bonuses as a fillip in their brown wage packets and this season had been no different. Upon winning the title, Gordon received a vast amount for the time; the astronomical sum of £500 in cash was placed in his brown envelope by Mr Swan!

14

INAUGURAL PLAYER OF THE YEAR AND CHAMPIONS FOR A THIRD TIME

IN MAY of 1951, accompanied by not only backroom staff and directors, but also by journalist Rex Kingsley from the *Daily Record*, Hibernian ventured on a two-match short tour in France, which included another game played under floodlights. The floodlit game in Paris, played at the Stade Olympique Yves-du-Manoir, was won 1–0 with Gordon Smith scoring the only goal – the second Hibernian footballer following Bobby Johnstone to score under lights.

Hibs Mini-Tour of France
May 2nd *Racing Clube de Paris 1–1*
May 6th *Olympique Nice 1–0*

Upon their return, the club joined in the celebrations for the 1951 Festival of Britain, hosting Sportsklub Rapid Wien at a packed Easter Road and losing 3–5 in a highly entertaining game.

On the invitation of golfing superstar Bobby Locke, Gordon stayed with the champion at the Royal Port Rush Golf Club in County Antrim, Northern Ireland. Locke was competing in the British Open Championship there, this year tying for sixth place, eight shots off the pace as England's Max Faulkner won it. The movie *Follow the Sun*, a biographical film about golfer Ben Hogan – another hero of Gordon's – was also released that summer and Gordon viewed it repeatedly.

The summer of 1951 also saw pianists Sam Price, Charlie Kunz and Pinetop Smith alongside other musicians, Leadbelly, Bessie Smith, Sidney Bechet, Jelly Roll Morton, Sister Rosetta Tharpe and Albert Ammons, all added to Gordon's now massive record collection. 'I Wish

I Could Shimmy Like My Sister Kate' was a surprise recent favourite of Gordon's, recorded by George Wettling's Chicago Rhythm Kings. He would buy his many records, not just predominantly from his favourite Edinburgh record shops Methven Simpson in Queensferry Street and The Clifton on Princes Street, but from visits to the London Jazz Club in the capital's Oxford Street, Russell's Piano Warehouse in Oxford, the Farley Radio Service in Woolwich, and from abroad, the Rue Lafayette's Phonorium in Paris.

Content with bachelorhood, the single Gordon had first met Nancy Croall, a girl from the Stenhouse area of Edinburgh, when she was still a seventeen-year-old schoolgirl attending James Gillespie's High. She was a Hibs fan and the pair would meet for lunch in 'discreet' cafés. That first summer, they would go to the pictures throughout the city, and on occasions to Portobello to Maison Demarco's American Soda Parlour and Café, where Gordon would enjoy listening to the resident piano player, always asking for Fats Waller tunes.

Although Nancy was to 'go out' with Gordon off and on for around eight years, with the two seen at many functions, by various accounts it was at her instigation more than his and nothing really serious ever came of the romance; the pair would both marry new partners within months of one another toward the end of the decade. Gordon always put football first before any serious romance until meeting his future wife and certainly held back any feelings he may or may not have had for Miss Croall. The taciturn Gordon could never express his true emotions at the best of times.

Cricket against the prestigious Grange Club at Raeburn Place preceded the new season, where 1951/52 would see Hibernian back-to-back champions of Scotland, with a team that would arguably be the finest ever in the history of the club. As always the Edinburgh Select Charities match was the initial football game – this year against Liverpool at Easter Road. With Gordon injuring his foot early on in the match, Jock Govan had 'to do tricks' on the wing for most of the encounter!

The first football magazine in the world, *Charles Buchan's Football Monthly*, started publication; priced 1/6, Gordon would enjoy reading the magazines in his new Citroën car before training. The magazines were the best way of keeping him informed of the goings-on in football outside of Scotland in the days before television.

Even though, in early autumn, the team were eliminated from the League Cup, they went on a nine game unbeaten run in the league through to November, with Gordon scoring in the opening encounter at Kirkcaldy and against Partick and Rangers.

However, the run came crashing to an end on 10 November when they lost 1–2 to Morton in Greenock. Six further straight victories followed, before two defeats in a row to Motherwell 1–3 at Fir Park and to Hearts 2–3 on New Year's Day 1952 at Easter Road. With freezing weather and heavy snow forecast, the attendance was a low 37,890 when Hearts' Alfie Conn wasn't even booked for a tackle on Smith on the touchline, where he bundled the Hibs winger into the boundary wall, knocking him unconscious.

Just prior to this game, Gordon had been selected to represent Scotland in a Rest of Britain Select against Wales in a game to commemorate the seventy-fifth anniversary of the Welsh Association of Football. He lined up alongside the likes of Nat Lofthouse, Billy Wright and Preston North End's Tommy Docherty, with the acclaimed Ivor Allchurch the Welsh star-attraction.

Gordon had travelled down to Cardiff from Glasgow airport with Jimmy Cowan, George Young and East Fife's Charlie Fleming for the game and, by all accounts, he was sensational – better than he had ever been for the Scotland national side or the Scottish League. Although Wales won 3–2, the Welsh newspapers were full of praise for Smith with Alf Sherwood, the Wales left back, commenting that he had never seen a player like him – 'he tormented me the whole game'. The Welsh manager backed this up, merely stating, 'Smith was great,' and Gordon's captain, Rangers' George Young, added it was Gordon's best performance in a representative game.

In his free time, Gordon's youthful love affair with 'going to the pictures' continued. He would either go alone or take Nancy to such varied theatres as his favourite, the Dominion in Morningside, Poole's Roxy in Gorgie, the New Victoria in Nicholson Street and the Salisbury Picture House under the giant shadow of Salisbury crags. Easter Road's Picturedome, where he'd first gone during his early days at Hibernian, had been renamed the Eastway and the nearest cinema to his grocer's business in Willowbrae Road was the Carlton at Piershill, where he received two free weekly tickets in return for the placement of an advert in his shop window. The Carlton, situated next to the Abercorn pub and the Piershill Dance Hall, was deemed too close to home for Gordon to relax, so he would often hand over 'the freebies' to his sister Rachel, who remembers he removed the ad – hence the free tickets – after a sibling argument had got out of hand one day.

Following the two defeats in succession, Hibs bounced back, taking the points in Glasgow with a win over Third Lanark on 2 January. However, as the players made their return to Edinburgh by train at Crosshill rail station, they were informed of a points failure on the railway. 'No points failure for us today, though!' spoke Willie Ormond, much to the players' amusement.

A shocking 1–3 defeat at Methil against East Fife was cancelled out by a 4–0 victory back in Edinburgh against Airdrie on 1 March. Although Hibs suffered their fifth defeat of the league campaign in a terrible 2–5 reverse to Queen of the South, with Rangers also losing games, Hibernian had only to beat Dundee at Easter Road to retain the championship. A four-week break ensued due to Scottish Cup matches and internationals and in that time, the team played without losing to St Mirren, Bolton Wanderers, Doncaster Rovers and Tottenham Hotspur, but Gordon's favourite was the 1–1 draw at Old Trafford against Matt Busby's Manchester United, with a massive 67,000 watching the friendly.

Before the end of the season, Gordon Smith won the inaugural *Sunday Mail* Player of the Year for 1951. Rex Kingsley and Lord Provost Miller presented the award at a ceremony held at Edinburgh's Waverley Market during the Festival of Sport exhibition.

'A player of exquisite ball control, club spirit and uncanny skill,' spoke Kingsley.

'The greatest honour to come my way in football,' replied Smith, who dedicated the award to his team-mates who 'had made it all possible'.

Four days before Hibs' penultimate league clash with Dundee, Gordon was chosen to represent Scotland alongside team-mates Bobby Johnstone and Lawrie Reilly. Lawrie scored but the English, including Finney and Lofthouse, won 2–1 in front of 134,504 fans at Hampden Park.

Around this time, Gordon received an offer from journalist Ross Fraser for him to write a biography on the famous Hibernian and Scotland winger. The letter contained 'sycophantic excerpts' from the proposed book. However, Gordon was unimpressed – possibly by Fraser's writing, the idea or both – and the stamped addressed envelope anticipating a reply was left untouched. It was a fairly rare event in the early 1950s for footballers to have books written about them, so Smith's complete disregard for the project was quite astonishing and especially disconcerting for the journalist.

On 9 April, Hibernian became champions for the second season in a row when they defeated Dundee 3–1 at Easter Road. By also beating Motherwell by the same score in their final game on spring holiday Monday in Edinburgh, they scored a record ninety-six goals in thirty matches and had used a mere seventeen players to retain their crown.

The triumph over Motherwell on 21 April was another glorious spring holiday football occasion that Gordon would remember for the rest of his life. That evening, as he drove up from Easter Road after the game, into the swirling mist at Abbeyhill, he was cheered all the way by fans young and old, waving and throwing caps. Small boys gathered and ran alongside his car, encircling him at red lights; patrons from the Artisan Bar left their drinks inside and lined the streets in admiration until his car had gone by. Even the police horses stood calm and, if legend is to be believed, they appeared to smile, bowing their long thin faces in recognition of an athlete at the peak of his powers, playing for a team at the peak of theirs.

Two days after the league season was completed, Hibernian travelled to London for an encounter that was billed as the match to decide 'The Champions of Britain'. They played Tottenham Hotspur, who two seasons ago were crowned English second division champions but were now incredibly top division champions, although they had finished runners-up to Manchester United this season. The Edinburgh side won 2–1 with a double from Gordon in front of a high-spirited 43,000 crowd, cheered on by an inspired performance by the Enfield Central Band at White Hart Lane.

Three days later, back in Edinburgh, Nat Lofthouse's Bolton Wanderers side drew 2–2, with Lawrie Reilly this time scoring a double. On the last day in April, Gordon played for Scotland again in a 6–0 rout of the USA with club-mate Lawrie Reilly scoring a hat-trick in front of another 100,000 plus fans.

The players had one week off before embarking on another tour of the continent. This year they ventured to the Netherlands and Germany, and then subsequently home to Scotland via Denmark to see team-mate Lawrie Reilly, who was playing for Scotland in Copenhagen.

Hibs Tour of the Netherlands, Germany and Denmark.

The Netherlands

May 10th *Limburg Select 4–2 (Limburg)*

May 11th *FC Köln 1–4 (Geleen)*

Germany

May 12th *Travelled to Germany*

May 14th *Borrusia DR 2–1 (Dortmund)*

May 17th *SV Werder Bremen 3–2 (Bremen)*

May 21st *St Pauli 1–1 (Hamburg)*

Denmark

May 25th *Denmark v Scotland 1–2 (Copenhagen)*

The players departed on 8 May from Edinburgh and travelled to the Netherlands, staying at the Belle Vue Hotel in Valkenburg. Two days later, Smith scored in a victory over a Limburg Select side. Next, although still in the Netherlands, the Hibs team played German side FC Köln at Geleen, losing 1–4.

Travelling by bus into Germany the day after, they met Borussia Dortmund in front of 38,678 fans, winning 2–1. A most bizarre incident occurred in a 3–2 victory over SV Werder Bremen. Willie Ormond had committed an innocuous foul and Eddie Turnbull jokingly suggested to the referee (in his best German) that maybe Willie should be sent off for the challenge. The referee, to the amazement of everyone, duly obliged and sent Ormond off. This was the one and only time Willie was sent off in his career – and it was all thanks to Eddie Turnbull!

The final game of the five-match tour was in Hamburg against St Pauli, where the game ended in a draw. The odd thing about this game was that the players had to get changed in rooms across a busy street from the stadium, which was situated in the city's red light district – home to the infamous Reeperbahn! Three days later, the Hibernian party arrived in Copenhagen and had ringside seats just a few feet away from the touchline to watch Scotland and more importantly Lawrie Reilly score in a 2–1 victory. The following day, 26 May, was Gordon's twenty-eighth birthday and the Hibernian party headed home to Scotland with a noon departure from Copenhagen by boat-train to Esbjerg, sailing on the *Kronprinsesse Ingrid*. On the sailing, Gordon celebrated his birthday in typically quiet fashion, although his team-mates did manage to pick up a cake – this year with a green jersey on!

The team bus arrived back at Easter Road in the afternoon of 27 May with Gordon's nineteen days in Europe enjoyable but more importantly eye-opening. The first thing he did after getting home was to order two pairs of German Adidas football boots – one with studs and one moulded. He had been very impressed with the German style, boots, strips and pitches on the tour, very impressed indeed.

Following a week in the south of France, Gordon drove down to Lytham for the year's British Golf Open Championship with his friend Bobby Locke winning for the third time by one stroke over his nemesis, the Australian Peter Thomson. Gordon was treated to a marvellous time in hospitality, obviously delighted with Locke's win. Over dinner, the two gents discussed what a great year it had been for them both professionally. In Locke's case, further success would follow soon after, but Gordon's Hibernian, although not knowing it then, had already peaked (certainly statistically). This was Hibernian Football Club at their most supreme. The club would never win the League Championship again – certainly for at least another sixty years – and Gordon's next League Championship medal would be eight years off, won with bitter rivals Heart of Midlothian.

15

TESTIMONIAL AND CORONATION CUP

The most accomplished, the most graceful footballer in Scotland.

– Waverley, *Daily Record*

When Smith stops playing for Hibs, they should re-turf the pitch.

– Rex Kingsley, *Sunday Mail*

Gordon Smith is to me, now and probably for the remainder of his career, the greatest footballer in the land.

– Bob Ferrier, *Daily Record*

ALTHOUGH TECHNICALLY having peaked in terms of silverware, the club would still have one more fantastic season, only finishing runners-up to Rangers on goal average. The 1952/53 campaign began once again with Gordon playing in the Edinburgh Select Charities match. This year the visitors were Portsmouth, and the 31,000 fans cheered on the home team to a 3–2 victory.

Four victories and two defeats for Hibs in their League Cup section in August meant they played Morton in the quarter-finals of the competition, winning by a massive 12–3 on aggregate over the two games.

On the opening league match on 6 September, Queen of the South were the visitors to the champions' Easter Road ground and humbled the Leith side by winning three goals to one. Gordon scored Hibs' solitary goal – his 292nd – on this, his 500th appearance for the club.

Gordon's luck improved the following day, as he took on his friend Bobby Locke in an Open Champion's Challenge played at Duddingston Golf Club and won.

In his *Scottish Daily Mail* column on 8 September, Smith praised the Hibs ground-staff and backroom staff for their gallant work behind the scenes at the football club – from head groundsman Harry Reading to Tommy Cannon and John Clapperton, through to trainer Jimmy McColl and his assistant Sammy Kean. Treasurer Mr Macintyre CA, Mr Terris, Mr Shaw and Mr Swan were also given commendation. He gave a special mention to director Tom Hartland, who he had always got on so well with since that first meeting eleven years previously in Arbroath. Tom Hartland had also become a good friend of Gordon's father Bob, with the pair of them avid stamp collectors (or philatelists to those in the know).

On Monday, 15 September 1952, Gordon Smith was awarded a testimonial by Hibernian FC for great service to the club. Harry Swan had wanted Arsenal to be the opponents but Gordon put his foot down and stipulated that English champions Manchester United were to be chosen. His close friendship with Matt Busby had swayed his decision and the Old Trafford side were eventually asked to play.

The vast sum for the time of £3,000 was given to Gordon from turnstile takings in the 28,000 crowd but he was to lose more than half in income tax and expenses. Gordon bought gift sets for the United players, presented his own team-mates with gift tokens and donated a percentage of proceeds from the sale of his testimonial programme to the Edinburgh Hospital Broadcasting Organisation. There had been a fair bit of resentment by some Hibs players prior to the game that Gordon had been awarded the benefit match and not them, but Gordon readily insisted that he had been responsible, not the club. A few months earlier, Chairman Swan and Smith had agreed in principle on a testimonial, but it was Smith who organised the event, the club's only involvement being the facilitation of holding the game at Easter Road. After 500 plus appearances in eleven years, few could deny he probably deserved it.

The game itself was magnificent. The final score was 7–3 to Hibernian, with some people saying it was (and still is) the finest ever match played between two British sides – three goals disallowed by referee Jack Mowat and a Manchester United missed penalty! Hibernian enthralled and played masterfully with Manchester United contributing a great deal in a classic football match.

The fans' chant from the terraces at Easter Road to the tune of 'A Gordon for Me' was raucously sung on the evening of the great Hibs number 7's testimonial match.

> A Gordon fur me, a Gordon fur me,
> If you're no a Gordon yir nae use tae me,
> Johnstone is braw, Reilly an' aw,
> But the cocky wee Gordon was the pride of them aw.

Referee Mowat, who was criticised in the press and harangued by the crowd, booked United's Jack Rowley and would later comment that it had been the 'fastest game' he'd ever officiated at. An Eddie Turnbull hat-trick (including two penalties), Lawrie Reilly with two, Willie Ormond and Smith himself were the scorers for the home team, with a Rowley double and Stan Pearson scoring for the Old Trafford side. Following the game, during a private reception at the North British Hotel for both sets of teams, Smith was affably given a standing ovation by Matt Busby and his team.

Smith was chosen to represent the Scottish Football League on 8 October at Celtic Park against the League of Ireland. He was selected alongside team-mates Jock Govan, Bobby Johnstone, Lawrie Reilly and Willie Ormond, but disgracefully – and some say because of 'west coast bitterness and jealousy' – Eddie Turnbull was omitted in favour of Dundee's Billy Steel, who, although a great player himself, agreed with the Hibs quartet of forwards and was humble enough to admit that Turnbull really ought to have been chosen in his place. To makes matter worse, Steel was only included at the last minute, when first choice Jimmy Bonthrone of East Fife had called off sick!

Had Turnbull been chosen, it would have been a unique event: all five forwards playing together for the national side – an event that many people (and not limited to fans of Hibernian) thought should have happened on numerous occasions throughout the years. What a feat it would have been. What an achievement by Hibernian Football Club to have the whole of a national team forward line represented by their players.

The game itself was won convincingly by the SFL 5–1, with a quartet from Lawrie Reilly and Steel scoring one, but Turnbull would probably have scored more. Following the game, Gordon made some derisory remarks about the omission of Turnbull to the waiting press and oddly enough, although he'd had a good game in the dark blue, this was to be Smith's last Scottish appearance for two and a half years, until his inexhaustible year for international football – 1955.

Three days later at Ibrox, Hibernian won 2–1 in a game famous for Gordon Smith's 'shushing' incident. When retrieving the ball from the corner flag, he allegedly tried to silence the hostile Ibrox crowd by putting two fingers to his mouth but they interpreted it differently, seeing it as a v-sign, and were livid! Smith spoke after the game: 'The Hampden roar had nothing on that din. Not for the rest of the game did they let up. Whenever I got the ball, there was a fresh storm of boos.'

He was tried by the newspapers and found guilty of inciting the crowd – newspaper editors who had sung his praises saw it as a deliberate act of provocation and attacked him in print. Even though he did try to explain to the press that he meant no harm with his actions – he was merely telling the crowd to be quiet and to stop shouting abuse as he took the corner – he wasn't believed by many, including his friend, the Rangers supporting Rex Kingsley, who vilified Smith for the one and only time in his career. Gordon always insisted that everybody had got him wrong.

Cheering him up in a turbulent week, a letter confirming the outcome of the Open Champion's Challenge arrived through the letterbox at Gordon's home.

The Daily Mail,
Editorial Dept
Northcliffe House
London EC4

G. Smith Esq
Gullane Golf Club
E. Lothian

October 1952

Dear Fellow Golfer,
I am very happy to send you attached, the winning certificate, recording your success over Bobby Locke as recognition of your beating his round against the scratch score of the course, in the Open Champion's challenge, which took place on September 6/7.

I should like to add my very sincere congratulations on a fine effort.

Best Wishes
Yours sincerely
F. G. Pignon. (Golf Correspondent)

The certificate read:

THE OPEN CHAMPION'S CHALLENGE
Sponsored by the *DAILY MAIL* in support of the
BRITISH GOLF FOUNDATION

This is to certify that
GORDON SMITH
With a net score of 60 beat me by 10 strokes
Bobby Locke.

Gordon, for the past few years, was becoming increasingly passionate about golf, as were most of the Hibs players. Every Tuesday, the players' day off, Jock Paterson, Lawrie Reilly, Willie Clark, Eddie Turnbull, Bobby Johnstone and Jimmy Cairns, amongst others, would arrive for breakfast at Gordon's house, adjacent to his grocery business and post office on Willowbrae Road. Gordon would then drive down with a lucky selected player in his sports car, leaving the rest to catch the SMT bus down to the coast, usually to Gullane. The players taking the bus, to keep them happy on their longer journey, would often receive some 'extra goodies' like chocolate and biscuits from Gordon's shop – possibly a little underhanded, as ration books were still in operation for sweet items until September the following year.

After their round of golf, they would often have lunch in the Wishing Well Café in the town's main street, with some of the players purchasing cigarettes from E. Munro's shop before catching the bus back up to Edinburgh. Once reaching Duddingston Crossroads, the players would often alight before catching a further bus home, in order to leave their clubs at Gordon's house, where his gullible sister washed them in readiness for the next week's outing.

On Wednesday, 22 October, Hibs travelled to London to take part in the unofficial Challenge of Britain match against Arsenal. The match was played in order to raise funds for the National Playing Fields Association.

For a side who had beaten the English champions 7–3 just weeks previously, they must have started as favourites against the third-placed English side from last season, yet they were annihilated 1–7 by the north London side in front of 56,000 fans, including future 'great train robber' Ronnie Biggs, who would later say this was his first ever game to see his local side Arsenal. After Arsenal's Don Roper had scored his side's last goal of the evening, Biggs apparently began to mock the Edinburgh team, shouting in a Scottish accent: 'Come on Hibs, we only want seven!'

Hibernian's fifth floodlit match result was all the more shocking as it was the very first game televised by the BBC outwith an international or a cup final. The second half was beamed live throughout the country, with more than one million viewers watching the game – for many it would be their first experience of football 'on the box'. Afterwards, at a post-game banquet, HRH the Duke of Edinburgh presented both teams with signed diplomas and a plaque commemorating the game.

Hibs next six games produced four victories and two defeats, and after the 1–1 draw against Celtic in early December, Smith enjoyed a purple patch of form. He scored in the annoying but entertaining 4–5 defeat at Firhill against Partick Thistle, which was followed by a 7–2 win in which he scored a hat-trick as Queen of the South suffered for beating Hibs back in August. Then, in the next game on 27 December against Aberdeen at Easter Road, Smith scored his 300th goal for Hibernian in a 3–0 triumph. Following the match, Gordon would receive a recording of his memorable goal from the commentator for the Edinburgh Hospitals Football Broadcast Committee, Wemyss Craigie.

A defeat of Hearts on New Year's Day 1953 was followed by an emphatic 7–2 conquest of Motherwell with goal number 301 for Gordon. Next came a loss at Kirkcaldy, with subsequent wins over Stenhousemuir 8–1 in the Scottish Cup, Falkirk and Queen's Park, and a home draw against title challengers, Rangers, sandwiched in between.

Another good spell for Gordon scoring-wise began on Valentine's Day, when he scored a double against Clyde. This was followed by his last ever hat-trick in a competitive game when scoring three of the four against Airdrie in the second round of the Scottish Cup. The following week, he scored his 308th goal for the Leith side, as Hibernian again slaughtered the vanquished cup-game losers 7–3 at Broomfield Park.

With Hibernian losing to Aberdeen in the next round of the cup in a replay, the final eight league matches of the season produced four wins, three draws and one defeat. The defeat against Dundee at Dens Park was the first game in the series, which left Hibs remaining undefeated for the remainder of the league contest. On the final day, 29 April, Hibs won 4–1 at Easter Road against Raith Rovers and by scoring a 'mere' four, this condemned Hibs to second place in the championship for the campaign. Had Hibs managed to score thirteen more, or had Rangers lost, they would have won the league title for a third consecutive season – and if the modern method of goal difference as opposed to goal average had been in operation then, Hibs would have been champions by a solitary goal!

Gordon was physically sick when news of the 2–2 draw for Rangers was announced, denying him and his team-mates three wins in a row. Hibs had scored a record ninety-three goals – thirteen more than Rangers. While not winning the league, Hibs were still arguably Scotland's finest team, deserving of the title. Their league form since the end of World War Two had been unparalleled in the history of the club (see list below) but although no one knew it at the time, Hibernian's fortunes would slowly decline from this moment on. From the minute they heard Rangers had drawn to snatch the title away, something was lost.

1946/47	2nd
1947/48	1st
1948/49	3rd
1949/50	2nd
1950/51	1st
1951/52	1st
1952/53	2nd

1952/53 League Table

	P	W	D	L	F	A	PTS
Rangers	30	18	7	5	80	39	43
Hibernian	30	19	5	6	93	51	43

Rangers' goal average: 2.05
Hibernian's goal average: 1.82
Rangers' goal difference: 41
Hibernian's goal difference: 42

Prior to the league conclusion, in mid-April, Hibernian had jetted to Brussels to play against Austria Vienna at the Heysel Stadium. Hibs lost 2–3 in front of 33,000 fans with Eddie Turnbull scoring both goals for the Scottish team. Then, on 7 May, just before the commencement of the Coronation Cup, Hibernian found a little solace by winning the East of Scotland Shield against bitter rivals Hearts 4–2 with goals from Smith, Turnbull and a pair from Lawrie Reilly.

In celebration of the forthcoming coronation of Queen Elizabeth II, the top eight British sides at the time would play in a knock-out competition vying for the trophy. Arsenal, Manchester United, Newcastle United and Tottenham Hotspur represented England whilst Rangers, Celtic, Aberdeen and Hibernian represented Scotland.

Hibs' results in the Coronation Cup of 1953
May 11th – 20th

Ibrox Park	**11th May**	Tottenham Hotspur	1–1 (52,000)
Celtic Park	**12th May**	Tottenham Hotspur	2–1 (45,000)
Ibrox Park	**16th May**	Newcastle United	4–0 (47,000)
Hampden Park	**20th May**	Celtic	0–2 (117,000)

Aberdeen lost to Newcastle United at Ibrox, Celtic defeated Arsenal, and Manchester United beat Rangers 2–1, then Celtic won by the same score against the Old Trafford side. Gordon Smith scored in Hibs' opening match at Ibrox against Spurs, which was replayed after a draw the following afternoon – this time resulting in a Hibernian victory. A 4–0 slaying of Newcastle United allowed the greens to contest the final against fellow greens and fellow Scottish side, Celtic.

On the day, goals by Jimmy Walsh and Neil Mochan gave Celtic an altogether undeserved victory. Hibs had attack after attack thwarted by the brilliance of Celtic goalkeeper John Bonnar, who was man of the match. Had it been another day, with Bonnar not having the game of his life, Hibs would have won the cup. Gordon said after the game: 'We could have scored a dozen.'

16

CAPTAIN AT THE MARACANÃ

IN THE summer of 1953, Hibernian were invited to go to Brazil to participate in the inaugural Torneio Octogonal Rivadavia Corrêa Meyer, which had been preceded by the Copa Rio the previous two years. Spanish champions Real Madrid and Uruguayan champions Nacional had withdrawn from this year's new tournament, paving the way for the Edinburgh side. Below is a list of the groups:

Group A: Games all played at the Maracanã Stadium in
Rio de Janeiro.
Vasco da Gama
Fluminense
Botafogo
Hibernian (Scotland)

Group B: Games all played at the Pacaembu Stadium in São Paulo.
São Paulo
Corinthians
Olimpia (Paraguay)
Sporting Lisbon (Portugal)

The team left Edinburgh on 1 June, travelling down south and staying overnight in a hotel in an exuberant central London, as the following morning of 2 June was the Coronation of Queen Elizabeth II at Westminster Abbey. The players watched the events on a television in their hotel, which also included the sensational news that Mount Everest had been conquered by a British-led expedition. The Hibernian team eventually left around 9pm from London airport, travelling through the night, through three continents and various time zones, until reaching the final destination of Rio de Janeiro in Brazil; they arrived in some style in a converted World War Two bomber, twenty-six hours after departing London, having survived the itinerary outlined below.

June 1st	Edinburgh to London (England)
June 2nd	London to Paris (France)
June 3rd	Paris to Lisbon (Portugal)
	Lisbon to Dakar (Senegal)
	Dakar to Recife (Brazil)
	Recife to Rio de Janeiro

After the gruelling trip, Hibernian arrived at the Galeão Airport in Rio de Janeiro, Brazil, on Wednesday, 3 June, at 11.50pm Rio time. Gordon, along with the fourteen other players, were taken directly to the Hotel Paysandu in the Flamengo district of the city in close proximity of the famous Copacabana beach.

Harry Swan had recently been elected president of the SFA, so chose not to travel but to attend to paperwork back in Scotland, leaving directors Wilson Terris, Tom Hartland and manager Hugh Shaw in charge. After a brief sleep on Thursday, 4 June, the team ventured to the beach and Gordon would later comment:

> The first day we went down onto the Copacabana, I thought they were playing netball. As I got nearer, I saw they were keeping the ball up with their bare feet. I was just a novice compared to these kids.
>
> I think we were the first team from Britain that realised just how good Brazil were going to be in the future.

That evening at half-time during the Bangu versus Flamengo league match, the fatigued Hibs players and backroom staff were introduced to the massive Maracanã Stadium crowd. Cheers rang out as they entered one by one. Directors: Wilson Terris and Tom Hartland; Manager: Hugh Shaw; Trainers: Jimmy McColl and Sammy Kean; club captain: Gordon Smith; players: Bobby Combe, Tommy Younger,

Lawrie Reilly, Eddie Turnbull, Bobby Johnstone, Willie Ormond, John Paterson, Hugh Howie, Willie MacFarlane, Archie Buchanan, Jock Govan, Pat Ward, Bill Anderson and Jimmy Shields. Below are some extracts from a notebook Gordon took with him to Brazil.

Thu 4th June: Sleep – then beach. Fantastic. Exhausted at the massive stadium at night.
Fri 5th June: Beach – dinner at Embassy.
Sat 6th June: Beach table tennis & golf.
Sun 7th June: Game in new strips – sweltering heat.

Hibernian's first game of the Rivadavia Corrêa Meyer tournament saw a still slightly jet-lagged Hibernian side draw 3–3 with Vasco da Gama. Following the contest, Gordon, as Hibernian club captain, came to the microphone and spoke a few words to the crowd (although not in Portuguese!), mentioning that they had enjoyed the game and expressed his appreciation for the wonderful reception the Scottish team had received from the Brazilian public.

In the intervening week between games, Gordon and the Hibs players continued to play golf on a daily basis, with venomous snakes often spotted sidling up to players as they were about to hit a shot! They also swam in the warm South Atlantic Ocean and attended a banquet held at the British Embassy to celebrate the coronation of Queen Elizabeth II. Down at the Copacabana beach, Gordon was constantly in awe of the kids playing football. Possibly one of these kids was a member of the great 1970 World Cup winning side?

Whilst swimming in the 'beautiful blue sea' Lawrie Reilly had managed to swallow quite a bit of putrid water and was taken to the Strangers Hospital for several days, only being released on the morning of the match against Botafogo. During the week, Tommy Younger had befriended a local celebrity tennis player who also owned an ice cream factory and the players, suffering in the sweltering Brazilian summer heat, took full advantage of the free cones!

Smith scored a disallowed goal in the second match of the tournament for Hibs but unfortunately they lost 1–3 against Botafogo, with Reilly coming out of his sick bed to score the only allowed goal for the Scottish side. The third and final game was another loss, this time 0–3 to

Fluminense, with young Bill Anderson collapsing near the end of the match due to heat exhaustion.

Gordon's football skills had astounded the Brazilians, as had Bobby Johnstone's. The pair had impressed Vasco da Gama and Botafogo so much that offers were made to keep both players in South America. 'Name your price for Gordon Smith,' the Botafogo chairman had said.

Remember, this was a country in 1953 with no favelas or Amazonian rainforest obliteration, but a country rich in minerals with emblematic exports such as coffee, rubber and cacao. Brazilian President Getúlio Vargas had just created Petrobras to explore and redeem oil. Gordon loved Rio and was impressed by the way of life, the weather, the women and the golf courses (not in that order). Many ex-pats lived there too and he wouldn't have been the first footballer from Scotland to have settled there, as Archie McLean from Paisley, known fondly as *Veadinho* and 'the father of Brazilian football', had lived in the country since 1912.

In reality, though, Gordon would have been lost in Brazil. He did admit, 'I was very flattered when I heard that Brazilian champions, Vasco da Gama were interested in buying me.' But although he loved travelling, he took pleasure in coming home to Scotland too much to ever seriously contemplate the extremely liberal offers. Reports that an armoured car drove up to the Hibernian tour party's plane as it was taxiing prior to take off, with the Vasco da Game chairman demanding by gunpoint that Smith and Johnstone leave the plane by the emergency chute, were slightly exaggerated – but only slightly!

Following another gruelling trip home, Gordon was worn out, but after a few days recuperation at his Willowbrae home, he travelled to see the British Open Golf Championship – this year held at Carnoustie golf links near Dundee. His friend Bobby Locke could only manage eighth position this year but the winner was Gordon's other hero, Ben Hogan.

Smith was honoured when Locke introduced the pair at a reception following Hogan's four-shot victory, with Gordon enthralled by this remarkable limping American. Hogan told Gordon about his car crash in 1949 and how, ever since that day, he had to endure enormous pain, treating his badly injured legs before and after every round of golf with a rigorous and agonizing training programme. This remarkable golfer was to win not only the 1953 British Open, but also five of the six tournaments he entered that year, including in the Masters and the US

Open. Normally the provider of autographs, on this rare occasion, Gordon was to come away from Tayside with Hogan's signature safely tucked away in his pocket.

Pre-season training and cricket games, with the players playing at both Raeburn Place and Leith Links this year, made Gordon's taste buds crave one of his biggest passions – football, golf, cars, films and records aside – ice cream! The mammoth helpings in Brazil couldn't have helped quell this longing and with his current favourite, Crolla's ice cream parlour on Easter Road, seconds away from training, he could be seen in there many times throughout the week.

At the commencement of the new season, Lawrie Reilly was very angry. He was angry and a tad envious of his friend Gordon Smith. Gordon's testimonial the previous season had made him want one – he felt he deserved one – yet he was flatly turned down by Harry Swan. There then followed an almighty wrangle over the matter, growing so heated that Lawrie refused to sign a new contract and was placed on the transfer list. Gordon was saddened by the whole affair but could see Lawrie's argument quite clearly.

Bobby Combe was made captain for the new season and Gordon would play once again in the Edinburgh Select side in the annual Edinburgh Charities Match. The game this year was against Billy Wright's Wolverhampton Wanderers with the Select side winning 3–2.

In the 1953/54 season, Hibernian would finish a lowly fifth and the seven years of magic had gone – injuries and lack of form combined to put paid to that. There was to be no riposte to challenge this year's winners Celtic in an unpredictable season for the Leith club. There was a feeling of ambivalence around the dressing room – the first time Gordon had felt such an atmosphere since he had signed over twelve years previously.

A decent League Cup run to the semi-finals was overshadowed by patchy league form including 0–4 hammerings by Raith Rovers and Hearts. Further defeats to Queen of the South and Partick Thistle saw Hibs just above mid-table by mid November. There was respite with challenge matches against Tottenham Hotspur, Manchester United and Derby County, and Leeds United for the opening of their new floodlighting system at Elland Road.

For the Manchester United friendly, Gordon and the Hibernian players had travelled down to their Southport hotel base to prepare for a benefit game for the United trainer, Tom Curry. Their training included a trip to Blackpool and the obligatory two rounds of golf. Just prior to the game, the arrival of Lawrie Reilly – who had driven down from Edinburgh – was greeted with a cheer and hand-shakes all round. Reilly had managed to sort out his differences with the club and was set to play for the first time this season, ironically in a testimonial match! Sir George Graham, secretary of the Scottish Football Association, had intervened in the matter, suggesting an international select could be arranged to play in a testimonial game for Reilly in due course.

Just prior to playing for Hibs in Paisley, Gordon travelled to a mining area in Midlothian with Bobby Johnstone to see local side Newtongrange Star defeat Dalkeith Thistle in what was Scotland's first ever cup tie under artificial light. The famous duo had a fantastic time and were given a rousing reception by the large crowd at Victoria Park attending the Murray Cup final, which 'Nitten' won 5–3. Gordon thought it a little odd that it was ok for junior teams to play official games under floodlights, but not professional ones.

A few days later, against St Mirren, Gordon Smith was booked for one of only three times in his whole career – for retaliation – and the following week he was castigated for his angry outburst when he was knocked-out cold by a stray boot in the home league victory over East Fife!

Further defeats at Dens Park and at home to Stirling Albion followed, but on 19 December, Hibs were coasting against Raith Rovers at Easter Road, with Smith having already scored two and looking to secure his hat-trick, when disaster struck. Gordon broke the tibia bone in his right leg in a collision with Rovers' goalkeeper, Charlie Drummond. He was rushed to hospital in an ambulance and sedated while his leg was put in plaster. A humorous tale then occurred, as he decided he wanted to go home, so telephoned his brother to collect him in one of the grocery vans used by his business. Gordon snuck out of the hospital by the back door and lay flat in the back of the van amongst apples, radishes and carrots as he was driven home by his brother.

As soon as he walked into the house, he fainted, hitting the side of his face. His brother panicked and called for Gordon's second ambulance of the day and Gordon was duly taken back to the hospital, then placed back in his bed in a private room. Furiously, the doctors told him not to move as the sedatives needed time to work.

No sooner than the medics had left the room, Gordon once again called his brother and again he arrived with the van, with Gordon making sure no hospital staff saw him as he hobbled back into the rear of the van for a second time surrounded by the fruit and vegetables, including a batch of newly arrived French onions.

Back home, he managed to last longer this time – he arrived, had a glass of water given to him by his sister, then proceeded to collapse again, missing the fire-place by a whisker. Once again, an ambulance was called for a still unconscious Gordon. Luckily he was ok and this was his third and final trip of the day! A nurse stood guard for the duration of his time in hospital and Smith said he could only remember vaguely the events following his injury, but it was a long time before he could stomach the smell of an onion again!

Once officially home, Gordon would be told his leg would be in plaster for at least six months, thus missing the remainder of the season. He was upset but realistically he had known this would be the outcome. The long lay-off also ruled Gordon out of any chance of participating in the 1954 World Cup. Gordon recuperated at home, listening to his jazz records and taking more of a front in the family business.

The spring of 1954 saw Gordon's youngest sibling, Brian, join the Royal Scots regiment for his national service. Brian, a very able amateur footballer with Preston Athletic followed by Selkirk Juniors, ended up in the jungles of Malaysia playing his football alongside Berwick Rangers goalkeeper and future Rangers boss, Jock Wallace, Jimmy Millar of Dunfermline, and soon-to-be Rangers hero and future Scotland manager, Third Lanark's Ally McLeod. The footballers, based at Batu Pahat, later said to Gordon that his brother was extremely talented.

The season ended with Hibernian finishing in fifth place, surprisingly only nine points behind champions, Celtic. It just goes to show that on the previous year's form, Hibs would have won the league by twenty points or more!

Gordon's friend Hugh Howie had retired to become a sports reporter for a newspaper and as the players embarked on a tour of West Germany, Gordon started light training alongside Archie Buchanan, who had also been sidelined with serious injury.

A little envious, Gordon read the reports from Hibs' further European adventures – this was an odd tour in the sense that the opening two games were against the West German and Czech World Cup sides (playing under the guise of Nuremberg and DSO), who were warming up for the 1954 World Cup in Sweden. The third game was against non-German opposition, drawing with AC Sparta Praha from Czechoslovakia.

Willie Ormond participated in the shambles that was the 1954 World Cup in Switzerland. The SFA took just thirteen players including one goalkeeper, Aberdeen's Fred Martin, and the team were slaughtered 7–0 in Basle by reigning World Champions, Uruguay, and 1–0 by Austria. A dismayed Gordon was appalled by the lack of planning that would see seventeen dignitaries from the SFA make the trip.

Despite these disappointments, Gordon did have one major highlight this year. Alfred Hitchcock's movie set on the French Riviera, *To Catch a Thief*, released the following year, should have read: 'starring Cary Grant, Grace Kelly and the legendary Scotland footballer extraordinaire, Gordon Smith'. Alas, although Gordon was in the film as an extra, he never received a billing! He had arrived in Cannes and stayed at his usual residence for a lengthy eighteen-day break when the offer of appearing came about after breakfast one morning. The film crew happened to be staying in the same hotel, and one of them was a keen football fan who recognised Gordon and promptly offered him the part!

Some people commented back home when he mentioned that he had appeared in a Hitchcock movie set in the south of France: 'You wouldn't need make up, Gordon, you'd just waltz right onto the set!' Such were the opinions of him – Gordon Smith, the man with the film-star looks.

Following this year's Royal Birkdale British Open Championship, with his friend Bobby Locke tying for second place, Smith was desperate to get back to playing football, having missed so many games. Smith's first match since December the previous year was playing for the Edinburgh Select team in the 1954 Edinburgh Charities match against Bolton Wanderers, which the Select side won 3–2 in front of 37,000 fans.

Eddie Turnbull was Hibernian's new captain for the 1954/55 season but the side started shabbily, losing to East Fife in the League Cup twice. However, they secured victories over Aberdeen, Queen of the South (with Gordon scoring his first goal since his broken leg) and Raith Rovers.

In early September, Rangers' Willie Woodburn was suspended by the referee committee of the Scottish Football Association, *sine die* –

Latin for 'without day' – in other words, for an indefinite period of time. He had head-butted a Stirling Albion player at the end of August, after being on the receiving-end of a rash tackle, but this was one too many sending-offs for the often volatile thirty-four-year-old player. Privately, Gordon was 'horrified' by the way his friend Woodburn had been treated by the SFA and, along with many other fellow players, including English star, Tom Finney, he was to write a letter to the SFA saying the ban ought to have been less severe and should be lifted. However, it wasn't lifted until three years later and by then, Woodburn, at thirty-seven, had decided he was too old to continue with his football career and concentrated instead on running his garage business. Gordon's sister, Rachel, who at the time was working as a cashier, remembers this 'very friendly and well-mannered chap', who from time to time would get his Ford car serviced, not at his own garage, but at Alexander's in Edinburgh's Semple Street.

Hibs, one of the British pioneers of the floodlit game for a number of years, had tried lighting systems in France, England and Switzerland, as well as at Ochilview Park, Larbert, the home of Stenhousemuir. On 18 October 1954, floodlights were first used at Easter Road. Heart of Midlothian was the team chosen to be the first to play under artificial light, unfortunately stealing Hibs' thunder by winning 2–0. Other unofficial floodlit challenge matches were played against AC Sparta Praha, where Smith scored a double with Tommy Preston and Willie Ormond doing likewise in the 6–2 victory, and against Leeds United at Elland Road.

Hibernian, Hearts, Newcastle United, Manchester City and Manchester United were all involved in the unofficial 'Floodlit League', which stuttered along without attracting too much attention or success. Hibs played on many Monday and Wednesday evenings, including a 1–1 draw at St James' Park, a 1–3 defeat at Easter Road to Manchester United and a 1–2 defeat also at home to Austrian champions Sportsklub Rapid Wien 1–2 on 13 December.

In the league, Hibs were playing quite well, including a fantastic series of six victories against Kilmarnock, Stirling Albion, Motherwell, Dundee, East Fife and St Mirren, which was then followed by a 0–5 humiliation by champions Celtic at Easter Road. The year of 1954 ended well, though, with a goal by Gordon securing a 3–0 triumph at Firhill on 18 December. Then, on Christmas Day, prior to kick-off, a recording of 'A Gordon for Me' sung by the broadcaster Wemyss Craigie on 11 October was presented to Gordon at Easter Road by the Alex Young Hibernian FC Supporters Association. The memorable match that followed resulted in a 2–1 conquest over Rangers, which gave all Hibernian fans the best present they would receive all day.

17

'THE BATTLE OF VIENNA' AND SCOTLAND CAPTAIN

> It is the proudest night in all my life. I never hoped to captain such a magnificent set of players, let alone lead them to such a great victory. I am unbelievably happy. It was a wonderful team . . . and now for Hungary.
>
> – Gordon Smith

ON PAPER, 1955 was to be Gordon's most prolific year in international football – odd for someone now at the age of thirty-one, whose appearances for the national side could be described as sporadic and undistinguished at best. He played an incredible eleven times for either the full national side or the Scottish Football League during the year, scoring six of the total of seven goals he scored internationally over his career.

Although Hibs were still a pretty decent side, they had lost the spark that made them champions a few years previously and with Bobby Johnstone departing for Manchester City soon after his last appearance for the team at the end of January, the 'five' were broken up.

After losing 1–5 against Hearts at Tynecastle on New Year's Day, Hibs suffered the ignominy again in the February, with the Gorgie side this time beating them 5–0, in the Scottish Cup. The following week, Gordon celebrated his 600th appearance for Hibernain in a 3–0 Lawrie Reilly hat-trick game against Kilmarnock at Rugby Park. Gordon scored two goals the week after at Fir Park and another at Dens Park in a 2–2 draw for the Edinburgh side.

It had been nearly three years since his last international appearance and suddenly he was back. He was picked for the Scottish Football

League's game against their English counterparts on 16 March at Hampden Park; with John Cumming, Alfie Conn and Jimmy Wardhaugh from Hearts travelling through with Smith, the team won 3–2.

After England hammered Scotland 7–2 at Wembley in early April, changes had to be made for the forthcoming May internationals; the 'old guard' had to be withdrawn, enabling an influx of fresh legs, including the return of Smith. He was to get his first full cap since the spring of 1952, being picked for an international at Hampden, then a three-game tour of Eastern Europe.

Preceding the first of these internationals, in the spring of 1955, a meeting took place in Paris to decide on the format for the forthcoming European Cup. The 1955 inaugural European Cup was the brainchild of French journalist, Gabriel Hanot, editor of the influential and widely read daily sports newspaper *L'Equipe*. Clubs right through Europe are indebted to him for such wonderful prescience.

The league season had ended for Hibernian with two victories, a draw and two losses, with Gordon scoring in successive weeks against St Mirren, Celtic and Partick Thistle. The Easter Road club ended up in fifth place – a massive fifteen points behind new champions Aberdeen.

Gordon's return to the international stage, alongside Hibs team-mates Tommy Younger and Lawrie Reilly, took place on 4 May at Hampden Park with Scotland beating Portugal 3–0. Precisely a week later, he embarked on the Scotland tour of Yugoslavia, Austria and Hungary to take part in what would be, without doubt, his three greatest games for the national side.

After spending the previous night at the airport hotel, the tour party departed from Prestwick Airport at 8am on Wednesday 11 May, flying on a chartered DC4 Swiss-Air four engine, fifty-five-seat plane bound for the Yugoslav capital, Belgrade, on what was probably the most important international series ever undertaken by a Scottish football team at the time.

The plane touched down in Manchester to take on extra passengers travelling to Zurich and after another quick touch-down in Zurich, it was straight to Belgrade, arriving at 5.30pm. The team headed on to the city's Majestic Hotel, allegedly the best hotel in the Balkans.

The Scotland Squad

Bobby Collins (Celtic)
Doug Cowie (Dundee)
John Cumming (Heart of Midlothian)
Tommy Docherty (Preston North End)
Bobby Evans (Celtic)
Tommy Gemmell (St Mirren)
Harry Haddock (Clyde)
Andy Kerr (Partick Thistle)
Billy Liddell (Liverpool)
Fred Martin (Aberdeen)
Alex Parker (Falkirk)
Lawrie Reilly (Hibernian)
Archie Robertson (Clyde)
Gordon Smith (Hibernian)
George Young (Rangers)
Tommy Younger (Hibernian)

The opening match of the three games would see Scotland taking on Yugoslavia in Belgrade's Partizan Stadion on Sunday, 15 May, with an early 5.30pm kick-off. The game finished 2–2 with goals coming from Hibs duo Reilly and Smith. After Scotland had twice been a goal down, the team played some adroit football in a very impressive performance.

'A Gordon for Me,' sang the happy Scottish players as their coach bounced up and down through the streets of Belgrade, after gaining a moral victory over Yugoslavia. Inside the bus, every eye turned to Smith – the man who had 'broken through' in the national side at long last. Thousands of Yugoslav fans stopped and waved to the players aboard the team bus as it meandered from the stadium to the Scotland team hotel. They had appreciated the good football played by the visiting nation so much that the atmosphere was that of a carnival nature. It was astounding that these were the opposing fans that were cheering and saluting the Scots!

The beginning of the tour was going remarkably well so far, especially considering the bad start Gordon had prior to the Yugoslavia game! He had split open his thumb when the head rest of a massage table clattered down, pinning him to the ground, just forty minutes prior to kick off. It was bloody and painful and according to Gordon, 'bloody painful'!

Trainer Alex Dowdells raced out for a brandy to give to the shocked Gordon but his request was interpreted by stadium officials as needing alcohol for massage purposes.

On his return with the 'medicine', the stench coming from the glass was utterly revolting, prompting Scots journalist George Aitken from the *Evening Citizen*, who was with the Scottish party in the visitors' dressing room, to push his way through the mass of fans at a stadium restaurant, where he was adept enough in the local lingo to purchase a glass of their best cognac. Allegedly teetotal, Smith lifted the glass to his lips in the dressing room, exclaiming: 'Here's my favourite drink – good luck to Scotland.' As his team-mates cheered, he knocked it back in one, just able to blurt out the infamous words: 'I feel better already!' before proceeding to cough and splutter, much to the amusement of all present.

A short two-hour flight to Vienna came after Belgrade and as the Scotland stars arrived in the city, they found it covered in flags and bunting, with an air of rejoicing. Had the Austrians heard how good the Scots team had been in Belgrade – or were the flags out to celebrate the signing of the state treaty and Austrian neutrality? Perhaps both.

A surprised yet very proud Gordon was chosen to replace the injured George Young as captain for the match in the Austrian capital. Prior to the game, about six or seven of the Scottish players, including Smith, had left their salubrious city centre hotel adjacent to the once Royal Palace of Schönbrunn to grab a breath of air and maybe a little culture in the old town, when one of the party mentioned that he thought he'd seen Billy Graham in the hotel lobby as they were leaving.

Billy Graham, the famous American evangelist, was all the rage in the mid-fifties and was currently on a European tour – so it was plausible. Out of curiosity, the delegation of players quickly headed back to the hotel, where true enough, a man resembling the legendary preacher stood at the far end of the lobby. The biggest joker in the squad, Tommy Docherty, went up to the preacher and asked him: 'Are you Doctor Graham, the Right Reverend Doctor Billy Graham, the famous American evangelist?'

The man stared at Docherty and in a high-pitched and exceedingly squeaky voice, replied with the most foul-mouthed half-German, half-English that he most certainly was not. It turned out the man was not the American evangelist, but an Austrian national.

Without Docherty's knowledge, another player had sidled up behind 'the evangelist' and was listening out for the conversation. As soon as he'd heard enough of the foul-mouthed tirade from the Austrian, he had quickly got back 'in position' with the rest of the players, telling them briefly what had happened, and awaited the Preston North End player's return with great delight and amusement.

When Docherty returned, his deadpan face didn't give anything away and when Gordon, who was frantically trying to keep it together, asked him what 'Doctor Graham' had said, Docherty merely replied, 'Oh, he was non-committal.'

Following this remark, Gordon and the remaining players were beside themselves, their shrieks of laughter echoing in the grand hotel. They laughed so much and with such volume that they were ordered to leave the lobby by a disciplinarian concierge clerk, who was closely followed by the now irate Austrian gentleman, squeaking in his odd language for a final time: 'These British are laughing at me!'

As you can imagine, this statement just ignited the fire of hilarity and the players were now almost crying with laughter! 'We're not British, we're Scottish,' came the reply in unison from the group as they headed back out onto the sunny Viennese street, all now teary-eyed. Could this be the highlight of the tour? This little bit of bedlam was nothing compared with what was to follow that evening during the game itself.

Gordon explained:

> The game in Vienna is memorable for a near riot I almost caused. Their full back fouled me and usually I jump up immediately so they do not think they'd hurt me. This time I was slower than usual and as he aggressively pulled me up by my shirt collar, I shoved him away and told him to leave me alone, whilst clenching my fist. This seemed to get the crowd going, and some invaded the pitch, with one irate fan heading for me, but luckily Lawrie, and then the police were able to stop him.

A shocking dose of enmity engulfed the 6pm game played on Thursday, 19 May, at the Prater Stadion in a match that became known as 'The Battle of Vienna'. Four changes had been made from the drawn match against Yugoslavia – Haddock, Young, Cumming and Gemmell were replaced by Kerr, Docherty, Cowie and Robertson. As an extremely emotional and almost tearful Smith walked out to lead his country for the first time in front of 65,000 fans, he was thrilled to have Tommy Younger and Lawrie Reilly by his side.

In a ninety-minute superlative and gritty performance in Vienna, Scotland's international team literally fought their way to a magnificent victory over Austria, winning 4–1 with goals from Robertson, Smith, Liddell and Reilly. The Austrian left back, Barschandt, was sent off with half an hour remaining, soon after Scotland's second goal was scored by the new skipper.

The Italian referee Giorgi Berdadi's night had got pretty busy. After Smith was mowed down by Barschandt, the Austrian defender grabbed him by the shirt and pulled him to his feet. At this rough treatment, the Scotland skipper came very close to losing his head, shouting 'Take your hands off me!' and drawing back his fist as if to emphasise the message. His big opponent took the hint but a section of the crowd took the shortest route to the field and charged towards Smith.

But so did Gordon's mates, especially Lawrie Reilly. As the fans advanced, one incensed hooligan took a kick at the suave captain, missing his chin by a fraction of an inch. Reilly, though, didn't miss the fan's chin, flooring him with a swift right-hook that current heavyweight boxing champ Rocky Marciano would have been proud to produce. As the on-field fighting continued amongst almost all the players, the police headed the mob back to the terraces and frog-marched Smith's attacker and Reilly's knockdown off to the cells. Bobby Collins almost had his jaw fractured by the boot of an Austrian defender just as the game was about to re-start.

At the end of the game, the Scottish dressing room looked like a war-zone as the players came in one by one to show evidence of the most unscrupulous and vicious tackling ever witnessed in an international match. Smith, Docherty and Collins were all bandaged up and to complete the scene, even one of the few Scottish spectators at the match was carried into the dressing room for sanctuary – the victim of a bottle assault by an enraged Viennese fan, after the final whistle had sounded.

When the Scottish players trooped out to the coach, they found an old-fashioned charabanc in its place, packed with police in riot gear and two motor-cycle outriders as escorts waiting to take them back to their hotel!

At an after-game banquet, the Austrian FA chairman played down the deplorable antics of his players and said that Scotland was on her way back to her rightful place in football. Scottish trainer Dowdells told Gordon he had never seen a Scottish team play better and Lawrie Reilly remarked that it was the best Scottish team he had ever played in – unquestionably the best team, he repeated to the euphoric but jaded players. Rangers' stalwart and usual Scotland captain hugged Smith, telling him that he could not have been more pleased even if he had been out there himself.

Gordon Smith would tell waiting journalists at the team hotel: 'It is the proudest night in all my life. I never hoped to captain such a magnificent set of players, let alone lead them to such a great victory. I am unbelievably happy. It was a wonderful team . . . and now for Hungary.'

And now for Hungary. The ominous score-line from Helsinki greeted the Scottish players as, in dribs and drabs, with one or two slightly worse for wear, they made their way to their hotel reception to collect room keys. They were all told the result by an astringent and slightly timorous Austrian night manager, hoping to succeed in putting the fear of God into them and certainly aiming to take the shine off a breathtaking night's work and Gordon's final comment to the press. 'Finland 1–9 Hungary,' he stated succinctly.

At the huge Népstadion in Budapest, unfortunately, Scotland were given a football lesson by the magnificent 'Magical Magyars' of Hungary when on Sunday, 29 May, the Scotland side lost 1–3, despite a successful first half. Through a goal scored once again by captain Gordon Smith, Scotland was leading at half-time and 102,000 fans howled their displeasure as Smith led his team down the tunnel – their howls delighting the Scots. After the break, however, goals from Hidegkuti, Kocsis and Feneyvesi, following a sneaky substitution, showed the class of the Hungarians, although Scotland put in a very decent performance – enough for the watching Hungarian president to say the Scotland team was at least four goals better than the present English side!

Captaining Scotland for the second time against one of the greatest players the world had ever known, Ferenc Puskás, was a thrill of a lifetime for Gordon, who sat with the illustrious player following the match when the two footballers, aided by an interpreter, 'chatted'. On the plane back, Gordon and his fellow players agreed that Puskás was 'short', 'stocky', 'barrel-chested', 'a little overweight', he 'couldn't head' and 'only used one foot' – 'but everything else about him was phenomenal – his balance, his ball skills, his poise and especially his deadly left foot'.

On Tuesday, 31 May, the Scots party arrived back at Prestwick at 8.55pm, right on schedule and in Gordon's words: 'happy', 'laughing at the hilarious Docherty's terrible jokes', 'in great mood' and 'delirious'. Gordon told waiting press that the trip had been fantastic from start to finish, with nobody wanting it to end. He said, 'The Scottish players on this trip reminded me so much of my own club, Hibernian, when we were at our best – a team of comrades ready to fight to the last for each other.'

Gordon had ordered a new sports car to replace the MG – a Porsche to be exact – and he flew to the German city of Stuttgart to collect it. He then proceeded to drive his new car back to Scotland, stopping en route at Le Mans for the world famous twenty-four-hour car race.

Gordon was not an avid motor racing fan but as he was driving back at the same time of the renowned race and because the media coverage was incredible, especially in mainland Europe, he decided to take a detour. When he arrived at this small town, he soon found it infested by hundreds of thousands of racing fans and he got caught up in the furore of this amazing spectacle.

This year, twenty-six-year-old British driver Mike Hawthorn, in the English-made Jaguar, partnered by the fifty-year-old Frenchman Pierre Levegh, were up against the German Mercedes team of Juan Antonio Fangio and the Brit Stirling Moss. It was billed as 'World War Two on the track' because of the bitter rivalry between the English and German manufacturers!

Such was the interest in motor sport in the mid 1950s that a throng of over 300,000 people packed in to the Le Mans race track and grandstands, with Gordon amongst them. The race itself on Saturday, 11 June, began at 4pm with sixty cars. The amazing spectacle of drivers sprinting to their cars with engines already running dumbfounded Gordon.

On lap thirty-five, the disaster occurred. After a collision, the Mercedes of Pierre Levegh went out of control at 150mph, decapitating many of the assembled throng of race-fans as it sliced through a mass of bodies in the grandstand. At least eighty-three people died, including many children, with over 200 injured.

The race continued, as organisers feared that ambulances and fire appliances would not be able to make their way to the dead and injured if the race was called off, as the road leaving Le Mans would be congested with cars driving away. Mercedes pulled out of the race but Jaguar continued; Mike Hawthorn went on to win but was vilified by the French newspapers.

Gordon, who was standing on the opposite side of the crash and subsequent fireball, was in shock and later admitted:

> I think that night all the tears in my body must've come out as I sat in my hotel room and watched the scenes on local television over and over again.
>
> When it became clearer what exactly had happened, I was just numbed to everything else around me.

Upon returning home, still shocked at what he had seen, he remained quiet about the appalling atrocity for some time after.

In early July, accompanied by good friend Bridget Gordon, the Hibs and Scotland number 7, showing off his new Porsche with the licence plate BMP 259 (distinctive in its day), as usual supported his pal Bobby Locke at the year's Open Golf Championship. Held at the home of golf, on the Old Course of St Andrews, this year it ended with Locke finishing in fourth place, losing out to the champion, Australian Peter Thomson, for the second successive year. Scotland's Johnny Fallon finished runner-up – he and Gordon 'talked football' in the players' tent, having been introduced by Locke.

Bridget Gordon from Bilston in nearby Midlothian had met the Hibernian player a few years previously at the Murphy's Pools offices at Greenside Place in Edinburgh, thinking he was a swarthy movie star and having no idea that he was a famous local football player. The pair had become colleagues when she worked alongside Gordon as he wrote his twice-weekly columns at the *Scottish Daily Mail*'s offices at the Canonmills area of the city.

They had a close, wonderfully affectionate, yet totally innocent rapport, and although their relationship was discreet and very personal, there was never anything inappropriate, with the pair solely good friends. Conceivably, the reason for this companionable relationship was due to the fact that Gordon was still dating girlfriend Nancy Croall and Bridget had a boyfriend as well.

At a recent annual Hibs dance held at the North British Hotel, Gordon had arrived on his own and seeing Bridget there, he spoke to her for a couple of minutes but then elusively disappeared, as was the norm. He wasn't seen again by Bridget (or anyone else) until just prior to the end of the evening, when he came skulking in and announced to her that he'd been for a walk on Princes Street. 'I wasn't going to return,' he told her with a wry smile, 'but you were so cheeky to me earlier that I just had to come back in and have a word with you, see that you were ok!'

There was a lot of frivolity and banter – such was the pair's relationship, never a bad word was said between them. Gordon also showed the appropriately named Miss Gordon down the players' tunnel at Easter Road during the close season, possibly in a move to impress her, but she was expecting something a bit grander apparently. Many an Edinburgh girl at the time would've been in 'seventh heaven' to have walked down the tunnel and out onto the pitch with the Hibernian right wing pin-up.

18

THE INAUGURAL EUROPEAN CUP

> If the European Cup had started, say, four or five years earlier, I am convinced Hibs would have been champions of Europe. No question about it.
>
> – Gordon Smith

JUST BEFORE the 1955/56 season began, the annual cricket match held at Leith Links attracted a huge crowd of well over 5,000. The match, between the Leith Franklin Cricket Club and Hibernian Football club, was obviously won by the footballers – by an impressive five wickets, no less!

Before the new season got underway with the Edinburgh Select Charities match – this year against Newcastle United at Easter Road – Gordon and his fellow Hibs players played at Meadowbank, again reaching the final of the now also annual prestigious five-a-side tournament. This year 13,000 fans watched the work-out; witnessing Hibs' victory over Hearts.

The 1955/56 season would herald a new dawn – Hibs would reach the semi-finals of the inaugural European Cup and their league position would improve to fourth in a term that would see Rangers champions again and local rivals Heart of Midlothian as Scottish Cup winners. Smith was once again installed as Hibs skipper for the new season, where in the initial five months up until the end of the year he would play an astonishing thirty-seven games, free from injury; this would be his most prolific period as a professional player:

League games	15
Floodlit Challenge matches	6
League Cup matches	6
SFL appearances	4
European Cup games	3
Scottish Caps	2
Edinburgh Charity Select games	1

Hibernian started badly, though; on 13 August in the League Cup, they lost to eventual winners Aberdeen, but Gordon secured goals in further League Cup games against Dunfermline and Clyde. The opening league match versus Aberdeen at Pittodrie was preceded by another Scottish Football League appearance, scoring again – for the fourth time in succession while wearing the dark blue. The SFL defeated the Irish Football League at Ibrox Park 3–0, with great friend and colleague, Lawrie Reilly, scoring alongside Smith.

Hibernian Football Club became the first British side to compete in a European Cup match. The team flew to Dusseldorf, then to Essen in Germany for the 14 September clash, playing against Rot-Weiss Essen and winning comfortably by four goals to nil. Over a thousand fans from the British Army on the Rhine were present among the relatively small 5,000 in attendance at the Georg Melches Stadion. Eddie Turnbull scored the first ever goal by a British player in a European competition and his two goals were complemented by a further two from Reilly and Ormond, with Smith scoring a goal in the last minute only for the referee to disallow it, claiming he had already blown his whistle.

In a 17 September interview with Howard Smart for the *Scottish Sporting Record*, Gordon remarked unequivocally when asked how long he thought he would play for:

> I'm looking for twenty-five years as a player for Hibs. I used to say a minimum of twenty, but it's ridiculous to think that I can't do twenty-five now; as long as I don't get any more serious injuries.
>
> I'd like to feel that my most enjoyable years have yet to come. I'm a great fellow for looking to the future.

What is the most memorable football game that you've played in?

It was in September 1950 when Hibs were in the quarter-final of the league cup against Aberdeen. We'd lost 1–4 at Pittodrie and faced a three-goal deficit in the second leg at Easter Road, with little likelihood of me playing.

I had been under continuous treatment for an injured shoulder, and no one dreamt that I could possibly be fit. Only I had hopes. At first I could not get any promise from the Hibs surgeon that I would be allowed to play, but on the day of the match I chased all around Edinburgh before I located him, and after pleading for twenty minutes, almost forced him to agree that I could play!

Even the rest of the players didn't know, and when I slipped into the dressing room and pulled off my coat my colleagues were incredulous.

My team-mates hooted with joy, but that was nothing to the roar that went up from the crowd when they heard I was playing.

In your opinion, what is the finest goal you ever scored?

Against Motherwell at Fir Park in November 1947. [The week before his five against Third Lanark.]

I just couldn't do anything wrong that day. I was told afterwards, that I beat seven men in the process. I don't remember that, but I do know I managed to walk the ball past goalkeeper Johnstone at the end.

Two days after the interview, following a 2–2 drawn match against Clyde, Hibernian defeated Manchester United 5–0 in a Floodlit Challenge match. An almost full strength United side included three players who would die in tragic circumstances in the 1958 Munich air disaster in two and a half years' time – Roger Byrne, Mark Jones and Tommy Taylor; a fourth, the incomparable Duncan Edwards, was an unused reserve. Smith with two, Ormond, Reilly and Turnbull would score in one of the best ever results for the Leith side.

Two nights later, Gordon was back playing for the Scottish Football

League alongside usual cohorts, Younger and Reilly. Smith didn't score this time but partner Lawrie did in a 4–2 victory in Dublin against the League of Ireland at Dalymount Park.

Following a win over Kilmarnock in the league, Hibs travelled to Preston to play North End at Deepdale, winning 4–0 and the following Saturday Gordon represented the full Scotland side for the first time since Budapest, with George Young re-installed as captain. The side lost 1–2 in Belfast to Northern Ireland but Lawrie Reilly would score yet again for his country. The usual Scotland Hibs trio were joined by their former Easter Road colleague, Manchester City's Bobby Johnstone, for this game and the quartet, alongside the rest of the Scottish players, would do a very much modern-day thing: attend a training camp in Belfast in the days after the game. The three Hibernian players missed the return European Cup match against Rot-Weis Essen in Edinburgh because fog had grounded all the planes in Belfast. An incredulous Smith wanted to charter a plane back to Edinburgh but forgot that fog delays had stopped *all* flights! So he, Younger and Reilly missed Hibs' match, sitting stranded in an airport lounge. In the last sixteen days, Gordon had spent only five at home, played seven games and travelled over 3,000 miles.

Hibs, without the Scotland three, drew 1–1 and comfortably went through to the next round 5–1 on aggregate. As mentioned in Tom Wright's book, *The Golden Years: Hibernian in the Days of the Famous Five*, Jock Buchanan had only found out less than an hour before kick-off that the Scottish trio were stranded in Belfast and wouldn't make the game, and that he was to wear Gordon Smith's number 7 jersey! Buchanan ran out to a huge cheer and scored. He scored the first European Cup goal on British soil, after he had, in his own words, 'just eaten a plate of mince and tatties that would have killed a store horse'!

The mist receded and after more league action, Gordon was back playing for the Scottish Football League with his two equally well-travelled Hibs colleagues, Younger and Reilly. This time it was the English Football League at Sheffield's Hillsborough ground with 37,788 seeing the English win 4–2 with Lofthouse and Finney among the scorers. Smith did score one for the SFL but against players in such fine form as Fulham's Johnny Haynes and Manchester United's Duncan Edwards, the Scotland team were outclassed.

After a 3–3 draw with Airdrie back in league business, Hibs played Bobby Johnstone's Manchester City in the Floodlit Football League on 1 November, winning 2–1 in front of the television cameras. This was the first ever game to be televised from Easter Road, when the whole of the second half was shown live. Many of the 18,987 had dressed up especially for the occasion – should they be shown on national TV!

Hibernian had been joined by neighbours Hearts, Glasgow's Partick Thistle and English sides Newcastle United, Manchester United and Manchester City in the new 'Anglo Scottish Football Floodlit League' that had been formed in the hope that the floodlit games would prove to be more of a success than the previous year.

It still struggled to achieve popularity – possibly because of the mouthful of the title – although Hibs were on a roll in the competition. The Leith side's next two ASFFL matches were both against Newcastle United, winning 2–1 at home and 2–0 at St James' Park.

On 9 November, Scotland defeated Wales 2–0 at Hampden Park with Bobby Johnstone scoring both. Fast becoming mainstays, Younger, Smith and Reilly all played against a Welsh team that included the illustrious John Charles, Ivor Allchurch and Cliff Jones.

Following a 3–1 league victory in Dumfries with Hibs' league form looking good, the club travelled to play their away game in the next round of the European Cup on 23 November against the Swedish champions, Stockholm club, FC Djurgarden – to all of Maryhill in Glasgow! Firhill, home to Partick Thistle, was chosen as the away ground as the severe Swedish winter had already closed in, not enabling football to be played in the country.

Hibs won 3–1 with goals from Bobby Combe, Jimmy Mulkerrin and Eddie Turnbull, with Eddie also missing a penalty, in front of 21,962 fans – not many of whom waved the blue and yellow of the Sverige national flag.

Turnbull did score a penalty in a 1–0 victory a few days later in front of 32,000 fans at Easter Road, putting the Edinburgh side through 4–1 on aggregate. And two days after the win, Gordon travelled to Copenhagen to play in what would turn out to be his last Scottish Football League match. Against the part-timers of the Danish Football Combination, the Scots won comfortably 4–0 and Gordon scored a goal in his final appearance – a parting shot, if you like.

In early December, following a league win over St Mirren at Paisley, Gordon Smith opened a public house he appropriately named 'The Right Wing', situated adjacent to his grocery and post office business on the corner of Willowbrae Road and Northfield Broadway. The plans for the opening of the public house had been in the works since the spring of that year, when Gordon had signed an agreement with John Fowler & Co, from Prestonpans to sell their beer. Flyers inviting guests to attend the noon opening had been printed by Mackenzie & Arthur of George Street, with excitable queues forming early on that frosty Monday morning. They snaked along Willowbrae Road and down Duddingston Road to the east, and stretched half way along Northfield Broadway to the west.

'Little Darlin'' by The Diamonds was the first 78 record placed on the turntable by Gordon, as the first guests frenetically danced. 'Only You' by the Platters was next, then Pat Boone and Nat King Cole discs, which were then followed by a selection of Gordon's favourite Fats Waller, Ink Spots and Sidney Bechet tunes. The merriment would continue long into the evening and probably way past Gordon's bed-time, even with an early 10pm closure akin to all licensed public houses of the era.

In Gordon's next game, he scored a wonder-strike against Dundee in a 6–3 victory and Hibs had now gone on a twelve-game unbeaten run stretching back to mid-October. However, two defeats by the Old Firm took the shine off this fantastic run of form, with both referees in the two matches allegedly biased.

In the Rangers game at Ibrox in a 1–4 defeat, even the Rangers-supporting journalist Rex Kingsley stated it was the worst performance he had ever seen by a referee, a Mr Liston of Larbert. The Celtic match at Easter Road was even worse as Hibs players, trailing 2–3 after only eighty-six minutes of the ninety played, were attacking the visitors' goal, when suddenly they heard the whistle blow and the referee Mr Younston from Aberdeen started walking toward the tunnel requesting the ball!

On Hogmanay 1955, pride was restored in a full ninety-minute match, as Hibs thrashed Stirling Albion 6–1 with a double from Smith, whose year in football had been quite extraordinary.

It had been quite a few months – he had made his 600th appearance for Hibs in February, played the first of five Scottish League matches in March, reclaimed his international jersey in April to play a further five times, played in the inaugural European Cup in September and defeated his favourite English side, Matt Busby's Manchester United 5–0 – scoring a double in that game the same month. He had almost scored for fun in national colours, after never having scored previously, and with Hibernian's current league form of nine wins in eleven and through to the European Cup semi-finals, things were certainly looking good down in Leith.

Gordon's highlight, however, was none of the above, nor even captaining his country on that famous night in Vienna, although in defeat; his highlight of 1955 was shaking the podgy hand of a certain Ferenc Puskás prior to joining him in kicking a football about on the same pitch.

19

JAZZ YEAR IN CANNES

FOLLOWING THE draw with Hearts on New Year's Day, two further narrow league wins and a defeat against Aberdeen were played before Smith scored his first goal of 1956, in the 7–0 trouncing of Motherwell at Easter Road. A 1–1 drawn match against Raith Rovers made history on 4 February, as it was the first Scottish Cup game to be played under floodlights.

Because of an injury picked up against Falkirk, Smith missed the replayed cup-tie against Raith Rovers, where Hibs lost 1–2 in Kirkcaldy. He returned for a challenge match against Bury at Gigg Lane, before scoring again in a 7–1 victory over Dunfermline in Leith. This was followed by further goals against Raith Rovers and Queen of the South. The Queen of the South game was famous as it was the first league game to be played under artificial light in Edinburgh.

In the middle of March, Gordon captained a Scottish Select XI against an Anglo/South African XI at Ibrox Park in Glasgow. The game ended 2–1 to the Scots with usual suspects Younger and Reilly also in the Select team. There were 60,000 mainly Rangers fans, who extraordinarily cheered for the 'away team' with more fervour than they did for the Scots XI (who included no Ibrox stars), with the reason for this being attributed to the fact that the Anglo/South African side had two Rangers players in the side – Johnny Hubbard and Don Kitchenbrand.

The massive crowd wasn't happy when Lawrie Reilly scored and especially when a Celtic player, Bobby Collins, scored the winner for the select! The match was in aid of the British Olympic Games Appeal, and Gordon invited a 'Miss James' to the game as his special guest in the stand to save her paying the 10/6 cost of a ticket.

Next up was the semi-finals of the European Cup and Hibernian travelled to France to play Stade de Reims in the inaugural elite tournament; Gordon's itinerary card below explains the details.

Reims v Hibernian in Paris for a Union des Associations
Européennes de Football match

Monday 2nd April
Depart Waverley station 10.40pm

Tuesday 3rd April
Waterloo Air Terminal S.E.1
(For coach to airport) report 10.30am
London Airport Central
Flight B.E. 331A take-off British time
12.15pm

Paris, Le Bourget Airport
Arrive (French Time) 14.35 hrs
Coach supplied by 'Transglobe',
14 Rue de Londres, Paris 9E
Will transfer passengers to Grand Hotel
Terminus, St Lazare, Paris.

Tuesday 3rd – Thursday 5th April
In Paris, at Grand Hotel Terminus, St Lazare

Thursday 5th April
Transfer by coach from Grand Hotel Terminus,
St Lazare to Bourget Airport, leaving hotel
at 16.00 hrs
Paris, Le Bourget Airport Flight BE 338
Take-off (French time) 17.30 hrs
Arrive at London Airport Central
(British time) 5.55pm

London Airport Central Flight B.E. 926 Take-off
7.45pm

Edinburgh Turnhouse Airport, arrive 9.20pm
Air Terminal, 133 George Street, Edinburgh
Coach arrives 10.00pm

Subject to Alteration

Unfortunately for Hibs, they lost the first leg to a very good Stade de Reims side at the Parc de Princes in Paris. Reims, who included the future Real Madrid playmaker, the great Raymond Kopa (at the time regarded as the best centre forward in Europe), won 2–0 with goals from Michel Leblond and Rene Bliarrd.

Two days after returning from Paris, Hibs won 2–0 at home to St Mirren in the league with a new scoreboard in operation at the ground. That same day, Gordon featured in an article in the *People's Journal* written by Gordon Gray.

> Ever since the Scottish team to play England was announced, all Scotland had been asking: 'How will Gordon Smith do at outside-left at Hampden?'
>
> Personally, I'm optimistic. England have successfully 'transplanted' a right winger on the left touchline by switching Tommy Finney – and you might call Finney the 'Gordon Smith of England'.
>
> What's more, that's a compliment to Finney – as you'd have agreed if you'd seen the Hibs skipper's dribbling, trapping and ballet-like pirouetting which made the ball do his bidding against Partick Thistle at Firhill. No, we should have fewer qualms over playing a player of Smith's ability out of position than we would with perhaps any other player in Scotland.
>
> He is a natural athlete. The first time he ever played golf, for example, Gordon astonished the local professional by his aptitude for the game.
>
> 'The pocket McGrory' he was called at school and two Scotland schoolboy caps at centre forward justified the description.
>
> 'The Gay Gordon' he was by the time he got to the junior Dundee North End and he lived up to it by grabbing a hat-trick against Bobby Baxter in that now famous Dundee Select v Hibs–Hearts Select match of April 1941.

> 'The Pride of Edinburgh.' That was to be Gordon's new name in a matter of weeks when, after signing for Hibs, he scored another hat-trick in his debut against Hearts at Tynecastle.
>
> He became the £40,000 player just after the war when Newcastle United, Aston Villa and Arsenal were reputed to be willing to offer a blank cheque for his transfer.
>
> Never out of the public eye, Gordon next astounded footballers and fans alike when he became the richest player in the country on netting the entire proceeds from his Hibs–Manchester United testimonial match.
>
> Today, he runs two businesses, his grocer's shop and his roadhouse, known as The Right Wing.
>
> He owns the house above the shop where his family now live. He runs a sports car. He holidays each year in Nice on the French Riviera. And he still finds time to divide his attention between his fan mail, his golf and his gramophone records.

The following Saturday, 14 April, was international week and Gordon, still in favour with the selectors, played as usual alongside Younger and Reilly in a 1–1 draw against England in front of 132,817 Hampden Park spectators. England included star players such as Roger Byrne, Duncan Edwards, Tom Finney, Nat Lofthouse, Johnny Haynes, Tommy Taylor and captain Billy Wright, with Bobby Johnstone collecting his seventeenth and final cap for Scotland. Aberdeen's Graham Legatt, on his debut, scored for his country, with Haynes returning the favour for England. For the first time in seventy-two years of the British Championship, all four countries finished level on points.

Gordon was to play only a further three games in the season, against Motherwell in a 1–1 draw at Fir Park, and his last league match coming in the 2–2 draw at Easter Road against newly crowned champions Rangers, where he suffered cartilage damage.

Sandwiched in-between was the return leg of the European Cup semi-final against Stade de Reims at Easter Road on 18 April. Imagine that: a European Cup semi-final at Easter Road! The 49,941 fans set a record attendance for a floodlit game in the UK at the time. Hibs lost 0–1 to lose 0–3 on aggregate, thus missing the chance to meet the mighty Real Madrid in the final. Among the record crowd was a future superstar of Scottish football, Jim Baxter, then a part-time player with

Raith Rovers, who had come from Hill of Beath in Fife to see his team Hibs and especially his favourite player – Gordon Smith.

Baxter and the rest of the Hibernian fans went home disappointed. Although losing on the night to a solitary early second-half goal, the Edinburgh side created numerous attempts to score the goals required to progress to the final. Smith, Turnbull and Reilly were all in great form and it required goalkeeper René-Jean Jacquet pulling off save after save to avert a goal feast for the home side before the interval.

Willie Ormond spurned many glorious chances in the second half and late in the game, Willie MacFarlane came very close too with a thunderbolt of a shot, but even if it had gone in, it would've been too 'eleventh-hour' to secure victory both on the night and on aggregate.

Gordon was utterly dejected following the game, desperately wishing to play in the final against the mighty Real Madrid; and for Hibs to get this close was galling for him. He was so disconsolate he had to be sweet-talked by his fellow players into attending the post-match reception, held at the North British Hotel. Had he had his way he would have walked out of the stadium and driven straight home without uttering a word to anyone!

Heart of Midlothian won the Scottish Cup on 21 April, the same day as Gordon's last match of the season, with Hibernian playing four games in the next nine days to wrap the season up, including a 3–1 challenge match against Brazilians Vasco da Gama, who bitterly disappointed by the non-appearance of Smith and Johnstone!

Gordon missed Hibernian's summer tour of France, staying at home following surgery on his knee, and as part of his recuperation, he jetted to Nice for three weeks. He had been making the pilgrimage to Cannes in the south of France for years now, introduced by his friend Willie Murphy just after World War Two, and he thought the place was like 'a little bit of heaven'. This year's fourteen days were to prove as exciting as other years – even more so than 'starring' in *To Catch a Thief* two summers previously.

This year was 'jazz year' in Cannes and along the coast in the little seaside bars of Theoule-sur-Mer and Juan-les-Pins, one of his heroes, the American saxophonist, clarinettist and composer, Sidney Bechet, was performing gigs alongside the Frenchman Claude Luter. Gordon had specially timed his vacation to coincide with the musical event. Upon arriving, the first thing he did was to take a minicab to Theoule and the vibrant venues – not returning till quite late, which was uncharacteristic for the sleep-loving Smith.

The next morning, Gordon struck up a friendship with the New-Orleans-born American. At fifty-nine, he was twenty-seven years older than the Scot, but they were both staying in the same hotel. Gordon couldn't believe his luck! The Martinez, the second best hotel in Cannes, only lagging behind the incomparable Carlton Hotel, was set overlooking the breathtaking Promenade de la Croisette. Once again, the introduction for Gordon was aided by the fact that he was pretty well known from previous trips and was now renowned as 'the man who almost beat Hungary' by the staff and regular clientele.

Although not conducive to Gordon's holiday mode, he was asked for a few autographs whilst sitting at breakfast; Bechet, who was sitting quite close, became aware of the practically clamouring girls in the room. He was more accustomed to being the one using a pen early in the morning!

Bechet, with his wife Elisabeth Ziegler, was intrigued by this young swarthy man who was attracting so much attention, and couldn't believe he was from Scotland when the two were introduced. Bechet enthralled Gordon and the two men hit it off immediately. From then on, Gordon would receive back-stage passes to the various venues Bechet was playing in – and on occasions would accompany the musician from the hotel to various events, including a wedding in Antibes where he performed. Parisian clarinettist and saxophonist, Claude Luter, was also a guest at the hotel. He loved football with a passion and Gordon was often seen demonstrating his skills in the vast lounge with Luter as an eager accomplice.

Just after dawn each morning, before the beach got too busy, Gordon would accompany Bechet for a swim in the cool but refreshing Mediterranean Sea, where the American would have the first of over 100 cigarettes of the day. His health was in decline and when Gordon suggested he should try to give up smoking, he looked horrified!

Smith and Bechet would then proceed to lie on sun loungers and listen to the gentle flapping of the tide as the sun broke through the clouds. The jazzman, lying back with his eyes tightly closed; would elatedly say: 'I can hear music in the sound of those waves, Gordon. The waves are talkin' to me, man. You must be able to hear it. You must.'

His persona very much reminded Gordon of Willie McCartney, a father figure to a degree, and he felt very comfortable in his presence. The two built up a great friendship that would unfortunately be short-lived, as the untimely death of Bechet was under three years away – from lung cancer. Bechet was quite astonished that this football player was so 'into' him and the two men, miles apart in many ways, did have a bond, which was as indisputable as each of their talents.

Five days after returning home, Gordon returned to Cannes, this time with his new 'friend', Joan Parry. He wanted her to meet Bechet and to experience the whole French Riviera scene, hopefully getting as much of a thrill out of it as he did.

The previous winter Gordon had met Joan Parry, an English-born girl brought up at Herriot Bridge in Edinburgh's Grassmarket, who in due course would become the love of his life. At this juncture, the pair had been 'just friends', with Gordon still continuing to see Nancy Croall from time to time.

He had met Miss Parry – an avid Hibs fan with season tickets to Easter Road – on the corner of Union Place and Forth Street when Joan dropped her purse – by all accounts accidentally! Although she, like many a girl at the time, admired, fancied and was a little in awe of Gordon, they did meet by pure chance.

As the months progressed, the couple's friendship was to reach another level as the couple holidayed together in Cannes with Joan taking her first ever flight – and hating every minute of it! The BEA Pinoair Dakota flight bulletin card from Captain Wilo, clutched in the perspiring palms of Miss Parry, informed the passengers that the test score was Australia 73 for 4 and the stewardess's name was Miss Lammas. It also told them to 'please pass on quickly', which Miss Parry did not, placing the card in her handbag instead. Miss Lammas would perhaps have lambasted her if she had found out!

Because of his two Cannes trips, Gordon missed the summer's British Open Golf Championship, which was held at Hoylake and won for the third time by Peter Thomson. During the summer, Gordon also began some 'business dealings' with Rangers star, Willie Waddell. The Rangers number 7 was seen arriving at The Right Wing on many occasions, where the two Scotland right wingers would talk in private for hours on end. The mention of stocks and shares were occasionally overheard by observant staff members but nothing further was ever disclosed – it was all very clandestine!

20

A BERNABÉU BIRTHDAY GOAL

THE 1956 Edinburgh Select Charities match found a fit-again Gordon raring to go. This year's game, Gordon's thirteenth Select game in succession, was against Birmingham City with Jimmy Wardhaugh and Lawrie Reilly scoring for the Select in a 2–1 victory in front of 34,000 at Tynecastle Park on 3 August.

His comeback following his cartilage treatment was to be short-lived. After losing the opening three League Cup matches, including a 1–6 defeat to Hearts at Tynecastle, Gordon's leg was broken during the fourth League Cup game, again against Hearts. In the game on 25 August at Easter Road, Hibs were 1–0 up following a goal from Gordon, when a tackle by Dave Mackay broke the smaller fibula bone in Gordon's right leg. Hibernian went on to again lose 1–2 against their mighty rivals.

Gordon was to be out of action until 3 October, when he played in a challenge match at St James' Park against Newcastle United in a 1–2 defeat. He returned to competitive action, playing his first league game of the season against Queen's Park in Edinburgh on 6 October. But at the next game at Kirkcaldy against Raith Rovers, he injured the bad leg again and was forced to miss a further match against Motherwell.

He returned for a 0–0 draw against Kilmarnock at Easter Road and four days later, on Halloween, Gordon travelled down to London with the team, back to Hibernian's favourite old haunt at White Hart Lane. Gordon came on as a second-half substitute and after the match, not for the first time, the Tottenham manager made enquiries about Smith's availability with Harry Swan. Gordon was still not 100 per cent fit again, though, and broke down in training the day before Hibs' next league match at Ibrox. He was to miss a further four matches before returning and scoring against Ayr United on 1 December in a 3–0 victory.

During Gordon's rehabilitation, he kept busy by following the news of the intriguing Suez Crisis involving Britain, France and Israel in conflict with Egypt's President Nasser. Aside from these political developments, Gordon was also pleased to hear the news that his old friend, Blackpool's Stanley Matthews, became the inaugural Ballon d'Or winner.

On 8 December at Broomfield against Airdrie, he injured his ankle in a 3–5 defeat and missed the next seven matches, including the New Year's Day derby win over Hearts at Tynecastle. In fact, Hibs had been undefeated in the seven, winning four and drawing three, but on Smith's return on 19 January, they lost 1–2 at Hampden Park against Queen's Park.

Gordon had his best game of the season against Aberdeen in the Scottish Cup, scoring in the 3–4 narrow defeat at Easter Road, but the following week in a season ravaged by injury, his ankle played up again and he missed even more matches. He returned on 9 March fully fit and played against Dundee at Dens Park and then in four more consecutive victories, but the Hibernian team, this time with the tables turned from earlier in the season, had been poor without him!

In a Challenge Match at Easter Road on 18 March, Hibs drew 3–3 with Leeds United, with Gordon scoring a right-foot chip. Also scoring that evening was John Charles, the Welsh internationalist who would sign for Italian club Juventus for £75,000 just a few weeks later.

On 6 April for the first time, Hibs played on a Saturday evening in front of 14,500 at Easter Road. Gordon scored two of his side's six in a convincing win but Hibs' mediocre season ended with two defeats and a draw, with the club finishing up in ninth place, twenty-two points behind Rangers.

Rumours circulated around Leith and in the press that Gordon Smith was being sold to Newcastle United. After Hibernian had played Celtic in Glasgow in the last league match of the season, Wilf Taylor – the Newcastle United chairman – travelled back with the Hibs party to Edinburgh, so he could discuss Smith's transfer. Hibs manager Hugh Shaw indicated a willingness to part with him but Harry Swan denied it.

Another shock a few days later occurred when, surprisingly – due to the amount of injuries he had recently had – Gordon was chosen to play for Scotland in a vital World Cup qualifier against Spain at Hampden Park on Wednesday, 8 May. It was Gordon's first international in a while without Lawrie by his side. However, Tommy Younger did play – although he was now the Liverpool goalkeeper.

In what was to be long-time Scotland skipper George Young's penultimate cap, Scotland, perhaps surprisingly, won 4–2, with goals including a hat-trick from Blackpool's Jackie Mudie. The game was played at Hampden Park in front of nearly 90,000 fans against a very good Spanish side, who had an array of scintillating players including Alfredo Di Stéfano, Francisco Gento, Ládisláo Kubala, Luis Suárez and José María Zárraga.

After the Spain game, the newspapers in Switzerland declared that Smith was the man to watch in Sunday's World Cup qualifying tie. At the airport, photographers and autograph-hunters made Smith, not George Young, their main target – but he was still angry about the Hibs' debacle and spoke to the *Evening Dispatch* on 18 May, when the plane touched down at Basle prior to the Switzerland World Cup Qualifier. He angrily remarked: 'I would play football anywhere for nothing, if it came to the push. My heart is in the game. I couldn't be happy, however, playing for a club who are rumoured to be willing to sell me at any time.'

The following night, in front of 48,000 fans, Scotland defeated the Swiss national side 2–1 with Celtic's Bobby Collins scoring the winner. This was to be George Young's last game for Scotland and Gordon Smith's penultimate cap. As Young was injured and pulled out of the friendly international in neighbouring West Germany, Gordon assumed he would possibly be made captain of the side for the remaining games as he had been two years prior; he was shocked, however, when not only was he overlooked for the captaincy in Stuttgart, but was also inexplicably dropped from the team altogether.

Picking Tommy Docherty for captain was 'fair enough' according to Smith, as Docherty had skippered the side on a few occasions when George Young had been injured, and Gordon didn't mind this one bit; but to be dropped from the side was infuriating to say the least, as he had, in his own words, 'had a pretty decent game against Switzerland'.

Scotland won the friendly match against West Germany 3–1 in Stuttgart in front of 80,000 fans at the Neckarstadion but Smith wasn't happy at all about being snubbed by the selectors. The Scots fielded the remaining nine players who had recorded a victory in Basle, with Celtic's Bobby Evans replacing Young, along with twenty-year-old Rangers winger Alex Scott making his third international appearance, replacing the bewildered Smith.

For the Spain international on 26 May, the Scots made two changes from the West Germany victory. Gordon Smith was recalled in place of Alex Scott, with twenty-two-year-old Dave Mackay, whose tackle had resulted in a broken leg for Gordon only last August, making his debut, replacing Rangers' Ian McColl.

The Spaniards made five changes from the team that had lost in Glasgow eighteen days previously, with Juan C Quincoces, Juan Segarra, Enric Gensana, Estanislao Basora and Enrique Mateos coming into the side. Three of the four Spanish goals were scored by captain Basora and Mateos, so you could say the changes in the team were vindicated!

Smith, on his thirty-third birthday, scored Scotland's only goal in the eightieth minute, to make the score 1–3, but with two minutes remaining, the Spaniards scored yet another to record a resounding victory in the sweltering early summer heat of Madrid.

Gordon had thought long and hard about whether to play in the Spain match but made the decision that if he was selected, he would play, as the honour of representing his country was too great to turn down, but he kept his doubts to himself. He was picked but the match would be his last for the national side.

Although not knowing it at the time, he bowed out from the international stage on his thirty-third birthday. Scoring for his country at the Bernabéu, in front of 90,000 fans and on the same pitch as the likes of Di Stéfano, Gento and Kubala, was an appropriate finale for the artistic and transcendent Smith.

Before his annual pilgrimage to the south of France this year, eagerly looking forward to meeting up with Sidney Bechet again, Gordon had been taking secret French lessons from a lady doctor at the French Consulate in Edinburgh's Randolph Crescent. The reason for this was possibly that he wanted to 'show off' to Miss Parry – or Bechet, who was fluent in French – or both of them!

On 6 June 1957, Gordon holidayed for a second time with Joan Parry in Cannes. Over the course of the holiday, Sidney Bechet arrived to stay for a few nights, as he had some gigs along the coast, with Joan meeting the famous musician after just missing him last year.

Bechet, of course, also soon familiarized Joan with the peaceful early morning Mediterranean Sea, where she too would listen out for the music in the waves. Gordon was to introduce her to another great friend of his that summer; upon returning from France, they headed to St Andrews, where they made it just in time to see Bobby Locke win the Open Golf Championship for the fourth time at the famous Old Course.

That victorious Saturday evening, Locke and Smith were reunited at Gordon's Right Wing public house, where it was reported by more than one person that a euphoric Gordon was seen drinking a brandy in celebration of his pal's victory!

21

WORST INJURY OF CAREER AND THE MUNICH AIR DISASTER

In early August 1957, Smith sat down with Harry Swan and thrashed out a new deal, with the Hibs chairman making Gordon an offer to re-sign for the new season.

The Hibernian Winger spoke to Charles Shankland from the *Sunday Pictorial.*

I AM not finished with football yet! It was enough when I was dropped from the Scottish team to play Germany on the continent during the summer. But I was even more deeply hurt when I read that Hibs were prepared to transfer me to Newcastle United – and I knew nothing about it!

Don't get me wrong. I am not so big headed to think Hibs and Scotland can't get on without Gordon Smith. Nor am I complaining that football owes me anything. But I'm not ready to be written off yet – by Hibs or Scotland. I'll go on playing for several years. In fact, barring serious injury, I see no reason why I shouldn't still be playing well into my forties.

Last season I came back to play for Hibs only seven weeks after I'd had my leg broken for the second time. I've always believed it takes at least a year to recover fully after you've had a broken leg. Everybody must admit that I know a little about that from my experience. But I wanted to play again, went out and broke down and was off again for a few weeks.

Then I was chosen to go on the World Cup tour and I was on top of the world . . . only to be dumped down again when

An early photo of Gordon, far right, with his siblings, from left Robert, William, Stanley and Rachel

A proud Montrose Roselea player

With older brother Robert

Gordon during his Dundee North End days

Hibernian, 1951/52 Scottish League Champions, featuring (in the front row) the Famous Five slightly out of sync; Johnstone, Smith, Reilly, Turnbull and Ormond, with the League Championship trophy in front of Chairman Harry Swan

Gordon enjoying his favourite salt water treatment with Bobby Combe

Inaugural Scottish Footballer of the Year in 1951

Scoring Hibs' only goal in the 1-2 defeat to rivals Hearts on 2nd January 1950 with the highest ever attendance at Easter Road, 65,840!

In action during Hibernian's 6-1 German tour mauling of FC Bayern Munich, May 1950

Introducing HRH The Duke of Edinburgh to Bobby Combe and the rest of the Hibernian players at Highbury, October 1952

The Famous Five in their heyday

Flash forward to 1979, for a reunion prior to the Rangers/ Hibernian trio of Scottish Cup Finals

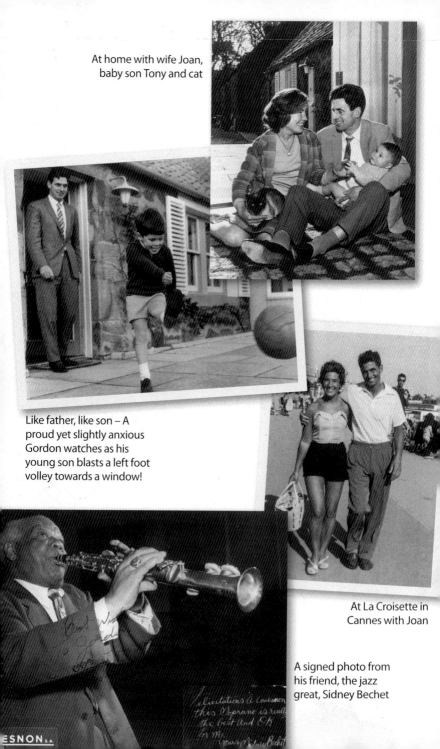

At home with wife Joan, baby son Tony and cat

Like father, like son – A proud yet slightly anxious Gordon watches as his young son blasts a left foot volley towards a window!

At La Croisette in Cannes with Joan

A signed photo from his friend, the jazz great, Sidney Bechet

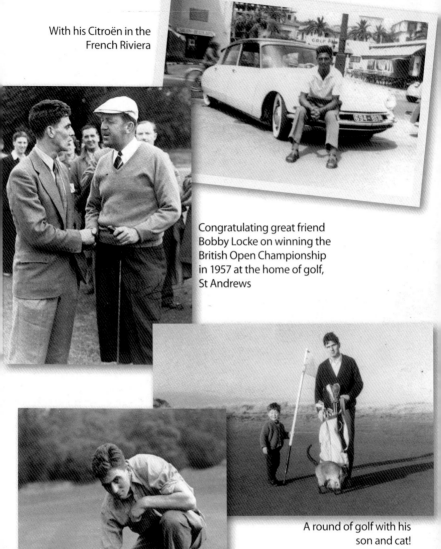

With his Citroën in the French Riviera

Congratulating great friend Bobby Locke on winning the British Open Championship in 1957 at the home of golf, St Andrews

A round of golf with his son and cat!

Eyeing up a putt

Shaking the hand of Ferenc Puskás, as Scotland captain, May 1955

Taking a free-kick against an English side featuring Wilf Manion, far right

The Heart of Midlothian 1959/60 League Championship and League Cup winning squad

Scoring for Hearts against St Mirren

Waitresses watch from above as Gordon holds the League Cup aloft in October 1959

A happy bunch of Dundee players – 1962 League Champions

Celebrating with Dundee coach, and ex-Hibs team-mate, Sammy Kean on the pitch at Muirton Park after winning the title seconds earlier – 28 April 1962

An exuberant Dundee squad after winning the league title

In his garden with wife Joan in 1990

Still kicking a ball, this time with his grandsons in 2002

Standing proudly with his son at the Hibernian FC supporters club at Sunnyside in June 1989

At the HFC Supporters Club again; this time with Eddie Turnbull in March 1997

I was dropped after playing against Switzerland. Only George Young and I were left out of the team to play against Germany – and Young had called off himself because of injury. That looked as if the selectors considered I was the only one who'd let them down against Switzerland. I know I didn't have a great game. But if I played badly, I certainly wasn't the worst man in the Scottish team. Not by a long way. I felt I had been treated unfairly. I was out of the international team and when it seemed my club didn't want me either I was really mad. That's why I waited until after I'd had a talk with our club chairman Mr Swan before re-signing this season.

On referees and football crowds:

There isn't enough protection for the ball player. Too many of our referees are what we call 'homers' – men who let the home team get away with practically anything. I don't expect to be treated like a privileged untouchable. I'll stand for the strongest tackle or a shoulder charge from anybody so long as it's fair. But I do say referees should take stronger steps to stop the man who goes out deliberately to injure another player.

Unfortunately for football there are some players of that type in the game getting away with it week after week. Unfortunately, too, some so-called supporters encourage these dirty players. You get little pockets of loud mouths at certain grounds that do nothing but hurl abuse at the visiting players. That's expected. But what are you to think when you hear, as I heard at one ground, 'Get stuck into that b*****d Smith and break his f*****g leg again'? What sort of mentality do these people have? One minute they're screaming for a body. Next, they're shouting for good football. They can't have both.

Gordon's outspoken comments did not make him the most popular player in Scotland – already criticised by some as a 'one-man show'. But there was too much truth in what he said to be ignored. This direct criticism ruffled the selectors' feathers and made one newspaper ask: 'Surely the SFA wasn't envious of Smith?'

During Smith's recent meeting with Harry Swan, he had been informed that his long-time friend and Hibs assistant-trainer Sammy Kean was not offered new terms for the forthcoming season after a heated exchange with the Hibs chairman. He was released and subsequently joined Dundee with Bobby Combe, at thirty-three, taking up Kean's position.

The new season, as always, began with the Edinburgh Select Charities match. This year, Gordon was captain of the Select side that played Preston North End, including the great Tom Finney in their side, and the visitors ran out 3–1 winners. North End also included Gordon's Scotland team-mate, moreover 'Battle of Vienna' accomplice-in-arms, Tommy Docherty, and Northern Ireland's Frank O'Farrell – two men who would become managers of Manchester United in the future.

Gordon, as captain of the Edinburgh Select side, wrote in the souvenir programme:

> I am sure that I speak for all the players when I say that footballers welcome any chance to do what they can for a worthy charity and, as I know from my long connection with this particular match, the Charities day game had a very fine record in helping deserving local charities.
>
> The very first time I played in a charity game was in 1942 when a Hibernian side met a RAF Select XI at Easter Road in the aid of the RAF Benevolent fund and local war charities.
>
> From these wartime games arose the present series and it is interesting to me – and perhaps to you – that apart from myself, only the incomparable Stanley Matthews is still in a First Division side of all the twenty-two players who took part in that match fifteen years ago.

During the week before the official commencement of the 1957/58 season, Gordon's new Porsche Speedster arrived in Edinburgh. Unlike two years ago, he didn't drive it back from Stuttgart – this time it had been shipped.

Also that week, *Scotsport* (STV's new sports show) arranged an unusual challenge after presenter Arthur Montford argued that goalkeepers ought to be able to save penalties more regularly. Montford, tweed jacket and all, asked Partick Thistle No. 1 John Fairbairn and Hibs winger Gordon Smith to take part in the televised penalty-kick event. The challenge was to take place at Firhill, with Fairbairn attempting to save five of Gordon's penalties. Gordon had 'sped through to Glasgow in his new speedster', scoring all his penalties against the hapless Fairbairn, even after telling the keeper which side he was going to place the ball prior to taking each penalty!

The season started with a Smith goal in a 4–0 defeat of East Fife in the League Cup at Easter Road, a 1–4 loss to Airdrie in the same competition, then a 3–1 victory over eventual winners Celtic, but Hibs were again knocked out from the tournament early. Initial league form was excellent, with five victories recorded in the opening six matches, with only a 1–3 defeat to neighbours and eventual League champions Hearts spoiling the perfect start.

Any thoughts that Smith may have ostracised himself with his erstwhile acerbic remarks to the press proved to be tenuous when he was selected to play in the international against Northern Ireland in Belfast on 5 October. Gordon called off at the last minute injured from a 'niggle' in training – although he was well enough to play and be selected 'man of the match' two nights later at Tynecastle for the official opening of Hearts' new floodlighting system in a 4–2 victory, mainly thanks to a Tommy Preston hat-trick.

Gordon's 700th appearance for Hibernian was against Dundee at Dens Park on 19 October. In a poor game for Hibs, he could not add to the 355 goals he had scored for the club in this 0–3 defeat and injured a foot in the process, missing the following week's game against Raith Rovers. Smith next played in Floodlit Challenge matches against Sheffield United, Wolverhampton Wanderers and a Liverpool side that included Scotland international, ex-Hibs goalkeeper Tommy Younger, Scotland's Billy Liddell and future captain, coach and caretaker manager, reds' legend, Ronnie Moran.

Again, possibly a little out of the blue, Gordon had been selected to play for Scotland in the forthcoming international to face Switzerland but had been slightly injured during the Wolves game. Hugh Shaw informed the SFA of the injury, as was the requirement, but told them it wasn't serious and he would be fit to play. Yet no sooner had he put down the phone than Smith was bizarrely removed from the squad, to be replaced by Rangers' Alex Scott. In a 3–2 victory, Scott scored the winner and the eventuality that Smith would never play for Scotland again was secured.

A bitterly disappointed Smith had decided, honour or no honour, that if ever picked again by the current regime in charge at the SFA, he *would not* play. The sardonic fact that Scott had scored the winner, and was in favour with the selectors, meant he would not have that call to make. Remarks made again to journalists did not go down well at the Scottish Football Association HQ in Glasgow. And in the six and a half further years he continued as a professional, between November 1957 and April 1964, despite playing at the highest level, winning two further League Championships, a Scottish League Cup medal and playing a further ten European Cup matches, the SFA selectors also never made that call.

Clearly, the ramifications of the West Germany 'dropping' never went away. The remarks that Gordon had made to journalists then, followed by the late Northern Ireland call-off and the further criticisms aired to reporters recently were not perceived to put the selection committee in a good light. Thus, the possibility of adding a further ten to fifteen caps never materialized.

Three days after playing at Anfield, on Saturday, 16 November, Smith was back playing for Hibernian in league duties at Broomfield when he received the worst injury of his career. Gordon had been man of the match once again before being seriously injured in a collision with the Airdrie full back, Jimmy Shanks. Smith's ankle was completely shattered. In agony, Smith was carried from the pitch to an awaiting ambulance and rushed to hospital. Prematurely, he returned six weeks later with the ankle appearing to have healed but his ankle would need many more operations to mend properly.

As his Hibs team-mates had enjoyed friendly matches in England against Manchester City and Middlesbrough, and Real Madrid's Alfredo Di Stéfano collected this year's Ballon D'or as the best player, Gordon had set his sights on returning to the Hibs team for the league match against Clyde at the end of December.

He was to miss the defeat to Clyde but returned for the New Year's Derby game against Hearts at Easter Road. This game would be the first of four in the first eleven days of the year – a tall order for a fit athlete but even taller for someone whose ankle had not long ago been shattered.

Four games and four defeats later, Gordon would be devastated, as was everyone else at Hibernian Football Club, upon hearing the news that former player and friend to many at the club, Hugh Howie, had been killed in a car crash. Hugh Howie had been a very close friend of Gordon's during his Hibernian playing career and had recently acquired a job working as a journalist for the *Daily Express*. He died tragically in a car crash on 14 January when, travelling between Blantyre and Cambuslang, he hit a lamppost whilst test driving a friend's car. He was trapped behind the wheel, later dying in hospital. A distressed Gordon sent a message of condolence to his bereaved wife Margaret and young son Douglas.

Before running out the Easter Road tunnel four days after Howie's death, the players said a prayer in respect of their former team-mate and friend. Hibernian were to honour him by halting the slide of defeats, drawing 3–3 against Falkirk with a Gordon Smith goal – direct from a corner-kick and the highlight of the afternoon. But all was not well at the club and talk that Lawrie Reilly and Gordon Smith were to be dropped to the reserves was rife.

The reports that Smith was to be dropped for the first time in his career were exaggerated – why drop a player who had scored in two successive games? His ankle had been troubling him so much that he had to have yet another operation, after which he wouldn't play again for ten months. Nevertheless, this was to be the longest lay-off in his professional career – one month more than after suffering a broken tibia during the 1953/54 season.

Incidentally, the goal scored against Falkirk direct from the corner-kick was to be Gordon's 362nd for the club and his last ever scored at Easter Road for Hibernian – his final pair for the club coming the following season at Stirling and Kirkcaldy.

As Gordon was recovering after another operation on his damaged ankle, he was to hear of even more dreadful news. On the way home from a European Cup quarter-final victory over Red Star Belgrade, the aircraft carrying the Manchester United players, officials and journalists, crashed into houses while attempting to take off after refuelling in Munich. Gordon, on hearing the news of the 'Munich air disaster' on 6 February, broke down and was very distraught. Matt Busby was on a life-support machine and Gordon felt helpless for his dear friend. Duncan Edwards, the young genial half back, whom

Gordon had once invited for post-match 'lemonades' back at The Right Wing, was also on a life-support machine.

The disaster claimed twenty-two lives, including seven players – seven players who Gordon knew very well both as opponents and socially. The trainer Tom Curry, whom Gordon had known for many years, with Hibs playing a testimonial game for him, also died in the crash. There were more players who did survive but were so maimed that they never kicked a ball again.

This news, just three weeks on the back of Hugh Howie's death, saw Gordon pretty despondent. To add to this anguish, the fact that the earliest he would be able to play again was next season exacerbated matters even more. He wanted to go out to Munich to see Busby and the survivors, and he probably would have but for his leg in plaster and the agony of his own ankle.

When, a fortnight later, Gordon received the news that Duncan Edwards' fifteen-day fight in the Rechts der Isar hospital had been in vain, with his name being added to the already long list of names that lived on forever with Gordon – Geoff Bent, Roger Byrne, Eddie Colman, Mark Jones, David Pegg, Tommy Taylor and Billy Whelan – he was inconsolable. Gordon had met and socialised with them all and just couldn't quite take it in. As well as the players, he had known the club secretary, Walter Crickmer, and Bert Whalley, the head coach, for many years. He and Willie Murphy had once socialised with another of the dead, Willie Satinoff – the racehorse owner and close friend of Matt Busby – and Bela Miklos, the Manchester travel agent, had visited Easter Road on a number of occasions. He had even known some of the eight journalists who were travelling with the team that fateful night who had not made it.

Busby was still too ill to move but the good news was that he was going to survive. This news aside, Gordon's *annus horribilis* continued, as he had to have yet another operation on his shattered ankle since it wasn't healing correctly after the second attempt. Also, the news that his great comrade and colleague, Lawrie Reilly, was retiring saddened Gordon incalculably.

Many letters were sent to Easter Road over the years, and many were simply addressed: 'Gordon Smith, footballer, Edinburgh'. Some were even just written, 'Gordon Smith, Edinburgh'! During his period of inactivity, there had been 'a mountain of mail' arriving daily at the club and in turn, they were delivered to Gordon's house by some very eager postmen.

Reading these letters from fans helped alleviate Gordon from the doldrums he was certainly in. It would take him hours to sift through them all, and he replied to many and signed photos by the sack-full! This certainly made the long hours spent in 'his own company' a little happier.

In early March, as Gordon was recuperating in a private hospital at 22 Moray Place in Edinburgh's West End, he received this letter from Hibernian manager and secretary, Hugh Shaw.

Hibernian Football Club

Dear Gordon,

In accordance with the normal practice when a player is incapacitated for an indefinite period, the club desires you to make arrangements for the Injury Benefit due to you under the National Insurance scheme to be made payable to the club. This, of course, requires in the first instance a Medical Certificate from the hospital to be forwarded to the Ministry of Pensions and National Insurance, 2 Commercial Street, Leith, and a claim form will then be returned to you for completion and authorisation for payment. This arrangement has operated quite smoothly in the past with A. Marshall, A. Buchanan, and J. Ogilvie etc.

I know the result at Tynecastle would give you as much pleasure as it gave us all here at Easter Road. Professor Bruce was there, as happy as a sand-boy and he described to me the details of your two op's, and he is very confident that your ankle will be tremendously improved.

Hoping to see you soon

Kind Regards

Yours sincerely

Hugh Shaw

Another letter received by Smith was from the Hibernian Supporters Association based at 7 Carlton Terrace, with their General Secretary worried about adverse press reports he'd read and he was extremely concerned for Gordon's welfare. Gordon, who was the President of the Supporters Association at this time, wrote back but couldn't alleviate the HSA's concerns about the rumours – as they were unfortunately true.

Wednesday, 19 March 1958, and *Evening Dispatch* reporter Jimmy Cowe wrote:

> Will Gordon Smith ever play for Hibs again? That's the burning question among Hibs' fans.
>
> Gordon has lost well over a stone in weight and the muscle and flesh have almost disappeared from his leg. He admitted that, of all his injuries and set-backs in football, this one had proved the most painful, the most discouraging.
>
> 'This third operation was my only chance of getting fit enough to play football again. Not until the ankle has healed will I know what my chances really are.
>
> 'When I will be able to start strengthening the leg again, I do not know. I may start very light remedial exercises in a month or it might even be three months. That shows you that I have no idea how it is all going to work out.'

Gordon, unable to go home, wrote to Lawrie and Matt from his hospital bed – saying to Lawrie that it was 'a tragedy' that it had to end the way it had, that it made him despondent to think that he would never play with his great partner again after the fantastic times they'd had together and the great service Lawrie had given to Hibs. To Matt, he continued to wish him a full recovery as he had done in previous correspondences and said everyone was 'praying for him, back home'.

On 21 April 1958, Lawrie Reilly played in what would turn out to be his last game for Hibernian. Fittingly, it was against Rangers at Easter Road and Hibs won 3–1. Gordon had managed to hobble along on crutches, against the wishes of the doctors, to watch his great friend and strike-partner in action one last time. He was just one of the 26,000 fans who saw the centre forward's glittering career come to an end. He had scored 185 goals in a mere 253 appearances, including eighteen hat-ticks, one more than Gordon's seventeen.

Five days later, Lawrie joined Gordon high in the stand at Hampden Park to watch their beloved Hibernian lose in the Scottish Cup final by a solitary goal against Clyde to end the most miserable of seasons.

Yet another parcel of mail would be delivered to Gordon's house day after day – with the poor postmen now having to undergo a special fitness programme just to enable them to carry the sacks full of mail. According to Gordon, it was like 'Christmas Day in a children's hospital' on a daily basis, with the amount of letters and packages they had to deliver to 233 Willowbrae Road!

In one of the parcels was a flat cap – a flat, tweed *Andy Capp* to be exact – sent by the *Daily Mirror* newspaper and specially approved by the football-loving, famous comic-book creator Reg Smythe, a Hartlepool FC fanatic. *Andy Capp*, the comic strip, had first been published by the Mirror newspaper group the previous August, initially as a single panelled cartoon (subsequently it became four panelled) and the title of the strip was a pun – a perfect phonetic interpretation of Hartlepool's pronunciation of the word 'handicap'. Smythe chose to call his character Andy Capp, as a handicap is exactly what Andy is to his hard-working spouse, Flo, as well as a reference to the main character's trademark flat cloth cap. Although synonymous with a loveable rogue and a bit of a layabout, he was endearing to the British public and Gordon treasured the cap, even sometimes wearing it on occasions and mimicking Mr Capp's northern English voice – but always indoors and always before he had combed his jet-black mane of hair!

On a foggy early May evening, Gordon watched his third game since coming out of hospital – this time Scotland playing the mighty Hungarians back at Hampden Park. The game ended in a draw and the Hibernian winger wrote this very interesting piece for the weekend's *Sunday People* and appeared to be way ahead of his time!

> It was a May evening in Glasgow . . . grey, murky and misty. From my seat in the stand it was difficult to distinguish what was happening on the field.
>
> But this wasn't an unimportant end-of-season affair. It was the Scotland v Hungary game at Hampden – the international

against the marvellous Magyars, who had thrilled us there nearly four years before.

And this match in the mist – was so vital to both countries as part of their World Cup warming-up plans – was being played with an ordinary ball . . . almost the same sort of football that has been used in Scotland for the last thirty years.

Why didn't we use a white ball which is so much easier to see and doesn't become heavy even in the wettest weather?

The answer is simple . . .

The heavier the ball, the more difficult it becomes for ball players – and to have played with a white ball would have been an advantage to the Hungarians.

As I sat there hardly able to follow the ball, my thoughts rolled back twelve years – to the time when I learned what I had always believed was, in fact, true.

We were using a ball which was ridiculously and unnecessarily hard.

AND WE ARE STILL USING IT.

At that time, when Scottish teams went abroad they always took their own supply of balls with them. And Hibs were no exception . . . we usually had half-a-dozen in the hamper. The idea was that the game would be played with OUR ball.

For by then (1946) the continentals were wise to the fact that if the ball is softer it has more 'give' in it, and can be manoeuvred easier . . . and that is the basic secret of their success at controlling the ball.

Naturally the Scots wanted their traditional brick hard ball to be used . . . and their insistence on that point always led to lengthy arguments . . . although we always won in the end. We were still respected as a no. 1 soccer nation at that time.

Our opponents pulled out every ruse they could muster to get their own ball on the field. On one tour in Czechoslovakia with Hibs our ball would go sailing over the terracing wall soon after the start of nearly every game . . . and theirs, lying ready, would be hurriedly rushed on from the sidelines.

That happened in almost every game . . . but the important point was we always kicked off with our own ball.

Gradually, however, as Scotland's stock in the football world slumped, Scottish touring sides found that half the game would be played with their ball – the other half with their opponents'.

And now, of course, it has reached the stage where if a Scottish team want to play abroad it's on their opponents' terms about the ball . . . take it or leave it.

I suppose many people will say that I attach too much importance to the question of what kind of ball should be used. But I must explain that I am quite certain that it is of vital importance if our standard of play is to improve.

A rule made many years ago states that the ball must be between fourteen and sixteen ounces, but, in fact, there is rarely a check to see if the ball exceeds that weight. And one club (Airdrie) makes the ball still heavier by soaking it in water – particularly if meeting a ball playing side.

All this means that the Continentals play with a ball which is fourteen ounces or less – I suspect very often less – and ours is invariably sixteen ounces or more. The disparity is just too great.

And I feel that unless we adopt the softer, lighter Continental ball we can forget all about World Cups.

Joe Baker was to be Hibernian top scorer this season – the first in seventeen seasons where it was not Gordon Smith or Lawrie Reilly – and Hibernian embarked on a short trip to Holland and Belgium to play German side FC Shalke and French team Valenciennes, without those two aforementioned stars and Eddie Turnbull, who had been chosen to represent Scotland in their World Cup domination bid! This miserable season for the Easter Road side continued as, in the penultimate game, they ended up conceding six goals in a heavy defeat, but at least the players ended on a high note with a 1–0 victory over the French side. Peter Thomson equalled his friend Bobby Locke's four British Open Golf Championships during the summer – a feat that further irked Gordon as his bad year continued. Injured or not, the summer was still to be dominated by football – good football.

Gordon was becoming more and more distant with Nancy and was seeing Joan increasingly often. This culminated in Nancy catching the pair out together. Nancy used subterfuge in dealing with 'the enemy'! She had arrived at Gordon's house at dusk, was let in by his mother and had waited for hours, hiding in the now almost dark bedroom for Gordon to arrive – and when he did, it was with Joan. At first, all hell broke loose, but not long after, Nancy realised that after many years together with Gordon, he appeared to be happier with this new romance than he'd ever been with her – she could see a look in his eye that she'd never witnessed before. The break-up wasn't acrimonious at all and Nancy remained friends with Gordon and, possibly surprisingly, with Joan; when she emigrated to Canada and married, she would send letters to the couple including a telegram on Gordon's Heart of Midlothian debut, as well as Christmas cards for years to come.

Once again, for a third successive year, Gordon and 'friend', Joan Parry, would jet to Nice, then hire a car to drive to Cannes and stay at the Martinez, with the couple, in the non-salacious 1950s, having separate rooms. From their favourite haunt, Brasserie du Casino, close to the famous Promenade de la Croisette, Gordon and Joan watched Scotland fare slightly better in this year's World Cup, held in Sweden, than they did during the previous shambolic disaster in 1954. Hearts star and future colleague of Gordon's, Jimmy Murray, became the first Scot to score at a World Cup finals, with the final ball being passed to Murray by none other than Eddie Turnbull, who played well for the national team. The madly in love pair cheered on Scotland from the heat of the Riviera but the game against Yugoslavia ended 1–1. The team ended up losing the other two to France and Paraguay but the games were very close and the Scottish players, although not world champions, held their heads up slightly higher than four years previously.

Once Scotland were eliminated, the couple's attention turned to Brazil, who were a joy to watch with the emergence of seventeen-year-old Pelé starring alongside Gordon's favourite, Garrincha. Brazil, using the novel 4–2–4 system (which had been recently trialled by FC São Paolo and FC Santos) for the first time in the World Cup finals, after drawing with England, had beaten the USSR and demolished home favourites Sweden 5–2 in the final in Stockholm. Gordon watched the game – up out of his seat in admiration for the Brazilians for most of it – at Cannes FC, where the couple had been cordially invited for a meal beforehand.

During the couple's stay, they once again met Gordon's 'jazz musician buddy', Sidney Bechet, who played an impromptu set in the foyer for the embarrassed pair one afternoon. Bechet had arrived at the hotel for the final week of the couple's holiday and the 'blue Mediterranean Sea early morning meetings', as Gordon referred to them, occurred for a third year in a row, with Bechet continuing to amuse Gordon as the tide ebbed and flowed with his 'wave-talk'. This summer, he was a little more vociferous than he'd previously been, and he would declare: 'Surely this year, you just must be able to hear that music, Gordon, you must be able to dig that rhythm, you just must!'

22

CONCLUDING MONTHS AT EASTER ROAD

THE GIRL who was turning into the love of Gordon's life, Joan Anne Parry, moved into a flat in Paisley Drive, near Gordon's Willowbrae Road businesses, and started to work for him in his grocers' shop and in The Right Wing, along with her sister Naomi and friends Terry and Lulu d'Angelo.

Talk amongst regulars in The Right Wing was that Gordon had paid Nancy off, helped her financially to emigrate to Canada, so it would be all 'plain sailing' for him and his 'new squeeze' Joan, but nothing could be further from the truth. Little did most people know that Joan and Gordon had been together off and on for over three years now and Nancy had also met someone else a long time ago, had fallen in love with him and found the prospect of a new life in Canada just too good to turn down.

Once again, Gordon tried to keep his relationship with Miss Parry quiet, as he had been doing, so the press wouldn't get hold of it. On many occasions, when going to his favourite cinema in Morningside, The Dominion, the Grassmarket girl would have to go in on her own, sit down and wait for Gordon, who would arrive five minutes later, buy a single ticket and discreetly join her!

The 1958/59 season – Gordon's eighteenth for Hibernian – would turn out to be his last for the east Edinburgh club. It started with Gordon unable to train, never mind play, thus missing his first ever Edinburgh Charities match, a 2–2 draw against Liverpool. The news that his dear friend Bobby Combe had left Easter Road to become a coach at Dumbarton did not help to alleviate his despondency. Gordon missed having Bobby around the place, as he too had been there since day one, signing the same afternoon in April 1941; both trialist and junior had done 'pretty well' that evening – and 'pretty well' in the two decades that followed!

Light remedial exercises started in September and over the next eight weeks, Gordon gradually built up to a reasonable fitness, enough for him to ask to try out in the reserves in the forthcoming Rangers match – the first and only time he was to play for the Hibernian second string.

The game went well and Gordon's ankle stood up to the test – although it was the reserves, it was still Rangers! One of his Famous Five partners in crime, Eddie Turnbull, was also playing for the second team that November Saturday but a crowd of just over 5,000 came predominantly to see the long-awaited return of the 'Gay Gordon'. Eddie unfortunately missed the chance to win the match for the home side – his penalty-kick saved by Rangers' keeper, Billy Ritchie, with the last kick of the game.

The following week, Gordon Smith returned to a Hibernian first team side that only lost three out of the next sixteen games. One newspaper reported that it was great to have Smith back in action and to see one of football's greatest sights – 'Gordon Smith in full cry going for goal'. The game against Third Lanark at Easter Road ended 4–4 with the 15,000 crowd cheering every time Smith touched the ball and with his name shouted throughout the lively encounter. However, it was Englishman Joe Baker who stole the show, scoring a hat-trick. Bobby Craig was definitely the most effective player for the visiting Glasgow side, scoring one goal and setting up the rest.

The end of the year saw Hibernian travel to London, losing to Tottenham Hotspur in a White Hart Lane friendly; Matt Busby replaced Dawson Walker as manager of Scotland; a Hibernian FC supporters rally at the Usher Hall featuring another friend of Gordon's – 'Hibs daft' Johnny Victory – and his repertoire company; and finally, Raymond Kopa, once of Reims, now of Real Madrid, win the year's Ballon d'Or.

However, Gordon's year-end highlight, sandwiched in between games against Partick Thistle and Stirling Albion, ought to have been playing alongside his great team-mate, Lawrie Reilly, one last time; albeit in a 'friendly' match in the former Hibernian number 9's testimonial match held on the Monday evening of 15 December 1958. Hibernian played against a Scottish International Select that featured

Tommy Docherty, Billy Liddell and ex-Hibernian players, George Farm and Bobby Johnstone, and won handsomely, 9–3. Gordon scored two goals, numbers eight and nine, and injured himself slightly in the process in a game that had become a farce of a match. 'Lawrie deserved so much better,' were Gordon's words after the debacle by the SFA. Reilly was forced by the officials from Glasgow to sit in the stand for his own testimonial game, as he couldn't receive the adequate insurance cover. The bureaucrats deemed further, for insurance purposes again, all the Scottish Select players had to be signed Hibernian FC players for the match – then sign back to their respective clubs the next morning! Consequently, there were twenty-two signed Hibernian players that evening! Four of the Famous Five played, with the one missing – the main man. Gordon thought that it was ludicrous and wrote a letter to the SFA telling them exactly what he thought of their decision making.

Gordon's last derby game as a Hibernian player took place on New Year's Day 1959 – and little did he know that the next time the two rivals met in early September, he would be a signed Hearts player, playing in Danny Paton's right wing position against Hibernian. The game ended in a win by three goals to one for the Tynecastle side. At the end of the long month of January, Gordon was to score his 364th and last ever goal for Hibernian against Raith Rovers in a drawn Scottish Cup-tie.

The day after winning the replay 2–1 against Raith Rovers, Gordon was invited to a screening of *The Captain's Table* by George James, the manager of the Gaumont Theatre in Edinburgh's Canning Street. The film, which preludes the *Carry On* films in its style, starred Donald Sinden, John Gregson, Joan Sims and John Le Mesurier, with an uncredited pairing of Steven Berkoff and Oliver Reed. Gordon thoroughly enjoyed the British comedy, although not normally his preferred cinematic category.

On Saturday, 28 February 1959, Hibernian entertained Partick Thistle in a 4–1 victory at Easter Road. This was to be Gordon's last home league game for the club, as his right ankle suffered severe bruising – an injury that would keep him out of the midweek Rangers' home draw and the Third Lanark away game on the first Saturday in March.

In a season in which he played twenty games, scoring two goals, 14 March saw Gordon play in his last ever competitive game for Hibernian.

Ironically, for the most part, he played at centre forward – where eighteen seasons ago he'd kicked off his Hibs career – after Joe Baker's return too quickly after injury didn't last long. Joe's recent knock flared up in the first few minutes and Gordon took over at number 9, interchanging with him until both players were basically unable to run! Accordingly, for the second successive week, Hibernian had returned to Cathkin Park, Glasgow, and this time for the quarter-final of the Scottish Cup. In a miserable afternoon, the greens lost 2–1 with Ormond scoring a consolatory goal. Eddie Turnbull was also badly injured alongside Baker and Smith – enough for him to decide to retire from the playing side of football – and his last appearance for the Leith club came in the early April Dundee visit to Easter Road. With Gordon out for the rest of the season due to his right ankle in need of more surgery, and with Hibs missing many other important players, the remainder of the league programme wasn't great to say the least – one win, one draw, four defeats and finishing up in tenth position – the club's lowest in twenty years.

In an edition of the *Evening Dispatch*, Gordon gave a candid Q & A to reporter John Gibson's generic queries. (Note: John Foster Dulles was the current US Secretary of State having worrying dealings with the Russian Premier Nikita Khrushchev, and Anita Ekberg was a Swedish model/movie star; about to take the world by storm with the sensational and iconic movie, *La Dolce Vita*.)

Duffle Coats:
Don't like them at all. I always feel it's a certain 'type' who wears them.

Emigration:
Seems to be a popular idea, but it has never appealed to me. The only thing wrong with this country is the climate.

The H Bomb:
Too big a problem for me to pass an opinion.

Temper:
Like everybody else, a bad one at times. I think I have lost it on occasions on the field, but over the years, on very few

occasions. Three or four times in fact and then only for an instant.

Glasgow:
I used to detest the place, but I like it now. I would say the Glasgow football fan while he can be very critical, is very knowledgeable. Nobody can deny they are crazy about the game.

Manners:
Far too many bad ones going about. What makes it so obvious is when you meet someone with really good manners. That person is rare.

Hogmanay:
For me, it's early to bed because we have a match the next day.

Gambling:
I'm not against it, in moderation, of course. Myself, I'm an ordinary gambler. We're not allowed to do the pools, but I go horse racing now and again. I usually can't resist having a flutter whenever I see a race on TV.

Drink:
All right in moderation. I'm more or less a teetotaller. Smoking? Never.

John Foster Dulles:
Not very impressed.

Anita Ekberg:
Very nice, to say the least.

Electric Shavers:
Like them a lot. I've used one for ten years now. A great invention.

Chic Murray:
Like him, I must say. I believe he's a Hibs fan. I'd like to meet him anytime he's around Easter Road.

Photography:
Don't dabble in it at all. And I detest having my own photograph taken. I always tell photographers that if they were good they wouldn't have to get me to pose. They get plenty of scope when I'm on the field.

Humphrey Bogart:
I must say, I admired him very much. The kind of fellow everybody misses. I probably saw all of his films. There's nothing I like more than a first class film. Laurence Olivier is my favourite actor. He watched Hibs at Easter Road a couple of years ago, and I was most annoyed to learn that he had been allowed to come and go with little fuss. I would very much liked to have met him.

Cars:
For me it provides a terrific amount of pleasure. A car is an essential part of my life. I've had one for twelve years. I'd like to see a much better standard of driving and a lot less carelessness.

Reading:
Don't read much at all, as far as books are concerned, although I take in most of the daily press.

Biggest Thrill:
My first comeback game after a nine month lay-off. Everybody seemed to be on my side; and meeting Bobby Locke.

Superstition:
I don't think you could call me superstitious. Lawrie Reilly always liked to come out last and other players tie a new lace before every game. Nothing like that for me.

Hobbies:
Jazz. I've got over 1500 records, mostly of the New Orleans and blues type. Fats Waller, George Lewis, Louis Armstrong and Sidney Bechet are among my favourites. You can say I appreciate all kinds of good music if it's well played. Golf, too. I play as often as I can, which is usually three times a week during the summer.

Ambition:
To remain healthy. To play football as long as possible.

23

RELEASE FROM HIBS AND A HEART-WRENCHING DECISION

> I'll never forget what that call from Willie Waddell meant to me. You know, he phoned me at something like six o'clock in the morning the very next day after I was released by Hibs and told me that as soon as I knew I was fit, Kilmarnock football club were waiting for me. He would love to have me on board, he said.
>
> – Gordon Smith

SATURDAY, 18 APRIL 1959, and following Hibernian's home defeat at the hands of Stirling Albion in their final league match of the season, an announcement was made by the club regarding Gordon Smith. They announced the unthinkable! Supporters, fellow players and the media were all equally shocked. Gordon Smith is no longer wanted at Easter Road and was free to go. Gordon recalled his reaction to the news:

> I was sick. I was absolutely shattered that Hibs didn't want me. I tried to put on a brave face, but it was hurtful to be released after what I'd gone through.
>
> I was absolutely devastated when I was told Harry Swan didn't want me. I really couldn't believe it.
>
> By spending so long at the club I had become a supporter too and it really hurt when they broke the news to me.
>
> The chairman couldn't even tell me to my face. Hugh Shaw had apparently argued my case for most of the previous night – but to no avail. Swan had said that having another operation would do more harm than good.

For fans young and old, this announcement bestowed a myriad of broken dreams; this was earth-shattering news. Harry Swan and Hugh Shaw had reached an impasse on negotiations and the chairman had the final say. Gordon did not malign Swan – far from it, although bitterly upset. Harry Swan had been very good to Gordon for eighteen years and they had built up a close bond – he was more shocked than maddened by the chairman's actions and final say. But when Hugh Shaw first told him of the chairman's decision, Gordon's first feelings were of anger and rage.

Knowing that these feelings would only exacerbate the already tense situation, Gordon tried to calm down but it was not easy. The very next morning, before 6am, Gordon's telephone rang. He was already awake and on the line was Willie Waddell, offering him a place in the Kilmarnock team. Gordon commented, 'Although Kilmarnock was to be the first club to show an interest in me, it was just too far away and I reluctantly declined the invitation after giving it a lot of thought in the weeks that followed.'

On the afternoon of Sunday, 19 April 1959, Gordon escaped from the media scrum that had formed outside his Willowbrae Road headquarters and jetted off to Nice, with his usual retreat of Cannes in the French Riviera – his personal sanctum – the destination. The reporters who had gathered ever since the 'unthinkable announcement' were eager for a story. 'I will play again!' was all an emotional and dour-faced Gordon had to say before speeding off up towards Jocks Lodge with older brother Willie at the wheel of his brother's Porsche.

Upon his return, he paid for an operation and the revered surgeon, Dr John Bruce, whom Gordon had asked to 'fix' his shattered ankle, said he would do his best. Curiously, Dr Bruce (ultimately Sir John Bruce) in due course became a Hibernian director.

On Sunday, 4 May 1959, Gordon travelled directly to the private hospital in Edinburgh's Moray Place, to be greeted as he exited his sports car by hordes of pressmen and the eminent surgeon, scalpel in hand, ready to operate on the ankle. Smith told the waiting media:

> I won't allow myself to become a responsibility to any club until I'm absolutely certain that I'm fit to give them my best in return.

This, I will promise. If and when I make my comeback and I find that my play doesn't measure up to the standards that the fans and my own judgement demand, I'll be the first to quit. Nothing will sway me from that.

So, yet another operation on Gordon's right ankle was carried out by Dr Bruce and after, Gordon continued his recuperation at the Braids Hills Hotel before returning home. He went quickly back to his favourite treatment, the icy cold water at Portobello beach, where he would endlessly walk up and down in the shadow of the giant power station.

Gordon had received in excess of an astonishing 5,000 letters in the three weeks since his release from Hibernian. All of them – mainly from Hibernian supporters – were on his side and very supportive, and he had had many letters from clubs, some with big money offers, asking him to sign for them. He, along with friends and family, took an age to go through all of them, with Gordon replying to as many as possible.

He wrote a letter to the *Edinburgh Evening News* stating:

I feel it is only right that I should ask you to express my very sincere appreciation to the very many people who have written to me and voiced their interest in other ways. I had no idea that so many people in Edinburgh were so genuinely concerned, and no matter what the future holds, it makes me feel very humble indeed to know that I have made so many friends.

Which club could he go to that would both satisfy his desire for first team football and provide him with the opportunity to still play at the highest level?

Willie Waddell had telephoned in the early hours of the day following his Hibernian release, doing his best to lure him to Kilmarnock, where he was now manager, and there was also a noted interest from Willie Thornton's Dundee at that time, too. The Dens Park side, coached by his friend Sammy Kean, was certainly the favourite for the winger's signature according to the media, and Gordon thought long and hard over the summer before coming to a decision.

Having taken holidays in the Côte d'Azur for many years now and having used the local football club's training facilities at one time or another, with the added attraction of the odd bounce match thrown in for good measure, Gordon was approached by the chairman of Cannes FC about signing up. The prospect of joining Cannes, who at that time played in the French second tier, appealed to him for an assortment of reasons. The lifestyle, the climate, the many jazz clubs scattered along the coast, the healthy eating, and the many friends he had in the area almost swayed Gordon to depart for the south of France. He had indeed taken secret French lessons for many years, maybe with the hope that one day an offer like this would come along? His girlfriend, Joan, also loved the idea of a permanent holiday in Cannes. If it wasn't for his business commitments in Scotland, many people assumed, he would have gone, thus denying the world of Scottish football a record that to this day has yet to be broken – winning the championship with three clubs, Hibernian (three times), Heart of Midlothian and Dundee, all outwith the Glasgow Old Firm.

The main reason he turned down Cannes was not solely a business one. Gordon still believed he had the ability and the fitness to ply his trade at a higher level. He was merely thirty-five years old with a shattered right ankle, having just had three successive operations in trying to mend it, and had been told by Dr Bruce that maybe he should never play again – why shouldn't he still aspire to play at the top!

The eventual decision to join Hibs' rivals Heart of Midlothian was not an easy one, having played the past eighteen seasons at Easter Road and having been part of the greatest days in the club's history. He was going to make his announcement in early August – for thousands of football supporters, not only a shocking choice, but also a betrayal from the man still widely acclaimed as being the greatest ever to don the green and white jersey of Hibernian Football Club. Although Smith publicly vindicated Hibernian chairman Harry Swan, the pair never spoke again. Could it have been possible that the added incentive of getting 'one over' on Harry Swan clouded his judgement and swayed his ultimate decision?

Cannes FC, although a mouth-watering prospect with the added incentive of a villa in the hills with swimming pool and sauna, could not offer football at the highest level. The Italian club, Fiorentina, were also showing an interest, as they had done many years previously. They played in Serie A, at the highest level, but Italy didn't appeal to Gordon, who worried about the language barrier. By now, contact had been made by Hearts; the serious offer and the prospect of playing in a very good team without having to move away from home and his Edinburgh business interests was to prove too strong an attraction, managing to beat out all the other contenders.

At the end of the day, was it a betrayal by Gordon Smith in joining Hearts, when really he could have played for almost any other team, or a betrayal by Harry Swan in not believing in his star player and in letting him go? Did Hibernian forsake him? Why did they not put their trust in him when he promised it would turn out 'just fine'? This was no ordinary player, so shouldn't they have believed what he had to say on such a crucial matter, at least taking into consideration his opinions?

Yet it certainly wasn't all Hibernian's fault, as is commonly stated. Smith justified Swan's decision completely, since his case did appear so hopeless in the beginning; but in the end, he did defy and astonish the medical profession, with his right ankle coming back from the dead after *five* operations in total on it, continuing to play for another five seasons.

Nor should Gordon take all the blame for choosing Hearts, as he took his time in picking his new club, having to start from scratch again after almost two decades in Leith. He was eventually swayed by the magnificently well-run Tynecastle set-up. In hindsight, he made the correct choice, making the switch across the city as Hearts went on to win the League Cup and the League Championship in his first nine months at the club!

Gordon, who had been freed by Hibernian since he was 'past it' and they believed he would never reach his incredible standard again, now ranked alongside of the likes of Lawrie Reilly, Sammy Kean, Archie Buchanan and Bobby Combe, who had all, in one way or another, been maltreated by Hibernian after they had given great service to the club. Many letters to the club, the press and to Gordon himself basically said Hibernian's administration were devoid of any common sense and sentiment whatsoever (although Gordon continued to exonerate his ex-chairman).

Recovering at home after his last operation, Gordon's downcast mood was not helped when he heard of the death of his friend, jazz great Sidney Bechet, whilst in hospital in the Garches suburb of Paris on his sixty-second birthday. He had nearly completed the writing of his autobiography, *Treat It Gentle,* when illness struck. Gordon had been aware that Bechet was writing a book and was desperate to read it. Once again, for the second time in two years whilst recovering from his own ankle injury, he had heard of the death of a good friend.

Ironically, Gordon was due to fly back to France the next day, for the second time in a matter of weeks, for a holiday with Joan. The couple arrived in Cannes after another near air-disaster during take-off from London airport in the second leg of their journey to the Riviera. The plane appeared to lose all power from its engines, dropping suddenly, before all returned to normal. Joan was petrified along with the majority of the other passengers.

Prior to arriving at the couple's usual Hotel Martinez, the first sound they heard on their taxi journey from the airport was Bechet's most famous tunes, 'Petite Fleur' and 'Les Oignons'. They were played continuously on car radios, in bars, hotels and restaurants – with Gordon despondent for an array of reasons, this didn't help! The Côte d'Azur was in mourning for the great jazz legend, whom they had adopted as one of their own. A man the existentialists had called 'Le Dieu' was gone. The hotel had a sombre feel to it too, from the many guests who, like Gordon, knew Bechet, through to the staff who had got to know the great man's many idiosyncrasies all too well over the years. Halfway through this trip, Gordon and Joan deemed it a necessity to move to the Hotel Splendid and were never to set foot in the Martinez again – the only reason being attributed to it holding too many memories of the now deceased Bechet. The jazz legend was buried during a private ceremony at the Cimetière de Garches, Hauts-de-Seine. Had it been a public affair Gordon and Joan would have undoubtedly attended.

As previously mentioned, whilst in Cannes, Gordon was offered terms for the forthcoming 1959/60 season by the French football club and he deliberated on this option for many a sleepless night – even doing some light and remedial training using the club's facilities to see if that would bring a solution. This was a serious offer that he couldn't quite decide a verdict on whilst he was there – it would have to be done with a telephone call at the end of the following month.

Over the next few weeks, Gordon regained a moderate level of fitness and he grew stronger. Moreover, upon his return from France, he was once again back down to Portobello beach at dawn, bathing his 'troublesome' ankle in the healing salty waters of the Forth and training

– now daily – at New Meadowbank, five minutes from his Willowbrae Road HQ.

One afternoon, whilst Gordon was playing golf at Gullane on a glorious summer's day in mid-July, his former colleagues, the Hibernian players, faced a sweltering start to the new season when they reported to new coach, Eddie Turnbull, at Easter Road. Sixteen players turned out for the first day's training and immediately on arrival, had their heights and weights taken before being given a word of welcome by manager Hugh Shaw in the dressing room. The sixteen players to report were: Aitken, Buchanan, Fox, Baxter, McClelland, Frye, Wilson, MacLeod, Leslie, Young, Baker, Wren, Anderson, Preston, Grant and Falconer. No Smith for the first pre-season since 1940!

As Gordon was getting near to full fitness, he had his lawyer draw up this document, which was open for any interested team to peruse.

July 1959; Gordon Smith's terms

(a) He would sign until 30 April 1960, after which he must be free.
(b) His wages during that period would be (unless he breaks down) £20 in the first team, £18 in the second team.
(c) If he breaks down, no wages will be paid.
(d) £20 signing bonus.
(e) If he is re-signed for season 1960/61, an extra £1,000 in wages will be added to this season's wages with an agreement that a similar sum will be added to his wages for the 1960/61 season provided he has no mishap.
(f) The player will have this assurance of an extra £1,000 when re-signed for a period not to exceed five years as from August 1959, provided always that the player does not break down.
(g) The Club will have the right to release or retain the player after April 1960 should the player decide to stay with this club.

It is interesting to note that (f) states from August 1959 not to exceed five years. That was a prophetic judgement, as Gordon did play his last professional match nearly five years later in April 1964.

What follows is a time-table of the days leading up to Gordon's decision to sign for Hearts.

Friday, 24 July 1959

Gordon telephoned the Chairman of the Côte d'Azur team, Cannes, informing him that he would not be joining them, after giving the matter serious consideration during the past few weeks.

Gordon received a very generous offer from English second division side, Huddersfield Town. Manager Bill Shankly, who a few months later went on to take over the reins at Liverpool, had known Gordon throughout the years and said he would be delighted to have him in the team to play alongside fellow Scots, Willie Sinclair, Les Massie, Gordon Low and the young Denis Law. 'Travelling would be an issue' Gordon scribbled onto a piece of notepaper; 'unlikely', he underlined beneath.

Saturday, 25 July 1959

Gordon received a letter from Bob Shankly the day after the one from his brother Bill. This time he considered it more of an option, as Glasgow's Third Lanark would only be a short distance from his Edinburgh base. After a lot of thought, he did turn down this very generous offer. Interestingly, the Glasgow side would meet the team he decided to sign for in the final of the League Cup a mere three months later, and Bob Shankly would try again to sign Gordon, this time for Dundee, in December 1960, before finally securing his signature in the summer of 1961.

Monday, 27 July 1959

Newly appointed Newcastle United manager Charlie Mitten had written to Gordon and offered very good terms that may have suited the veteran – pay when you play, plus a hefty signing-on fee. This must've been the twentieth (and final) attempt to secure Gordon's services by the St James' Park side! Mitten, a former Manchester United left winger, had known Gordon for many years, playing against him for Manchester United, and so easily could've been a team-mate of Gordon's just after the war, when Busby had wanted Smith to join his Old Trafford set-up.

Once again, Gordon had taken this offer very seriously – this bid had come out of the blue and taken Gordon by surprise a little, as he believed the Tyneside giants had given up hope in signing him. There had always been a part of Gordon that had wanted to ply his trade in England and Newcastle United, like Tottenham Hotspur and Manchester United, were his favourites – and the proximity of Newcastle to Edinburgh made this a more realistic opportunity. In deciding to stay in Edinburgh and turning down them and Huddersfield, amongst other English teams, he realised that he would probably never play in England at the highest level, as the travel issue would not go away – but he assured himself he was doing the right thing in joining Hibernian's city rivals Hearts.

He had been impressed by the Hearts' offer and their welcome when he secretly went along to meet manager Tommy Walker and Chairman Nicol Kilgour, realising that he would be joining a very good team. That was what had been the final and main selling point – the standard of the players.

Final League positions:
Hearts vs Hibernian
1953/54 Hearts 2nd vs Hibs 5th
1954/55 Hearts 4th vs Hibs 5th
1955/56 Hearts 3rd vs Hibs 4th
1956/57 Hearts 2nd vs Hibs 9th
1957/58 Hearts 1st vs Hibs 9th
1958/59 Hearts 2nd vs Hibs 10th

If Hibernian had been 'world beaters' between 1946 and 1953 – champions three times, runners-up three times and a 'lowly' third once – the league positions since then showed Hearts had gained the upper hand and dominance in the previous six seasons. Hibs were on the slide, whilst Hearts were on the rise – and within those first nine glorious months at Tynecastle, those statistics were to make even better reading for fans of Heart of Midlothian: another first compared to Hibernian's seventh!

Thursday, 30 July 1959

Gordon informed Willie Waddell at Kilmarnock that he wouldn't be joining his team, as the offer from March was still open. Waddell already knew in his heart that the travel was a problem and the chances were very slim but had held out hope, as the former Hibernian player hadn't reached a decision about joining any other team. Gordon, once and for all, turned Kilmarnock down, also telling the ex-Rangers winger of his decision to join Hearts during that call – knowing that the secret was safe with his great friend until he was to officially notify the west Edinburgh club. He also informed and disappointed both Shankly brothers at Third Lanark and Huddersfield Town.

Friday, 31 July 1959

Gordon enlightened Willie Thornton and Charlie Mitten by phone that he would not be joining Dundee or Newcastle United football clubs, and had made a decision to join another team.

Saturday, 1 August 1959

Around 8am, Gordon telephoned Heart of Midlothian chairman, Nicol Kilgour, at his home to inform him that he would like to join his team and therefore end months of speculation. At 10am on the dot, Gordon arrived at Tynecastle and was met by the jovial manager, Tommy Walker, before going inside and putting pen to paper, signing for Hearts, eighteen and a half years after the Tynecastle club became interested in him for the first time.

At the culmination of the summer break, it appeared that six teams had been front runners and serious contenders for Gordon's signature: Kilmarnock, Dundee, Hearts and the French club, Cannes, with possibly the biggest surprises being Newcastle United and Third Lanark. There were many others, possibly as many as thirty in all; letters had arrived almost daily throughout the summer from managers and chairmen up and down the UK and Europe, from Aberdeen to London, from Nice to Munich, with invitations to join their various teams. But in the end, Gordon stayed in Edinburgh, joining, without a doubt, the strongest of all the teams who had showed an interest in him.

TOP NEWS

St Mirren's triumph, Busby's plane;
Dame Margot's husband and John Wayne;
These all are themes to conjure with,
But none like the news of Gordon Smith.

Our nation, making up the leeway;
The start of the St Lawrence Seaway;
Such stories lack the power and pith
Of the news concerning Gordon Smith.

Young Brian London's fighting chance;
The latest Margaret romance;
Such stories (Be they fact or myth)
Are dimmed by the news of Gordon Smith.

The variously reported scene
Of the return of Terry Dene;
A Russian gunboat up the Nith
Would scarce compete with Gordon Smith.

MacNib © 1959

24

IMMEDIATE REWARDS AT TYNECASTLE

> I had become a fanatical Hibs supporter and so I was very apprehensive about the move to Hearts . . . but I needn't have worried. Everyone at the club was fantastic to me. I was a wee bit worried about what sort of reception I would get, but they took to me quickly. Everybody was great to me . . . including the Hibs fans!
>
> – Gordon Smith

ON SATURDAY, 1 August, Gordon signed for Heart of Midlothian, whilst across the city at Easter Road, 27,000 fans were enthralled by a seven-goal thriller as an Edinburgh Select side defeated Newcastle United 4–3. This was only the second Edinburgh Charities Match since 1941 that Gordon had not played in – but he had now missed two in a row.

Four months after Gordon's Hibernian release and Harry Swan's comments that another operation would do him more harm than good, Hearts' boss, Tommy Walker, said something completely different. He felt that Gordon could give excellent service for some time yet and his ability as a player and as an example would be of immense help to the club. Gordon did give great service in two full seasons at Tynecastle – particularly in the incredibly successful first season.

The first Monday in August, two days later, Gordon was back at Tynecastle to start pre-season training and meet up with his new colleagues. He had arrived too early for training, so sat in his Porsche quite a distance away from the club entrance in a quiet backstreet, scanning a Heart of Midlothian booklet that he had picked up on

Saturday, which detailed everything about the Gorgie side. The Earl of Roseberry KT was the Honorary President, it stated, and it occurred to Gordon that the club appeared to be very well run, from Nicol Kilgour's chairmanship; A Wilson Strachan's vice chairmanship; and directors, Mr R. Tait, Mr W. Eadie and one Mr Alex Irvine. Now that name rang a bell for Gordon. Through the grapevine, Gordon had heard that the former Hearts manager – who, in April 1941, had almost signed him – was a little reticent towards Gordon. He was possibly still a little bitter all these years later but Gordon hoped he would in time succumb as his talent shone through at Tynecastle. Manager and club secretary, Tommy Walker, had of course known Gordon since that fateful night back in 1941 when both had scored hat-tricks, and the two had been quite close friends over the years – having been linesmen together once in a charity game. Walker was ably supported by trainer Johnny Harvey and his assistant Donald McLeod.

Gordon was more than a little fearful as he walked in to the club as a player for the first time at just after 9am. As soon as he opened the dressing room door, he received a standing ovation from the whole of the waiting Heart of Midlothian squad, who had arrived early to welcome their new fellow player. Gordon became quite emotional, as he had not expected such a welcome, and it certainly settled him down. Although one or two players, like Mr Irvine, were a little resentful about the great man's arrival, they were still aware that they were in the presence of a genius. His signing was cause to exult – certainly in the eyes of most at the club.

Gordon's first day at new club Hearts commenced with sprints at Saughton Enclosure with his new colleagues. Near the end of training, Gordon suddenly had his doubts about his decision to join Hibs' greatest rivals. An off-the-cuff remark by one of the players, possibly not meaning to undermine Gordon, had nevertheless hit a raw nerve with him and he felt physically sick for the last period of that first day's workout.

The afternoon was spent back at Smith's old stomping ground. He sped back to Easter Road and visited the Easter Road Ice Cream Parlour situated at the Albion Road junction, where many Hibs players were sitting having some post-training food. Gordon was treated like a hero by all of them, too, whilst voicing his own doubts and the merits of his move across the city. After a discouraging ending, following his great start to the first day's training, he had grave concerns.

Maybe he ought to have gone for 'La Dolce Vita' in the French Riviera or to an English club, away from Edinburgh and Scotland. But, thankfully, he didn't remain worried for too long, and after a few more days training at Tynecastle, he didn't visit his former team-mates as often. He was seen with a glowing air about him, and certainly appeared more relaxed after the stressful changeover of football teams, as he played golf down the coast at Kilspindie, Gullane or North Berwick. The remark made by the player had been forgotten, with an apology made, and that gave Gordon the boost he needed. The former Hibernian star was to miss only five games in all competitions throughout the entire season for his new club, and was to play in thirty-eight games in total, scoring a respectable thirteen goals.

The edition of the *Sunday Post* from 16 August highlighted Gordon in their 'The Honest Truth' feature.

> *Were you surprised and let down when Hibs gave you a free transfer?*
> No. I was more disappointed because Hibs didn't trust my judgement about my ankle.
>
> *At what ground do fans give you the best reception?*
> Firhill.
>
> *Who is the greatest character you have met in football?*
> Sammy Kean, now trainer at Dundee. He has been my friend for eighteen years and is the kind of fellow money can't buy. A good mixer, he always has a happy outlook, which seems to be infectious.
>
> *What was your worst moment in football?*
> I bracket two together. One was when I heard of the death of Hibs manager Willie McCartney. The other was when I was carried off after kicking a ball at Airdrie two seasons ago. Many months of pain and disappointment followed and it was almost a year before I played again.

What are your hobbies?
Golf and collecting records – mostly jazz, although I like good music of any kind.

Do you go to church?
Only on special occasions.

Have you had many anonymous letters in your career and if yes, which of them stands out in your memory?
The letter which advised me for my own good not to play well in a certain game. Such letters don't upset me. I know they're written by fools.

If you weren't a famous footballer what would you like to be?
A great pianist.

If you could invite three people to your home for a weekend, who would they be?
Bobby Locke, Louis Armstrong and Bob Hope. All have been at the top of the tree for a long time, have travelled all over the world and must have wonderful tales to tell.

Who is the most unforgettable person you've met?
Undoubtedly, the late Willie McCartney. What a personality he had. When I was playing as a junior, the only senior club I wanted to play for was Hearts. Although I knew I was due to play a trial at Tynecastle, the McCartney magic was so strong that when he came along and asked me, I signed for Hibs.

What was your proudest moment?
Two answers. The occasions when I captained Scotland against Austria and Hungary. I was also proud of the way other clubs and the public rallied round me after I was given a free transfer from Hibs and was fighting to regain fitness before signing for another club. I was proud that so many clubs were willing to sign me and that hundreds of fans thought enough of me to write wishing me good luck.

What is the greatest compliment you've ever been paid?

The fact that a club like Hearts should have enough faith in me to sign me after being eighteen years with their greatest rivals.

Gordon made his debut for the club that had paid him his greatest compliment against Dundee in a reserve game at Tynecastle, with a 3pm kick-off on a sun-drenched Tuesday afternoon in high summer. A crowd approaching 13,000 had come to witness the cross-over, the debut of arguably Edinburgh's most talented footballer of all time now plying his trade in the maroon of Heart of Midlothian.

'Before the kick-off I was feeling more nervous than I was in my first international,' Gordon told the press later that evening – but he needn't have worried.

It was vintage Smith as he scored a second-half 'bullet' header, after running in at speed, and he helped new signing Bobby Walker score a hat-trick, including two penalties. It was ironic that the name of this new inside forward should be Bobby Walker, the name of one of Hearts' most famous players of all time – the one, if you recall, that the midwife who delivered Gordon referred to when she said that he had 'strong legs like Bobby Walker' way back in May 1924!

Playing in the Dundee reserves were two future team-mates of Gordon's – Andy Penman and, making his debut, the awesomely talented Alan Gilzean, who had just completed his national service.

Dundee boss, Willie Thornton, was noticeably delighted with the huge crowd for a reserve game (Dundee received a cheque for half the gate money) and commented later that most of his players had never played with such a huge crowd watching. It was ironic that Gordon should meet Thornton, boss of one of the 'nearly teams' from just a few weeks previously. Even more incongruous was the fact that the next game Gordon would play was against Kilmarnock and Willie Waddell.

Following the Dundee game, the crowd that had gathered to wish Gordon well was so large that Hearts officials decided it would be better for Smith to climb the terracing and leave unnoticed at the other end of the ground.

Gordon clambered through the fence upon reaching the top where, just like in the movies, he proceeded to turn round and wave to the Hearts directors, players and staff. He waved and they all waved back!

It was as if he were escaping from a prison and going on the run, as following his bag, which he'd thrown over the stadium wall, he then disappeared head-first through a gap and into the night.

Various editions of the next morning's newspapers carried these words from Smith:

> I have had many, many magic moments in my football career and certainly one which I will recall with a lot of pleasure materialised last night – the night I first played on Tynecastle Park as a Heart of Midlothian player.
>
> It was a thrill to don the number 7 maroon jersey, but that was completely overwhelmed by the reception I was given by the crowd which turned up for the game.
>
> I felt that every one of the thousands on the terracing were willing me to be a success in my come-back and their tremendous ovation when I scored my first goal was something I shall never forget.
>
> All through my fight back to fitness I have received more encouragement and good wishes than I believed possible and that magic moment last night – on the evening of 18 August when the fans welcomed me to the Tynecastle fold will never be forgotten.

Later that afternoon – unscathed and glowing after his great escape the previous evening – he was included in a fourteen-man squad that travelled to Dundee to play in that evening's league match for the first team. He wasn't, however, selected to play and sat alongside youngster Andy Fraser, and old adversary and Scotland associate, Jimmy Wardhaugh, witnessing a 3–1 win.

His first team debut on Hearts' fifth game of the season was Saturday, 22 August 1959 and it was in a Scottish League Cup tie at Tynecastle Park. Heart of Midlothian defeated Kilmarnock 2–0 in front of 28,000 fans, including the new Scotland manager Andy Beattie, who was watching from the stand.

Amongst the many telegrams Gordon received prior to playing in his first team debut were ones from his friends Bobby Locke, Willie Waddell and Matt Busby who simply stated: 'Good luck, Gordon.' Two from his former Hibernian team-mates stood out; full backs John Grant and Joe McClelland wished Gordon 'all the very best of luck'. Another telegram that arrived at Tynecastle Park – this one with a Canadian stamp – read: 'Best wishes for this new season, love Nancy.' It maybe wasn't expected but still adorned the mantelpiece!

Jimmy Cowe from the *Evening Dispatch* wrote:

> It did not take long for Gordon Smith to show that he is still as brilliant a ball player as ever. His well known strategies, cute flicks and pin-point passes helped Hearts to a sound win. The two goals which finally killed any hopes which Killie might have had were engineered by Smith.

With the Edinburgh Festival in full swing, the *Edinburgh Evening News* final sports edition printed:

FESTIVAL STAR

Auld Reekie now begins her binge
Around the Festival and Fringe
With famous names to conjure with
Bur none compares with Gordon Smith

Duncan Macrae surpasses all
The rest at the Assembly Hall
Yet even his most dazzling myth
Fades beside that of Gordon Smith

The lamps in Princes Street shine bright
And draw the crowd to walk at night
Yet haven't half the pulling pith
Of swift and twinkling Gordon Smith

The highbrow fest is underway
But middlebrows still have their day
From brig o don to banks of Nith
No star's as bright as Gordon Smith

MacNib © 1959

Four days after playing in his debut, he featured in a Hearts team that won 4–1, once again in the League Cup, this time at Aberdeen's home venue, Pittodrie. Gordon had scored his second goal for the club in his opening three appearances and this initial first-team goal was greeted by cheers in the packed 31,400 crowd, including applause from Aberdeen fans.

Another League Cup match against Stirling Albion was drawn at Tynecastle toward the end of the month, where the following Monday afternoon, Gordon scored again in an 8–1 victory over a British Army side in front of 8,500 fans at Tynecastle.

The next game would be a league match, Heart of Midlothian's first home top division game of the 1959/60 season – and Gordon's first league game for his new club – and would be against Hibernian, of all teams! In a hard-fought 2–2 draw at Tynecastle, Gordon played well but later admitted that he ought to have scored the winner with minutes remaining on the clock – that would surely have produced tumultuous emotions.

Following yet another draw, this time back in the League Cup at Fir Park, Hearts travelled to Glasgow to play Celtic in a top of the division clash, winning 4–3 in a pulsating match, and four days later, defeated Motherwell in the return Cup encounter at Tynecastle, winning 6–2 in front of a massive 44,201 evening attendance on a clammy Wednesday in September.

Hearts, now unbeaten in eleven, entertained Dunfermline Athletic back in league action, winning 3–1, and on the last Saturday of the month, Gordon scored a brace for his new team in an away draw against Stirling Albion. Gordon would later reveal that there was a 'feel-good factor' about his new team, that he knew 'in his bones' they were going to have a successful season by the middle of September. 'Lucky thirteen' games played with eight wins and five draws may have had something to do with the premonition.

The draw in Stirling was followed by another four victories, the run only spoiled by a 0–0 Floodlit Challenge match against English opponents, Norwich City. Three subsequent wins in league action against Ayr United, Airdrie and Arbroath and a mammoth 9–3 League Cup semi-final demolition of Cowdenbeath, with Gordon back playing on his hallowed turf at Easter Road for the first time since his move across the great divide and scoring the eighth goal, ensured the Tynecastle bandwagon rolled on.

As well as being provider, Gordon had scored a goal in each of these games (except the Norwich City friendly match), making his tally read nine scored for his new club in sixteen appearances – not bad for a player who, according to some people, ought to have retired from the game – with the ankle holding out well.

In a poll carried out by the *Sunday Mail* in October, Gordon was chosen as one of Scotland's ten most attractive men, alongside Jimmy Logan, Kenneth McKellar, the Earl of Dalkeith, Jay Scott, James Robertson Justice, Sir Compton McKenzie, Joe Gordon, Hugh Fraser and Lord Lovat, and a few days later, in keeping with the article, he featured on the front page of many newspapers for his 'alleged engagement shenanigans'! They wrote that at thirty-five, Gordon Smith was Scotland's most eligible footballer bachelor – but he was secretly engaged. They reported that the closely guarded secret ended yesterday with an admission of 'guilt' from his fiancée, attractive fair-haired Joan Parry of Meadowfield House, Paisley Drive, an assistant in Gordon's shop in Willowbrae Road, Edinburgh.

'Yes, we have become engaged, but there are no plans for a wedding in the near future,' she was reported as saying from behind the counter of the combined post office, newsagents and grocery. 'There is no secret about our romance. I met Gordon three years ago and we have been going out together ever since.'

Gordon, who had allegedly given her an engagement ring with a sparkling solitaire set in a circle of diamonds, was more reticent. After a game of golf with the Hearts team at Kilspindie in East Lothian, he stowed his clubs in his Porsche and said crisply: 'There's no chance of a comment from me.' The car turned and he sped off towards Edinburgh. The couple, it was further reported, had known each other for years and had been seen a lot together.

The twentieth game for the club in the 1959/60 season was at Hampden Park, for the final of the Scottish League Cup against Third Lanark. The Tynecastle club remained undefeated, with Gordon having scored in his last five successive league and cup games, as they headed into 'medal territory' on Saturday, 24 October.

Heart of Midlothian's great season reached new heights after they won the cup, defeating the Cathkin Park side 2–1, with both goals for the Edinburgh team coming in a two-minute period in the second half. Johnny Hamilton and Alex Young were the scorers, following an early

Third Lanark goal in the first two minutes of the game scored by Matt Gray when an error by goalkeeper Gordon Marshall had worried the maroons.

In a game dominated by Hearts, winning twenty corners to Third Lanark's five, they thoroughly deserved the spoils of victory. In the most sporting of finals, during which the referee did not have to speak to even one player, the defeated Third Lanark men, as a team, stood and clapped Hearts off the field as they received the cup. Harry Andrew scribed in the *Scottish Sunday Express*: 'Gordon Smith, master craftsman – as great a player as ever he was in his best Hibs days, used the ball superbly throughout the final.' Gordon's old Scotland companion George Young had just taken over as Third Lanark manager from Bob Shankly and was sportingly one of the first to congratulate Gordon on his success following the full-time whistle.

Contrary to most reports, this wasn't Gordon's first major cup medal; he did win the League Cup back in 1944 with Hibernian – when it was then called the Scottish Southern League Cup – 'but that was won on corners,' retorted a delirious Smith. This was to be Gordon's second and final League Cup winner's medal, in a career in which the big one was to elude him: the Scottish Cup.

Gordon, yet to play in a losing match for his new club, had been one of Hearts' stars since signing from Hibs in August and his display brought a special cheer from the crowd as he stepped up to receive his medal. The cheers were continued back in Edinburgh as thousands braved an icy wind to give Hearts a great welcome home. As the floodlit bus, glistening with 100-watt bulbs, looking like 'a showground on wheels', swept into Charlotte Square for a celebration dinner, maroon scarves were thrown into the air and above the noise of the fireworks came the song everyone was singing – 'A Gordon for Me'.

A beaming Gordon Smith pronounced: 'My father gave me some lucky charms to take to the game this morning. A piece of coal, a bent and battered penny, and a couple of foreign coins – it looks like they worked a treat!' The club themselves were also a tad superstitious, with reports saying that they had apparently hurried to Hampden early to claim the 'lucky' dressing room at Hampden Park.

With Smith winning a medal, he rounded off the hat-trick of players who had made the Hibs–Hearts move and went on to win a cup within months of arriving at Tynecastle. Jim Souness was first, winning a League Cup medal after transferring in 1953, and then there was Ian Crawford, who also won medals after joining Hearts in 1954 – now Gordon made it three in a row!

A week following the cup win, on a misty Halloween in Glasgow, Gordon and his team-mates were back in Glasgow – this time to play Rangers at Ibrox Park. In front of a 71,000 crowd, Hearts bewitched the home side, winning 2–0, and made it twenty-two games without a defeat – there appeared to be no stopping them.

Two more home games were played next and two more victories were recorded. This time Partick Thistle and Kilmarnock were the unlucky teams, who were to lose eight goals between them. This was followed by a tricky away game in Aberdeen but the Edinburgh men convincingly won 3–1 without an injured Gordon. His right ankle was fine, but it was a niggling muscle spasm in his lower back that kept him out of his first game in a run of twenty matches.

Gordon's return in the 2–2 draw a week later against Clyde at Shawfield Park made it:

Played 26
Won 19
Drawn 7
Lost 0
Goals scored 91
Goals conceded 38
Goals scored by Gordon 9

On 5 December, with a party planned for later that evening at Gordon's public house to celebrate a combination of his fourth anniversary of opening The Right Wing and his 'alleged' engagement, Hearts finally lost a football match.

A victory-expectant home crowd packed into Tynecastle Park were to see a sight they hadn't witnessed in nearly a year – a home defeat for their team. Hearts lost 0–2 to St Mirren, and worse was to follow the week later, when they conceded three goals without reply to a Motherwell side at Fir Park.

Had the bubble burst? Gordon was in no doubt it hadn't, that it was just 'a little glitch' that needed tweaking, as he put it.

How right he was. The club were only to lose two more games out of the remaining twenty games they played – both games to a club that Gordon nearly signed for, Willie Waddell's Kilmarnock. With one of these defeats occurring in a Scottish Cup replay, Hearts would win the League Championship by four points over their 'bogey team' from Ayrshire. Important victories over Hibs, Dundee, Celtic, Aberdeen and Clyde, as well as a win against Partick Thistle at Firhill in mid-March, were also to prove crucial.

But for now, the new year of 1960 was rung in by Real Madrid legend, and Gordon Smith's favourite, Alfredo Di Stéfano winning 1959's Ballon d'Or, just prior to Gordon making his twenty-fourth appearance for Hearts at the New Year's Day derby. This triumph for Hearts would turn out to be one of the highlights from the second half of the championship-winning season. Gordon returned to Easter Road for the second time since being released by Hibernian the previous spring, scoring in an astonishingly one-sided 5–1 Hearts' victory that was to help the team stay three points clear of Rangers at the top of the league.

This win was pivotal, as, with fellow Famous Five legend Bobby Johnstone's return to Hibernian from Manchester City, Smith's old club were pouring the goals in, scoring eleven at Broomfield against Airdrie and ten at Firhill against Partick Thistle.

A cartoon appeared in a national newspaper with the words:

> 'Here comes Bobby . . . good old Bobby, welcome home . . .'
>
> 'We get Sammy Kean back as trainer to release Turnbull, bring Ormond up from the reserves . . . coax Reilly out of retirement . . . apologise to Smith and buy him back from Hearts, for say, thirty thousand . . .'
>
> 'There's only one snag!'
>
> 'What's that?'
>
> 'You're only allowed to turn the clock back at the end of summer-time!'

Whilst it would be fair to say that, on the field, Hearts' winter was a success, off the field, it could be called 'The Winter of Romance'. Firstly, Gordon started the ball rolling with his talk-of-the-town engagement; this was then followed in January with Hearts' left winger Johnny Hamilton's marriage in Edinburgh to Miss Betty Farquar. Hamilton's best man was Tynecastle right back, Bobby Kirk, with guests also including fellow team-mate, Gordon Smith, who was accompanied by fiancée Joan Parry. A few weeks later, in early March at 3pm precisely, Jimmy Murray married his fiancée Jean at Cairns Memorial Church in Gorgie Road, with a reception later held at the city's Grosvenor Hotel. The same day, Gordon received a letter from journalist Hugh Taylor with a 'draft' of an idea for *Biography on Gordon Smith*. This was the second offer of a book to be written about the player's life but Smith put the idea on hold.

The thirty-five-year-old Gordon almost made a sensational return to the Scotland team, not playing at right wing, but back in his old schoolboy position of centre forward! Selector Haig Gordon and Scotland manager Andy Beattie had been impressed by Gordon in the 24 February cup match, where Gordon had excelled whilst playing at number 9 in the one and only time he was to play for Hearts in that position throughout the season, but in the end, the selectors went for youth and Ian St John was chosen instead. In the weeks prior to the international, many sports journalists and current players had called for Smith's return to the international arena – but the most debonair and accomplished player in the country didn't quite fit the bill.

Kilmarnock centre half, Willie Toner, had said that Gordon was easily the best centre forward he had faced all season and that he was a genius. 'You can't get near him. He's always thinking of that move ahead,' he added. Bobby Evans at Celtic echoed the opinion, saying that Smith was a wonderful player and he knew he could be just as good at centre forward as on the right wing. The Scotland centre half continued: 'Some critics may say he's too old, but that's just silly. It's skill and form that count, not age, and Gordon is still terrific.'

The international against England duly took place on Saturday, 9 April, with Gordon there – but only as a spectator alongside his Hearts team-mates who all went to see colleagues John Cumming and Alex Young play at Hampden Park. The 1–1 draw in front of over 113,000 fans was a fair result with Scotland's Graham Leggat and England's Bobby Charlton the scorers. The Scotland side, apart from Gordon's two Tynecastle team-mates, included Frank Haffey in goal, old adversary Dave Mackay, Rangers' Eric Caldow, great admirer Bobby Evans and sensational number 10, Denis Law. The England team, led by Charlton, had Hibs' Joe Baker at centre forward.

Exactly one week later at Love Street, Paisley, on Saturday, 16 April 1960, Heart of Midlothian became champions of Scotland. Needing just a point to secure the title, an amazing 4–4 draw was fought out in an end-to-end battle against St Mirren with the Hearts' goals coming from a Young double, Crawford and Willie Bauld's late equaliser from a corner taken by Gordon Smith.

Hearts added the League Championship to the League Cup in an incredible first season for Gordon. They lost only three games – one at Tynecastle and two away. Second-placed Kilmarnock, who Gordon almost signed for, were the main threat to Hearts during the season, and had also knocked them out of the Scottish Cup in a replay during an incredible twenty-one match unbeaten run. Ironically, Gordon's first team debut for Hearts was in the League Cup game against Willie Waddell's men in the only time they managed to beat the Ayrshire team all season.

Listed below are the top four positions. Hibernian, in the first season in nineteen without Gordon on their books, finished seventh.

	Played	Points
HEARTS	34	54
Kilmarnock	34	50
Rangers	34	42
Dundee	34	42

So, three of Gordon's final group of teams that he considered signing for finished first, second and fourth, but it certainly looked like he chose the correct one. Would his signing have made the difference to Kilmarnock's title bid had he chosen to join his first interested club, Willie Waddell's men?

With the League Championship in the bag, Hearts entertained Aston Villa, with Gordon providing the crosses for Jimmy Murray and Willie Bauld's pair of headers in an entertaining 2–2 draw in front of over 21,000 joyous fans on the misty spring bank holiday evening of 25 April.

In a carnival atmosphere, the old stone smoke-blackened walls reverberated with wave after wave of cheering. Women threw maroon rosettes to the team as if they were Spanish toreadors. At McLeod

Street, where part of the Monday evening throng had surged into Tynecastle, there were crowds of people singing outside the public houses, where the fans had drunk their last hurried pint on their way to the match and returned to have their first to celebrate a glorious season afterwards. This time it was undoubtedly the crowning victory roar and the foaming pint tumblers of Gorgie were raised in salute to a most wonderful season.

In the last league game on 30 April, Gordon scored his thirteenth goal of the campaign as Hearts drew 2–2 in a relatively meaningless but nonetheless exhilarating Kirkcaldy fixture for the players.

In all, Gordon had played in thirty-nine games, including League, Scottish Cup and League Cup games and three friendly matches. Not bad for a player who was, as Harry Swan stated, 'finished from the game' twelve months before. As Labour Prime Minister Harold Wilson would be quoted as saying, 'A week's a long time in politics.' It could also be said: 'A year's a long time in football, especially where Gordon Smith is concerned.'

The emancipation of Gordon Smith by Hibernian was an immeasurable windfall for city rivals Heart of Midlothian and didn't Gordon, Harry Swan and all the Edinburgh football fans know it. When asked by a media scrum, following his overwhelming first season at Tynecastle, how he compared the Heart of Midlothian winning team to that of Hibernian's previous championship teams, a buoyant Gordon, possibly even a tad gung-ho, was quoted as saying:

> It's maybe interesting to note that both the league winning teams I've been associated with placed the accent on attacking play.
>
> At Easter Road we often won our matches by such scores as 4–3, with the emphasis very much on the fabulous Famous Five scoring machine.
>
> I'm not saying this is the only formula for league success. Rangers, after all, have for long played a defensive game, and the recent great run by Kilmarnock has been built on sound defence.
>
> But I rate Hearts the better all-round team. This championship win has been more of a combined victory by the *whole* team than was the case at Easter Road.

25

EXTENSIVE NORTH AMERICAN TOUR

The Squad
Gordon Marshall
Bobby Kirk
George Thomson
Jimmy Murray
Jimmy Milne
Andy Bowman
Gordon Smith
Bobby Blackwood
Willie Bauld
Ian Crawford
Johnny Hamilton
Danny Ferguson
Allan Finlay
Andy Kelly
John Lough
Jim McFadzean
George Robertson

Members of the party
Nicol Kilgour (Chairman)
Wilson Strachan (Vice Chairman)
Tommy Walker (Manager/Secretary)
John Harvey (Trainer)
Donald Macleod (Assistant Trainer)

The Flights

1 Prestwick to Toronto
2 Toronto to Ottawa
3 Ottawa to Montreal
4 Montreal to New York City
5 New York City to Toronto
6 Toronto to Calgary
7 Calgary to Vancouver
8 Vancouver to Seattle
9 Seattle to San Francisco
10 San Francisco to Los Angeles
11 Los Angeles to San Francisco
12 San Francisco to Seattle
13 Seattle to Vancouver
14 Vancouver to Victoria
15 Victoria to Vancouver
16 Vancouver to Edmonton
17 Edmonton to Toronto
18 Toronto to Montreal
19 Montreal to Prestwick

The Hotels

1 Royal York Hotel, Toronto, Saturday, 14 May
2 The Lord Elgin Hotel, Ottawa, Sunday, 15 May
3 The Laurentien, Montreal, Tuesday, 17 May
4 Hotel Governor Clinton, New York City, Friday, 20 May
5 Hotel Royal, Calgary, Monday, 23 May
6 Hotel Devonshire, Vancouver, Friday, 27 May
7 Hollywood Roosevelt Hotel, Los Angeles, Monday, 30 May
8 Hotel Devonshire, Vancouver, Friday, 3 June
9 Empress Hotel, Victoria, Sunday, 5 June
10 King Edward Hotel, Edmonton, Tuesday, 7 June
11 Royal York Hotel, Toronto, Wednesday, 8 June

The Tour Games

P	W	D	L	F	A
10	5	2	3	25	14

14 May: Manchester United (Toronto) Canada	2–2	17,849
16 May: Montreal Cantalia (Ottawa) Canada	3–0	3,000
18 May: Montreal Concordia (Montreal) Canada	2–0	5,000
22 May: Manchester United (New York) U.S.A.	0–3	10,411
28 May: Manchester United (Vancouver) Canada	2–3	18,644
1 June: Manchester United (Los Angeles) U.S.A.	4–0	10,500
4 June: B.C. All Stars (Brit.Columbia) Canada	2–2	17,500
6 June: Victoria All Stars (Victoria) Canada	3–0	2,500
8 June: Alberta All Stars (Edmonton) Canada	6–2	7,000
9 June: Burnley (Toronto) Canada	1–2	15,020

THE CHAMPAGNE had hardly time to take effect when Heart of Midlothian, the best football team in Scotland, headed off on a summer jaunt. A five-week-long summer jaunt no less, to Canada and the USA, taking with them seventeen players but omitting the injured Billy Higgins along with Alex Young and John Cumming, who had been selected for the forthcoming Scotland international tour of Turkey, Hungary and Austria. The omitted players also missed the singing; each player had been given a Heart of Midlothian songbook for, as it stated, 'community singing when on tour'.

The players assembled at Tynecastle Park on Tuesday, 10 May, at 3pm before travelling by bus to Prestwick Airport. Before anyone could even begin to feel a little forlorn in leaving loved-ones and home behind, the songbooks were brought out on the instruction of the chairman and everyone was singing. The tartan-covered book comprised about fifty songs, mainly Scottish ones, possibly on the premise that eleven Scotsmen singing during a game may frighten off their opponents!

As well as the Scottish favourites back catalogue, there was a smattering of current hits with the likes of Adam Faith's 'What Do You Want', Jerry Keller's 'Here Comes Summer', 'Dream Lover' by Bobby Darin, 'Peggie Sue' by Buddy Holly and the Crickets, but the firm favourite en route to the airport was Cliff Richard's 'Living Doll', with even Gordon coaxed into crooning a little!

Their 9.25pm departure arrived at 5.40am in Toronto the following morning and they headed straight to their first of nine hotels on the trip where Gordon was to room with George Thomson for the duration. The jet-lagged players were joined at a formal dinner later that evening by George Anderson, the secretary of the SFA, where a sad Gordon was already homesick just hours after leaving Scotland and more importantly his fiancée, Joan.

On Friday, 13 May, Gordon met up with Matt Busby, whom he had seen only once since the Munich air disaster of two years previously; unbelievably, the pair went shopping downtown, checking out the malls for bargains. Jean, Matt's wife, had 'ordered' him to look for new curtains. The following day, Matt's Manchester United drew 2–2 against the Scottish champions, in the first of four games the two teams would play against each other in just over a fortnight at various venues throughout Canada and the US. Next stop was Ottawa, the Canadian capital, and a visit to the Houses of Parliament didn't quite bore the players to death but came within a whisker of doing so! Luckily the day was saved with a 'French lunch' followed by a game of golf for those who wished to play.

Subsequent to the next tour match, a 3–0 win over Montreal Cantalia, Gordon wrote back to fiancée Joan that he was disappointed with the poor turnout. Only 3,000 fans had turned up for this game.

The players were glued to the hotel lobby television on the afternoon of 18 May. Due to the five-hour time difference, they were able to watch the European Cup Final, this year staged back home in Scotland at Glasgow's Hampden Park, before their evening tour game against another Montreal side, Concordia.

The Hearts squad were captivated by the likes of Ferenc Puskás, Alfredo Di Stéfano, Francisco Gento, Argentinean José Santamaría and Captain José María Zárraga as Real Madrid and Eintracht Frankfurt entertained majestically in what was arguably the greatest ever club football match played. The atmosphere in the hotel lobby was electric with the volume button turned up to its peak on a state of the art television; as the commentary blasted out, it appeared to get louder and louder as the game continued and most other observing guests were enthralled too – it was as if they were part of the 135,000 Hampden Park crowd.

The final was officiated by Scottish referee Jack Mowat, who was obviously well known to all the players and during the course of the game, he had his fair share of boos from some of the Hearts' stronger tacklers! The game ended with ten goals being scored; 7–3 in favour of Real Madrid, with Gordon's favourites Di Stéfano scoring a hat-trick and Hungarian captain Puskás going one better with four. Eintracht Frankfurt's goals were scored by Erwin Stein with a pair and Richard Kress, who had opened the scoring with the first of the match's ten in the eighteenth minute. Gordon took great delight in watching Real's emphatic win, with the majority of the team old adversaries from his Hibernian and Scotland days.

Another win, this time 2–0, followed for the Hearts' touring team in their game that evening in front of a slightly better crowd, and the players then enjoyed a day off in Montreal with Concordia's Scots ex-pat players Tommy Barrett, who had played in the previous night's match, and squad player George Savage showing them the sights of the French Canadian city.

The next day, the Scottish champions flew to New York City, staying midtown and visiting the Radio City Theatre in the evening. The Manchester United touring party had arrived back from their travels and after checking in to their rooms in the same hotel, the two teams went on a night out to the Latin Quarter nightclub as guests of the American Soccer League. Gordon left early with a couple of United players and headed off in a yellow taxi in search of the jazz clubs in downtown Brooklyn. Gordon was in his element!

Hearts lost by three goals to nil in the next afternoon's Triborough Stadium encounter with the English side, with some players from both teams still a little 'fragile' from their 'exertions on the dance floor' the night before. It was reported that 'loud and extensive' cheering could be heard when it was realised it would be nearly a week until the next match for both teams! Again, Hearts would play against Manchester United, but this time in Vancouver on the Pacific coast.

The Hearts players touched down in Toronto around lunchtime the following day, then proceeded, after refuelling, to Calgary – 'Indian territory' as Gordon called it, where he bought a pair of hand-made moccasins for Joan. Everyone was told to relax for three days in the area, which included playing rounds of golf and visiting the Banff Health Resort in the Rockies.

On Thursday, 26 May, Gordon's thirty-sixth birthday, the team arrived in Vancouver to prepare for the next Man United encounter. Matt and Gordon once again went out – this time for dinner as both players celebrated the same birthday. Gordon presented Matt, the older man by fifteen years, with a bright yellow tie for his birthday.

Gordon, in turn, received nothing back from the Old Trafford boss – possibly as punishment for turning down his lucrative offer all those years ago!

The next day, the players went to the beach and cinema and on 28 May, in the third of four encounters with Matt Busby's side, Hearts narrowly lost 2–3 at the Empire Stadium in Vancouver in front of a near 20,000 crowd – the biggest of the tour so far and in Gordon's opinion, 'easily the best pitch'.

Prior to departing to catch yet another plane, on the afternoon of 29 May, the Hearts players and staff were joined by some of the Manchester United squad to watch another televised match from Europe. This time they were looking forward to watching two of their own, as Scotland played in Vienna, bringing back happy memories for Gordon from the 1955 match. Although the team lost 1–4 on this occasion, every time Hearts players Young and Cumming touched the ball, there was an almighty roar from the group in the dining room of Vancouver's Hotel Devonshire. Alex Young had replaced Manchester City's Denis Law after only eleven minutes and this brought howls of delight from both sets of players watching from thousands of miles away. Yet, as Matt Busby watched the encounter quietly with Gordon in the corner of the room, he was maybe already hatching a plan to sign the City striker, who in years to come would become one of the greatest players in the history of Manchester United.

As soon as this game finished, both clubs travelled together, chartering a plane to take them to Los Angeles after refuelling in Seattle and San Francisco. At one refuelling, out came the dreaded tartan song-books once more, and the Hearts players were even benevolent enough to share their books with their Manchester United foes, as both sets of players and staff belted out Shirley Bassey's 'Kiss Me, Honey, Honey'! The two teams were again staying in the same hotel, in the city's Hollywood district.

The players from both clubs socialised together during their three days off, going to Long Beach, Santa Monica and visiting the set of MGM Pictures near their Hollywood HQ. They went to a baseball game, cheering for the LA Dodgers, and Gordon found there was great camaraderie amongst the players of both Hearts and Manchester United when off the field. Smith, as well as knowing United's Matt Busby, had played against Bobby Charlton, Bill Foulkes and Dennis

Viollet in the past. Young Johnny Giles, who would later be a star for Leeds United and the Republic of Ireland, impressed Gordon particularly and later it would be reported by Busby that transferring him to the famous Yorkshire team was 'the worst mistake of my managerial career'.

The fourth and final Heart of Midlothian encounter against the grandiose Manchester United ended in an incredible 4–0 rout for the Edinburgh side; goals from Bauld with two, Crawford and a Thomson penalty making it an equal 8–8 between the clubs in the quartet of matches. Both sets of players let their hair down during a night out in nearby Marina del Rey after being presented personalised statuettes by the Los Angeles Scots AC.

Also while in LA, Gordon had the pleasure of meeting the English singer, Frankie Vaughan, and actor, Herbert Marshall. Vaughan (a 'Gordon Smith fan' ever since seeing the winger at Easter Road when he was appearing on stage in Edinburgh in the mid-fifties) was in Hollywood making a movie with Marilyn Monroe, *Let's Make Love.* Twenty years down the line, the 1980s dance-pop stars Frankie Goes To Hollywood named themselves after the Liverpool superstar's working sojourn to California, when they discovered an old copy of the *New Yorker* magazine from June 1960 with a headline stating just exactly where Frankie had gone! Marshall, on the other hand, was an icon from a much earlier era and had starred alongside the likes of Basil Rathbone, Greta Garbo and Marlene Dietrich. Old black and white movie buff, Gordon, was captivated and spellbound by his scandalous tales and gregarious nature.

The next day, the Edinburgh team's tour party had returned to Vancouver and the monotonous travelling was beginning to take its toll on the players – particularly a fatigued Gordon, who just wanted to go home to his fiancée. The golfers in the group enjoyed another round, in the now quite familiar surroundings of the Canadian city, before an additional tour game against British Columbia All Stars back at the Empire Stadium. Again, this game attracted around 18,000 fans and Gordon admitted being happiest in Vancouver, as according to him, the fans appeared quite knowledgeable and seemed to enjoy their football there with the playing surface 'almost perfect'.

The Empress Hotel in Victoria was the setting for a further squad get-together in front of the television to watch their national side in action. This time it was the 5 June encounter from Budapest against the might of Hungary. Once again, Gordon's memories of his exploits were shared with his team-mates, who were charmed by his accounts of a peerless night captaining his country.

Tonight, this Scotland side were to fare even better than his team of five years previously, as they held the Hungarians 3–3 with the loudest cheer of the day reserved for a goal by Heart of Midlothian's Alexander Young.

A 3–0 Hearts' victory against Victoria All Stars the following night was quickly followed by yet another flight, this time to Edmonton, Alberta, to prepare for the penultimate game against another local side, All Stars Select.

The afternoon of Wednesday, 8 June, found the players congregated in, thankfully, an enormous cinema room of the King Edward Hotel. It was filled with the whole touring party eager for Alex Young to score for the Scotland international side again. The venue for this third and final international was Ankara in Turkey, with the Scots losing 2–4, but the cheers did ring out once more as Young at least scored another goal in the defeat.

Later that day, against the All Stars on a cold evening, Gordon scored his first and only goal of the tour in a 6–2 victory. The following evening, the touring party arrived back at the hotel where they had started the tour – the Royal York in downtown Toronto. Gordon's brother, Stanley, was waiting for the arrival of the Scottish football club. Stanley, who had emigrated to Canada some years previously, joined the players for a meal before he and Gordon took a golf lesson in his room. Following the lesson, the pair headed out in search of the many jazz clubs in Toronto, where they incredibly met a bass player from a trio that had been the resident band at the Marine Hotel in North Berwick.

Before noon the following day, Gordon visited his brother's home in Toronto to say farewell, meeting his wife Marjory and another old friend who turned up for lunch – Nancy Croall, his old girlfriend, who lived in the Canadian city as well. Gordon jokingly wrote to Joan that Nancy didn't fancy him anymore – and that he was quite hurt! He then went on to explain that Nancy was genuinely happy for the couple on hearing the news about their forthcoming marriage.

The evening game at Toronto's Varsity Stadium, with a 15,000 crowd, was the last of the long tour and played against current English champions, Burnley – so it was billed in some newspapers as 'The Battle of Britain'. Unfortunately, Willie Bauld's goal for the Scottish team was not enough to crown Hearts as the Kings of Britain, as they conceded two. The day after that final match, as the Edinburgh team headed for the airport, news reached the party that their manager, Tommy Walker, was to be made an OBE later in the year for his services to football. This brought great cheering and yet another spontaneous burst of singing on the bus with players clambering for their songbooks for a rousing edition of 'Scots Wha Hae', which slightly alleviated their long journey home across the North Atlantic.

As the exhausted and hoarse Heart of Midlothian contingent arrived back in Prestwick – with Smith, Bowman and Thomson hiring a car to arrive back earlier than the scheduled return of around 4pm on Monday, 13 June – all twenty-two members of the touring party were delighted to be back home following an extremely enjoyable but quite gruelling tour.

26

SECRET MARRIAGE AND LAST SEASON WITH HEARTS

GORDON, ALTHOUGH on the face of things content and affable on the North American tour, wasn't happy at all. His cheerfulness was a facade. Singing or no singing, he was desperate to return home. The tour had lasted over a month and Gordon was in love. His fiancée, Joan, was waiting for him back in Scotland and he was due to be secretly married to her in a few days' time. He had informed Matt Busby of his intentions and Matt was deliriously happy for him and Joan, but he had decided not to tell his fellow Hearts players for fear the news would leak out to 'the press'.

The lovebirds had sent each other over a dozen letters and in one correspondence, Joan insisted that every time she visited their impending new home, she felt closer to Gordon; and in another, she insisted Gordon watch himself. 'Tell George [Thomson], Jim [Murray] and Jim [Milne] not too many parties for you – tell Andy [Bowman], I'm putting him in charge!' Gordon wrote back saying he was too busy for parties, and that Andy said to tell Joan he'd look after Gordon and that she was 'a good judge'!

Although he had enjoyed the North American cuisine – especially the steaks and fruit salads – and got a lot of pleasure from meeting some of his film and music idols, he was homesick from day one, describing California as 'beautiful, but very artificial and nothing like Cannes'. He 'longed to be home' he would continue in a letter to his 'soon-to-be betrothed'.

With Gordon on tour in North America, Joan Parry had been busying herself, on the instruction of her husband-to-be, to 'get things ready' for the big day and the move. She had been sworn to secrecy by her very private yet famous partner, and told not to even think about speaking to the press as they may 'worm something out of you' regarding the impending marriage.

Gordon had acquired, in his words, an 'enchanted cottage' to escape from the attention he attracted. The cottage was situated just over twenty miles from Edinburgh, down the coast, but city-loving Miss Parry had serious reservations on the move. Her life was in the city, her friends lived in the city and she was an extrovert, as opposed to the introverted Gordon. She wanted to be seen with him here, there and everywhere, whilst he just wanted the quiet life. She had promised him she would give it a go and see how it went and he had agreed if they weren't happy after a year, they would move back to the city.

Three days after Gordon's return from the lengthy North American tour, on Thursday, 16 June 1960, he married his fiancée, Joan Ann Parry, at Morningside Registrar's office and the only people to see the ceremony were the best man, Gordon's brother Robert, and Joan's sister Naomi. As soon as the short ritual was over, the newlyweds were driven off by the new Mrs Smith's brother-in-law, Frank O'Rourke, to Turnhouse Airport, where an awaiting flight took them to Nice. The happy couple later returned bronzed and radiant from their honeymoon in the south of France, although Gordon had to help a 'shaky' Joan from the plane after what would be her last ever flight, having been uncomfortable during almost all of the flights she'd ever undertaken.

They moved into their new cottage near North Berwick and, more importantly, near to the beach. The proximity to the beach was the main factor for Gordon, who still believed very much in the 'healing powers' of the salt water. The renovated cottage was set in a couple of acres of old farmland adjacent to the West Links golf course, which also suited the low-handicap golfer. Gordon had his heart set on the property after viewing it over the years when spending time at the nearby Westerdunes Hotel with Hibernian Football Club. The club would be regular visitors to the area and would alternate between the Westerdunes and the more cosmopolitan Marine Hotel. Westerdunes was only a minute or so up the road from the secluded cottage and Gordon would be a frequent diner that first summer of marriage. The couple thoroughly enjoyed these visits with the young football-adoring Italian chefs Giuseppe Amato and Cosmo Tambouro, the latter becoming a firm family friend.

* * *

The 1960/61 season began on 6 August, with Gordon playing in what would be his sixteenth and final Edinburgh Select Charities match. Out of a possible eighteen, Gordon had missed only two, the previous two in fact. This year, the Select were visited by a Chelsea side containing Peter Bonetti, Jimmy Greaves, Terry Venables and Gordon's friend, Bobby Evans.

Gordon dazzled on the wing as did his old Famous Five partner, Willie Ormond, on the opposite flank, although Hearts' reserve goalkeeper, Jim Cruickshank, was certainly kept busy between the sticks. Gordon was to finish his charity match run in great style, providing crosses for two of the home side's goals in a 5–4 victory over the south-west London side at a packed and sun-drenched Tynecastle Park. Goals by former Hibs colleagues Ormond, centre forward Joe Baker and John Baxter, along with two penalties from team-mate George Thomson, sealed the closely fought victory.

The Olympic Games in Rome distracted Gordon a little; he was in awe of a new sporting hero for him and for millions throughout the world. Cassius Clay (who would later change his name to Muhammad Ali) won the light heavyweight gold medal with exquisite style. Gordon, who had always quite enjoyed boxing, was hooked and the great boxer would captivate the footballer for years to come.

Gordon's second and what would turn out to be his last season for Heart of Midlothian wasn't in any way, shape or form as rewarding or successful as the previous fairytale season had been. League Cup holders Hearts were knocked out of that competition in early September after a play-off against a Clyde side that would be relegated from the division at the end of the season, even before they had kicked a ball in their European adventure.

With the former League Champions Hearts due to entertain the mighty Portuguese champions, Benfica, in a European Cup adventure for the second time in three years, everyone at Tynecastle was hoping for a better outcome than the 3–6 aggregate reversal suffered against the Belgians, Standard Liege, with first round elimination in the 1958/59 season.

Hearts stayed at Peebles Hydro Hotel for a few days prior to this vital match whilst using the facilities of local team Peebles Rovers and training at their Whitesone Park ground. Alas, this season was to be a repeat of their previous European experience, with Hearts once again being knocked out in the opening round, going down 1–5 on aggregate to a great Benfica side.

Gordon was played at no. 11, on the left wing, for the first leg at Tynecastle, with Alex Young on the right wing, in a bid to possibly confuse the Lisbon side. Unfortunately, it didn't confuse them enough and the Edinburgh side suffered a 1–2 defeat in front of a 45,000 partisan Scottish crowd. Gordon's new wife, Joan, rubbed salt into the wound in an interview given to Tom Nicholson of the *Daily Record* following the match. She was quoted as saying: 'Hearts didn't go for the ball like Benfica. I thought Benfica were a wonderfully fit team.' Say it like it is, dear!

For the return match in Lisbon, Willie Bauld had been replaced by Ian Crawford, Alex Young moved from the right wing to centre forward and Gordon was back in his customary position, but the team were sadly to lose by three goals to nil in the Portuguese heat, and that was the end of Gordon's further adventures in Europe – for now anyway.

Hearts then lost five of their next six matches and the season was looking pretty grim. Smith had been injured in a 1–3 defeat to Rangers – a game in which he scored what would turn out to be his last goal for the club; he himself was despondent.

The news, a few weeks later, that the 1960 Ballon d'Or winner was to be Barça great, Luis Suarez, was overshadowed by a letter Gordon received in that morning's post. The postmark was from the 'City of Discovery'. It was a letter from Bob Shankly, who had tried to sign him for Third Lanark in the summer of 1959 and was now manager at Dundee. He asked Gordon if he would be willing to leave Hearts and join Dundee, mid-season at the turn of the year, and said that they would see to the 'paperwork'. It was as if the 'January transfer window' that exists today had existed fifty years ago.

In the letter, Shankly also stated that Gordon's great old friend, Sammy Kean, would very much like to work with Gordon again and both men had been aware that Gordon's drive and desire from the previous season had somewhat petered out in recent months. Gordon replied and thanked Shankly very much for his offer but he said that he would see the season out with Hearts and he would make a decision once it was over. This was the third time during his career that Dundee had tried yet failed to land their target, Gordon Smith.

As Smith stayed, for the time being, Alex Young and George Thomson departed to Everton, and the great championship-winning side was officially broken up. The loss preceded more woe for the maroon side. Although doing slightly better in the Scottish Cup, only losing in the quarter-finals to St Mirren after crushing Tarff Rovers 9–0, and Kilmarnock and Partick Thistle both by 2–1, they finished the league campaign way down on the previous year in eighth place, with even rivals Hibernian finishing one place ahead of them – higher in the league table for the first time in eight seasons.

Gordon played only thirteen league matches and a total of twenty-two in all competitions from a maximum forty-seven, scoring a meagre two goals in the course of a season dogged by injury. Hamstrings, neck injuries and his perennial affliction, the ankle, would plague him once more.

He would play his final Hearts game, his seventy-sixth for the club, back at his old favourite position of centre forward, the fifth time he had done so with the club – against Third Lanark at Tynecastle on 8 April. John Cumming scored a penalty to give the home side a 1–0 victory as 15,000 fans witnessed the end for Smith. Struggling with a calf injury and hobbling with his right leg, he missed the final three matches of the season. It is interesting to note that less than half of the great championship-winning side of 1959/60 played for Hearts in Gordon's final game for the club.

His right ankle was ravaged and he was in severe pain, and this time it was thought by most managers and players alike that he was definitely on his way out of top-flight football when released by Hearts. On Thursday, 4 May 1961, he had received the letter containing his P45 and a note from manager and secretary, Tommy Walker, saying that Hearts thanked Gordon for his service to the club and politely wishing him every success should he want to find a new club next season. Little did they or anyone else know that over the course of the next two seasons, that wish would come true and Gordon was to be as phenomenal a player as he had ever been, and in a career that had already spanned twenty years, debatably and quite sensationally, his best two were yet to come – though perhaps one manager may have had an idea?

27

FOURTH TIME LUCKY

I WAS very proud of winning the league championship – it was quite an achievement to be honest. Dundee had a marvellous team when I was there and I really enjoyed playing up front with Alan Gilzean and Alan Cousin. I really felt that Dundee team was on a par with Hibs at their best.

– Gordon Smith

<u>Dundee Squad</u>
Pat Liney
Alex Hamilton
Bobby Cox
Bobby Seith
Ian Ure
Bobby Wishart
Gordon Smith
Andy Penman
Alan Gilzean
Alan Cousin
Hugh Robertson
Alec Stuart
George McGeachie
Craig Brown
Bobby Waddell

THE FIFTEEN players listed above who were to play in the championship season of 1961/62 were to become legendary as arguably the greatest team in the history of Dundee Football Club; Gordon had once again 'backed the right horse'. He was given a free transfer from Heart of Midlothian and made Bob Shankly's summer by finally agreeing to sign for the dark blues. Attempts in 1941, 1959 and just the previous December had all ended up in failure for one reason or another – but this time, at long last, Gordon Smith was a Dundee player. What a move it would turn out to be for both club and winger.

His reasons for joining were primarily because his good friend and old Hibs player and coach Sammy Kean was there, and he saw it as a sort of homecoming – also feeling in some way that it was his duty to play for the Angus club, as a piece of his heart still belonged in this region. The district and the city that catapulted him to fame as a raw sixteen-year-old still evoked many memories from all those years ago when Gordon was a boy.

Another important reason was that the club allowed him to train at home in North Berwick most of the week, only driving to Dens Park on a Thursday for training and going over arrangements for the Saturday game. Initially, though, for pre-season training, Gordon was up and down the coast daily, travelling with Edinburgh-based player Bobby Wishart. Smith did admit, however, that not being based in the team's home city did take its toll:

> When I said to Bob Shankly, that a sensible solution would be that I would train at home but journey up, say, twice a week, he shook his head but reluctantly agreed. Looking back, I was in the team, but not part of it . . . I did miss the camaraderie that I had enjoyed so much at Hibs and also Hearts.

But the most pivotal reason of all for Gordon was the talent of the players. With Hearts the previous two seasons, Gordon had seen Dundee at first hand and could see the potential at the club. Manager Bob Shankly had seen his side finish in a discouraging tenth place the previous season and knew he would have to do something special to challenge for honours. As it turned out, Smith was the missing link, as the other players who made up Dundee's most famous line-up were already there.

In the *Evening Dispatch* on 3 June 1961, Gordon Smith talked to John Gibson.

Did you find any differences between Hibs and Hearts supporters?
It's hard to say. I'd say this and it's quite true, that the main fear when I decided to move to Hearts from Easter Road was that I wouldn't be well received by the Tynecastle faithful. That worried me most of all.

I thought it would be a terrific challenge, but, to my astonishment, I found I didn't have to win them over at all. Both sets of supporters have been marvellous to me, and if they're half as good in Dundee, I'll have no complaints.

When the time comes for you to hang up your boots, will you stay on in the game?
I haven't given that much thought. Indeed, I've never thought for a second of not playing. I intend to play as long as I can without struggling. April 28th this year marked my twentieth anniversary as a professional player and I hope to add a few to the tally.

How do you feel about teaming up with trainer Sammy Kean again?
It's no secret that Sammy and I were always great pals. I knew him from the moment I arrived at Easter Road until the moment I left, and I'd go as far as to say that as far as I was concerned, it was a tragedy when he left. Sammy was a great mixer with the players, and somehow always in a good mood. I never had a wrong word with him in sixteen years.

How do you keep in trim these days? Still a salt-water man?
I live almost on the beach itself at North Berwick, which is not purely coincidental. Yes, the site of our cottage ties in with the fitness angle. There'll be plenty days in the coming season when I won't manage to Dens for training, on these days you'll find me on the beach and the grass just on our doorstep. We've been there since last July, and I reckon we'll be staying on indefinitely . . . forever.

How do you feel about the wages situation?
It's quite a problem. You can argue both ways. Everybody admits there are players who deserve more than others, but,

after all, it's a team game, and that's where it's awkward varying the wage packets.

I rather admire the Tottenham Hotspur arrangement, whereby they have a private agreement with their players, and only their players know about it. Each individual's performance is reviewed at the end of the year, I've read, and paid accordingly.

Any young players who have particularly impressed you?
Motherwell's Willie Hunter, Dundee's Andy Penman, and lads of that class, though they've almost proved themselves. Then there's a player at the other end of the scale, you might say, in Ronnie Simpson. Simpson is the one man who made all the difference to Hibs last season. You can't underestimate the effect he had on the team as a whole.

It's grand to feel that you've a good goalkeeper behind you. I remember Jimmy Kerr at Easter Road . . . the best I've ever seen. He was fantastic for three or four years. I think there was one season when we lost only six goals at Easter Road, thanks to Jimmy.

Anything to say on your stay at Tynecastle?
The first season was most enjoyable, probably because it was successful from Hearts' point of view in winning the League and League Cup. The second season was perhaps not quite so enjoyable.

How about Dens Park?
It's home territory for me, almost, and just as important, a lovely big pitch. One of my grievances is that pitches are not uniform. There's such a difference between minimum and maximum. Dens Park is probably the best pitch in Scotland. Yes, I'm happy to be going . . .

Gordon signed for Dundee on the same Wednesday, 31 May, evening as Hearts' sublime conquerors, Benfica, defeated Barcelona to win the European Cup. The signing took place in the unchanged North British Hotel in Edinburgh, where he had marked his name for Hibernian twenty years prior and then journeyed across town to Tynecastle, reminiscent of that April 1941 night. There, his old boss Tommy Walker and the Dundee boss discussed the transfer further, thrashing out miscellaneous terms – and as soon as the ink was dry on all the forms, his new manager Bob Shankly went on holiday for two weeks a happy man.

On 27 June, after his usual invigorating pilgrimage to the south of France, Gordon travelled north for training for the first time – a gruelling day spent under his friend and new coach Sammy Kean's command, involving a practice game at Stobswell Recreation Park. Gordon drove his Porsche to Edinburgh, where he picked up Bobby Wishart, the ex-Aberdeen star, and the two gents talked football all the way to Dundee.

A week-long tour to Iceland began on 4 July as the Dundee party flew out of Scotland to Reykjavik, with Smith and Wishart room-mates for the week. The trip started badly as the flight was delayed by five hours due to seagulls disabling an engine. Overall, the pre-season tour of Iceland wasn't one of Gordon's favourite tours. He didn't like the place: the weather, the sparseness of the terrain, the fact that it never got dark and especially the food – specifically the salty fish dishes. He had pre-empted the situation by taking it upon himself to pack fresh fruit alongside tins of fruit and jams, packets of raisins and shortbread biscuits so he didn't go too hungry when turning down the local cuisine. Whilst most of the players would be eating the local dishes, Gordon would try out local delicatessens for tastier, healthier options. He was to be a revolutionary at Dens Park, bringing his ideas on boots and diets, including introducing the players to pasta and the benefits of it. Another avant-garde gizmo was Smith's electric razor. The future Scotland manager, Craig Brown, a young Dundee player at the time, remembers Gordon using a Ronson with all the players being greatly impressed by this state of the art device, none more so than Brown himself, and he would stand in awe, staring, as Smith plugged in and shaved 'US style'!

Although he enjoyed his first games with his new team-mates and took great delight in scoring for his new club in his first two matches, his Iceland tour was further marred by a foot injury picked up in the third and final match. He did, however, write down on his tour itinerary card that he 'must buy a pair of Gola Pacemaker boots' on his return.

The players stayed in the Hotel Garden in Reykjavik and the first game was against KR Reykjavik on 6 July. Dundee won the match 3–1 and along with Gordon, Penman and Waddell also scored. The Tayside team enjoyed a tour to Gullfoss, lunching at the Hotel Geysir, followed by a sightseeing tour of Reykjavik before the next game against Arkranes. Dundee won 4–0 with goals by Smith again, Cousin and this time a double by Andy Penman. Willie Reid, the St Mirren manager, had accompanied Dundee on the tour, predominantly to watch Thorolf Beck who played in the Icelandic side, with the Paisley boss hoping to acquire his signature for the start of the new season.

With their performance and free-flowing style of play, the Dundee touring side prompted the local press to describe them as, apart from Moscow Dynamo, 'the best side ever to play in Iceland' and Dundee *Courier* sports writer Tommy Gallacher, an ex-Dundee star himself during the 1950s, was principally flattering with his praise for the side and, in particular, was impressed with the start made by the ex-Hibs and Hearts icon.

On the penultimate day of the visit, the touring party were treated to a bus tour to Thingvellir at the invitation of the Reykjavik Municipal Authorities. The following evening, the third and final game of the short tour was played out at Laugardalur – where all the games were based. This game, in which Gordon injured his foot, was played against an Iceland International Select, with Dundee winning again 3–1. Following the match, all the players were presented with a sheepskin rug at the dinner/dance held at the tour sponsor FC Thoroltor's ground.

Returning to Scotland, the injury picked up against the Iceland International Select was to limit the time Gordon spent on the pitch for his Dens Park debut, disappointing the 5,500 or so fans, with a lot coming along especially to see him perform. Dundee held their annual public trial, their 'show occasion', on 7 August, in which the entire playing staff competed in a full-scale practice match – three thirty-minute periods, which was the norm for trial matches. The Dundee first team wore white and the reserves blue, with the whites coming out on top 5–2. Prior to the public trial match in the changing room on Craig Brown's peg was his strip and below it a package wrapped up in brown paper. Upon opening it an excited Brown unveiled a Ronson electric razor with 'Best wishes Craig from Gordon' signed on the box.

Missing the opening two games of the season, the League Cup ties against Airdrie and Rangers, Gordon made his official debut for Dundee in Scotland by scoring alongside Alan Gilzean and travelling buddy Bobby Wishart in 2–3 away defeat to Third Lanark, on Saturday, 19 August, also in the League Cup. The only problem with Wishart's goal was that it was an own goal for the Glasgow side!

The following Wednesday evening, 23 August, Gordon made his league debut at Brockville against Falkirk, opening the scoring in a 3–1 victory in a game that ended in almost complete darkness, as the home side's floodlights had not been switched on due to an oversight. Appearing from the gloom in the Falkirk side was former Famous Five co-star Willie Ormond, and John Lambie, who would many years later become coach at Easter Road.

Smith continued his goal scoring for the third successive match on Saturday, 26 August, away to Airdrie in the League Cup again. On his home league debut, with a 20,000 crowd roaring him on against rivals Dundee United, Gordon scored yet again in a 4–1 win – their largest win over United since 1926. His scoring salvo read: six goals in his first nine games for the club – an impressive start for the winger!

In their subsequent match against Aberdeen, Charlie Cooke, the future Dundee centre forward, taught the 'City of Discovery' men a harsh lesson by outplaying everybody on the pitch. He had a hand in all Aberdeen goals as Dundee lost 1–3 at Pittodrie – their first league defeat of the season. Incredibly, though, it was to be their last loss until February the next year. Dundee went on to go twenty games undefeated in all competitions. This record stood until March 2011 – just less than half a century later – when the 2010/11 Dundee side bettered this winning run. The 2011 team played in the second tier and their players openly admitted the run by the 1961/62 team far outweighed their feat.

The first of the twenty games was against Gordon's recent team, Hearts, at Dens Park, and through the preceding week, Gordon admitted that he may be unable to play against his former colleagues. The reason was not because he felt a little ill at ease, nor was it due to an injury to his knee, back or his 'dodgy ankle'. The embarrassing explanation was he had a gigantic boil, the size, in his own words, 'of a horse shoe', on his backside! Smith eventually decided he would risk it and said to fellow players that he would be ok as long as the ball didn't hit his 'sore bum with a direct hit'. As it turned out, the game went ahead uneventfully, with a 2–0 victory for Dundee.

Smith scored again for his new club, this time at one of his favourite grounds, the wide and expansive Fir Park. However, the following week, in a 2–1 victory over Dunfermline at East End Park, Gordon received an injury in the first seconds of the match. In the days before substitutes, he soldiered on, completing the full ninety minutes, but was to miss the next game – a 3–1 home win over Partick Thistle.

Looking back, the next four games probably went a long way in deciding the outcome of the Scottish League Championship of 1961/62. A victory over Celtic was followed by one of the most astonishing and pleasing for Gordon in all his years as a professional. Once again, it was against his old foes, Rangers, and this time it wasn't Hibs who humbled the Glasgow giants.

Rangers 1–5 Dundee, played on a foggy November afternoon, with some fans turning back after hearing rumours that the game had been called off. Gilzean, scorer of an amazing four on the day, said: 'It was my third goal that made me jump for joy for I had been trying out the move all season with Gordon Smith – a low corner out to me just inside the box. Usually a defender gets in the way but this time it came off and I hit the ball home first time.' The score-line was made all the more remarkable as all six goals were scored in the second-half!

Rangers, who themselves had been unbeaten in twenty-one games, were humbled by Dundee, whose 5–1 victory is still undoubtedly the most supreme and grandest league result in the history of the dark blues. Smith was quoted as saying in many newspapers: 'I felt as if I was playing for Hibs again back in the glory days.'

Gordon's next game, a week later, was another sensational match, with Dundee back at home beating Raith Rovers in an incredible 5–4 match. Smith scored the winner with seconds remaining and was duly mobbed by fans and team-mates alike. Although Gordon enjoyed the Ibrox exploits the week before, this game, he would later allege, was the one that won them the title. In an after-match chat with Kean and Shankly, Smith said all three of them reckoned the team had the potential to win the league.

Gordon didn't play in a midweek friendly against Swedish opposition Elfsborg Boras, but returned to haunt his old team Hibernian at Easter Road the follow Saturday with a goal direct from the corner – similar to his last at the ground for the Leith side back in January 1958. Next came a home draw in a wintry Dundee against Stirling Albion, followed by yet another Smith goal for Dundee in a 5–1 win over Airdrie, with Gordon taking over centre forward duties as Gilzean's jaw had been broken. A 1–1 draw two days before Christmas, against ex-Dundee player Bobby Flavell's St Mirren, meant that Dundee finished 1961 undefeated in their last fifteen matches.

The following is an extract from an interview with Gordon in the *People's Journal* of 16 December 1961.

> *To whom do you owe most for putting you on your football career?*
> The schoolteachers who ran the Montrose Southesk team with such enthusiasm. They were Mr James Edward, Mr Ian Russell and Mr Peter Clark.
>
> The first, Mr Edward, was typical of all three. He was sport-minded, and took a terrific interest in the school team, even to the extent of paying our bus fares to away games at Johnshaven, Stonehaven and Brechin.
>
> Nothing was too much trouble to them and their enthusiasm was infectious. They knew the game. I idolised them and they gave me every encouragement to play football.
>
> And a word of praise to schoolmaster Major Lawrie Kerr, of Laurencekirk. As a selector, he pitched for me at a time when there was terrific competition. He also accompanied me to all schoolboy international games.
>
> *When, and why did you switch from centre to right wing?*
> My two school internationals were as a right winger, but this was because of my lack of height. I was small for my age and they decided to play me on the wing. I was the smallest boy in our school team.
>
> Of course I'd grown a bit by the time I went to Hibs, and I was still a centre. But Mr McCartney played me on the wing. I don't really know why.
>
> It was much to my disgust. I really didn't fancy it at all. But Arthur Milne was at centre forward. He wasn't always available – he was in the RAF – and I got a game at centre when he couldn't make it.

Which position did you prefer?
Centre forward.

How did Dundee North End get you in preference to Hillside United and Forfar Celtic?
I was living in Montrose and it was something to play for Dundee North End. They had a high standard. I did have one game for Hillside, and scored nine goals. But even the thirty-mile journey didn't mean a thing. When North End came along, I had no hesitation in signing for them.

What's your top score in a senior game, and against whom?
Five goals against Third Lanark at Easter Road in the late 40s.

What's the best team you ever played against?
Hungary, in Budapest in 1955.

Who, in your opinion, is the finest left back in the Scottish League at present?
I know players like to mention their own team-mates, but, in all sincerity, I think it's easily Bobby Cox.

Some folk say you're more injury prone than most players. Would you say this is true?
No. I had no serious injuries until 1954 when I broke my leg. Since then, I've broken it again. Through the years my right ankle suffered so much damage that eventually in 1958 I had two operations on it.

This was the beginning of the ankle trouble which led to my free transfer from Hibs. I had a third operation on the ankle in 1959. I missed one game in two years with Hearts. I don't think that's an injury-prone record.

Was it easy to fit into the scheme of things at Dens Park?
Yes. They're a football playing side from goalkeeper out, which suits me very well.

How many more years would you say you have in senior football?
It's impossible to say. If you'd asked me ten years ago, I couldn't

have said I'd still be playing today. As long as I feel as I feel now, I'll be playing.

How do you account for the fact that you never really managed to produce your true form in international matches?
I don't think I played too badly in internationals. But it may have been because there was never quite the same understanding in any international game. It was generally agreed I played well in the 1955 tour against Hungary etc.

Do you find the pace a bit fast for you nowadays?
If I did I wouldn't be playing.

That fabulous forward line of Smith, Johnstone, Reilly, Turnbull and Ormond turned in some devastating performances. Any match you specially recall?
The game against Rangers in the Scottish Cup at Ibrox about 1954. We won 3–2 after twice being down. Then, of course, there were the fabulous cup replays with Aberdeen at Ibrox and Hampden. These, too, were wonderful games, for Aberdeen were playing very good football at that time.

As Juventus' star player, Omar Sivori, won the Ballon d'Or for 1961, Dundee youngster Andy Penman got engaged to his sweetheart, Sandra Watson, with an 'impromptu party' in a Dundee Hotel with a hint of Christmas snow in the air. Penman, who made his Dundee debut aged just fifteen in 1958, was understandably in a buoyant mood – but then talked football:

> I've learned more about the game in the past few weeks than in ten years prior. And it's all thanks to Gordon Smith. Time and time again, Gordon has taken me out for half an hour to iron out some fault in my play. As my right wing partner, he'd be continually working out plots with me, even during a match. In fact we cooked up something special for Rangers during the interval at Ibrox, recently.

28

DUNDEE, CHAMPIONS OF SCOTLAND WITH SEVEN DEADLY WINS

VICTORIES OVER Falkirk and Hearts started 1962 well and Gordon was man of the match, back playing at Tynecastle for the first time since he left the club the previous May. He set up both goals for Cousin and Gilzean, with many people presuming he wouldn't play, as the previous afternoon he'd been involved in a serious car accident travelling to his North Berwick home from Edinburgh, when a car swerved in front of him, forcing Smith off the road and into a ditch, where he apparently lay unconscious for several minutes. Taken by ambulance to hospital, he was found to be suffering from a mild concussion and some bruising of the chest – he was lucky and informed Shankly he could play.

Extracts below are from a 16 January 1962 article from the *Toronto Telegram* by Rex Kingsley of the *Sunday Mail*.

> Scotland has its own Stanley Matthews. Indeed, many people declare him to be a better all round football-player than the immortal Stanley – and there are facts to prove it.
>
> He is none other than the equally immortal (in Scottish eyes at any rate) Gordon Smith.
>
> Exploding into the Scottish soccer scene as a star right winger of that one-time famous Hibs attacking five card trick Smith, Johnstone, Reilly, Turnbull and Ormond (all full internationals), he created a record for a winger that Stanley Matthews couldn't look at – he scored more than 350 goals. And made many more – as Lawrie Reilly, now retired, could testify.

He is the dream player model for all other performers and idolized by them as the greatest football thoroughbred Scotland has ever produced.

Yet three years ago, Hibs thought they'd had all Gordon could give them, so in gratitude, they gave him a free transfer. Neighbouring Edinburgh club, Hearts, snapped him up.

But Gordon, although oozing the same poise, positional sense and precision as of yore, was never happy with Hearts due to the player shuffling the team suffered.

And last April, after two seasons, Hearts also gave him a 'free'.

He said to me: 'Rex, I always told you I'd hang up my boots when I thought I had nothing further to contribute to the game. Maybe you think that time has come. But I don't, and I'll prove it to you.'

Shrewd manager Bob Shankly of Dundee took a chance by signing him for this season.

Smith told him: 'I don't want any signing fee. I'll play my way into your team or go of my own accord.'

Right now, six months later, Gordon Smith is the toast of Dundee, idol of his colleagues, and the sensation of the season – at thirty-seven years of age.

No player in the country has such perfect balance or such unflappable no-panic poise. The Dundee team wraps itself around him, and strides elegantly towards the first league championship in its history.

I watched him make the two goals that defeated Hearts at Tynecastle last Saturday – on the very ground where last season he played for the home team unhappily.

The Hearts fans blinked in astonishment, as he feinted, dummied and tore down the line to lay the ball deliberately towards the scorer. No wonder Dundee are playing the most distinguished soccer seen by a home side in years.

Two more home wins against Third Lanark and St Johnstone followed, and with the latter on 24 January 1962, Dundee had set a new club record – twenty games undefeated – with a 2–1 winning score. Unfortunately, three days later, this fabulous Dundee team were to lose at Dens Park in the Scottish Cup to St Mirren, a team struggling in the league. The only goal of the game was scored by George McLean from a mere five yards out. The Lanarkshire club manager, Bobby Flavell, had done his homework on Scotland's top side. Apparently, the Paisley side's boss had his players out on the beach at Broughty Ferry early in the morning – and it certainly paid off.

The following Saturday, Gordon drove down to Kilmarnock early to meet up with the upcoming opposition's manager! His friend, Willie Waddell, knew that if the proximity of Kilmarnock had been different, Gordon, without a doubt, would've signed for his team – instead of either Hearts or Dundee. The two gents discussed the stock exchange and other secret business deals that they had going on but football business was never talked about. They had far too much respect for each other for that. When the Dundee team bus arrived, Bob Shankly joined the pair for a 'cup of tea and a good blether', before the ensuing 1–1 draw.

Disaster struck for Dundee the following week – and this time it wasn't the cup but the league. Once again, they went down 1–3 at Dens Park. They were up against a decent Motherwell team.

The subsequent week was a free week for Dundee because they'd been eliminated from the Scottish Cup, so the team headed down to London to play Arsenal at Highbury in a friendly match on Saturday, 17 February. A crowd of 16,340 witnessed a competitive 2–2 draw against the Londoners, who, like Dundee, had also lost in the English FA Cup two weeks previously. The next evening, Gordon was coaxed into going to the Usher Hall in Edinburgh (straight from the airport after his London jaunt) to see his former Hearts colleague, John Cumming, win the *Sunday Mail* Scottish Football Player of the Year for 1961.

After losing the Motherwell match, the next three games continued in the same vein – away defeats against Partick Thistle and Celtic, and then for the third loss in succession at Dens Park, to Dunfermline Athletic.

A startling early spring slump had taken place: twenty games undefeated and now four defeats in a row. Against Partick, Dundee frighteningly had only two attempts at goal in the entire match. Then, against a Celtic side that included players such as Jim Brogan, Paddy Crerand, John Hughes and debutant Bobby Lennox, they lost out to a late header scored by captain Billy McNeill, with Gordon carrying a thigh injury for most of the match. Gordon's dream of winning yet another league title was foundering and he discovered the most upsetting of the quartet of loses was the fourth, against Dunfermline Athletic – a game he had to watch from the sidelines as his thigh injury received against Celtic hadn't recovered in time for him to play.

The next eight games proved to be more pivotal than the twenty games without defeat. This time they had to perform knowing it would be the difference between winning the league or not. There was a lot of pressure after four straight defeats, yet Gordon described this octet of games as: 'Eight of the best I've ever played in; eight of the best I've ever experienced.'

Gordon rose from his sick-bed in the mid-afternoon of Wednesday 14 March. He had been feeling under the weather, which had stopped him training for a few days, but at least the injury incurred against Celtic had healed. He drove his Porsche to Queensferry and transferred across to Fife, then up to Dundee, probably driving faster than he ought to have.

He pulled over before reaching the city. Craig Brown, driving up from Glasgow to Dens Park, stopped his car too after noticing the parked sports car and was amazed to see Gordon sprinting up and down a farm field – 'getting in some extra pre-match training!' This was a big one, a huge game in the season. It was against Rangers and the outcome of the title could be determined that evening. It would appear that Gordon was leaving nothing to chance.

In all likelihood, the victory flag would fly high above Ibrox Park in August like so many times before – or was there still a chance? Would it be, for the first time, at Dens Park with a cold North Sea wind blowing the standard? It looked like it was a two-horse race. Dundee, who had at one point been six points clear at the top of the league, now trailed three points behind new leaders Rangers before this game.

Dundee, by drawing a game at home, had 'stopped the rot' as Gordon put it and this would have been celebrated almost like a victory had it not been against main title rivals Rangers. With seven games to go, time was running out for Dundee to catch up with Rangers, who were still three points ahead in the title race. Bob Shankly told Gordon: 'We need to win most of them, if not them all, to have any chance.' Gordon was as desperate as he'd ever been to win a championship medal, and told Bob he thought they needed to win them all and hope Rangers would stumble a little.

Their hopes were not in vain. Dundee, without a victory in any competition in over two months, won all seven remaining matches, whilst Rangers did stumble – the lowest point of the Govan side's season was a 0–1 defeat at home against, of all teams, Dundee's city rivals Dundee United!

Dundee's Seven Deadly Wins

1) Raith Rovers 3–2
2) Hibernian 1–0
3) Stirling Albion 3–2
4) Airdrie 2–1
5) Dundee United 2–1
6) St Mirren 2–0
7) St Johnstone 3–0

Following Gordon's goal against Stirling Albion on 31 March – the first he had scored since the middle of December – they defeated local rivals Dundee United on Easter Monday, 9 April. The same afternoon, Rangers dropped a point by drawing with rivals Celtic. This was followed by a sixteen-day wait to play again and in that time, the whole Dundee first team squad journeyed to Hampden to watch club-mate Alex Hamilton play in a 2–0 victory for Scotland against England.

Rangers, on the penultimate evening of the Scottish Football League campaign, were to play away in Aberdeen and then Kilmarnock at Ibrox the following Saturday. They had a vastly superior goal difference, with the likelihood that they would retain the title in three days' time.

At half-time in their second-last match at home to St Mirren, Dundee were 1–0 up from an Alan Cousin goal scored two minutes from the interval. Then, news reached the players that Aberdeen were beating Rangers by the same score through Englishman Bobby Cummings' goal, scored after fifty minutes in a game that had started slightly earlier.

A potential disaster occurred when Smith handled in the penalty area with ten minutes to go at Dens Park and referee Willie Syme pointed to the penalty spot. This could have been the end of Dundee's title bid but Pat Liney made a miraculous save to deny St Mirren captain Jim Clunie. Two minutes later, Dundee scored again and news came through from Pittodrie that 1–0 was the final score. Pat Liney was a hero upon the final whistle blowing; the pitch was submerged in a sea of fans, with police doing their utmost to cordon-off an area for the players to escape down the tunnel. One woman broke free of the cordon and ran up to veteran Dundee winger Gordon Smith, hugging and kissing him, exhilarated on a night that no Dundee fan would ever forget – it was his wife.

The dressing room was euphoric, with a relieved Gordon hugging Liney as if he'd saved his life, telling him: 'You realise that if we win the League on Saturday Pat, you will be famous in Dundee forever.' Meanwhile, outside in the street, there was a lot of dancing to be seen and the players could hear the joyous singing of 'Up Wi' the Bonnets of Bonnie Dundee' as the PA system had informed the masses waiting to hear the happy news of the result from Aberdeen.

Saturday, 28 April 1962, is a day that will always stand out in the memory of every Dundee fan – for those who were there especially but even for those who were not and those who were not even born; it will be etched on their minds with indelible ink. Just before 5pm, Dundee became Scottish League Champions for the first (and only) time in their history.

With the Dens Park side only needing a point to secure the title, they headed to Perth for the last game of the season. The attendance at Muirton Park that day was a record 26,856, with the majority of fans wearing the dark blue of Dundee, having made the short trip along the Tay. On the morning prior to the game, Gordon had attended a family wedding in Edinburgh. He then sped up the road in his gleaming sports car to join the already assembled and expectant throng of Dundee players.

Bribery was becoming rife in the game and before the match, the entire Dundee squad was offered £50 each (a big sum in 1962) by an unknown Perth businessman, who had been allowed to infiltrate the away dressing room, to make sure the result ended in a draw – thus enabling St Johnstone to avoid relegation with the point they required. Each and every one of the players became more determined than ever to win after this took place. Lining up in the soon-to-be-relegated Perth team was twenty-year-old Alex Ferguson, who went on to play for Rangers, amongst other teams, before gaining huge success as manager of East Stirlingshire, St Mirren, Aberdeen, Scotland, and now, of course, Manchester United. In fact, he had a goal disallowed in this game when

Dundee led 3–0 and it was thought that the goal might have been enough to keep St Johnstone up on goal average. As it turned out, even if the goal had stood, it wouldn't have made any difference to the eventual outcome in terms of the relegated sides. Ferguson recalled:

'We had a lad [Lawrie] Thomson playing out of position on the left wing – playing more like a left back, who was trying to whack Smith constantly.

'I remember at one point Thomson was chasing the famous winger; still trying to kick him at the side of the pitch as the game continued in full-flow on it!

'At every opportunity he would try and foul him. Anyhow he failed miserably, with Gordon getting away from him almost all the time and one of his trademark crosses found the head of Alan Gilzean to score the opening goal.'

Rangers had drawn 1-1, leaving Dundee with a three-point margin at the top of the league. But for St Johnstone, it was a disaster as all the other teams in the relegation battle had won.

The Dundee players were carried off shoulder-high; Bob Shankly ran onto the park as soon as the final whistle blew and made a bee-line for Gordon, then started congratulating the rest of his team but was engulfed by ecstatic fans! A delirious Sammy Kean lifted Gordon into the air. Like at the St Mirren game, the police had to assist players back to the dressing room through the mass of overjoyed dark blues fans and into the sanctuary.

'The team will not appear,' exclaimed the announcement over the Tannoy, as fans shouted for their heroes to re-emerge from the darkness of the dressing room to take a bow in what had become a rapturous park blazed in sunlight for the fans. However, seconds later, Bobby Cox led his team up into the main stand to acknowledge the cheering masses. It was a moment that could have gone on forever. A perpetual moment that, to be savoured fully, ought to have been frozen in time.

The players' bus back to Dundee crawled along at speeds often as low as five miles an hour for most of the way. Gordon was in his Porsche directly behind with wife Joan and fans at the roadside were clamouring for autographs from him as he posed for photographs. Then the supporters ran up alongside the team bus and some of them even managed to get on board to greet their heroes. It was the longest journey ever recorded in the short distance from Perth to Dundee but for all those fans and players alike, it was the best and most unforgettable trip they'd ever make on the road.

As soon as the bus and the Porsche reached Dundee, they headed firstly to the City Chambers to be greeted by Lord Provost, Maurice McManus and Dundee MP Morgan Thomson, then to chairman James Gellatly's house in Broughty Ferry, followed by a meal and private party at the Queen's Hotel. Gordon relaxed with fellow Dundee players and, for once, 'let his hair down'!

In twenty-one years as a player, Gordon had never felt so appreciated by his fellow players. He told his brother: 'I have never experienced anything like it before – it feels like something that would only occur in *The Rover*.'

On 18 May, Dundee took the plane across the pond to New York City for the International Soccer League. Scotland normally sent over the runners-up and the SFA, pre-empting the outcome, had informed the Americans that Dundee would be coming across (it was perhaps presumed by the SFA that Rangers would emerge as champions – enabling second-place Dundee to participate in this tournament). For the first and only time, it was the champions of Scotland who participated and there was much consternation at the SFA headquarters.

Alongside the players, Dundee chairman James Gellatly was joined by Jack Swadel, his vice chairman, club secretary Bob Crighton and, to keep the players in order of course, were Sammy Kean, physiotherapist Lawrie Smith and Jacky Kay, the boot room assistant.

Gordon roomed with Andy Penman for this trip and the club stayed at the Hotel Empire, on Broadway at 63rd Street. When the players arrived at the airport, the incessant heat greeted them, reading 94°F (34.5°C) on the clock tower. This was an ominous sign of things to come. That evening, for what would be the highlight of the tour, Gordon attended 'the fights', as the New Yorkers called them. This was no ordinary boxing bout: along with Sammy Kean and journalist Tommy Gallacher from the Dundee *Courier*, the trio managed somehow to procure tickets, went to the famous St Nicks Arena and saw, up close and personal, arguably the greatest boxer in the history of the sport, Muhammad Ali, or as he was still known then, Cassius Clay. Clay defeated Billy Daniel, another contender for the heavyweight title, and

Gordon was enthralled when they briefly met the champ through the connections of ex-Dundee player Gallacher.

Dundee's first game on 20 May, with the thermometer now reading 99°F (37°C), was played at Randall's Island against West German opponents, Reulingen. Dundee lost 0–2 in front of an 18,000 crowd on a sweltering evening in the Big Apple. Following the match, Gordon was rushed to a nearby hospital, suffering from severe dehydration. He vowed to Bob Shankly that he would go home, 'back on the first plane away from here' in the morning, but the Dundee players managed to coax him into staying. Before leaving the hospital, he was weighed and was found to have lost over a stone (sixteen lbs in total) during the opening game in the stiflingly hot and sultry conditions! Trips to Coney Island and training in Central Park followed throughout the following week, and Gordon was visited by an old school-friend from Montrose now domiciled in the US, Conn Henderson.

The team then flew to Detroit, briefly escaping the unrelenting heat, staying at the classy Wolverine Hotel. Here they played against another West German side, Saarbrucken, on 25 May in front of a smallish crowd of 5,311 at the giant Tiger Stadium – and were humbled 1–5 in the process.

Lyall Smith interviewed Gordon for the *Detroit Free Press* on the day of the game.

SOCCER'S IRON MAN TELLS HIS SECRET

> How old are you, Gordon?
>
> 'I'm 37,' he offered warily. [His thirty-eighth birthday was the very next day!]
>
> With fifteen other members of the Dundee soccer team, he's here in Michigan to kick the ball around at Detroit's 52,416 all-seated Tiger Stadium on Friday night in a game against Saarbrucken of Germany.
>
> Gordon is a tousle-haired character with a wide grin, weighing 168 pounds and stands about 5 feet 9 inches tall.
>
> How does he explain his record of longevity in a gruelling sport?
>
> 'I try to take fine care of it. I don't smoke, drink spirits, or even coffee. I always take at least a five hour interval between any kind of meals.'

Have you received many bad injuries?

'Broken legs . . . two,' he grinned. 'Operations on right ankle . . . three. Facial stitches . . . more than a dozen times. Cuts, bruises, sprains . . . too many to count. But it's been fun!'

Can you still run fast?

'As the number 7 for Dundee I have to be quick. My partner, Andy Penman is only nineteen. That means I was playing professionally two years before he was born. I have to be able to run!'

How much do you receive in your weekly pay-checks?

'Seventy-five dollars a week. That's tops for the course. It might not sound like a lot over here in the States,' he suggested. 'You are used to hearing about athletes getting fabulous salaries for playing your football and baseball. But over in Scotland, our soccer salaries put us in the same financial scale as doctors and dentists and other professional men. The average wage for all persons back home is less than forty-five dollars a week and there are thousands, many thousands, who get much less than that.'

Gordon is one of the few soccer professionals who have their own business enterprises. 'It's difficult for us to get into such things,' he explained. 'We start our training season in July. Our season opens in August. Then we play regularly until the end of April and into May. As a result, we just don't have time to work at any other job. But I finally invested in a roadhouse . . . an Inn, I guess you'd call it over here. Something for me to fall back on when I really get too old and can't play anymore.'

When do you think that may be?

'One more broken leg could be enough,' he figured. 'That would set another Scottish record . . .'

Upon returning to a little cooler New York City, Dundee drew with Yugoslavian champions Hajduk Split at the end of the month and this was followed by Gordon's last game of the trip. He played in a 3–2 win over Mexican side Guadalajara. Gordon, still suffering from the heat, was excused by Bob Shankly and flew back home, promising to return should Dundee win their qualifying group.

When Smith arrived back in Edinburgh, he was still a bit dehydrated from his NYC adventures, certainly lighter, and at times, 'talkin' American', but most of all he returned with a huge smile on his face. It was just beginning to sink in that he had won a Scottish League title for the fifth time and was due to play in the European Cup for a third time.

A return to the US would not be necessary, as following the drawn match against Italians Palermo, the final game of the six-week excursion was against the Brazilian side FC America, where Dundee lost 2–3. Gordon received airmail from his club manager, Shankly, who wrote:

> As you now know, we didn't win yesterday, so there will be no need for your return as we can't now win the section. Perhaps it's just as well with this heat, as we may well have been held to our contracts. This was a game I did want to win, though, as I'm afraid have no love for 'the tallies' [Italians] after the show they put up against the Mexicans.

As soon as Gordon heard the news from his Dundee boss, he headed off to Cannes with wife Joan and marvelled at the talent on display at the 1962 World Cup Finals, which were held in Chile. They would watch the football on small black and white televisions in the bars and *tabacs* of the old town and in restaurants; for some of the games, they were invited by Cannes FC to attend showings at the clubrooms overlooking their ground, where predominantly at half-time Gordon would run out onto the bone-dry pitch, taking a ball or two, and soon there would be a throng of youngsters deserting the 'TV room' to join him!

Just prior to pre-season training and upon his return from holiday, there were two letters that stood out from the others awaiting Gordon amongst bills and the usual hordes of fan mail. One was from the SFA, informing him quite bluntly that he would not be able to play in a charity match alongside Johnstone, Reilly, Turnbull and Ormond. The other letter read:

June 26th 1962
Re: Progressive Candidate for the Town Council

Dear Gordon,
It has been suggested that you would be a most likely candidate for Craigentinny and perhaps you would care to consider the matter.

ON BEHALF OF BAILIE STEWART

Gordon was to politely turn down the offer to run for political office and he regretfully phoned up his old Easter Road partners in crime, passing on the news from the SFA letter.

He had no ambition to be a demagogue in a political world but was quite happy to be one in the only world of which he knew – a football world. A football world in which Smith had, for the second time, confounded those who had written him off; a football world in which now, at the age of thirty-eight, he felt he was once again at the summit.

29

ONE GAME TOO MANY

IN AN August 1962 interview with John Gibson for the *Evening Dispatch*, Gordon discussed training and his ambitions.

Do you train at Dens Park every day?

John, when it comes to training, I do what I think is best for me. And the fact that you think it's best for you does you good even if it's not true. Maybe it all boils down to Psychology or autosuggestion.

Generally Dundee see me twice a week; on Thursdays for practice with the rest of the team and on Saturdays for the match. They trust me to train conscientiously on my own. The arrangement proved a happy one last season, and I think I can say it was to our mutual benefit.

I think the salt water helps my bones. I like to think so. Even when I was at Easter Road I nipped down to Portobello beach at every opportunity. Salt water strengthens the ankles. At least I can prove it doesn't do them any harm!

When I was asked to turn out in the charity match I wrote straight back saying that if they could get the other four (from the Famous Five) I would be delighted to do so. Then came the ban. But I could have played in spite of the league, for I hadn't then re-signed for Dundee.

Anyway, I always live in hope that the five of us will get out again as a line. Now that these days are over, people seem to think more of us, even more than they did at the time.

What's your ambition?

I could and probably should say to win that elusive Scottish Cup medal. The truth is I want most of all to keep as fit as I felt twenty-two years ago. I prefer not to make forecasts . . . just to take each season as it comes.

The season of 1962/63 stands out for some Dundee fans as the most memorable ever – they didn't win the League Championship this season, but they went within one game of becoming the first British club to reach the final of the European Cup. It was Gordon's middle season at the club and it was sensational. He played in forty-eight games, scoring ten goals – three of which were in Europe.

In the league, the team were unable to match the glorious exploits of the previous season and languished around mid table for most of the season, finishing in ninth place with Gordon missing only five games from thirty-four played. Some say their league form deteriorated because their exertions in Europe took their toll on the team both physically and mentally, but the players were quick enough to repudiate this and during the course of the season, they recorded their biggest ever victory – the 10–2 hammering of Queen of the South.

Their League Cup campaign was poor, finishing bottom of their group, although Gordon scored two goals in his five appearances. This chapter will mention other games briefly, including a decent run in the Scottish Cup, but will concentrate primarily on the amazing run in the European Cup.

On 15 August, the League Championship flag was unfurled for the one and only time in the history of Dundee Football Club as 21,000 fans cheered and sang prior to the League Cup victory over Celtic. The following Sunday, at a civic reception staged by the Dundee Council, the club was honoured at Dundee City Chambers.

Dundee had been drawn against West German Champions, FC Köln, in the first round of the European Cup and prior to the first match, Gordon sat down with the players one day after training and helped plan the tactics for the European tie. Now in his thirty-ninth year, his vast knowledge of the game was immeasurable and the squad would attentively listen to his advice as much as they would to their bosses Kean and Shankly. Everyone at the club was well aware that Gordon was better advised in the exploits of European adventures, having played in seven European Cup games already with Hibs and Hearts.

The two games played by Dundee against the West German opposition in New York City last summer gave great insight to the method of formation play favoured by the Continentals, which would prove to be a pivotal key to the Tayside team's future success. At training matches, as the initial European match drew closer, Smith would teach the players some of his 'tricks' and sitting watching approvingly was Shankly, who was preparing a big adjustment – he wanted to alter the team formation for the forthcoming match in Europe to a 4–2–4 system. The system had operated on the Continent for a few years now but was now becoming common in Britain. However, at training, the 4–2–4 system wasn't working out with the Dundee players 'all over the place'. Just hours before kick-off, Shankly was still indecisive, but conceded in the end, saying to the players to just 'go out and play as you know best'.

On Wednesday, 5 September 1962, Dundee Football Club created shockwaves throughout Europe. The bonnets of bonnie Dundee were tossed skyward-bound, as their team won 8–1 against FC Köln – the second favourites to win the tournament. Three goals from Alan Gilzean and one each from Wishart, Robertson, Smith and Penman, and an own goal by Hemmersbach, sealed an empathic victory, with the West Germans only reply coming from a Dundee player – a deflection scored by an unfortunate Alex Hamilton. The 25,000 Dundee fans were completely stunned by the incredible final score and were in total disbelief by the end of the game.

The club from the Rhine had started as favourites with ten internationals in their starting line-up, including skipper Hans Shäfer who was the West German leader when they won the World Cup in 1954 and Karl-Heinz Schnellinger, who was named best left back at the 1962 World Cup. The amazing score-line was a record defeat for the opposition, which prevails to this day. The score will stand as one of the greatest in the history of the European Cup.

FC Köln goalkeeper, Fritz Ewert, was carried off after an innocuous clash with Andy Penman in only the second minute and couldn't remember much after, thinking that the game was over at half-time; he was concussed enough to think the score was only 0–2 against his team – so subsequently he wasn't allowed back for the remaining forty-five minutes. Their right back, Anton Regh, took over in goal after the interval, with the score at 5–0 for the home side, as Smith had scored the fifth with seconds remaining of the first half.

Although the incident between Ewert and Penman was an accident, the German side made a great deal of it and accused all the Dundee players of being cheats, with Gordon being kicked up and down the park for a lot of the second period – but this was nothing compared to what was to follow in the second leg in three weeks' time.

An almost diffident Karl Frohlich, the FC Köln manager, remarked after the game: 'Our team did nothing right. They did not play according to plan and they did not tackle well enough. Dundee were wonderful and Gordon Smith is a professor of football.' The West German press, however, were not as articulate and rational as the team boss and were raging – making out the Penman/Ewert clash was deliberate.

On the plane across to West Germany for the return leg in the Mungersdorf Stadium in Cologne, Gordon sat next to his new goalkeeper, Bert Slater – who strangely wore his old team Liverpool's blazer for the trip. Bob Shankly stood up mid flight and told the seated squad not to treat the game like a 'walk-over'. Upon arrival in Cologne the day before the game, the Scottish team had an inauspicious start as they were told they had nowhere to train before the match. Worse was to follow with the terrible accommodation. When arriving for the evening match, the Dundee directors and officials were shunned by their German counterparts and not even offered a glass of water, never mind anything stronger! The Dundee side was jeered and humiliated from the minute they stepped on the pitch, yet that was nothing in comparison to what would occur during the game itself – the game that would become known as 'The Battle of Cologne'.

Another ominous sign was the stretcher-bearers, who had taken up position behind the goal of Bert Slater. The scurrilous West German media had been full of despicable remarks almost instructing the FC Köln players to 'knock out the Dundee goalkeeper' to 'make things even'. It would appear that Slater was a definite target, long before a ball had even been kicked.

Gordon described the game as the most menacing he had ever played in; even more intimidating than the other infamous battle when he played for Scotland in Vienna seven years previously.

The home team scored after just seven minutes and unfortunately, as the West German press and stretcher-bearers had heralded, Slater was carried off with blood pouring from his ear after a not-so-innocent challenge from a German boot minutes earlier. According to Smith, it was a 'quite deplorable challenge and quite intentional'.

Ironically, it was villain to North Rhine team, Andy Penman, who replaced Slater in goal, but was 'absolutely useless' according to his team-mates, letting in two further goals, making the score at half-time 3–0 to Köln.

Slater, who had been lying flat-out in a near-comatose state in the dressing-room, incredibly defied the orders of a waiting German doctor who had ordered an ambulance for him; he ran back out at the commencement of the second half with his head bandaged and started playing outfield on Gordon Smith's wing!

He was ushered back into goal soon after, as Penman had conceded another goal by then, and a penalty for FC Köln luckily hit the bar and rebounded to safety. Had it gone in, the West Germans would have only required two more goals to ensure a third match 'replay'. Severely concussed, to this day, Slater can still remember nothing from the second-half in which he saved shot after shot. If his gargantuan performance, alongside the brave tackling of Ure and Cox, hadn't been so good, the hosts could easily have won by double-figures, as some of the Dundee players froze on the night, completely losing their composure in the hostile atmosphere.

The game ended in an almighty mêlée, with Penman, Wishart and Ure having chairs wielded at them by irate fans and Gordon being tripped up and kicked as he lay on the ground at the end of the game. The German officials did not intervene and simply stood by as the Dundee number 7 hobbled back into the away dressing room, aided by two of his team-mates, with his legs and body bruised black and blue. It had taken the mediation of off-duty British servicemen to throw a cordon around the team, enabling them to escape.

Scuffles then broke out down the players' tunnel; fists were flying with the players, coaching staff and directors now all involved and it was unanimously decided that they would just go back to their own hotel and opt out of the official reception. Incredibly, FC Köln then bewilderingly invited some travelling Dundee supporters to the after-match banquet in the team's place; although flabbergasted and a little apprehensive by the peculiar request, they duly went, and were duly ignored and treated with the revulsion they had expected. But the supporters did nonetheless enjoy the meal – no self-respecting Scotsman would ever turn down free food!

The game will be remembered as one of the dirtiest and most brutal ever witnessed – both on and off the park – and for the performance of Bert Slater. The incredible goalie, sitting next to Gordon again on the return trip with a head that had ballooned-up overnight, was in an awful state awaiting hospitalisation back in Scotland – but this game, this 4–0 defeat, made Bert 'Punchy' Slater a hero.

One month later, on 24 October, Dundee lost to the Sporting Clube de Portugal in Lisbon by a solitary, dubious goal scored by Geo in the ninetieth minute. The French referee awarded a goal when Bobby Wishart had quite clearly kicked the ball from the goal line, but no amount of remonstrating by the Dundee players would alter the decision and the bizarre goal stood. As soon as the match was over, the Portuguese club arranged a banquet at a local restaurant for the Dundee players, coaching staff and directors; this time they went, although displeased by the unfortunate ending of the match! The menu for the sumptuous looking meal (if you can understand Portuguese) is below.

'O FAIA RESTAURANTE TÍPICO'
BANQUET DE HOMENAGEM DO SPORTING CLUBE DE PORTUGAL AO DUNDEE F.C. REALIZADO NO RESTAUTANTE TÍPICO < O FAIA> APÓS A PARTIDA DISPUTADA PELAS DUAS EQUIPAS, PARA A TAÇA DOS CLUBES CAMPEÓES EUROPEUS.
Lisboa, 24–10–1962

EMENTA

CALDO VERDE

BACALHAU À BRÁS

VITELA ASSADA C/ GUARNIÇÃO

PUDIM

MELÃO

CAFÉ e BRANDY

VIHNOS BRANCO e TINTO da CASA

The green cabbage soup, cod with scrambled eggs and baked veal were all deemed too dodgy to enter Gordon's mouth, so he asked for and received a plain omelette, followed by fresh fruit salad, complemented by a glass of still bottled water, and had retired for the night before the rest of the players and dignitaries were half-way through the banquet. Ever the adventurer!

One week later, on another bewitching Halloween, Dundee beat the champions of Portugal 4–1 in the return leg in the second round of the European Cup. The 32,000 crowd were entertained with no tricks, just treats. Well, maybe some tricks. Alan Gilzean scored a hat-trick but it was that old man of magic, Gordon Smith, the Merlin of Scottish Football, who brought a dream to reality. Gordon tantalised and tormented the bewildered Portuguese, as he helped create Dundee's first three goals with an assortment of his trickery.

Left back and captain Hilário da Conceição conceded to the press after the match that Gordon Smith was the man who caused their downfall. 'Smith was impossible all the game – I had to decide whether to follow him, or wait for him, but whatever I did was wrong. Smith is a wonderful player. He gave me a much harder game than Garrincha.'

Sporting Clube de Portugal left half, David Júlio, asked: 'How can we mark a man like Smith? He is too unorthodox and wily for planning!'

'No one in Portugal would believe that Smith is thirty-eight years old!' added the Lisbon coach, Juca.

Gordon checked the teams that had made it through to the quarter-finals of the elite cup alongside Dundee: AC Milan, Galatasaray, Feyenoord, Dukla Prague, Anderlecht, Hearts' conquerors Benfica and the team that beat Hibs in the 1956 semi-finals, Reims. They were all good, he thought, but told his brother he would prefer it if Dundee could avoid Benfica, Anderlecht or AC Milan – they looked the best teams. In the end, Dundee avoided only Benfica from this trio.

As has been already stated, the league season was up and down, but on 1 December, Dundee made another little piece of history – winning by their highest ever margin. The hapless Queen of the South were the unfortunate team that lost ten goals at Dens Park, seven scored by Alan Gilzean – four from Gordon Smith crosses, with Penman, Ryden and Houston scoring the remainder. Alan Gilzean had been a huge Hibernian fan as a boy and moreover a Gordon Smith fan, and the two had played against one another when Gordon made his Hearts' debut in the reserves and Gilzean, just returning from National Service, played for Dundee reserves. Both had scored that day and both made their respective full team debuts a few days later on 22 August 1959. Gilzean would later attribute a lot of his goals, on days like that of the Queen of the South game, to the pinpoint crosses by Smith.

Two days following this mammoth victory, as Dukla Prague player Josef Masopust won the Ballon d'Or for 1962, the draw was made for the European Cup quarter-finals. Dundee had been paired with one of Gordon's three teams to avoid – Belgian champions Anderlecht, who had previously defeated the majestic Real Madrid in the competition.

The winter of 1963 was the coldest on record and football was a casualty of the relentless snow and ice. Dundee only played two games in nine weeks – both Scottish Cup ties.

Friday evening of 11 January 1963, as the players slept in the team hotel in Inverness, Sammy Kean and Bob Shankly sneaked out in the middle of the night to inspect the pitch for the following day's cup tie! Outrageously, they had to break into Telford Park as it was obviously locked up for the night, Kean standing on Shankly's hands before being shoved up and over a boundary wall in order to view the pitch. 'All ok boss,' he had reported, 'no snow on the pitch – it's been cleared.' Kean then opened a gate from the inside to let an unbelieving Shankly see for himself. The following day, Dundee won 5–1 against Inverness Caledonian, with two goals by Andy Penman and one each from Robertson, Gilzean, and Cousin.

The weather was getting worse and no further games were played until the early February visit from Gordon's old hometown team of Montrose. The minnows were no match for their mighty neighbours, who crushed them 8–0, with Gordon scoring a spectacular goal against his early childhood heroes.

There was a further five-week hiatus from any form of football as the weather deteriorated further and Britain almost came to a standstill.

It was during these dark, snowy, bleak and miserable weeks that Gordon and his wife Joan conceived what was to be their one and only offspring, who would come into the world nine months or so later on 16 November.

On the evening of Sunday, 24 February, Gordon managed to drag himself away from his love-nest to applaud team-mate Ian Ure, who had won the 1962 Player of the Year award, with the celebratory event being staged at Dundee's Caird Hall. The weather closed in with severe blizzards and heavy snow, forcing Smith to stay in Dundee for a further four days at club chairman James Gellatly's home.

Belgian side, RSC Anderlecht, were Dundee's next opponents and they included the celebrated internationalists Laurent Verbiest, Martin Lippens, Jef Jurion, Jacques Stockman and wonder kid, nineteen-year-old Belgian player of the year, Paul Van Himst – who already had sixteen caps for Belgium. In recent years, Anderlecht had supplied almost the whole international Belgian team. Only goalkeeper Fazekas, the Hungarian, and number 7 Jassens had not been capped.

By the time Dundee played at Brussels, they had only played two Scottish Cup matches in two months due to the inclement weather, yet nonetheless they were to play like kings. The Dundee team arrived in the Belgian capital with Gordon and room-mate Andy Penman staying at the Palace Hotel, room number 75. Prior to the 6 March game, the players and officials visited the fields of Waterloo and then the players trained at Anderlecht's ground in the evening. The match had been moved to the grander Heysel Stadium to accommodate the expected 68,000 fans. Gordon would admit that night in Brussels was his favourite European game as Dundee beat the home side 4–1, with the team playing 'the best football they had ever played', according to Smith.

Just before kick-off, both Hector Nicol's Dundee song AND the Tannadice song were played to a bemused and laughing Dundee players before the game, as the Belgians didn't know which one to play; but their Scottish visitors sure knew what to play – scintillating football. Two goals for Alan Gilzean in the first half, and one each from Alan Cousin and Smith in the second, encapsulated a night of great possession play.

At the end of the game, not only did the whole stadium rise to applaud Dundee off the pitch, but each of the sporting Anderlecht players applauded, too – a very rare occurrence in the world of football. Dundee had been, for want of a better word, phenomenal.

During the after-match reception, each player was presented with a cigar box and silver cigarette lighter. Centre forward Alan Gilzean missed out on the reception, as he had been taken to hospital directly from the stadium to receive six stitches in an ankle wound. Concerned players waited back at the hotel for information, fearing the injury may have been worse.

The second game in the following week was a bit of an anti-climax after the tremendous effort that had been made in Belgium. Trainer Sammy Kean went ballistic at the players during the half-time interval, as they trailed 1–0 on the night to a Jacques Stockman strike. In the second half, Dundee were much improved, but without scoring – until, with ten minutes remaining, Cousin equalised and Smith scored from the right-hand edge of the penalty area, where he hit a left-foot shot that flew through the defence, struck the far post and settled into the net. His second and match-winning goal, scored six minutes from time, sent 40,000 Dundonians home ecstatically proud. Their team was in the semi-final, of the European Cup. 'Dundee are a great football team – even better than Real Madrid,' the Anderlecht coach conceded.

Five days later, in the third round of the Scottish Cup, Dundee defeated a vibrant Hibs side 1–0 in a pulsating match, with the solitary goal coming from the head of Alan Gilzean just before half-time. Rangers were next up in the quarter-finals and although drawing, Dundee lost the replay at Ibrox to a Ralph Brand goal scored in the last minute in front of an astonishing 83,000 fans. The defeat at Ibrox was Dundee's first in six years in Glasgow and it meant that they could now win only one cup: the European Cup – the final of which was to be held this year in London at Wembley Stadium. With Gordon and a few of his team-mates accustomed to playing there, it was felt that advantage could be crucial.

For the 24 April first leg semi-final of the European Cup, Dundee had been drawn against the illustrious Italian champions, AC Milan. Their sides, with crowds often exceeding 90,000, could earn as much as £70,000 for a game at the San Siro Stadium – an astronomical amount of money in 1963. They paid fantastic wages, with José Altafini, for instance, making at least £25,000 a year since moving over from Brazil. On a bonus of £700 a man to win, Milan, with nine internationalists including Cesare Maldini, Giovanni Trapattoni and Gianni Rivera in their line-up, 79,500 fans shouting and screaming their support, and certainly aided by a Spanish referee who was subsequently banned for accepting 'gifts', outclassed the Dundee side in a devastating second-half performance. Dundee players did receive a gift, too, but above board and not entirely useful – a 'nurse's watch' from the renowned downtown Milano gioielliere, R. Russo, with AC Milan written on the face!

Dundee had matched the Italians during the first half, when Cousin had cancelled out an early Dino Sani goal for the Italians; but a half-time team talk ruined Dundee's chances of beating AC over the two legs. Some players, now over-confident, thought they were invincible. Previous success had gone to their heads and there was reckless talk of going out to 'beat the dirty bastard Italians'.

A cataclysmic collapse ensued and they were to lose four second-half goals – all brilliantly executed – without scoring in reply. Again, without the exploits of Slater in goal, it could have been, according to Gordon, 'annihilation'. Although a fine side, they were a filthy 'spitting at every opportunity' team, according to Smith, who along with Alan Gilzean, had been kicked up and down the pitch all night by defenders Mario Trebbi and the Peruvian, Victor Benitez.

The atmosphere in Dundee was electric on 1 May, the day of the Milan return game. Although down by four goals, an early one tonight for the home side could change things completely; there was still hope of a miracle. Realistically, the fans, the players – everyone involved – was hoping for sunshine but preparing for rain. What they witnessed was one of the most bruising battles ever seen at Dens Park.

Dundee defeated AC Milan 1–0 and it could and should have been a lot more in another hostile European Cup match, with both sets of players sporadically fighting throughout the ninety minutes. Rivera kicked Gordon at the start of the game and the normally restrained number 7 had to held back by team-mate Alex Hamilton. This was a sign of things to come.

Dundee scored at a great time – on the stroke of half-time – from a Smith free kick perfectly placed on the head of Gilzean. Just after the re-start, Penman had the ball in the net as Dens Park went wild but the referee ruled the goal to be offside.

The home team pressed forward time and time again, requiring three more goals, and when a penalty claim for the Scottish side was rejected, another brawl between the players broke out. Alan Gilzean was sent from the field with six minutes remaining for attacking a defender who had felled Gordon Smith with a deliberate right-hander. Smith had again been targeted by the Italians and was fouled constantly – but this was the final straw for Gilzean. Nereo Rocco, the Milan coach, said after the game that Dundee had been a far improved side from the previous week in Italy. If the Dundee defence had been as strong then and if that half-time talk had been more restrained, who knows, it might have been a different story.

So AC Milan defeated Dundee 5–2 on aggregate but were then beaten by Benfica in the final at Wembley – if they'd got through instead, Dundee would probably have beaten the Lisbon side and won the European Cup. Imagine that: Dundee Football Club, European Champions! They would've been the first British club to win the trophy, four years before Celtic's magical night in Lisbon. If only that half-time team talk had taken a different shape in the away dressing room at the San Siro and Dundee had played with a different style in the second half. If only some of the impetuous players hadn't got carried away with the occasion and realised that the score at half-time was only the score at half-time; there were still forty-five minutes of play to follow! If only.

With hindsight, maybe Gordon ought to have called it a day after beating Milan at Dens Park that May Day evening, yet he was to continue playing top-flight football for one more season – rightly or wrongly. Nevertheless, this was Dundee's finest hour, and what an hour it had been. The 'hour' that had commenced in August 1961, ended on 1 May 1963.

30

THE FINAL SEASON

> With the three other clubs I had earned the right to play in Europe – I was with them the season they qualified – I haven't earned it with Glentoran – although the offer was very tempting.
>
> – Gordon Smith

FINALLY, to the mercurial Gordon Smith's last season in professional football. A season in which he played only twelve games for Dundee before walking out on the club because he wasn't getting a regular game and he felt guilty about taking wages without earning them. Then, a little bizarrely, he proceeded to make cameo appearances for Greenock Morton and north Dublin club, Drumcondra.

He ended his illustrious career playing on the wing for an All Stars XI in a charity game, donning, some would say appropriately, the green and white strip of Hibernian for this, his fond farewell, his football finale.

The same people would say that perhaps he played one season too many and should've ended his career at the top, following the 1–0 victory over the prodigious AC Milan, instead of playing alongside journeymen players and amateurs in his final few games. It did seem an odd way to end such a glittering career. On the other hand, should he possibly have continued – maybe even for a half a season further – when he could have represented a fourth team, Glentoran, in the European Cup?

When asked if he thought he had possibly made the wrong decision in fundamentally walking out on Dundee, his answer was simple: no. When asked if he thought, with hindsight, maybe he should've signed up for another foray into the European Cup, his answer was also an emphatic no.

When newly signed Arsenal and Scotland star Ian Ure was asked: 'Is there perhaps any one person you admire more than anyone else?' he replied:

> I think, perhaps, Dundee winger Gordon Smith. To me he is a symbol of everything that is good in football. Many people don't like him. I can't understand why. I have always regarded him, for want of a better phrase, as a paragon of all the football virtues.

Season 1963/64, Gordon's twenty-third and final as a professional footballer, started as always with pre-season training and Sammy Kean putting the players through their paces. This year, after Dundee's great European Cup run, Ian Ure had gone to London. He had been sold for a then world-record transfer fee for a centre-half: £62,500.

In the 29 September edition of the *Sunday Mail*, when asked, alongside other 'celebrities' including Jimmy Logan, Kenneth McKellar, Billy Butlin and Sir Compton McKenzie, 'Would you like to live to be 100?' Gordon, at thirty-nine, replied:

> It's not a question I can answer easily. Too much depends on physical fitness. I'd hate to live till I was 100 if I was going to be unfit . . . a drag to everyone. Maybe if you ask me the question when I become a fit seventy-year-old I could give you a straight yes. At the moment, I am too young to give you a simple answer.

On 7 October 1963, the Beatles topped the charts with 'She Loves You' and that night they played to a sell-out crowd at Dundee's Caird Hall. A group of the Dundee players went to the concert and were invited backstage to meet John, Paul, George and Ringo. The musical superstars were 'deeply honoured' to meet some of the 'fabulous Dundee FC players' whose European Cup exploits they'd apparently closely followed during the previous season.

Gordon, however, was at home in North Berwick, listening to 'real' music. Ironically, if you were to ask any of the Beatles backstage that night in Dundee what they thought of the likes of Fats Waller, Louis Armstrong, Sidney Bechet and Leadbelly, they would have said all of these artists had inspired them. This was 'real' music to them, too. These musicians had acted as forerunners and were heroes to the likes of Elvis Presley, Hank Williams, Buddy Holly and Little Richard, with the Beatles stating many times that they were influenced by such performers. Gordon at thirty-nine was too set in his ways, too stubborn to give the 'Liverpudlians with the long hair' a chance.

On 19 October, Dundee defeated Gordon's old team, Hibernian, by another decisive score-line. The 4–0 victory at Easter Road, one of Gordon's last matches for Dundee, featured future Hibs legend, Pat Stanton, making his home debut for the Edinburgh team. It was also a game in which Alan Gilzean scored all four Dundee goals – three of which were scored from inch-perfect crosses by Smith.

One month later, Gordon's wife Joan gave birth to the couple's only son, Anthony Gordon, born on Saturday, 16 November. Joan and the baby boy were assigned a private room at the hospital to allow Gordon to visit without any 'extra attention'. A few days later, John F. Kennedy was assassinated in Dallas – a day and time that most people of a certain age will never forget. As Gordon arrived to visit his wife and new son, news of the tragedy was breaking and in the ensuing days, many mothers changed their boys' names to 'John' in remembrance of the favoured US President – but not Joan and Gordon; they liked the name Anthony, for an assortment of reasons, and they were sticking to it!

A few weeks later, Gordon made one more appearance for Dundee at the New Year derby game on 1 January 1964 against Aberdeen at Dens Park. Gordon would play his last ever game for the dark blues in a 1–4 defeat in front of 15,000 carousing fans.

Interestingly, on the last few occasions that Gordon drove his Porsche to Dundee for training, he was accompanied by sixteen-year-old new Dens' signing George Stewart. Stewart would play for the Tayside club for twelve years and also win a trophy for the dark blues – the 1973 League Cup. Later in his career, he was an influential player at Easter Road and was part of the Hibernian team in 1979 that unluckily lost to Rangers in the 'three game cup final'.

Goalkeeper extraordinaire, Pat Liney, also departed Dundee at this time, amazingly having played only two games for the team since being nigh on invincible during the course of the championship season. He joined his hometown Paisley team, St Mirren, for £4,000 – the team he had supported as a youngster. Gordon had always thought it a crime that Liney, who had been superb in the championship season of 1961/62, had been unceremoniously dumped when Liverpool's Bert Slater arrived in the close season. Pat had saved a penalty in the penultimate game of that glorious season – had it gone in, history may have been altered. Gordon never forgot that and felt it was shameful the way he had been treated; yet he also acknowledged the brilliance of Bert Slater, too.

As Gordon, too, saw no future at Dundee, on Friday, 7 February, he spoke to Bob Shankly and asked to be released from the club. Gordon wasn't contracted to the club and had received no signing-on fee – this was part of the deal, unwritten, but secured with a handshake back in the early summer of 1961, therefore he was free to leave.

Gordon told the waiting journalists:

> I don't intend to play for any other club until the start of next season. If Dundee called on me between now and the end of April, I would willingly go back. I feel I owe it to them. Frankly, I've been ashamed to take their money recently. There's no satisfaction in receiving wages you haven't earned.
>
> Mr Shankly sincerely believed that it is in my own interests that I should play only once every few weeks. I don't agree with that. I'll be forty in May, but I'm thoroughly fit and I've never felt better. To lie off for long spells can only be detrimental to my play.
>
> It's as simple as that. Dundee have been wonderful to me. From chairman down to groundsman, they are a great club. My only difference with Mr Shankly was on this question of playing. I believe him to be sincere, but to me it doesn't make sense.

The Dundee/Smith parting was strange, as both sides appeared to be so unhappy about it. After nearly a hundred games, in two and a half seasons, Gordon would never pull on the dark blue of Dundee again. The end of yet another golden era for the thirty-nine-year-old had come.

He had been too upset to speak to his team-mates but personally sent a farewell and good-luck message to Dundee before their game against Motherwell the next morning. He said: 'I felt the parting too deeply to say goodbye to the lads personally on Friday.'

In another newspaper the following day, there appeared a cartoon with the then Hibernian boss, Walter Galbraith, sitting in his office and someone opening the door showing him the headline in the paper: 'GORDON SMITH IS FREE'.

The following morning, Gordon received this letter from his now ex-Dundee team-mate Bobby Seith.

> *Dear Gordon,*
> *I just had to write a few lines to say how sorry I was not to have been able to see you before you left. I got quite a shock when I first read that you were leaving us, but when I thought over how you were feeling the last time we had a talk – it seems ages ago – your decision to ask for your release is really not so surprising. It goes without saying that I am sorry to see you go as we had many happy times on the field and many interesting discussions off it. I hope however that we may still remain friends and that we may see each other many more times in the future both on and off the field. I hope too that if you are ever up this way that you will find time to pay us a visit.*
>
> *It only remains for me to wish you, Joan and Anthony the very best of luck in the future.*
>
> *Yours Aye,*
>
> *Bob Seith*

Gordon played, as a 'guest player', in a challenge match for second division Greenock Morton against top division Queen of the South. Smith had been enticed to play by Morton director/manager Hal Stewart and he proceeded to score in the 2–0 victory for his new side – his 403rd senior goal – which delighted the 3,000 crowd. Gordon gave his match fee of £20 to journalist Rex Kingsley for his 'charity for the blind'. By scoring in that game, he had completed a remarkable record that was only to be spoilt weeks later. He had scored on his debut for every single club team he had ever represented from schoolboy to Hibs, Hearts, Dundee, and now Greenock Morton.

On Sunday, 23 February, Gordon attended the 1963 Player of the Year show at the Glasgow Concert Hall. He sat alongside Willie Thornton, George Young, Willie Toner, Harry Haddock, Ian Ure and Dave Mackay, all previous winners who attended the show, which was headlined by variety act, Andy Stewart. The 1963 winner was Ian McMillan of Rangers.

The following week Gordon was offered terms by Canadian side, Toronto City.

TORONTO CITY SOCCER CLUB LTD
Varsity Stadium, Toronto, Canada

March 6th 1964

Dear Mr Smith,

Following your discussions with Bob Pennington, Rex Kingsley and George Cross and assuming that you are a free player, we are very pleased to invite you to play for our club for the 1964 Canadian soccer season.

We have been following your soccer career through the writings of Mr Kingsley and other columnists and would consider it a real honor if you would decide to accept our invitation.

Taking into consideration that we are a small club struggling to gain recognition, we would be prepared to offer you the following:

1 *Air passage for yourself, Mrs Smith and the baby to Toronto and return*
2 *Weekly salary of $125.00*
3 *Game bonus of $10 for a win or $5 for a tie.*

Hoping that you'll be able to accept our invitation to play for our club from May 8th until September 15th and looking forward to hearing from you at your convenience.

Yours very sincerely,

Steve Stavro

President

Gordon declined the offer and instead took up another one, nearer to home. On Friday, 6 March, he 'guested' for Drumcondra in the Football Association of Ireland Cup quarter-final clash with Drogheda at Tolka Park. His new team were to win 1–0 in front of 8,000 fans, but alas, Smith didn't score on his debut for this club, but did injure his notorious right ankle! Drumcondra were a north Dublin side and the arrangement was set up by Willie Murphy, Gordon's old friend, who knew the club chairman, Stephen Prole. He was to play two further games for the Irish club, scoring in a drawn league game against Shamrock Rovers on 22 March, but then losing to Cork in the semi-finals of the FAI Cup on Sunday, 5 April.

Two Sundays later, on 19 April, he was asked by the SFA not to play in an Edinburgh Students Charities match at Powderhall Stadium; the SFA frowned upon the match, as they opposed Sunday football. Whilst other stars of earlier years, who were still full-time professionals, called off, Gordon turned down their request and played nonetheless, saying, 'I am not registered with the SFA just now so don't see how it could affect me. I promised the students over two months ago and I am not letting them down now.' Heavy rain poured from the heavens throughout the match, with Gordon's team wearing Hibernian jerseys for what would turn out to be his final appearance, witnessed by more than 2,000 soaked fans.

Written in the match programme were the words: 'We apologise for the changes in the advertised teams. This has been caused by an SFA ban.'

The bunch of rogues who turned out with Gordon were: Jimmy Brown (Kilmarnock), Bobby Parker (Hearts), Jimmy McColl (Queen's Park), Tommy Gallacher (Dundee), Willie Woodburn (Rangers), John Paterson (Hibernian), Gordon Smith (Hibernian, Hearts & Dundee), Jimmy Wardhaugh (Hearts & Dunfermline), Harry Toff (mystery deputy for Lawrie Reilly, who was ill), Vic Rickis (Millwall) and an Edinburgh University player named Haynes who was a late representative in place of Dundee's Dave Curlett.

Following the game, won by the odd goal in nineteen by the Showbiz XI, Gordon received a letter from the 'sanctimonious SFA' stating that he was banned from playing football in Scotland for a 'period of time'. He was told he would have to write to them should he wish to 'rescind this assessment'. Imagine that – a player who was nearing forty and had given his heart, soul and twenty-three years as a professional to Scottish football had been banned for playing on a Sunday.

Nineteen years earlier, in 1945, he'd played for a Scottish Select in Celle on a Sunday, and again for Scotland's international side in 1948 in Paris, then in 1955 at Belgrade and Budapest. So it was ok then, in these European cities, but not in cheery Presbyterian Scotland during the swinging sixties!

The next day, Gordon received a letter from the Drumcondra Chairman.

DRUMCONDRA FOOTBALL CLUB
TOLKA PARK, DUBLIN 3

Dear Gordon,
My apologies for having omitted to write sooner, but time has simply flown. We picked up 4 points, winning at Sligo and Cork, so got 'a lift' up the table. If you hear of a good big centre half who would be willing to play over here we would be very interested. By the way, Roy had been expecting to hear from Mr Murphy.

It was very nice having you here and we wish to thank you for coming. It was also nice meeting Mr Murphy. I am sure we will be in touch with each other again in the future. Enclosed find cheque for last trip. With kind regards and best wishes also again very many thanks.

Yours sincerely,

S Prole

The following Saturday, Dundee lost to Rangers at Hampden Park in the 1964 Scottish Cup final by three goals to one. Would Smith have made a difference had he stayed? Would he have been chosen? Might he have won an elusive Scottish Cup medal at long last . . . three weeks away from his fortieth birthday? We'll never know.

At the end of May, Smith was seen back at Easter Road as the guest of manager Jock Stein, watching the current team defeat Kilmarnock 3–0 in the resurgent Summer Cup semi-final. Players such as Pat Stanton, Jimmy O'Rourke, John Fraser, Eric Stevenson and Neil Martin had caught his eye. This got the tongues wagging in press rooms up and down the country!

In June, Gordon Smith gave new Raith Rovers manager, George Farm, his first big disappointment. George wanted his former Hibs team-mate to join him at Kirkcaldy next season but it wasn't going to happen. Gordon told the Raith boss that he wasn't interested in playing second division football and a few days later it was reported that Gordon had been offered professional terms by Irish champions, Glentoran.

The east Belfast club wanted the veteran to play for them next season, when they would be taking part in the European Cup, and, if Gordon agreed, he would set up an amazing new record for the competition. But the bad news was, he was officially banned in Northern Ireland after playing on *that* Sunday and would have to go a-begging to the SFA and request they remove the ban.

Throughout the summer, the press were full of stories that Smith was going to apologise to the SFA and ask them to end his ban. Falkirk and Greenock Morton were both extremely interested, it was reported – but he was not interested.

Reports said also that Drumcondra wanted to take him back on a full-time basis for the forthcoming season. And the good news was, his ban had no jurisdiction there and *they* played on Sunday! This was an option he considered seriously after receiving another letter from Mr Prole, the Drums' chief.

On 1 July 1964, Gordon wrote to the Glentoran chairman declining his offer to sign for them, as he felt he would be a cheat by walking straight into the team without firstly earning that place. Had Gordon accepted Glentoran's offer, he could've then played for a fourth team in the preliminary round of the European Cup early the next month against Greek champions, Panathinaikos, who narrowly defeated the Northern Irish team 5–4 over two legs. Even more incredibly, had he returned to Drumcondra and played in the upcoming season, he may have been part of their Irish League Championship-winning side, thus enabling him to play in the 1965/66 European Cup at age forty-one without feeling he was 'cheating' anybody!

The media reported that maybe Gordon's SFA ban was for life, so he would have to play in Ireland, England or in Europe – and at forty, with business interests, it looked unlikely. The media were right.

On Monday, 20 July 1964, Gordon announced his retirement from the game with a valedictory statement:

From now on, I won't be kicking a football except in fun; it's going to be a tremendous wrench. It's going to be a complete break. I don't plan to have anything to do with football in any other capacity. Playing was my life; I wouldn't want to have any other part in the game.

You know, I always said I would quit when I was struggling, when I found it difficult to keep up with the pace of the game. Strangely enough, I am not struggling at all – I have just made the decision. The decision to give up playing has been a very difficult one to make.

I am retiring from football.

The very next day, as the newspapers were full of Smith's revelatory retirement news, the news reached Gordon of the death of Tottenham Hotspur and Scotland star John White, aged only twenty-seven. He had been playing golf during a storm and was sheltering beneath a tree when he was struck by lightning. Gordon was deeply upset upon hearing the tragic news.

At the end of that shocking week for Scottish football, *Daily Express* writer Brian Meek wrote an article on Gordon Smith.

He picked up a stone between his shoes, transferred it from one foot to the other, and smashed it towards an imaginary goal. Gordon Smith was still practising; but now it's just for fun. Smith, the finest thoroughbred Scottish football has sired in a century, has put himself out to graze.

At forty, the padlocks have finally snapped shut on his football boots. Yet, as Gordon Smith received me at his North Berwick bungalow, he seemed not to have changed at all. The same dark, wavy locks, the same tooth-paste-ad smile, the same age-defying vigour. It was all there, just as I had seen it eighteen years ago when I first watched him in a Hibs green and white jersey. It was then he first convinced me football was so much more than kicking and running.

To all little boys who stood in the rain and sleet and snow in green and white scarves, Gordon Smith was a weekly ticket to paradise. He was impersonated in every two-a-side match within cheering distance of Easter Road.

> To Hibs, he gave his heart and most of the skin on his legs. He was 'The Gay Gordon', 'Football's gentleman' and the number one of the Famous Five. He, more than any other player, made Hibs one of the greatest teams in the world.

So, as Gordon's football career ended on such a sad day for him personally, with news of the death of John White, the demise of Gordon's career was, to a lot of people, akin to that. Scottish football would certainly not be the same without him. He left behind a million memories etched in the minds of a million supporters across the land – for Scotland, for Heart of Midlothian, for Dundee, but most of all, for Hibernian.

Bob Crampsey, veteran football writer and historian would comment:

> Smith was the most complete Scottish player I ever saw. He was ahead of his time and a wonderful athlete and footballer. He looked after himself so well that he was able to enjoy a phenomenally lengthy career at the top level. It is the fact that he gained Championship medals at Hibernian, Heart of Midlothian and Dundee that makes him so special in my book.

Not only could he play a bit, he looked good, too. In the recent publication, *The Fashion of Football*, Gordon was named the 'First Metrosexual' by the former Scotland and Arsenal player Frank McLintock. 'One of the best-dressed footballers of his era, he looked great every time you saw him; fantastic style about the man,' said Frank.

Booked only three times in his twenty-three year career, he deemed two of these cautions to be 'totally unfair', but granted the retribution was spot on for a retaliatory foul on Rangers' nemesis Scott Symon. Hearts' Tam Mackenzie and Sammy Stewart from East Fife were possibly two left backs who, on occasion, held their own against Gordon but in the main, he came out on top.

In a mock interview arranged by his son many years later, Gordon would answer a few questions about his career.

On training and injuries:
I was always fairly fit, although you could only do the normal training at the club as they didn't encourage you to do your own thing. I had some bad injuries in my career. One thing that interested me was the way in which broken legs were covered in the newspapers. The tibia is the shin bone, and a few inches wide. If it breaks, then playing is impossible. However, the fibula was the smaller bone and players used to play on even if they were broken. I remember you would go to the likes of Airdrie, and they would pump the ball up until it was like a stone, then if it got wet, it got even heavier. Also, players wore toe-caps, so all in all, I reckon broken bones were more common, and the game was certainly different in many ways.

Most goals are actually made by somebody – and credit is not given enough to the creator, just the scorer.

I also once heard that McLaren of Raith Rovers had wanted to break my leg – he may have wanted to, but he never succeeded!

On his major memory of the Brazilians of 1953:
I think the Brazilians were then, and still are, the best in the world and it was fantastic to stand on the Copacabana beach and watch young boys keep the ball up in the air indefinitely.

On the Scotland international scene:
I always felt I was on trial for Scotland except for the 1955 tour – which was fantastic. A lot of people maybe don't realise that I played at numbers 7, 8, 9 and 11 for the international team over the years.

On his feelings toward retirement from the game he loved so much, a sometimes esoteric Gordon scribbled down:

Over the dusty years they come
Swiftly, their glory wanes;
Champions have but their day,
While the sport itself remains.

On his League Championship winning teams:

1 Hibernian 1947/48: Jimmy Kerr, Jock Govan, Davie Shaw, Hugh Howie, Peter Aird, Sammy Kean, Gordon Smith, Willie Finnegan, John Cuthbertson, Eddie Turnbull, Willie Ormond, George Farm, Archie Buchanan, Bobby Combe, Alec Linwood, Lawrie Reilly.

2 Hibernian: 1950/51 Tommy Younger, Jock Govan, John Ogilvie, Archie Buchanan, John Paterson, Bobby Combe, Gordon Smith, Bobby Johnstone, Lawrie Reilly, Eddie Turnbull, Willie Ormond, Mick Gallagher, Jim Souness.

3 Hibernian 1951/52: Tommy Younger, Jock Govan, Hugh Howie, Archie Buchanan, John Paterson, Bobby Combe, Gordon Smith, Bobby Johnstone, Lawrie Reilly, Eddie Turnbull, Willie Ormond, Mick Gallagher.

4 Heart of Midlothian 1959/60: Gordon Marshall, Bobby Kirk, George Thomson, John Cumming, Jimmy Milne, Andy Bowman, Gordon Smith, Jimmy Murray, Willie Bauld, Bobby Blackwood, Johnny Hamilton, Alex Young, Ian Crawford, Billy Higgins, Jim McFadzean, Wilson Brown.

5 Dundee 1961/62: Pat Liney, Alex Hamilton, Bobby Cox, Bobby Seith, Ian Ure, Bobby Wishart, Gordon Smith, Andy Penman, Alan Cousin, Alan Gilzean, Hugh Robertson, Alec Stuart, George McGeachie, Craig Brown, Bobby Waddell.

When asked which one was the greatest, a tactful Gordon, a little indignant at first by the question, sighed, and then all of a sudden smiled, before saying thoughtfully:

I think they were all pretty good, pretty sensational to be honest, in their own way, don't you?

31

LIFE AFTER FOOTBALL: FEMMES FATALES AND OPEN CHAMPIONS

WITH BOBBY JOHNSTONE retiring in December 1964 from Oldham Athletic – the last of 'the five' remaining – it was now well and truly the end of an incredible era. There was an abundance of 'press talk' regarding Gordon and the Scotland manager's job – with some papers intimating that he, at the very least, should be given a role in a coaching capacity, but Smith was having none of it. He had retired from football and that was that. Denis Law was crowned king of Europe as footballer of the year and it was time for the young Scots – the likes of the Manchester United number 10, Rangers' star Jim Baxter and Celtic's Jimmy Johnstone – to have their successes without any advice from 'a forgotten old man', as he thought of himself.

Although a private person, from time to time Gordon, coaxed by wife Joan, was talked into inviting luminaries from the golden days of the Scottish music hall and variety theatre to the Smith household, such as Hibs' fans Chic and Maidie Murray, Kathie Kay and on one occasion, Mr Moonlight himself, Frankie Vaughan. Joan herself had trod the boards during the 1940s and 1950s in Scotland as a 'crooner' in a singing variety combo. She had made her debut as a raw teenager on 4 August 1943, singing at the Central Halls in Edinburgh's Tollcross, with her favourite song being Hoagy Carmichael and Mitchell Parish's 'Stardust'. She predominantly performed in the west coast, in Glasgow and Ayrshire and, at times, in England at holiday resorts, where she would always end the dances and summer shows, 'giving it laldy' with her signature tune, 'Whispering Grass'. But it was performing back in her home city of Edinburgh, where she sang in an all-girl trio for her workplace firm, Alexander's, that she enjoyed the most.

The Smiths became especially friendly with the Murrays, recognised by millions through the years for their famous stage name, 'The Tall Droll with the Small Doll'. As the couple's bond grew, Gordon was presented with a photo of himself taken by Chic at St Andrews in 1957, showing Gordon and golfer Bobby Locke shaking hands following the South African's victory. When invited to Gordon's North Berwick home, Chic would entertain the couple with his always amusing stories – not too dissimilar to his stage act. On one occasion, he apparently borrowed Gordon's *Andy Capp* 'bunnet' during an impromptu performance that almost left Joan requiring hospital treatment for a swollen jawbone! Humour would even come into their sending of Christmas cards to each other. Chic's would be signed, 'It's Christmas. Chic Murray and Maidie, "The Giant and the Midget"' and a witty Gordon, not to be outdone, would retort, 'Yes, it's Christmas, from The Gay Gordon and the JAPS' – an acronym of his wife's full name, Joan Anne Parry Smith!

Another Hibernian-supporting husband and wife team in the showbiz scene, Johnny Victory and his Belfast-born wife, Betty, also became great friends of the Smiths, with Joan and Betty often going away for weekends together in the course of the 'swinging sixties'.

The Smiths would venture from time to time to the Palladium at Fountainbridge in Edinburgh, where, after shows, Gordon would regale the cast and crew with his tales, leaving them open-mouthed and in awe of the legendary footballer.

In early summer the following year, Gordon did have his boots back on once again alongside three of his old Famous Five colleagues: Eddie Turnbull, Willie Ormond and Bobby Johnstone. This account of the occasion by features writer John Fairgrieve is taken from the *Sunday Express*.

THE FAMOUS FOUR AT THE VILLAGE FIVES.

> If you don't happen to look right as you pass the road end on the A68, you'd never know there was such a place as Ancrum, in the county of Roxburghshire. There's a football field, a little bit farther on, however, and there among the cowpats, there played on Saturday, four-fifths of the finest club forward line of our time.

There was Gordon Smith, and there was Bobby Johnstone, and there was Eddie Turnbull, and there was Willie Ormond. Lawrie Reilly unhappily couldn't make it, as he was playing golf, but Lawrie Leslie, who played instead, was as able a centre forward as you might expect a high-class goal keeper to be!

The occasion was the annual five-a-side tournament of the Ancrum Amateur Football Club, and in the eighteen-year history of the event, there was surely never a five like this.

Smith still looks as if he could walk into any First Division team.

The five won their first three ties against some enthusiastic and not unskilful amateurs, by the simple and obvious expedient of making sure the other lot didn't get the ball!

Even remembering the quality of the opposition, and this is not intended as unkind comparison, it wasn't at all hard to see how, not so long ago, these former Hibernian players had carved up the best defences and earned themselves a place in football legend.

The skill was still there for the final but the steam wasn't, and they missed too many chances anyway. It was a pity, somehow, because by that time we were taking their eventual victory for granted.

But the host club, Ancrum Amateurs, won worthily and have plenty to boast about now.

Meanwhile, my five-year-old son, who stuffed himself with ice-cream and crisps and was very sick, will at least be able to say, in years to come, that the first outside right he ever saw was Gordon Smith. That's something to boast about too.

The autumn of 1966 brought an international superstar into the Smith household, completely by chance. Bridget Bardot, the French movie icon, was in Scotland shooting part of the film *Two Weeks in September* (*À Coeur Joie*) in East Lothian and stayed nearby Gordon's house in the village of Dirleton at The Open Arms Hotel.

On a day off from filming, whilst out for a walk with her new husband, Gunther Sachs, she encroached onto Gordon's property. Joan instantly recognised her and invited the couple in for coffee and some of her special bread pudding which she had just made. Bardot and Sachs accepted, and the following evening, the Smiths were invited by Bardot to dine with her and her husband at their hotel, where the two couples were joined by the hotel owner, Arthur Neil and his wife. The thirty-one-year-old Bardot, who was based in the French Riviera in St Tropez, was intrigued by Gordon's stories – not so much his football tales, but by his knowledge of the Cote d'Azur, and the two talked fondly of the late Sidney Bechet whom Bardot had also met on numerous occasions.

A few months later, in the summer of 1967, Gordon was the week's feature in the *Sunday Mirror.* They ran a serious of interviews with eleven players, who, in their opinion, were the finest from days gone by.

> *This is the £1 million line-up whose successes are being recaptured every week – Jimmy Cowan, George Young, Eric Caldow, Bill Shankly, Willie Woodburn, Bobby Evans, Gordon Smith, Bobby Collins, Lawrie Reilly, Billy Steel, Billy Liddell. This week: Gordon Smith.*
>
> *Who is your current favourite player to watch?*
> What is more exciting than a winger moving at speed past the full back, reaching the bye-line and then crossing a ball fast, hard and accurately for a centre forward to head into the net?
>
> The most impressive orthodox winger right now is Jimmy Johnstone of Celtic. I reckon he is the finest winger in Britain.
>
> *Why do you think you never reproduced your club form for the national team?*
> Mainly it was because I was not the first choice man for the Scottish teams. Willie Waddell was the man in possession and he never let Scotland down. As far as I was concerned I always admired Waddell and there was no doubt he was always a great player for Scotland. When I came into the international team it was because Willie had maybe lost form or because he was injured. I never seemed to be picked as the first choice and I never felt happy in these circumstances. Then it became the case that people said Gordon Smith never

played well for Scotland ... They accepted that ... and I accepted it too!

Only once did Smith escape this second-best tag ... the tour of Yugoslavia, Austria and Hungary in 1955.

For the first time, I was with Scotland knowing that for the three games, I would be outside-right, for I was the only right winger in their party!

Then George Young was injured against Yugoslavia and I was made captain for the other two games. That increased my confidence.

I played my best football for Scotland in these matches. Even at club level, I always had to feel that I had the confidence of the men picking the team, otherwise I did not play well. On that 1955 tour, I felt this confidence for the first time from Sir George Graham and the selectors.

Favourite players?

The most complete player I have ever seen was Di Stéfano. He had everything. And he had that quality that only great players have. The quality to take control of a game and make it go the way he wanted it.

I used to motor hundreds of miles to watch Stanley Matthews play. If I knew I could see a game with him in it, then I would be off to watch him. Matthews perfected the art of beating a man on the outside. No one in the world has ever been able to touch him on that.

As had been the case since the spring of 1949, golf had been Gordon's other major sporting interest. Following his retirement from football, he would play almost constantly for the next thirty years, with his handicap around the 5 mark for a great part of this, at one point reaching 2, then 1 for a number of years. With a little more drive (forgive the pun) perhaps he could have been a professional golfer; such was his love for the sport.

He would play with his old Hibernian team-mates and friends, Willie Murphy and Bill Brittee, in North Berwick and he would play in his own pub team, 'The 20 Club', at various venues throughout the summers. He would also still play a few rounds with four-time British Open champion, Bobby Locke – at least biannually until the South African's health impeded his wonderful ability and he was unable to play.

In between the running of his business interests in Edinburgh and his own golf schedule, he would venture to countless golf tournaments throughout the UK and Europe to watch the world's finest as a spectator, usually meeting up with Locke, who would introduce him to the current stars.

The same summer of 1967 saw Gordon travel to the Royal Liverpool Golf Club at Hoylake where Jack Nicklaus came second to Gordon's bet to win, Argentinean Roberto De Vicenzo. Following the tournament, a jubilant Smith, along with Locke, attended pre-season matches at Anfield and at Old Trafford, at the behest of Bill Shankly and Matt Busby.

A few weeks later, Gordon received an invitation from the captain of the Cunard ocean-going liner, the RMS *Queen Mary,* to sail on the ship's final voyage to Gibraltar, Lisbon and Las Palmas. On 29 September, accompanied by his wife and son, he embarked from Southampton on the massive Clyde-built ship – of which Gordon had many memories of seeing depart the west coast during his early years at Hibernian.

Cabin A15 was to be their home for the next three weeks, with the highlight of the trip, apart from Bay of Biscay sea-sickness, being their son's winning of the *Top of the Pops* competition – according to the four-year-old anyway!

The following year, Gordon's golf was improving so much that, according to Gullane professional Hugh Watt, he would be a 'scratch' player before the year was out. He continued to travel all over Britain to tournaments, watching his new 'hero', two-time US Open Champion and current PGA tour-leader Billy Casper. Bobby Locke was still suffering the after-effects of his 1959 car crash and was starting to take a back seat in major competitions; hence the American, now at the forefront of Smith's affections.

Gordon was disappointed as Casper finished in fourth place at the year's Carnoustie Open Golf Championship, with Locke's fellow countryman, Gary Player, the victor. Following the Tayside event, Gordon held an impromptu putting competition on his own private putting green in his garden for Ryder Cup star, Englishman Malcolm Gregson, Billy Casper and Bobby Locke. By all accounts, the contest was a serious affair, with Smith, having home advantage, winning after Locke suffered from 'the yips' at the 18th hole.

Daily Record sports journalist Cyril Horne wrote that he was the one who had the great pleasure of introducing Casper to former Scotland outside-right, Gordon Smith:

> Gordon, his wife and little son had travelled overnight to Wentworth for the primary purpose of watching Casper, Gordon's current golfing hero, in action. They had made the same kind of pilgrimage to Carnoustie in July and to Royal Birkdale last week for the ALCAN Golfer of the Year championship.
>
> When Gordon met Casper he told him:
>
> 'I have always been a fitness fan and I have great admiration for your self-discipline in keeping your weight down and retaining full physical fitness.
>
> 'I know that I speak for many people all over Britain when I say that they have a feeling for you, that they believe that you are a man of principles and scruples as well as a super golfer.
>
> 'I have seen you take the bad with the good with the greatest of good grace. I can assure you that you will have a wonderful welcome everywhere you go if you become a regular visitor to these islands.'
>
> Casper replied:
>
> 'Well, Gordon, I have had many kind things said to me in Britain – but this sure has been the nicest of them all.'

The end of 1968 marked the golden wedding of Gordon's parents but joy was to turn to sorrow when, a few months later, whilst on holiday in Cannes, Gordon received a telephone call late one night, informing him that his father had died, aged seventy-eight. Through that very night, there had been a massive thunderstorm in the French Riviera and both Gordon and wife Joan had been woken by an enormous rattling in the wardrobe. They were convinced they witnessed a shape, a figure in the form of a young boy, heading toward their son Anthony's bed; both were frozen to the spot when a knock at the door, informing Gordon of the phone call from home, disturbed 'the figure'. Had this been an omen, a premonition of the bad news to follow?

Just before the end of the 1960s, a Brazilian football encyclopaedia was published devoting an entire chapter to the skills of Hibernian FC and, as usual, commended the Famous Five during their visit to the South American country sixteen years prior. The chapter in question came with graphics illustrating the positional interchanging with which the Hibs' attack bewildered defences and won three league titles in five years. With Gordon and his fellow Hibernian players credited for inspiring part of the success of the wonderful 1970 Brazilian team, it was certainly something to be proud of.

A decade was ending, a decade at the start of which Gordon had been told he was finished. A decade in which he won two further League Championships, a Scottish League Cup and played in the European Cup on a further two occasions; only ceasing to be a professional player at forty years old, when he knew that he would not be able to give a club what he had 'been capable of in the past' – though many a team would've been glad of his services, even then, at the age of forty-five.

Although now out of the game completely, Gordon was very pleased that three of his most respected friends in the sport were to be the main beneficiaries of glory in the mid-to-late 1960s since his retirement: ex-Tottenham Hotspur opponent Alf Ramsey, ex-Celtic rival Jock Stein and former Hibernian colleague Matt Busby, now household names throughout the football world. Ramsey's England were to be first in 1966, winning the World Cup on their own patch with Gordon especially pleased for Bobby Charlton and Bobby Moore, who he had a lot of respect for as opponents in his playing days.

The following May, on the eve of his forty-third birthday, Gordon watched Celtic become the first British club to win the European Cup – four years after it could have so easily been Gordon himself holding the gleaming and magnificent cup aloft, with Bob Shankly's Dundee coming to within ninety minutes of a Wembley final. But it was to be Lisbon's Estádio Nacional that was the setting for the Celtic team's famous victory, and again players such as Billy McNeill, Bobby Murdoch, Bobby Lennox and Ronnie Simpson had played against Gordon, with Stein receiving an extra large congratulatory telegram.

One year later and it was Matt Busby's turn to receive a laudatory message from Gordon. His Manchester United team followed on from Celtic's success by winning the 1968 trophy with 1966 heroes, Nobby Stiles and Bobby Charlton, once more in a 1960s' groundbreaking side. As well as Charlton from the victorious team, Smith knew Paddy Crerand well as an opponent from his days at Celtic; he'd also played against and socialised with Bill Foulkes and Shay Brennan whilst on Hearts' tour of the USA and Canada; and he knew man of the match John Aston's father, also called John Aston, very well since his Old Trafford days during the 1950s. Gordon was as absolutely delighted with this result, as he had been with the previous two, enough to feel compelled to make a 2am congratulatory telephone call to Busby and his players.

On Wednesday, 10 February 1971, Gordon was back playing the game he loved best. Alongside luminaries and old friends such as Stanley Matthews, Ferenc Puskás, Tom Finney, Nat Lofthouse, John Charles and Nándor Hidegkuti, he starred alongside fellow Scots, George Farm, Willie Fernie, Graham Leggat, Bert McCann, Jimmy Wardhaugh and Willie Woodburn in the Ford Fives European Festival at Meadowbank Stadium, with the trophy presented to winners by the 1969 world champion racing driver, Jackie Stewart.

That summer, to commemorate fifty glorious years at Easter Road, Gordon presented a medal to Hibernian coach Jimmy McColl. With the arrival of new manager Eddie Turnbull, fresh from great success at Aberdeen, Gordon was back on the scene at the Leith club and would take his seat in the directors box for the new glory years – the years of 'Turnbull's Tornadoes' as they became known – the greatest Hibs team since the 1950s.

During the spell of the new glory years at Easter Road, Gordon would have lunch at the Braid Hills Hotel before dropping his son off at his sister's tenement flat in Bothwell Street. The 'Braids' had great memories for Gordon, as he had often stayed there overnight before a prominent game during Hibernian's halcyon days in the late 1940s and '50s, becoming well acquainted with Irish waitress Agnes, cocktail barman Martin Rowell and especially with the owners, Mr and Mrs Grant.

It was whilst at Muirfield in 1972, with his three golfing buddies, Bobby Locke, Malcolm Gregson and Billy Casper all playing, that

Gordon was introduced to ace RAF World War Two fighter pilot, Group Captain Sir Douglas Bader. Locke, who himself had been a first-rate pilot for the South African defence force during the war, introduced the pair. They got on so well that Bader invited Gordon down to his home near Wentworth golf course, where Gordon, by all reports, had a superb time; in addition to golfing, the gents went to football games in London and socialised in top Knightsbridge restaurants.

In the next few years, Gordon spent even more leisure time on the golf course than before, playing in most months of the year on a daily basis. He was playing more and more with Bobby Locke, who wrote in one letter:

Frinlay Hall Hotel
Camberley
Surrey
14th June 1975

Dear Gordon,

Just a few lines to let you know that I arrived over – three days ago. After a good flight from Johannesburg.

I will be arriving at North Berwick (at the Marine Hotel) on Thursday 26th June, and was wondering if we could have a game at Duddingston on the 27th – I want you to put me right – am hitting the ball with no 'EFFORT' and getting no 'DISTANCE'.

Will give you a ring when I arrive on the 26th.

Must close with Kindest Regards and Best Wishes to Joan, Gordon Jnr, and yourself.

From your friend,

Bobby Locke

Gordon wrote back a long letter, which – quite extraordinarily – included some tips for the former World Number 1 golfer! Part of the letter and the advice read:

Dear Bobby,

Check grip very carefully, turning hands into each other, and very relaxed. Stand to full height with knees relaxed and pointing inwards; right foot square to line of flight – push back with left hand-arm-shoulder . . . pull down, concentration on head position, (on to both feet) checking that shoulders are square when hit is made; mainly with right hand, with left hand squaring to the ball, and continue straight through.

Later the same year, Hibernian Football Club celebrated their centenary with a night to remember at their usual venue for grand events, the North British Hotel in Edinburgh's east end, with, as usual, Gordon and his Famous Five cohorts taking most of the plaudits. Amongst the hundreds of invited guests were two former Hibs managers, and two great friends of Gordon's, Jock Stein and Bob Shankly. Earlier that year, they had both been involved in a serious car crash when a car travelling in the opposite direction on the A74 (now M74) careered into their path, hitting them head-on – Stein, especially, was lucky to survive.

Over the course of the next few years, Gordon's golf travels would take him to Gleneagles, Carnoustie and Royal Birkdale. He especially enjoyed the 'duel in the sun' between Jack Nicklaus and Tom Watson at the Ayrshire course of Turnberry.

As the decade drew to a close, Gordon's son – who everyone thought would play football professionally and emulate his illustrious father – was showing a decent level of playing ability with local juvenile teams Belhaven, Haddington Star and then Salvesen Boys' Club. He trained with Hibernian on Tuesday and Thursday evenings, being put through his paces by the talented and assiduous coaches Stan Vincent, John Fraser, Jimmy O'Rourke (ex-Hibs players) and John Lambie; whilst his old man's Famous Five colleague (now legendary Easter Road manager) Eddie Turnbull would on occasion oversee proceedings like a boorish, malevolent and vociferous Mafia don; screaming abuse whenever he deemed it necessary to do so – which happened to be incessantly. Yet in spite of his hostile demeanour, Eddie unquestionably knew the game he loved inside out and with a passion.

From time to time he would heap praise on the teenager and the other trainees for 'doing what he'd told them to do', albeit perhaps a little grudgingly! The young Smith ended up playing semi-pro soccer in the USA for the San Francisco Scots XI – but regrettably wasn't to make the grade.

At the end of that season in May 1979, Hibernian reached the final of the Scottish Cup and played against Rangers in a dynamic trio of matches watched by a total of 114,716 fans. Sadly, they were to lose by the odd goal in five in the third encounter of the extravaganza, which lasted sixteen days from the initial Saturday final through to the second replay. Gordon was deeply upset at the outcome, as he had been caught up in the whole ordeal, even relenting enough to be pictured at Easter Road alongside 'the other four' with a 'Hibs for the Cup' rosette embellishing his jacket.

The following season, with Hibernian struggling in the top division, the club chairman, Tom Hart, made an audacious signing in that of the legendary ex-Manchester United and Northern Ireland hero, George Best, who, unfortunately, failed to keep Hibs from being relegated that season but certainly paid for himself by the huge rise in attendances that would come out predominantly to see him play.

The genial Belfast boy's twenty-five appearances for the Easter Road side were unfortunately overshadowed by his well-publicised drinking exploits in bars such as the hotel he stayed in when in Edinburgh, the North British Hotel, and the Jinglin' Geordie bar in Fleshmarket Close. There were reports that Best had ventured down to Willowbrae Road in search of Gordon and was seen having a couple of 'shandies' in The Right Wing, but it was a week night and Gordon wasn't in. George and Gordon did meet whilst Best played for Hibs – as they had done previously some years before – and although Gordon appreciated George's talent for what it was and found him to be a charming and gracious person, he found it difficult to excuse him for what he had put his friend, Matt Busby, through at Manchester United.

On 4 May 1984, Gordon was devastated by the death of Famous Five associate, Willie Ormond, who he had been very close to, often seen at his Musselburgh public house The Footballer's Bar, discussing tactics with the great former Scotland manager.

As well as Best's visit to The Right Wing, some other celebrities were seen on occasion having 'a jar or two', including Gordon's old golfing superstar, Bobby Locke, comedian Chic Murray and local Duddingston-based former Scottish Amateur Champion golfer, Ronnie Shade.

Another local boy, Northfield's World Boxing Champion, Ken Buchanan, would pop in every so often for a soft drink and world famous actor, Richard Burton, would come in from time to time, as his brother and niece lived locally on Milton Road.

Towards the end of 1985, news that Gordon was thinking of selling The Right Wing was rife amongst the locals and, fittingly, one of Hearts' greatest ever players, John Robertson – then only twenty – was one of the last customers to be served. 'Robbo', from a Hibernian supporting family, is the only player to have eventually scored more goals than Gordon in Edinburgh derbies. Gordon's fifteen equalled Hearts' Tommy Walker but were dwarfed by the twenty-seven scored by Robertson for the Tynecastle club, though Smith's fifteen goals do make him the top Hibernian scorer of all time against Heart of Midlothian.

32

PRIZED BOOTS SENT TO THE CRUSHER!

IN 1985 GORDON SMITH sold his public house to Edinburgh businessman Jimmy Doonan, after running it from its conception for thirty years. He still owned his Willowbrae Road house and grocers' business, which still included a post office and newsagents shop – well established since 1947, but he had leased them out a few years previously. He was sixty-one and planned to enjoy his retirement. A retirement that would be traumatized by the onset of Alzheimer's a mere six years later.

Gordon, of course, continued to play golf at Longniddry most Sundays through the summers with a number of his former Hibernian team-mates, and he still enjoyed his excursions to London to watch Test Match cricket and to Cannes. One year, he was even tempted by his wife Joan to go on a coach tour to Holland instead of his beloved Riviera! He would watch football predominantly on television, including the sensational Diego Maradonna's magic at the 1986 Mexico World Cup and took much pleasure in tending to his garden. The quiet life was all he really craved now.

He saw Bobby Locke, his great friend, for the last time the year before Locke's untimely death aged just sixty-nine in the spring of 1987. They had played golf at Duddingston and at Muirfield but Gordon noticed Bobby was growing frailer and had lost weight. The friends parted after the golfing superstar had visited the Smith household one last time – losing in a putting competition in Gordon's garden, reminiscent of the famous one back in the late sixties. This time he was to lose at the 18th hole again – this time to Anthony, Gordon's son, who was on sparkling form that day. Tragically, a few years after his friend's death, Gordon was to receive word of the 'champagne suicide' of Locke's wife and daughter – who had struggled to cope after the death of the South African golfer. Mary and Caroline, who had, over the years, become close friends of the Smith family, were found together hand in hand after drinking champagne laced with cyanide.

Gordon was an honoured visitor to Rangers Football Club in September 1987 with Jim Blair of the *Daily Record* writing the following:

> Two of the best right wingers Scotland has ever produced came face to face on Saturday at Ibrox Park; and all they did was talk football!
>
> The Willie Waddell Suite at the Rangers stadium has been a tremendous success, and it prompted the one-time winger, manager and Scotland international to invite the great Gordon Smith as his guest.
>
> In fact, I'm told it was Smith's first look at a top class Scottish game in seventeen years! (Probably nearer a dozen).
>
> It was also something completely different to see a queue of autograph hunters who were aged between forty-five and fifty-five.

Two years later, he attended the Famous Five presentation night in the summer of 1989 – the honouring of the five legends by the Hibernian FC Supporters Association.

The following year, he was enthralled by World Cup – Italia 90. He was impressed by the teams, especially Italy, Argentina and England, as well as enjoying the football played by Paul Gascoigne. Along with the amazing football, it also helped Gordon find a new genre of music at a late age – opera! It was brought to him and millions of others by The Three Tenors – Luciano Pavarotti, Plácido Domingo and José Carreras – during their iconic concert from Rome in the midst of the tournament alongside the constant playing of Pavarotti's 'Nessun Dorma' played on TV throughout the contest. This World Cup would be one of his all-time favourites, ranking alongside the 1962 and 1970 events. STV producer, Alan Pender, had made a documentary on Scottish football and Gordon had recorded his part in his garden during the course of the tournament in Italy, with Pender invited to watch some of the action with the former Hibernian superstar.

While mainly watching football on television, he was coaxed from time to time to attend live games, and on one occasion later that year, it was the turn of his ex-Dundee team-mate, Bobby Wishart, to entice Gordon to a game. The alluring Meadowbank Thistle versus their old team, Dundee, was the spectacle; both men had a great time catching up, sharing the vivid memories of their great days in the early 1960s.

The spring of 1994 was to bring his last ever interview before his wife's untimely death and his own Alzheimer's took hold. He once again spoke to his great admirer, the journalist John Gibson of the *Edinburgh Evening News*.

> I reckon I experienced the last of the good days in the Scottish game. Even in '64 it compared favourably with the great stuff that the likes of Hibs, Hearts and Rangers had served up to crowds of 50–60,000. I see all my football on TV now and it's the Italians on Channel 4 who show us how the game should be played, not that they're perfect.
>
> Football gave me a lot, though I like to think I put a lot into it in return. For the last sixteen years of my playing days, I combined football with a business, a grocer's/post office at Willowbrae, and for the last nine years, I also had The Right Wing, a successful bar.
>
> I gave all that up a long time ago and I've been relishing the simple life with Joan, the girl I married thirty-four years ago. She was a fanatical Hibs follower, a Gordon Smith fan. She had been a regular at Easter Road before we met.
>
> I'd have liked it if my son Anthony had stuck with football. I felt he had plenty of ability. He was a centre half, with strong legs like his father's. But he didn't really apply himself, didn't appreciate that he really had to make a great effort to get somewhere in football. Mind you, he'll tell you that too many people kept telling him he'd never be as good as his dad and he didn't enjoy living in my shadow. Anyway, he chose music for a living. He loves what he's doing and that's fine by us. His music gives me a lot of pleasure and I'm very proud of him.
>
> I can't see Joan and me ever moving from East Lothian. We've spent all our married life there and enjoyed the peace and quiet, the air, the proximity of salt water. I walk a lot; do a wee bit of jogging . . . I can still run.

One hot, sunny afternoon, as Gordon and Joan cleared out the garage, they found a pair of the former player's old moulded Adidas football boots – boots that Gordon remembered he had worn, putting 'an early '50s' date on them.

After trying them on for the first time in years, he said that they 'fitted like a glove'. His son, who had just arrived, was invited to have a kick-about in the garden, where the pair proceeded to keep the ball up on countless occasions as well as play a game of 'head tennis', with Gordon running around like he was thirty years younger but with even more grace, agility and fervour than was customary.

Later that evening, Gordon and Joan discussed the find and came to a decision to have the 'precious boots' cleaned up and put in a display cabinet, as they held so much sentimental value; but after placing them in a plastic carrier bag in the kitchen, the boots were never to be seen again! The next day was 'bin day', and for some inexplicable reason, the boots in all probability found themselves in the rubbish lorry; the plastic carrier bag must have inadvertently been placed in 'the big black bag' by an unaware Joan, Gordon or Anthony whilst rushing to take the refuse out.

That afternoon, once it had dawned on everyone what must have happened, and only hours after the rubbish was lifted, the Smith family were to be seen at the local dump for approximately four hours searching for the old boots – but to no avail. Despite the aid of 'helpers galore', as word got round the town, no one was to come out lucky in the futile search. At one point, Gordon was standing on top of a mass of 'unsavoury matter', rummaging with a stick in desperation, but the boots were never seen again.

To think that these boots could have won three, possibly four League Championships, and were worn by, in today's market, the '£50 million pound feet' of such a superstar at countless magnificent football parks all over the world. Could these have been the boots that kicked a ball in British football's opening European Cup night in Essen in 1955? Could these have been the boots that were worn in Gordon's last European Cup match against AC Milan in 1963? Could the boots have possibly scored Gordon's last international goal at the Estadio Santiago Bernabéu on a sultry May evening in Madrid? Nevertheless, they ended up in the crusher. Maybe somebody did find them, but more than likely proceeded to throw them away instantly as they looked like an old pair of boots!

The death of Sir Matt Busby at the age of eighty-four in early January 1994 upset Gordon terribly with a bout of influenza stopping him from attending the funeral, but on a much happier note, he and Joan became extremely proud grandparents later in the year, thoroughly enjoying their 'elder role', playing with the little boy named Danaan Patrick whenever they could. But their blissful happiness was rocked two years later and Gordon was completely confounded and devastated by the death of his wife Joan in October of that year, after a short yet horrendous battle with liver cancer.

For months after her death, he would try to contact her through the medium of spiritualists, going to meetings all across Scotland, whilst tending to her grave on an almost daily basis at the beginning. Eventually, however, as Alzheimer's took hold, his moral fibre diminished and his desire to contact her waned. As his illness grew worse, he would still continue to travel around the country watching his son, now a professional musician, and took great enjoyment from the trips all over Scotland and the UK.

At one local gig at North Berwick's Marine Hotel, international music superstars the Bee Gees were in town and Gordon's son was playing an opening solo piano set for Barry Gibb's parents-in-law's Golden Wedding celebrations. Gordon turned up to watch his son in action playing alongside the music legends but on this occasion, he was thrown out by heavy-handed police officers who thought he was merely a 'gate-crashing disco fan' – if only they had known who he really was, rather than 'the receding piano player's father', he should have said: 'Gordon Smith, the ex-footballer!'

Cale Jackson, a second grandson for Gordon, was born in early 1998. However, over the next two or three years, Gordon's health deteriorated a great deal and he became unpredictable at best. The year of 1999 brought a sudden and severe decline to this most proud of men. He had been forgetting names and places and suffering what turned out to be the early stages of dementia for seven years or so now, but this year the brain disease proliferated and he took a turn for the worse.

He increasingly stayed within the confines of his home and garden in the following years and his final get-togethers were attending 'The Golden Years' at Easter Road – a celebration of his Hibernian team at their and his peak – and he attended the official 125th Hibernian Football Club dinner in May 2001, where long queues formed for his prized signature. Unbeknown at the time, these were to be the last autographs he was ever to inscribe.

Days later, on his seventy-seventh birthday, Gordon attended his final Hibs match, the Hibernian versus Celtic Scottish Cup final. His final act for the 'Hibs family' was turning out for the funeral of his former co-star, Bobby Johnstone, in Selkirk later the same summer, the second of the five to die, following Willie Ormond's extremely premature death in 1984. The following April, in 2002, Smith attended his last ever football function – the fortieth anniversary of the celebrated Dundee champions of 1962, arguably his and Scotland's finest ever side.

During the course of the subsequent nine months, Gordon's health deteriorated dramatically, so much so that his son was strongly advised by doctors to place his father in a residential care home. The first of two care homes in East Lothian was in Haddington; the latter, Copper Beech in North Berwick, back near his seaside home, was where he would draw his final breath.

On Friday, 5 December 2003, he was inducted into the Scottish Sports Hall of Fame at the National Museum of Scotland, and whilst too ill to attend in person, his son and eldest grandson accepted the honour on his behalf.

In the spring of the following year, he became a granddad on a third occasion, this time to a little girl called Marly Lia, the first female Smith in seventy-five years, who, along with his two grandsons, would visit him on a regular basis at the residential home. Just under two years later, another granddaughter, Jaiden Aiyana, would be born; regrettably, Gordon would not survive to see her first smile.

Amongst Gordon's last visitors outside immediate family were Bridget Gordon (now Bridget Hill), his great friend since the early 1950s, who would come through from her Glasgow home to visit him, and his old Hibernian team-mates, Tommy Preston and Lawrie Reilly, who would do their best to reminisce about great football stories with their former dear companion – hoping to trigger a reaction. All were distraught on seeing Gordon like he was – listless and unresponsive – and felt at times their journeys may have been futile, yet they would come back time and time again to see Gordon.

The last ever photo of Gordon was taken at his eightieth birthday 'celebrations' on 26 May, portraying him holding baby Marly – and a football! By his side were son, Anthony, and his two older grandchildren, Danaan and Cale. He just sat there staring into space until the football came into the room. When the football was brought out, he remarkably appeared to perk up and when given the ball, he started keeping it up in the air with his head – whilst sitting down in his chair! This continued for a ten-minute period, with the whole family throwing the ball at 'Granddad' and he repeatedly headed it with precision timing like the true athlete he was. It was if he had 'come alive' one last time though this, sadly, was to be his final game.

A few weeks later, he fell and broke the femur bone in his right leg and was in and out of hospital during the early part of the summer; the change in his surroundings proved too much for him and he never recovered. By the last Friday in July, he had stopped eating and whilst his son did his best to spoon-feed him, he was told that his father was dying. Gordon Smith had given up.

On 7 August 2004, the opening day of the new SPL season, Gordon died in the care home after nearly eight days in a close to comatose state, clinging on to dear life by a thread.

Six days following his passing, a funeral attracted a huge turn-out, with a large number of his football friends in attendance and appropriate eulogies superbly read by the renowned cerebral genius, Bob Crampsey, and Gordon's old Hibernian-supporting *Edinburgh Evening News* columnist, the genial and inquisitive, yet unobtrusive, John Gibson.

Two weeks later, he was honoured by two of his clubs, Hibernian and Dundee, as they fought out an entertaining 4–4 draw in Leith, with his grandsons running out at the start of the game as club mascots with current Hibernian heroes, Garry O'Connor and Derek Riordan by their side. During the half-time interval, a dazzling array of old players, representing each of Gordon's three teams, along with family members, was paraded on the pitch.

Stars from Hibernian's great 1940s and '50s side – including the two remaining legendary Famous Five colleagues, Lawrie Reilly and Eddie Turnbull – Heart of Midlothian legends from the 1960 championship-winning side, and greats from the Dundee champions of 1962, lined up in Smith's honour. Gordon's son, Anthony, with his girlfriend Louise, grandsons Danaan and Cale and granddaughter baby Marly mingled with the quite visibly upset ex-players in the centre-circle and accepted the standing ovation and cheering from both sets of supporters honouring this great servant to Scottish football on one last occasion at his spiritual home, Easter Road.

A week later, in what was to be the ultimate of only two Festival Cup competitions, this year fittingly renamed. The Gordon Smith Cup, Tony Mowbray's Hibernian lost at Tynecastle to Craig Levein's Hearts, in a closely fought game, with Gordon's son presenting the trophy to the winning Hearts captain on the day, Robbie Neilson.

Gordon Smith was posthumously inducted into the Hibernian Football Club Hall of Fame in October 2010 alongside fourteen others including his old visionary chairman, Harry Swan; Leith legends, Joe Baker and Pat Stanton; and the four other Famous Five members. On 29 April 2012, Gordon was installed into the Dundee FC Hall of Fame, flanking other Dens Park heroes such as Alan Gilzean, Pat Linney and Ian Ure.

His name had previously been added to the list of greats in the Scottish Sports Hall of Fame joining the likes of Kenny Dalglish, rugby union's Andy Irvine, former motor racing world champion Sir Jackie Stewart and he was accepted into the inaugural Scottish Football Hall of Fame next to some of the exceptional players he'd played against toward the end of his career. These included Jim Baxter, Denis Law, Billy McNeill, John Greig, and his old comrades from the early days: Willie Woodburn, Jock Stein, Bill Shankly and, some would say his most influential contemporary and treasured friend, Matt Busby.

EPILOGUE

ENJOYING THE SUN

ANTHONY IS the name on my birth certificate. My friends call me Tony, but Gordon Smith called me Anton. Gordon Smith was my dad. He once told me that the reason he quite liked the shortened version of my name was mainly due to the Austrian musician, Anton Karas, the world famous zither player whose Harry Lime theme tune was made famous in the 1949 film *The Third Man*. Dad loved that film and he loved that music, telling me he had once met Karas in Cannes where he was performing and that the Austrian had been very interested in football. Although he used Anton as a term of endearment, Anthony was (and still is) my Sunday name.

Even though, as you've read in this book, my dad was twice asked by journalists of the epoch, Ross Fraser and Hugh Taylor, if they could write his life story and he declined, I'm amazed no one in recent years has considered it. With that said, I'm delighted to have been the one to write it (albeit from a slightly different perspective) and proud his name is once again up there in the lights, where it belongs, among the greats of Scottish football.

The writing of this book has been very time-consuming, painstaking, interesting, yet heart-wrenching; I've experienced my fair share of torrid moments but most of all the writing of this book has been extremely rewarding.

In this epilogue, in which the biographer has suddenly become the son, I will endeavour to paint a picture of what life was like with this wonderful and gifted man.

Toward the end of his life, he was blighted by Alzheimer's, and I have included some stories here that concern that period in his life –

not too many, as, to be honest, that could be another book in itself and some are too personal, as you will understand. Yet, even traumatised by dementia, he still had the charm and humour that made him a remarkable human being. There was always humour – and there was always football.

My dad was quite an astonishing man, and more importantly to me, a great father. Growing up with a famous dad was amazing. It would open up all sorts of doors for you! I remember his fast driving in his sports cars, and many a policeman happily accepting an autograph for his misdemeanour of speeding when a 'normal mortal' would've been fined or worse. I recall as a child going on holidays to the south of France, and the fact he would play football and cricket with me often for hours on end, even table tennis – until I started beating him! He despaired that I had little or no interest in golf, but I did enjoy putting, so that cheered him up a little.

When I was very young – a mere two years old – I bounced up and down on Bridget Bardot's knee. Even though I was a couple of months short of my third birthday, I can still remember it clearly! As I got older, I met renowned people such as the then Manchester United manager and Dad's old Hibernian colleague Sir Matt Busby, Sir Douglas Bader and the world-famous golfers, Malcolm Gregson, Bobby Locke and Billy Casper. But mostly I met football men such as Lawrie Reilly, Bobby Johnstone, Eddie Turnbull, Jimmy Kerr, the three Willies – Ormond, Clark and MacFarlane, the two Tommy's – Preston and Younger, Celtic boss Jock Stein and Rangers boss Willie Waddell, to name a few.

I had a great experience in 1972, aged nearly nine, when Hibs played in the Cup Winners Cup in Portugal against Sporting Lisbon. Sharing a chartered plane with my heroes – the likes of Pat Stanton, Jimmy O'Rourke, Alan Gordon and Alex Cropley – was a great thrill, and I remember Dad having a ball too. We stayed at a hotel in Estoril on the outskirts of Lisbon, with Tommy Preston, Willie Clark, Lawrie Reilly and Willie MacFarlane all trying to teach me to swim; ultimately they failed, and I remember cheating by pretending to them that I was swimming by moving my arms like a real swimmer would, whilst unknown to them (or so I thought), keeping my feet on terra firma. Although Hibs lost 1–2, I loved the fact that I was up late at night – the game was played around 10pm to diminish the effects of the searing Portuguese heat.

The following year, I had the immense thrill and great honour of training with the 'black panther', better known as simply Eusébio, along with his Benfica team-mates. He was, and still is, one of my all-time football heroes. We were on holiday at Estoril again – this time as a family – and Dad had got talking to Jimmy Hagan, the Durham-born coach of the Lisbon club, who was dining at a nearby table; the previous season he had guided the Lisbon club to an incredible twenty-eight victories out of thirty matches played and won the league. Hagan and my dad talked football for what seemed like hours and during their often-heated parley, they arranged for me to 'train' with the team the following day. History shows that this squad of players was Benfica's best ever and looking back, it was an incredible privilege to play with them.

Early the next morning, I was whisked off in a car by this strange Portuguese man and deposited at the club's training facility high in the hills outside of Lisbon. I had the most fantastic day – playing five-a-side games – and as the session ended, my parents arrived and they were *both* coaxed into joining in with some 'head tennis' alongside the first team squad! I remember my mum blaming her hair for her considerable failings, much to the hilarity of the charming Eusébio and team-mates such as the legendary left winger, António Simões, who I was already taller than, and star strikers, Nené and Toni.

A few days later, we all went to see these players again as they took on a Rest of the World XI for Eusébio's testimonial match, with an array of star players in the World XI line-up, including even more heroes of mine: George Best, Gordon Banks (recently signed Real Madrid star), the West German Günter Netzer and the Charlton brothers, Bobby and Jack.

I would get taken around the UK to countless golf tournaments, which I hated, cricket at Lord's, which I loved, and to football games all over Europe, especially at Easter Road, which were fantastic. Meeting Dad's other friends, like the celebrated Tottenham Hotspur manager Bill Nicholson, and my dad's old Dundee colleague, the legendary Alan Gilzean, was a delight. I remember a club director, or other such dignitary, castigating them when they played football with a ball made of a scrunched-up match-day programme in the club's illustrious boardroom. Smith kicked an inch-perfect cross and Gilzean headed a perfectly directed goal beyond the reach of the hapless but stranded half back, Nicholson, who was in goal!

My father's one failing in life, if you can call it a failing, is that he was an overly private person, possibly slightly esoteric – 'very deep' as his old teacher Miss Nairn had said all those years ago. Fans were just wanting a bit of his time, or clubs wanted to show him off to his still adoring public, but he would have none of it a lot of the time. He maybe ought to have put more back into the game that made him so famous? On countless occasions, he would walk away from restaurants because he was being 'hassled' and so my mum and I had to follow him, with her often shouting as we walked away, 'Gordon, I was really enjoying that meal!'

Although my dad was not a huge fan of boxing, I recall many a night when I was growing up when he would stay up late to watch another of his sporting heroes, Muhammad Ali, in action. Along with many people, Gordon thought the heavyweight boxer from Louisville, Kentucky, was the most amazing human that had ever walked the planet and was captivated by the man who he had met briefly in New York City.

He would reminisce about his favourite games he had played in, like the days of winning each of his league titles, many Hibernian games, his great reception at Hearts and his favourite Scotland games – especially the tour in '55. He enjoyed watching TV – his old films from the '30s, '40s and '50s undoubtedly were his favourites – probably bringing back lots of memories from when he first saw them in picture houses. He also loved watching tennis, particularly the volatility of his favourites, Pancho Gonzales, Ilie Nastase and John McEnroe, whilst still watching a lot of cricket, too, with a passion.

I recall one summer, I think it was 'the scorcher' of 1976, when we had travelled through to Ayrshire to see the Open Golf Championship at Turnberry; I remember him – quite possibly out of character – enjoying the cabaret-style shows we went to see in the evenings. Dad laughed so much at the Gaiety Theatre in Ayr, where Johnny Beattie was starring in the 'Gaiety Whirl' alongside Grant Frazer and Anna Desti, enjoying it so much he went back three nights from five. The other two nights we went to see the 'Andy Stewart Show' – again Dad had a great time and he met the great entertainer backstage after the performance, as he'd been recognised by some footballer who was also in the audience.

My mum hadn't flown since her honeymoon in June 1960, so we had to travel by train to his beloved south of France every year on holiday.

The boat trains used to be the bane of his life, as I recall – they were always stopping just outside of Folkstone or Dover and it was always a rush to make the Channel crossing. In the days before segregated smoking coaches on trains, he would abhor the compartments that were cordoned off; should someone come in and light up a cigarette, Dad would start coughing and spluttering (quite embarrassingly for me) way over the top and most of the time the person would leave as they would obviously have felt uneasy.

He cherished his holidays in Cannes, though, treating it almost like a second home, as hardly anyone recognised him there and he would be quite content to just lie in the sun in the mornings and take a walk with my mum around the old harbour in the afternoons. The evenings would be spent at his favourite restaurant, Brasserie du Casino, at the Marimée Square near Rue d'Antibes, with the owners becoming good friends of ours over the years.

My parents had two cats, Ting and Pelé as I was growing up, which they loved and we would constantly play with them in our garden. He and my mum were always laughing and I can still picture their smiling faces; they were always laughing and joking and happy. Wonderful times, wonderful memories and I keep thinking about just how much my dad loved my mum.

As I left home and pursued my love of music, I travelled all over but would always enjoy coming home to see them and to kick a ball about with my mum, dad and the cats in the garden. By this time the cats were more skilled than my mum (especially Pelé)!

They were overjoyed to become grandparents for the first time in 1994 when my first child, a strapping boy named Danaan, was born. When, in October 1996, my mum died after suffering all that year from what we eventually knew was cancer of the liver, my dad was heart-broken. Her death affected him considerably and the pain and sorrow he suffered in the ensuing weeks and months after her death was immeasurable and can't be put into words.

The next three years were to be his last, as I knew him anyway – for the remaining five years of his life, the Alzheimer's that had been creeping in ever-so-slowly began to overtake and change him as if he was somebody completely different.

Four years after his first grandchild was born, he was once again proud to be a grandfather for a second time, with another grandson,

Cale, joining the Smith family. This event cheered him up and he enjoyed kicking a ball about with my sons and me, but he was mentally on the slide for great periods at a time.

He had stopped going to football matches, except for the odd invitation from his friend, Lawrie Reilly, who would accompany him. He did attend the opening of The Famous Five stand in July 1998 at Easter Road as Hibernian were defeated by Barnsley, yet because of the hooliganism and rowdy crowd behaviour in general that had crept into the game, he would prefer to watch his football on TV. He was a huge admirer of the likes of Paul Gascoigne, Ruud Gullit, Marco van Basten and Eric Cantona – his favourites in the modern era.

By the time his first granddaughter, Marly Lia, was born, my dad was in a residential care home and in, for the most part, a somewhat perplexed state. To those around him, to those who cared and certainly to me, it was a blessing when, a few months later, he peacefully passed away.

There has been some research into if there is a link between heading the old-fashioned ball and footballers of this era developing dementia. Ex-Rangers and Scotland player, George Young; Celtic's Billy McPhail; Manchester United and Northern Ireland captain, Danny Blanchflower; West Bromwich Albion's Jeff Astle – to name but a few – all suffered from Alzheimer's, too. My dad used to tell me how some clubs would even soak the ball overnight in a bath to make it even harder.

Only recently, as I was nearing completion of this book in March 2011, a primary school in Huyton, Liverpool, in an area known for producing footballers, banned leather footballs from its playground for 'health and safety reasons'.

Chronic traumatic encephalopathy – a degenerative brain disease associated with years of repeated blows to the head – is another ailment that some ex-footballers have succumbed to. Although there is no evidence proving that heading a ball can cause this to develop, there has been plenty of research into finding an answer. On the other hand, there are plenty more people who suffer from these diseases each year that have never headed a football in their lives.

The very first time that I was aware there was something wrong with Dad was a summer's day in 1991. I took a train from Edinburgh to North Berwick and he picked me up, as usual, in his car. As soon as I opened the door, I felt something wasn't right. I sat in the passenger seat, but he also just sat there, with the engine running, quite motionless for what seemed like an eternity but couldn't have been more than ten or fifteen seconds; yet it was enough time for the situation to become unnerving. He moved eventually, but only to turn off the ignition key, so the deep purr of his Honda Accord engine stopped, and now we endured this absolute silence. I asked him if he was ok; there was no response. I asked him what was wrong, what the matter was – but again, no response. By then I was getting a little worried.

My dad's sixty-seventh birthday had come and gone, yet he still looked like he was in his forties – still lithe, an extremely fit man, running every morning in all weathers – and here he was, sitting in his car in silence, just staring through the windscreen. I had never seen my dad like this before and was getting quite agitated, repeatedly asking him to please tell me what the problem was. After what seemed like an eternity, he started crying hysterically. He pushed his head onto the steering wheel and held on to the wheel very tightly with both hands.

'What's the matter?' I begged him to tell me.

'I'm forgetting things, having terrible memory lapses and I'm so worried,' he replied, his face still buried on the wheel. His voice trembled as he told me and it was my turn to just sit there motionless.

'I'm so scared,' he continued, 'I just don't know what to do. The doctor told me it's just my age, said he can give me pills to take, but I'm petrified to be honest.'

To be honest, so was I. To see my dad like this was alarming to say the least. I tugged and pulled a little at his dark blue jumper, coaxed him to stir from his position over the steering wheel, and we both turned around in our seats and hugged. I had never been aware of him being forgetful whatsoever.

We hugged in his car and it started raining – from the engine noise to silence to quite heavy rainfall, all those sounds were so vivid. We embraced for ages and not a word was said between us. Then he half-sobbed: 'Please, whatever happens, promise me you won't ever put me in a home, don't ever let me get like that.'

I promised him I wouldn't put him in a 'home'.

Another five minutes or so must have passed before he was in a fit state to drive back and we went in to the house to see my mum, who was worried and asked us why we were so delayed. Before I could say anything, Dad blurted out: 'The train was late, Joan. Anton's train was late again.'

And we all sat down to eat and my mum was laughing and joking and my dad, too, laughed and joked. He never again mentioned to me anything like what he'd said in the station car park – that day was the one and only time. Humorists amongst you may hypothesize it was because he forgot to tell me, as his memory degenerated! Regrettably, I think there may be some truth in that.

The next few years, without being too aware of how bad things were, he obviously got decidedly worse. With the sudden death of my mother in 1996, his doctor had warned me to expect a sharp decline, but he actually seemed to improve for a short spell and his time was taken up with visiting my mum's grave, travelling around watching me play the piano and his gardening. At one point, I almost believed he was coping so well, it was almost as if the illness had receded!

Gradually, however, it reappeared, such as the times we'd arranged to meet and he wouldn't show up, or the time I was playing a gig in London and we had planned to meet at Edinburgh's Waverley station; I waited and waited for him, missing my train and eventually got so worried that I cancelled my gig and drove down the coast to his house in North Berwick, assuming the worse. When I got there, he wasn't in and so some friends and I raised the alarm and looked for him in the surrounding area, only for him to call my mobile from London asking where I was. He'd been up at the crack of dawn apparently and got the train he thought he was supposed to take!

Episodes like these were happening repeatedly. He started to play fewer rounds of golf with the likes of Lawrie Reilly, as he forgot to turn up more often than not, with his behaviour now quite disconcerting for his friends. Pilmar Smith, once the vice-chairman of Heart of Midlothian was a great friend of my dad's and told the story of receiving a lift from him – following Hibs' legend Tommy Preston's birthday celebrations – from Edinburgh to North Berwick where they both lived. Pilmar stated that at every opportunity on the twenty-mile journey an agitated Gordon would make a left-turn at an exit and they would be back where they started more than once! Pilmar had to placate Dad enlightening him which roads to take to get home. My dad told Pilmar 'this nightmare' had been occurring for quite some time, and on one occasion he had to sleep in his car as he had driven around and around so often his car had run out of petrol.

Another sad, but in some ways quite amusing episode took place the following summer, when his degeneration was now visibly noticeable to everyone. I had meandered from the woods, passing the burn, which was almost bone dry, to the adjacent farm field only a couple of minutes away from my dad's property. The property consisted of a large acre-and-a-half garden and an unused, unkempt two-and-a-half acre field. A few sheep ran and a few seemed indifferent as I approached, marching onward.

Suddenly I heard shrieking. A discordant combination of sounds resonated from his garden. I could hear gasping, loud puffing and panting. I was aware of Dad's agitated voice yelling: 'Come on, keep going!'

I panicked and ran, and in no time, I had reached the field that led to the garden and I sprinted in the direction of it. That's when I saw it first: a small black Bible. A Bible on the lawn! Next to it, which if anything was even stranger, was a neatly folded coffee-coloured jacket with a name badge gleaming from the top pocket. The odd aspect about this was that Dad owned neither a Bible, nor a coffee-coloured jacket, and also, although he used to be, he was never that neat and tidy these days. His jacket would have been flung onto the grass in a heap. I could still hear panting and the deep breathing was getting increasingly louder.

Then I saw a strange sight. It was a hot day and Dad was sprinting. Dad was seventy-seven years old and he was sprinting with two Caucasian men in their mid-to-late twenties, one of whom was carrying another Bible in his left hand and sweating profusely, wearing a tie tied tightly on a shirt that was so drenched with perspiration that I have no idea what colour it was supposed to be! The other man wore a battleship-grey jacket and red tie and was overheating so much that steam rose from his neck and the back of his head. I deduced his faith wasn't as important to him as his comrade's, as he'd put down his Bible in the face of adversity, whilst his colleague had only removed his jacket.

'Sir, can you help us, sir, if you can?' One of them voiced in an American accent, almost out of breath. They greeted me with such bonhomie that I took an instant dislike to them.

'We, sir,' he exclaimed, 'are members of the Church of Jesus Christ of Latter-day Saints and sir, we are very tired and hot. This gentleman has made us run with him round and round his beautiful garden but we are a little weary.'

Weary, I thought. I could think of some other words to describe you.

'Just take your Bibles and your jackets and go back where you came from!' I exclaimed. Then I remembered the outer gate was locked.

'How did you get in?' I inquired, presuming they'd jumped.

'Oh, the gentleman let us in, sir.' He gestured in the direction of Dad, who had stopped running and was standing statuesque, monitoring the situation.

'He opened the gate for us [pointing] up there, with a key.'

'Oh really,' I replied in an exasperated tone.

Another nightmare! I thought I'd taken all the keys from my dad, as he was prone to walking on the road and taking the neighbours' wheelie-bins for walks – long walks – and often the wheelie-bins would end up in some very odd places. I once found one of his neighbour's bins, full of stinking rubbish, I may add, in my old bedroom. On a different occasion, he got stuck climbing over the gate while still holding onto one of his beloved bins, and ended up splitting his trousers in two, eventually getting over (with the wheelie-bin, naturally) after being in an elevated position for over twenty minutes! His doctor had asked me to try and stop him from going out the gate – for that reason and possibly one or two other more serious ones.

I took pity on the two members of the Church of Jesus Christ of Latter-day Saints and walked up the field with them, leaving Dad still motionless, with the intention of unlocking the gate and letting them 'escape', as I don't think they had had the energy to vault over it.

The coup de grace of this whole escapade now occurred as Dad started sprinting, once again, up the field towards us. I chuckled, as I could hear him shouting.

'Bloody bastards. Get away from here, you bastards,' he yelled, and he gained ground on us at an alarming rate. Was I being included in this virulent attack? Hopefully not! The Americans looked at me. They appeared petrified and were rooted to the spot. They had been outfoxed by a professional athlete, masquerading as a senile old man with a filthy tongue (very much due to his illness). I turned around in the direction of Speedy Gonzales, leaving the men standing, still unmoved, and eventually coaxed my incessant father to go back and wait for me in the garden. After promising I would get rid of them, he sprinted (naturally) back to the garden, while I escorted the sweaty do-gooders from the premises.

'Thank you, sir,' they said in unison.

'Don't come back,' I retorted, almost starting to enjoy the shenanigans, as we reached the gate.

'No sir, we sure won't be bothering you again. Oh, and thank you again, for helping us – by the way, is the gentleman your father?'

'Yes.'

'My word, sir, he is indeed a very fit man for his age.'

'Yes, he is.'

'Charles, here, said he needed to lose a few pounds the other day, so I guess we can declare without a lie he'll have made his target,' uttered the taller of the two.

'He probably exceeded it,' I added. They found this an amusing comment, but probably were laughing more with relief at finally being set free. 'If I hadn't come along, this road here [I pointed up Abbotsford Road], could've been your Via Dolorosa!' I pronounced.

'Yes, the good Lord works in mysterious ways,' Chuck chuckled, as they toddled off, waving to me like maniacs, whilst ambling up the road.

Doesn't He just, I thought, as I headed back down to see Dad who, believe it or not, was still running in the garden. Around and around, doing lap after lap. I'll have to get that bloody key off him somehow, I reckoned, but I'll leave it just now. It was far too hot for a plan.

'Those American bastards with their Bibles, just who do they think they are?' spoke Dad breathlessly, as I approached him and guided him over to the garden sun-beds.

'Mormons, Dad!'

'I've always been wary of them. I've never liked them. They're a smarmy lot,' he declared.

I didn't want to remind him but up until recently, he was very close to Billy Casper, who was a 'smarmy Mormon' I'd met on numerous occasions as a child in the very same garden these men had been forced to run in today. You couldn't possibly have met a nicer man.

'By Jove, it's hot,' he exclaimed.

'It is indeed,' I affirmed. Undeniably a lot hotter with all that running you've been doing, I thought to myself!

I calmed Dad down, telling him it was nonsensical to be running on such a scorching day as today; he at last succumbed to my wise words and we planted ourselves in the garden. He, on his green sun-bed and me, on the red sun-bed that used to be my mother's, where we proceeded to drink cola with miniature footballer-shaped ice-cubes.

It was scorching and in no time we had our tops off. The fragrance from the pink and yellow roses in the garden was abundant and I could smell peppermint and the pungent aroma of freshly cut grass.

'What a beautiful day, isn't it, Dad?'

I squinted to my left, noticing beads of sweat trickling down his nose, as we both fried in the searing heat of the sun.

'Beautiful, Anton,' he responded sleepily.

A few minutes went by until I again interrupted the serenity.

'You must've got a hell of a shock with those two turning up this morning. Don't think we'll be seeing them again, mind you – you've exhausted them! You should've seen the look on their faces when you had them doing their paces round and round the garden.' I laughed aloud as I remembered the anxious and troubled sweaty expressions on the faces of the running, puffing 'Bible-bashing yanks'.

Dad sat up from his sun-bed abruptly. 'What do you mean?' he questioned, in a slightly vexed and aggressive manner, as I continued to laugh with hysterical abandon. 'What are you talking about? Whose faces?' He looked straight at me and enquired: 'Were there people here in the garden?'

I gradually stopped laughing and could see the bewildered look on his face. He was very confused and lay back down again. Just over ten minutes after they'd gone, my dad had no recollection of the Mormons. I turned and faced away, as I was aware my joy and happiness had directly turned to that unforeseen shocking sadness I was getting all too used to lately and a couple of my tears descended onto the parched grass.

'It doesn't matter, Dad,' I managed to articulate. 'Let's just enjoy the sun.'

During the course of that summer, Sky TV reporter James Mathews came down to the house to record footage and interview Dad for his forthcoming *Famous Five* DVD, and early the next summer, my friend David Ross would try to repeat what James had done in getting an interview from him. But a year is a long time for someone suffering from Alzheimer's and he didn't really make too much sense, with David's account having to be aborted. Nonetheless, the footage shot by him, which proved to be the final footage of Dad playing football, is astonishing! His dexterity was incredible – keeping the ball from touching the ground up to fifty times at a go and then heading it in the air without the ball touching the ground for at least another twenty or so. It took me until only a few months ago to actually bring myself to watch the footage and it took my breath away – just how good a football player he still was at seventy-seven! He may not have known what he was saying a lot of the time but he still knew how to be in command of a football, that's for sure. There was talk of a 'star related' video being shot, as through my friends Norrie Preston and Sandy Jones, the celebrated author and Hibs fanatic Irvine Welsh was approached and was said to be very interested in fronting the project, but time had run out – it had been left too late.

Although he passed away on the 7 August 2004 at a North Berwick care home, fittingly in room number 7, he had 'died' to me a very long time before. It's quite hard to put an exact date on this occurrence but certainly during the summer and early autumn of 1998, he started deteriorating quite badly – and when visiting him after that, he became quite irrational, with severe mood swings and very odd, often quite belligerent, behaviour. Behaviour that was so out of character, it was terrible to see him like that – such is the scourge of dementia. Looking back, I suppose the day I now realise I 'lost' him was another hot day during the previous summer of 1999. A day I remember for all the wrong reasons. I had visited my dad and was preparing lunch for us when I went through to his bedroom to inform him it was almost ready. When I walked in, he was lying on his bed holding a photograph, with a perplexed look, half-smiling, but bemused and puzzled.

I asked him what the photo was and he replied: 'That's the thing Anton, it's some woman but I'm not sure who she is.'

'Let me see,' I said, and I walked across to his bed and sat beside him. To my horror and disbelief, the photo was of my mum.

'She's a smasher, mind you, isn't she?' he added, still clutching at the photo. 'You wouldn't happen to know who she is, by any chance, would you? It's got me baffled.'

How do you answer a question like that? What do you say? What can your response possibly be? Not recognising the love of his life, 'his girl' of nearly forty years, the mother of his only child, his sweetheart and his wife. I didn't say anything – I couldn't speak – aghast and astounded, I speedily headed to the bathroom, locking myself away for so long that when I did move again, my body was numbed – partly from being sat motionless and partly from mental anguish.

When I managed to compose myself, I went through to the kitchen. He had the photo up on the windowsill in pride of place, – alongside a golf ball, a golf tee, a chocolate-covered nut from a bar of Cadbury's Fruit and Nut and an album of my piano music – and he had not only eaten his meal, but mine also.

'That was a very tasty lunch, thanks, Anton.' He smiled and continued, 'Think I'll go for a wee lie down now.'

No bloody wonder, with all that food you've eaten, I thought to myself!

With hindsight, maybe he ought to have been in residential care a little sooner than when he eventually went, quite close to Christmas of 2002; but in a way, I'm also pleased that I waited until then to make that very difficult decision. That difficult decision had become easier to make by then.

The last few weeks that he lived in his house had become a nightmare and at times he acted like a feral animal, such was the erosion of the mind. I would visit him on a daily basis, trying to be emollient, but would struggle at times. I knew I maybe ought to have stayed longer than I did on certain days, but I just couldn't bring myself to, and would depart back to Edinburgh after about an hour or so. As soon as I arrived to see him, I just wanted to go; yet when travelling back to Edinburgh, I wanted to be back with him – but back with the 'normal' him. It was torturous seeing my dad like he was. Had he been aware, I know he would've begged me to end it all for him.

On the day of reckoning, the day he was to begin a new life in a Haddington care home, my friend Rod McPhail and I arrived early and drove him away for the last time – away from his home of forty-four years. He was in tears and very confused when we eventually managed to coax him to the car; I was grief-stricken and so was Rod.

As we drove to the care home, Dad suddenly blurted: 'Anton, are you taking me home? I want to go home.'

Knowing that I couldn't take him back to his home, I just nodded quietly, whispering a lie that had to be said: 'Dad, yes I am.'

This emotionally charged atmosphere seemed to last forever as we drove further and further away from his home. The band Coldplay's song 'The Scientist' played on the radio, with the chorus containing the somewhat prophetic lyrics: 'Nobody said it was easy, it's such a shame for us to part; nobody said it was easy, no one ever said it would be this hard.'

As it played, reminiscent of a dirge, the hammer-blows continued, as Dad kept repeating: 'I want to go home, Anton. I want to go home. You're taking me home, Anton, aren't you?' Incredibly, the home he meant was not back to his house in North Berwick – not even Edinburgh where he'd lived for eighteen years in his football prime: 'I want to go back home, to Montrose,' he sobbed. 'Oh, I've missed it so much.'

This was a great shock to me and the sudden realisation of just exactly where his mind was knocked me for six, filling my heart with overwhelming sadness. Then he fell silent and became quite serene; the least agitated he'd been in weeks after being reassured he was going 'home'. I still felt like he would become very agitated again, that this respite was only temporary – the calm before the storm – but no storm came. As we continued to drive, he rested his head against the side window and he almost smiled. I was so pleased – this wasn't what I'd expected to happen at all. He should've been distraught, but quite amazingly he wasn't. Coldplay's poignant singing finished and he appeared to have found some peace at last – his daydream was a happy one.

Could he have been playing a round of golf with Bobby Locke, or crossing a ball for Lawrie Reilly or Alan Gilzean to direct into the back of the net? Perhaps he was keeping the ball up whilst running down the right wing at Easter Road or listening to his favourite Fats Waller records on his radiogram back at Willowbrae Road? Maybe he was actually back home in Montrose, kicking that ball at the corrugated shed again and again. There's a good chance he was simply with my mum, in their garden, with his beloved cats and roses and they were deliriously content. All I know is that he looked at ease and wasn't disconcerted at all. It was as if a great weight had been lifted from his shoulders, as if he'd found his own nirvana somewhere.

As I sat there next to my dad that dank December Tuesday, I watched him closely. This was the first time that I'd mustered up the courage to look at his face directly for such a long time for fear of catching his eye.

I wondered, could he have been lying on the beach in the south of France alongside his jazz buddy, the celebrated Sidney Bechet? Perhaps it was early in the morning, just after dawn. Could they have been listening out for the beautiful music made by the tranquil Mediterranean Sea, with an exuberant Bechet inviting an answer: 'Do you hear that Gordon? Can you dig the rhythm of the waves?'

APPENDIX

FACTS, FIGURES AND MEMORABLE GAMES

Born:	26th May 1924, Edinburgh
Died:	7th August 2004, North Berwick
Height:	5 feet 9 inches
Weight:	11 stones 6 pounds
Football Teams supported as a boy:	Montrose and Heart of Midlothian
Positions:	Centre Forward and Right Wing
Professional Debut:	Hibernian v Heart of Midlothian, 28th April 1941, aged 16, scoring 3 goals in a 5–3 win at Tynecastle Park, Edinburgh
Retired from football:	July 1964 (after 23 years as a professional)

Inducted into the Halls of Fame of the Scottish Sports (2003), The Scottish Football (2004), Hibernian FC (2010) and Dundee FC (2012)

Inaugural Scotland Footballer of the Year: 1951

CLUB FOOTBALL

Remains to this day the only British footballer to have won the League Championship for three different clubs then subsequently played in the European Cup the following season with them.

Scottish Southern League Cup winner with Hibernian.	6–5 on corners at Hampden Park on 20th May 1944 v Rangers
Played in front of Hibernian's largest away crowd of all time (a British record for a club game other than a final).	143,570 v Rangers at Hampden Park, Glasgow, 27th March 1948
Played, on his Hibernian debut, in the lowest Edinburgh derby crowd of the 20th century, for any senior match between the two teams.	3,004 v Heart of Midlothian at Tynecastle Park, Edinburgh, 28th April 1941
Holds the record in Scottish football history for the number of goals scored by a winger during one match.	5 v Third Lanark on 8th November 1947
Played in front of Hibernian's largest home crowd of all time.	65,840 v Heart of Midlothian on 2nd January 1950
All-time leading Hibernian goal-scorer.	364 goals
No player for Hibernian has scored more goals against Heart of Midlothian.	15 goals in 37 games
Scottish League Cup winner with Heart of Midlothian.	2–1 at Hampden Park on 24th October 1959 v Third Lanark
Played in Dundee's biggest win of all time.	10–2 v Queen of the South

5 SCOTTISH LEAGUE CHAMPIONSHIP MEDALS

Hibernian: (1946/47) (1950/51) (1951/52); Heart of Midlothian: (1959/60); Dundee: (1961/62)

ALL TEAMS FROM CHILDHOOD TO RETIREMENT

TEAM	TOWN	YEAR	AGE	GAMES	GOALS
South Esk Primary School	Montrose	1932–1935	8–11	68*	204*
Montrose Academy	Montrose	1935–1939	11–15	81*	236*
Bromford	Arbroath	1935–1937	11–13	60*	186*
Kirriemuir Harp	Kirriemuir	1937–1939	13–15	65*	189*
Montrose Roselea	Montrose	1939–1940	15–16	32	60
Hillside United	Dundee	1940	16	1	9
Dundee North End	Dundee	1940–1941	16	23	58
Hibernian	Edinburgh	1941–1959	16–34	674	364
Heart of Midlothian	Edinburgh	1959–1961	35–36	76	17
Dundee	Dundee	1961–1964	37–39	105	21
Greenock Morton	Greenock	1964	39	1	1
Drumcondra	Dublin	1964	39	3	1

	GAMES	GOALS
Amateur: 1932–1941	330*	942*
Professional: 1941–1964	859*	404

* Indicates estimated games and goals

PROFESSIONAL CLUB GAMES AND GOALS SCORED

SEASON	TEAM	LEAGUE GAMES	LEAGUE GOALS	OTHER GAMES	OTHER GOALS	TOTAL GAMES PLAYED	TOTAL GOALS SCORED
1940/41	Hibernian	1	3	3	2	4	5
1941/42	Hibernian	29	24	11	17	40	41
1942/43	Hibernian	29	26	11	8	40	34
1943/44	Hibernian	26	13	11	7	37	20
1944/45	Hibernian	29	21	11	14	40	35
1945/46	Hibernian	25	15	13	5	38	20
1946/47	Hibernian	27	8	20	16	47	24
1947/48	Hibernian	29	19	16	12	45	31
1948/49	Hibernian	29	15	10	7	39	22
1949/50	Hibernian	29	25	17	11	46	36
1950/51	Hibernian	25	10	22	8	47	18
1951/52	Hibernian	29	9	15	6	44	15
1952/53	Hibernian	28	13	17	11	45	24
1953/54	Hibernian	12	5	9	4	21	9
1954/55	Hibernian	28	9	7	0	35	9
1955/56	Hibernian	30	7	12	2	42	9
1956/57	Hibernian	17	3	5	2	22	5
1957/58	Hibernian	16	3	6	2	22	5
1958/59	Hibernian	15	1	5	1	20	2
1959/60	Heart of Midlothian	29	11	20	4	49	15
1960/61	Heart of Midlothian	13	2	14	0	27	2
1961/62	Dundee	32	7	13	4	45	11
1962/63	Dundee	29	4	19	6	48	10
1963/64	Dundee	9	0	3	0	12	0
	Greenock Morton	1	1	0	0	1	1
	Drumcondra	1	0	2	1	3	1

SCORED 17 HAT-TRICKS, ALL WITH HIBERNIAN

DATE	YEAR	GOALS	AGAINST	COMPETITION
28th April	1941	3	Heart of Midlothian	Southern League
23rd January	1943	3	Airdrie	Southern League
30th January	1943	3	Partick Thistle	Southern League
18th September	1943	3	Dumbarton	Southern League
4th December	1943	3	Albion Rovers	Southern League
11th November	1944	3	Airdrie	Southern League
13th January	1945	3	Falkirk	Southern League
20th April	1946	3	Dundee	Victory Cup
1st March	1947	3	Airdrie	League Cup
16th August	1947	3	Clyde	League Cup
8th November	1947	5	Third Lanark	League
10th December	1949	4	Falkirk	League
18th February	1950	3	Motherwell	League
1st April	1950	3	Stirling Albion	League
19th August	1950	3	Falkirk	League Cup
20th December	1952	3	Queen of the South	League
21st February	1953	3	Airdrie	Scottish cup

EUROPEAN GAMES

European Cup games: 15 appearances, 3 goals

Played in the very first European Cup match by a British team: Hibernian, in September 1955.

First British footballer to play in two semi-finals of the European Cup competition, also holding the record in May 1963 for the most European Cup games played by a British footballer at that time.

DATE	YEAR	FOR	AGAINST	VENUE	CITY/ COUNTRY	SCORE	CROWD	G.S. GOALS MISC.
Wed 14th Sep	1955	Hibernian	Rot Weiss Essen	Georg Melches Stadion	Essen, Germany	4–0	5,000	0
Wed 23rd Nov	1955	Hibernian	FC Djurgården	Firhill	Glasgow, Scotland	3–1	21,962	0
Mon 28th Nov	1955	Hibernian	FC Djurgården	Easter Road	Edinburgh, Scotland	1–1	31,346	1 goal
Wed 4th Apr	1956	Hibernian	Stade De Reims	Parc de Princes	Paris, France	0–2	35,486	0
Wed 18th Apr	1956	Hibernian	Stade de Reims	Easter Road	Edinburgh, Scotland	0–1	44,941	0
Thu 29th Sep	1960	Heart of Midlothian	SL Benfica	Tynecastle Park	Edinburgh, Scotland	1–2	29,500	No. 11
Wed 5th Oct	1960	Heart of Midlothian	SL Benfica	Stadio do Luz	Lisbon, Portugal	0–3	30,122	0
Wed 5th Sep	1962	Dundee	FC Köln	Dens Park	Dundee, Scotland	8–1	23,821	1 goal
Wed 26th Sep	1962	Dundee	FC Köln	Müngersdorfer stadion	Köln, Germany	0–4	37,998	0
Wed 24th Oct	1962	Dundee	Sporting Clube de Portugal	Estádio José Avalade	Lisbon, Portugal	0–1	45,000	0

DATE	YEAR	FOR	AGAINST	VENUE	CITY/ COUNTRY	SCORE	CROWD	G.S. GOALS MISC.
Wed 31st Oct	1962	Dundee	Sporting Clube de Portugal	Dens Park	Dundee, Scotland	4–1	30,596	0
Wed 6th Mar	1963	Dundee	RSC Anderlecht	Heysel Stadium	Brussels, Belgium	4–1	64,703	0
Wed 13th Mar	1963	Dundee	RSC Anderlecht	Dens Park	Dundee, Scotland	2–1	38,232	1 goal
Wed 24th Apr	1963	Dundee	AC Milan	San Siro	Milan, Italy	1–5	73,993	0
Wed 1st May	1963	Dundee	AC Milan	Dens Park	Dundee, Scotland	1–0	35,169	0

INTERNATIONAL

Gordon represented his country on 39 occasions
Played in four different positions for Scotland – numbers 7, 8, 9, and 11
2 Schoolboy International caps for Scotland
3 Wartime caps for Scotland
4 Scottish Select X1 appearances
1 Rest of Britain games
11 Scottish Football League appearances
18 Full International appearances for Scotland
9 goals: 4 for Scotland in Full Internationals, 3 for the Scottish Football League and 2 for in Scottish Schoolboy Internationals
In 1955 played 11 games for Scotland or the Scottish League, scoring 6 goals

DATE	YEAR	VERSUS	VENUE	CITY/ COUNTRY	SCORE	CROWD	G.S. GOALS/ MISC.	TYPE OF MATCH
Apr 30th	1938	Ireland	Starks Park	Kircaldy, Scotland	5–2	9,471	2	Schoolboy
May 14th	1938	England	Roker Park	Sunderland, England	1–0	23,897	0	Schoolboy
Nov 6th	1943	RAF International X1	Hampden Park	Glasgow, Scotland	1–2	50,000	First game for Scotland at Hampden	Scottish Select X1
Oct 14th	1944	England	Wembley Stadium	London, England	2–6	100,000	0	Wartime
Nov 10th	1945	Wales	Hampden Park	Glasgow, Scotland	2–0	92,323	0 No. 8	Wartime
Nov 17th	1945	Combined Military Services XI	Highbury	Celle, Germany	4–2	12,000	0	Scottish Select XI
Nov 18th	1945	Combined Military Services XI	Millerntor Stadion	Hamburg, Germany	1–1	35,000	0	Scottish Select X1
Jan 23rd	1946	Belgium	Hampden Park	Glasgow, Scotland	2–2	48,830	0	Wartime
Nov 27th	1946	Northern Ireland	Hampden Park	Glasgow, Scotland	0–0	98,776	0	Home International Championship

DATE	YEAR	VERSUS	VENUE	CITY/ COUNTRY	SCORE	CROWD	G.S. GOALS/ MISC.	TYPE OF MATCH
Apr 12th	1947	England	Wembley Stadium	London, England	1–1	98,250	0	Home International Championship
Nov 12th	1947	Wales	Hampden Park	Glasgow, Scotland	1–2	86,582	0	Home International Championship
Jan 14th	1948	The Irish League	Celtic Park	Glasgow, Scotland	3–0	40,000	0	SFL
Apr 24th	1948	The League Of Ireland	Dalymount Park	Dublin, Ireland	2–0	17,000	0	SFL
Apr 28th	1948	Belgium	Hampden Park	Glasgow, Scotland	2–0	67,447	0	Friendly
May 17th	1948	Switzerland	Wankdorf Stadium	Berne, Switzerland	1–2	30,000	0	Friendly
May 23rd	1948	France	Stade Olympique	Paris, France	0–3	46,032	0 No. 9	Friendly
Oct 19th	1949	The League Of Ireland	Dalymount Park	Dublin, Ireland	1–0	17,000	0	SFL
Mar 22nd	1950	The English League	Ayresome Park	Middlesbrough, England	1–3	39,352	0	SFL
Nov 29th	1950	The English League	Ibrox Park	Glasgow, Scotland	1–0	72,000	0	SFL
Dec 3rd	1951	Wales	Ninian Park	Cardiff, Wales	2–3	26,454	0	Rest of Britain Select
Apr 5th	1952	England	Hampden Park	Glasgow, Scotland	1–2	134,504	0	Home International Championship
Apr 30th	1952	USA	Hampden Park	Glasgow, Scotland	6–0	107,809	0	Friendly
Oct 8th	1952	The League Of Ireland	Celtic Park	Glasgow, Scotland	5–1	10,000	0	SFL
Mar 16th	1955	The English Football League	Hampden Park	Glasgow, Scotland	3–2	29,834	0	SFL
Apr 4th	1955	Portugal	Hampden Park	Glasgow, Scotland	3–0	20,858	0	Friendly
May 15th	1955	Yugoslavia	Partizan Stadion	Belgrade, Yugoslavia	2–2	20,000	1 goal	Friendly
May 19th	1955	Austria	Prater Stadion	Vienna, Austria	4–1	65,000	1 goal (Captain)	Friendly
May 29th	1955	Hungary	Nepstadion	Budapest, Hungary	1–3	102,000	1 goal (Captain)	Friendly
Sep 7th	1955	The Irish League	Ibrox Park	Glasgow, Scotland	3–0	33,500	1 goal	SFL
Sep 21st	1955	The League Of Ireland	Dalymount Park	Dublin, Ireland	4–2	16,756	0	SFL
Oct 8th	1955	Northern Ireland	Windsor Park	Belfast, Northern Ireland	1–2	58,000	0	Home International Championship

DATE	YEAR	VERSUS	VENUE	CITY/ COUNTRY	SCORE	CROWD	G.S. GOALS/ MISC.	TYPE OF MATCH
Oct 26th	1955	The English Football League	Hillsborough	Sheffield, England	2–4	37,778	1 goal	SFL
Oct 30th	1955	The Danish Football Combination	Idraetsparken	Kobenhavn, Denmark	4–0	16,000	1 goal	SFL
Nov 9th	1955	Wales	Hampden Park	Glasgow, Scotland	2–0	53,887	0	Home International Championship
Mar 12th	1956	Anglo/ South African XI	Ibrox Park	Glasgow, Scotland	2–1	60,000	0 (Captain)	Scottish Select XI
Apr 14th	1956	England	Hampden Park	Glasgow, Scotland	1–1	132,817	0 No. 11	Home International Championship
May 8th	1957	Spain	Hampden Park	Glasgow, Scotland	4–2	88,980	0	World Cup Qualifier
May 19th	1957	Switzerland	St Jakob's Stadion	Basle, Switzerland	2–1	48,000	0	World Cup Qualifier
May 26th	1957	Spain	Estadio Santiago Bernabeu	Madrid, Spain	1–4	90,000	1 goal	World Cup Qualifier

17 EDINBURGH SELECT CHARITIES MATCHES

YEAR	VERSUS	VENUE	SCORE
1942	RAF International	Easter Road	1–3
1943	RAF International XI	Tynecastle Park	3–2
1944	Aston Villa	Tynecastle Park	3–4
1945	Huddersfield Town	Tynecastle Park	4–0
1946	Aston Villa	Easter Road	3–3
1947	Derby County	Easter Road	4–5
1948	Blackpool	Tynecastle Park	1–1
1949	Wolverhampton Wanderers	Easter Road	2–3
1950	Newcastle United	Tynecastle Park	1–1
1951	Liverpool	Easter Road	1–2
1952	Portsmouth	Tynecastle Park	3–2
1953	Wolverhampton Wanderers	Easter Road	3–2
1954	Bolton Wanderers	Tynecastle Park	3–2
1955	Newcastle United	Easter Road	1–1
1956	Birmingham City	Tynecastle Park	2–1
1957	Preston North End	Easter Road	1–3
1960	Chelsea	Tynecastle Park	5–4

TIMELINE OF GORDON SMITH'S MOST MEMORABLE GAMES

SCOTLAND SCHOOLBOY INTERNATIONAL

30th April 1938	*Starks Park, Kircaldy*	9,471
Scottish Schools FA	5 (Smith 2, Combe)	
Irish Schools FA	2	

SCOTLAND SCHOOLBOY INTERNATIONAL

14th May 1938 *Roker Park, Sunderland* 23,897
English Schools FA 0
Scottish Schools FA 1

DEBUT FOR HIBERNIAN

28th April 1941 *Tynecastle Park, Edinburgh* 3,004
Heart of Midlothian 3 (Walker 3)
Hibernian 5 (Smith 3, Combe, Adams)
Heart of Midlothian: Willie Waugh; Duncan McClure, Archie Miller, Jimmy Phillip, Jimmy Dykes, Tommy Brown, Tommy Dougan, Tommy Walker, George Hamilton, Alex Massie, Robert Christie.
Hibernian: Jimmy Kerr; Davie Shaw, Alex Hall, Sammy Kean, Bobby Baxter, Willie Rice, Jock Weir, Bobby Combe, Gordon Smith, Willie Finnegan, Tommy Adams.

LEAGUE MATCH, AND RANGERS HEAVIEST EVER DEFEAT

27th September 1941 *Easter Road Park, Edinburgh* 14,800
Hibernian 8 (Milne 2, Combe 4, Smith 2)
Rangers 1 (Venters pen)
Hibernian: Crozier; Shaw, Hall, Hardisty, Baxter, Kean, Smith, Finnegan, Milne, Combe, Caskie.
Rangers: Dawson; Grey, Shaw, Bolt, Woodburn, Little, McIntosh, Gillick, Smith, Venters, Johnstone.
Referee – M Hutton (Glasgow)

SUMMER CUP FINAL

14th July 1942 *Hampden Park, Glasgow* 40,000
Rangers 0
Hibernian 0 (Rangers won on the toss of a coin)
Hibernian: Joe Crozier; Davy Shaw, Alex Hall, Matt Busby, Bobby Baxter, Sammy Kean, Gordon Smith, Willie Finnegan, Arthur Milne, Bobby Combe, Jimmy Caskie.
Rangers: Dawson; Gray, Shaw, Little, Young, Symon, Waddell, Thornton, Gillick, Venters, Johnston.

AGED 19, HIS FIRST ADULT APPEARANCE FOR THE NATIONAL SIDE

6th November 1943 *Hampden Park, Glasgow* 50,000
Scotland XI 1 (Fagan)
RAF International XI 2 (Carter, Drake)
No team listings available due to wartime security measures.

SOUTHERN LEAGUE CUP FINAL

20th May 1944 *Hampden Park, Glasgow* 50,000
Hibernian 0
Rangers 0 (Hibernian won 6–5 on corner kicks)
Hibernian: Mitchell Downie; Bobby Fraser, Alex Hall, Willie Finnegan, Bobby Baxter, Sammy Kean, Gordon Smith, Tommy Bogan, Jimmy Nelson, Jimmy Woodburn, Jimmy Caskie.
Rangers: Jerry Dawson; Douglas Gray, Jock Shaw, Dr. Adam Little, George Young, Scott Symon, Willie Waddell, Torry Gillick, Jimmy Smith, Jimmy Duncanson, Joe Johnston.

FIRST FULL INTERNATIONAL CAP

14th October 1944 *Wembley Stadium, London* 100,000
England 6 (Lawton 3, Goulden, Carter, Smith)
Scotland 2 (Milne, Walker)

England: Frank Swift (Manchester City); Laurie Scott (Arsenal), George Hardwick (Middlesbrough), Frank Soo (Stoke City), Bernard Joy (Arsenal), Joe Mercer (Everton), Stanley Matthews (Stoke City), Horatio Carter (Sunderland), Tommy Lawton (Everton), Leonard Goulden (West Ham United), Leslie Smith (Brentford).

Scotland: David Cumming (Newcastle United); James Stephen (Bradford City), George Cummings (Aston Villa), Bobby Thyne (Darlington), Bobby Baxter (Hibernian), Archie Macauley (West Ham United), Gordon Smith (Hibernian), Tommy Walker (Heart of Midlothian), Arthur Milne (Hibernian), Andy Black (Heart of Midlothian), Jimmy Caskie (Hibernian).

ROSEBERY CUP FINAL – HIBERNIAN WON 7–6 ON CORNERS

9th May 1945 *Easter Road, Edinburgh* 15,252
Hibernian 2 (Weir 2)
Heart of Midlothian 2 (Black 2)

Hibernian: Mitchell Downie; Jock Govan, Alex Hall, Willie Finnegan, Bobby Baxter, Sammy Kean, Gordon Smith, Bobby Combe, Jock Weir, Willie Peat, Jimmy Caskie.

Heart of Midlothian: Brown; McAra, McClure, Cox, Baxter, Neilson, Briscoe, Walker, Garret, McRae, Black.

ONLY CAP ALONGSIDE WILLIE WADDELL

10th November 1945 *Hampden Park, Glasgow* 97,323
Scotland 2 (Dodds, Waddell)
Wales 0

Scotland: Brown (Queen's Park); McPhie (Falkirk), Shaw (Rangers), Campbell (Greenock Morton), Paton (Motherwell), Paterson (Celtic), Waddell (Rangers), Smith (Hibernian), Dodds (Blackpool), Deakin (St Mirren), Liddell (Liverpool).

Wales: Sidlow (Wolverhampton Wanderers); Dearson (Birmingham City), Hughes (Birmingham City), Witcomb (WBA), R Davies (Nottingham Forest), Burgess (Tottenham Hotspur), J Jones (Swansea), Squires (Swansea), Lowrie (Coventry City), Cumner (Arsenal), G Edwards (Birmingham City).

Referee – M Dale (Glasgow)

SCOTTISH XI SELECT GAME

17th November 1945 *Highbury, Celle, Germany* 12,000
Combined Military Services XI 2
Scottish Select XI 4 (Delaney, Garth, Walker 2)

Combined Military Services XI: Swindon; Compton, Hughes, Russell, Mould, Ward, Whittinghame, Lewis, Westcott, Dorset, Ormston.

Scottish Select XI: Brown (Queens Park), McPhie (Falkirk), McGowan (Partick Thistle), Campbell (Clyde), Husband (Partick Thistle), Cox (Dundee), Smith (Hibs), Baird (Aberdeen), Delaney (Celtic), Garth (Morton), Walker (Hearts)

ANOTHER SELECT GAME – THE FOLLOWING DAY

18th November 1945 *Hamburg, Germany* 35,000
Combined Military Services 1 (Westcott)
Scottish Select XI 1 (Garth)

Combined Military Services XI: Swindon; Hughes, Westwood, Russell, Mould, Percival, Robinson, Lewis, Westcott, Hume, Wardle.

Scottish Select XI: Brown; McGowan, McPhie, Campbell, Husband, MacDonald, Smith, Baird, Delaney, Garth, Walker.

Referee – Lieutenant Commander FG Davis, RNVR

FIRST PEACE-TIME INTERNATIONAL

23rd January 1946 *Hampden Park, Glasgow* 48,830
Scotland 2 (Delaney 2)
Belgium 2 (Lemberechts, D'Aguilar)

Scotland: Brown (Queens Park), McGowan (Partick Thistle), Shaw (Rangers), Campbell (Clyde), Paton (Motherwell), Paterson (Celtic), Smith (Hibernian), Baird (Aberdeen), Delaney (Manchester Utd), Deakin (St Mirren), Walker (Heart of Midlothian).

Belgium: Daenen; Paverick, Pannaye, Puttaert, Vercammen, Devos, Lemberechts, Coppens, Declyn, D'Aguilar, Sermon.

Referee – J Jackson (Glasgow)

CHALLENGE MATCH

1st May 1946 *Highbury, Celle, Germany* 14,000
British Army on the Rhine 0
Hibernian 3 (Smith, Weir 2)

The British Army On The Rhine: Bly (Hull City); Brinkwater (St Mirren), Widdowfield (Halifax), Williams (Chester City), Compton (Arsenal), Rickaby (Middlesbrough), Parsons (West Ham United), Duggan (Luton Town), Harrison (Burnley), Dymond (Bristol City), Steel (Morton).

Hibernian: Kerr; Howie, Shaw, Fraser, Aird, Kean, Smith, Finnegan, Milne, Weir, Nutley.

VICTORY CUP FINAL

15th June 1946 *Hampden Park, Glasgow* 67,000
Rangers 3 (Finnegan og, Duncanson 2)
Hibernian 1 (Aitkenhead)

Rangers: Brown; Cox, Shaw, Watkins, Young, Symon, Waddell, Gillick, Thornton, Duncanson, Caskie.

Hibernian: Kerr; Govan, Shaw, Howie, Aird, Finnegan, Smith, Peat, Milne, Aitkenhead, Nutley.

Referee – J Martin (Blairgowrie)

TECHNICALLY, HIS FIRST OFFICIAL 'CAP' ALTHOUGH THIS WAS THE 9TH TIME HE'D REPRESENTED HIS COUNTRY

27th November 1946 *Hampden Park, Glasgow* 98,776
Scotland 0
Northern Ireland 0

Scotland: Brown (Rangers); Young (Rangers), Shaw (Hibernian), Campbell (Morton), Frennan (Newcastle United), Long (Clyde), Smith (Hibernian), Hamilton (Aberdeen), Thornton (Rangers), Duncanson (Rangers), Liddell (Liverpool).

Northern Ireland: Hinton (Fulham); Gorman (Brentford), Feeney (Linfield), Martin (Glentoran), Vernon (Belfast Celtic), Farrell (Everton), Cochrane (Leeds United), Carey (Manchester United), Walsh (WBA), Stevenson (Everton), Eglington (Everton)

Referee – G Reader (Southampton)

INTERNATIONAL

12th April 1947 *Wembley Stadium, London* 98,250
England 1 (Carter)
Scotland 1 (MacLaren)

England: Swift (Manchester City); Scott (Arsenal), Hardwick (Middlesbrough), Wright (Wolverhampton Wanderers), Franklin (Stoke City), Johnson (Blackpool), Matthews (Stoke City), Carter (Derby County), Lawton (Chelsea), Mannion (Middlesbrough), Mullen (Wolverhampton Wanderers).

Scotland: Miller (Celtic); Young (Rangers), Shaw (Rangers), Macauley (Brentford), Woodburn (Rangers), Forbes (Sheffield United), Smith (Hibernian),MacLaren (Preston), Delaney (Manchester United), Steel (Morton), Pearson (Newcastle United).

Referee – C Delasalle (France)

SCOTTISH CUP FINAL

19th April 1947 *Hampden Park, Glasgow* 82,140
Hibernian 1 (Cuthbertson)
Aberdeen 2 (Hamilton, Williams)

Hibernian: Kerr; Govan, Shaw, Howie, Aird, Kean, Smith, Finnegan, Cuthbertson, Turnbull, Ormond.
Aberdeen: Johnstone; McKenna, Taylor, McLaughlin, Dunlop, Waddell, Harris, Hamilton, Williams, Baird, McCall.
Referee – R Calder (Rutherglen)

HIS FAVOURITE EVER GOAL

1st November 1947 Fir Park, Motherwell 16,000
Motherwell 0
Hibernian 2 (Smith 2)

Hibernian: Brown; Govan, Shaw, Buchanan, Waldie, Kean, Smith, Combe, Linwood, Turnbull, Ormond.

SCORED 5 GOALS – A RECORD FOR A WINGER IN SCOTTISH FOOTBALL

8th November 1947 *Easter Road, Edinburgh* 25,000
Hibernian 8 (Smith 5, Linwood 3)
Third Lanark 0

Hibernian: Brown; Govan, Shaw, Buchanan, Waldie, Finnegan, Smith, Combe, Linwood, Turnbull, Ormond.

INTERNATIONAL

12th November 1947 *Hampden Park, Glasgow* 88,592
Scotland 1 (MacLaren)
Wales 2 (Ford, Lowrie)

Scotland: Miller (Celtic); Govan (Hibernian), Stephen Arsenal), Macauley (Arsenal), Woodburn (Rangers), Forbes (Sheffield United), Smith (Hibernian), MacLaren (Preston North End), Delaney (Manchester United), Steel (Derby County)
Wales: Sidlow; Sherwood, Barnes, Powell, Jones, Burgess, Thomas, Powell, Ford, Lowrie, Edwards.
Referee – A Ellis (Halifax)

FIRST GAME FOR THE SCOTTISH FOOTBALL LEAGUE

14th January 1948 *Celtic Park, Glasgow* 40,000
Scottish Football League 3 (Houliston 2, Duncanson)
Irish Football League 0

SFL: Willie Miller (Celtic); Sammy Cox (Rangers), Tommy Deans (Clyde), Andy Cowie (Aberdeen), George Young (Rangers), Pat McAulay (Celtic), Gordon Smith (Hibernian), Torry Gillick (Rangers), Billy Houliston (Queen of the South), Jimmy Duncanson (Rangers), Willie Ormond (Hibernian).
IFL: Smyth; McMillan, McMichael, Leggett, Currie, Lawlor, McKenna, McCormack, Bradford, O'Neil, Kelly.
Referee – W Webb

LARGEST EVER CROWD AT A BRITISH FOOTBALL MATCH – OUT WITH AN INTERNATIONAL

27th March 1948 *Ibrox Park, Glasgow* 143,570
Rangers 1 (Thornton)
Hibernian 0

Rangers: Brown; Young, Shaw, McColl, Woodburn, Cox, Rutherford, Gillick, Thornton, Findlay, Duncanson.
Hibernian: Farm; Govan, Shaw, Kean, Howie, Buchanan, Smith, Combe, Linwood, Cuthbertson, Ormond.

SFL INTERNATIONAL

24th April 1948 *Dalymount Park, Dublin* 17,000
League of Ireland 0
Scottish Football League 2 (Aikman, Hamilton)

SFL: Willie Miller (Celtic); Jock Govan (Hibernian), Davie Shaw (Hibernian), Hugh Brown (Partick Thistle), George Young (Rangers), Willie Redpath (Motherwell), Gordon Smith (Hibernian), George Hamilton (Hearts), Archie Aikman (Falkirk), Johnny Deakin (St Mirren), Tommy Pearson (Aberdeen).

INTERNATIONAL

28th April 1948 *Hampden Park, Glasgow* 67,447
Scotland 2 (Combe, Duncan)
Belgium 0

Scotland: Jimmy Cowan (Greenock Morton); Jock Govan (Hibernian), Davie Shaw (Hibernian), Willie Campbell (Greenock Morton), George Young (Rangers), Archie Macauley (Arsenal), Gordon Smith (Hibernian), Bobby Combe (Hibernian), Leslie Johnston (Clyde), Eddie Turnbull (Hibernian), David Duncan (East Fife).

Belgium: Daenen; Aernaudts, Erroelen, Anoul, De Buck, Henriet, Lemberechts, Govard, Mermans, Van Steelant, De Cleyn.

Referee – W Ling (Stapleford)

INTERNATIONAL

17th May 1948 *Wankdorf Stadium, Berne* 30,000
Switzerland 2 (Maillard, Fatton)
Scotland 1 (Johnston)

Switzerland: Corrodi; Belli, Steffen, Lisenti, Eggimann, Bocquet, Bickel, Friedlander, Amado, Maillard, Fatton.

Scotland: Jimmy Cowan (Greenock Morton); Jock Govan (Hibernian), Davie Shaw (Hibernian), Willie Campbell (Greenock Morton), George Young (Rangers), Archie Macauley (Arsenal), Gordon Smith (Hibernian), Bobby Combe (Hibernian), Leslie Johnston (Clyde), Eddie Turnbull (Hibernian), David Duncan (East Fife).

Referee – A Bernanek (Austria)

INTERNATIONAL

23rd May 1948 *Stade Olympique, Paris* 46,032
France 3 (Bongiorni, Flamion, Baratte)
Scotland 0

France: Darui; Huguet, Marche, Cuissard, Gregoire, Prouff, Sesia, Baratte, Bongiorni, Barek, Flamion.

Scotland: Jimmy Cowan (Greenock Morton); Jock Govan (Hibernian), Davie Shaw (Hibernian), Eddie Turnbull (Hibernian), George Young (Rangers), Archie Macauley (Arsenal), Eddie Rutherford (Rangers), Billy Steel (Derby County), Gordon Smith (Hibernian), Sammy Cox (Rangers), David Duncan (East Fife)

Referee – K Van Der Meer (Holland)

WILLIE MCCARTNEY'S TESTIMONIAL

22nd September 1948 *Easter Road, Edinburgh* 35,098
Hibernian 0
Manchester United 1 (Buckle)

Hibernian: Kerr; Howie, Shaw, Finnegan, Aird, Kean, Smith, Cuthbertson, Linwood, Turnbull, Ormond.

Manchester United: Crompton; Ball, Carey, Anderson, Chilton, McGlen, Delaney, Buckle, Rowley, Pearson, Mitten.

'CHAMPIONS OF BRITAIN' MATCH.

25th April 1949 *White Hart Lane, London* 40,000
Tottenham Hotspur 2 (Duquemin, Bennett)
Hibernian 5 (Johnstone, Ogilvie 2, Turnbull, Smith)

Tottenham Hotspur: Ditchburn; Tickridge, Withers, Garwood, Clarke, Trailer, Walters, Bennett, Duquemin, Bailey, Medley

Hibernian: Younger; Govan, Cairns, Gallacher, Paterson, Ogilvie, Smith, Johnstone, Cuthbertson, Turnbull, Ormond.

FIRST EVER LEAGUE MATCH THE 'FAMOUS FIVE' APPEARED TOGETHER.

15th October1949 *Easter Road, Edinburgh* 25,000
Hibernian 2 (Smith, Turnbull)
Queen of the South 0

Hibernian: Younger; Govan, Cairns, Combe, Paterson, Buchanan, Smith, Johnstone, Reilly, Turnbull, Ormond.

SFL INTERNATIONAL

19th October 1949 *Dalymount Park, Dublin* 17,000
League of Ireland 0
Scottish Football League 1 (Reilly)

SFL: Jimmy Cowan (Greenock Morton); George Young (Rangers), Sammy Cox (Rangers), Bobby Evans (Celtic), Willie Woodburn (Rangers), Willie Redpath (Motherwell), Gordon Smith (Hibernian), Jimmy Mason (Third Lanark), Billy Houliston (Queen of the South), Johnny Deakin (St Mirren), Lawrie Reilly (Hibernian).

LOI: Kirch; Clarke, O'Byrne, Murphy, Daly, Broadly, Charoll, Lawler, Killfeather, Mullen, Colven.

LARGEST EVER ATTENDANCE AT A GAME PLAYED AT EASTER ROAD

2nd January 1950 *Easter Road, Edinburgh* 65,840
Hibernian 1 (Smith)
Heart of Midlothian 2 (Conn, Wardhaugh)

Hibernian: Younger; Shaw, Cairns, Combe, Paterson, Buchanan, Smith, Johnstone, Reilly, Turnbull, Ormond.

Heart of Midlothian: Brown; Parker, McKenzie, Cox, Dougan, Laing, Sloan, Conn, Bauld, Wardhaugh, Flavell.

SFL INTERNATIONAL

22nd March 1950 *Ayresome Park, Middlesbrough* 39,352
English Football League 3 (Mortensen 2, Bailey)
Scottish Football League 1 (Young)

SFL: Bobby Brown (Rangers); George Young (Rangers), Sammy Cox (Rangers), Bobby Evans (Celtic), Willie Woodburn (Rangers), Willie Hewitt (Partick Thistle), Gordon Smith (Hibernian), Jimmy Mason (Third Lanark), Willie Bauld (Hearts), Alan Brown (East Fife), Lawrie Reilly (Hibernian).

EFL: William; Ramsey, Aston, Wright, Franklin, Dickinson, Hancocks, Mannion, Mortensen, Bailey, Langton.

Referee – W Holt

CHALLENGE MATCH

1st May 1950 *White Hart Lane, London* 33,000
Tottenham Hotspur 0
Hibernian 1 (Ramsay og)

Tottenham Hotspur: Ditchburn; Ramsay, Willis, Nicholson, Clarke, Burgess, Watters, Bennett, Duquemin, Rees, Medley.

Hibernian: Younger; Govan, Cairns, Howie, Paterson, Ogilvie, Smith, Combe, Reilly, Turnbull, Ormond.

SCOTTISH LEAGUE CUP QUARTER-FINAL (SECOND-LEG)

20th September 1950 *Easter Road, Edinburgh* 41,789
Hibernian 4 (Johnstone, Reilly, Ormond, Anderson og)
Aberdeen 1 (Yorston)
Hibernian: Younger; Govan, Ogilvie, Howie, Paterson, Combe, Smith, Johnstone, Reilly, Turnbull, Ormond.
Aberdeen: Martin, Emery, Shaw, Anderson, Young, Bakie, Boyd, Yorston, Hamilton, Baird, Hather.
Referee – J Jackson

SCOTTISH LEAGUE CUP QUARTER-FINAL (REPLAY)

2nd October 1950 *Ibrox Park, Glasgow* 52,000
Hibernian 1 (Turnbull)
Aberdeen 1 (Baird)
Hibernian: Younger; Govan, Ogilvie, Buchanan. Paterson, Combe, Smith, Johnstone, Reilly, Turnbull, Ormond.
Aberdeen: Martin; Emery, Shaw, Anderson, Young, Glen, Boyd, Yorston, Hamilton, Baird, Hather.
Referee – J Jackson

SCOTTISH LEAGUE CUP QUARTER-FINAL (SECOND-REPLAY)

3rd October 1950 *Hampden Park, Glasgow* 22,803
Hibernian 5 (Smith, Johnstone 2, Reilly, Turnbull)
Aberdeen 1 (Baird)
Hibernian: Younger; Govan, Ogilvie, Buchanan, Paterson, Combe, Smith, Johnstone, Reilly, Turnbull, Ormond.
Aberdeen: Martin; Emery, Shaw, Anderson, Young, Glen, Boyd, Yorston, Hamilton, Baird, Hather.
Referee – J Jackson

SCOTTISH LEAGUE CUP FINAL

28th October 1950 *Hampden Park, Glasgow* 67,000
Hibernian 0
Motherwell 3 (Young, Forrest, Watters)
Hibernian: Younger; Govan, Ogilvie, Buchanan, Paterson, Combe, Smith, Johnstone, Reilly, Ormond, Bradley.
Motherwell: Johnston; Kilmarnock, Shaw, McLeod, Paton, Redpath, Watters, Forrest, Kelly, Watson, Aitkenhead.
Referee – J Mowat

SFL INTERNATIONAL

29th November 1950 *Ibrox Park, Glasgow* 72,000
Scottish Football League 1 (McPhail)
English Football League 0
SFL: Bobby Brown (Rangers); George Young (Rangers), Willie McNaught (Raith Rovers), Bobby Evans (Celtic), Willie Woodburn (Rangers), Willie Redpath (Motherwell), Gordon Smith (Hibernian), Eddie Turnbull, (Hibernian), John McPhail (Celtic), Billy Steel (Dundee), Willie Ormond (Hibernian).
EFL: Ditchburn; Robinson, Aston, Wright, Taylor, Cockburn, Hancocks, Mortensen, Lofthouse, Morris, Finney.
Referee – J Mowat

SCOTTISH CUP MATCH

10th February 1951 *Ibrox Park, Glasgow* 102,342
Rangers 2 (Simpson 2)
Hibernian 3 (Smith, Turnbull, Johnstone)
Rangers: Brown; Young, Shaw, McColl, Woodburn, Cox, Waddell, Thornton, Simpson, Rae, Paton.
Hibernian: Younger; Govan, Ogilvie, Buchanan, Paterson, Gallacher, Smith, Johnstone, Reilly, Turnbull, Ormond.

FLOODLIT GAME

2nd May 1951 *Stade Olympique, Paris* 31,000
Racing Clube de Paris 1
Hibernian 1 (Smith)
Hibernian: Kerr; Howie, Cairns, Gallagher, Paterson, Buchanan, Smith, Johnstone, Reilly, Turnbull, Combe.

TOUR MATCH

6th May 1951 *Stade Municipal du Ray, Nice.* 30,000
Olympique Nice 0
Hibernian 1 (Reilly)
Hibernian: Kerr; Howie, Cairns, Govan, Paterson, Buchanan, Smith, Johnstone, Reilly, Turnbull, Combe.

FESTIVAL OF BRITAIN GAME

19th May 1951 *Easter Road, Edinburgh* 31,000
Hibernian 3 (Buchanan, McDonald, Turnbull)
Sportsklub Rapid Wien 5
Hibernian: Younger; Govan, Cairns, Buchanan, Paterson, Howie, McDonald, Johnstone, Smith, Turnbull, Combe.
Sportsklub Rapid Wien: Zemman; Happel, Markel, Gemhardt, Hannappi, Müeller, R Köerner, Reigler, Deinst, Pröbst, A Köerner.

MATCH COMMEMORATING THE 75TH ANNIVERSARY OF THE WELSH FOOTBALL ASSOCIATION.

3rd December 1951 *Ninian Park, Cardiff* 26,454
Wales 3 (Allchurch 2, Ford)
Rest of Britain Select 2 (Fleming, Medley)
Wales: Short (Plymouth Argyle); Barnes (Arsenal), Sherwood (Cardiff City), Paul (Manchester City), Daniel (Arsenal), Burgess (Tottenham Hotspur), Foulkes (Newcastle United), Morris (Burnley), Ford (Sunderland), Allchurch (Swansea Town), Clarke (Manchester City).
Rest of Britain Select: Cowan (Greenock Morton & Scotland); Young (Rangers & Scotland), McMichael (Newcastle United & Northern Ireland), Docherty (Preston North End & Scotland), Vernon (WBA & Northern Ireland), Wright (Wolverhampton Wanderers & England), Smith (Hibernian & Scotland), Fleming (East Fife & Scotland), Lofthouse (Bolton Wanderers & England), Bailey (Tottenham Hotspur & England), Medley (Tottenham Hotspur & England).

INTERNATIONAL

5th April 1952 *Hampden Park, Glasgow* 134,504
Scotland 1 (Reilly)
England 2 (Pearson 2)
Scotland: Bobby Brown (Rangers); George Young (Rangers), Willie McNaught (Raith Rovers), James Scoular (Portsmouth), Willie Woodburn (Rangers), Willie Redpath (Motherwell), Gordon Smith (Hibernian), Bobby Johnstone (Hibernian), Lawrie Reilly (Hibernian), Ian McMillan (Airdrie), Billy Liddell (Liverpool).
England: Merrick; Ramsey, Garrett, Wright, Froggatt, Dickinson, Finney, Broadis, Lofthouse, Pearson, Rowley.
Referee – P Morris (Belfast)

HIBS – CHAMPIONS FOR 2ND SEASON IN A ROW

9th April 1952 *Easter Road, Edinburgh* 26,000
Hibernian 3 (Ormond 2, Combe)
Dundee 1 (Christie)
Hibernian: Younger; Govan, Howie, Buchanan, Paterson, Gallacher, Smith, Combe, Reilly, Turnbull, Ormond.
Dundee: Henderson; Follon, Cowan, Gallacher, Cowie, Bøyd, Burrell, Ziesing, Flavell, Steel, Christie.
Referee – G Mitchell

UNOFFICIAL BRITISH CHAMPIONS GAME

23rd April 1952 *White Hart Lane, London* 43,000
Tottenham Hotspur 1 (Ramsay)
Hibernian 2 (Smith 2)
Tottenham Hotspur: Ditchburn; Ramsay, Withers, Nicholson, Clarke, Burgess, Walters, Bennett, Duquemin, Bailey, McLellan.
Hibernian: Younger; Govan, Howie, Buchanan, Paterson, Gallacher, Smith, Combe, Reilly, Turnbull, Ormond.

CHALLENGE MATCH

26th April 1952 *Easter Road, Edinburgh* 24,000
Hibernian 2 (Reilly 2)
Bolton Wanderers 2 (Lofthouse 2)
Hibernian: McQueen; Govan, Howie, Buchanan, Paterson, Gallagher, Smith, Combe, Reilly, Turnbull, Ormond.
Bolton Wanderers: Hanson; Ball, Higgins, Bell, Barrass, Edwards, Holden, Moir, Lofthouse, Hassall, Webster.

INTERNATIONAL

30th April 1952 *Hampden Park, Glasgow* 107,809
Scotland 6 (Reilly 3, McMillan 2, O'Connell og)
USA 0
Scotland: Jimmy Cowan (Greenock Morton); George Young (Rangers), Sammy Cox (Rangers), James Scoular (Portsmouth), Willie Woodburn (Rangers), Hugh Kelly (Blackpool), Gordon Smith (Hibernian), Ian McMillan (Airdrie), Lawrie Reilly (Hibernian), Alan Brown (Blackpool), Billy Liddell (Liverpool).
USA: Borghi; Keough, O'Connell, Sheppell, Colombo, Bahr, Monsen, Souza, McLaughlin, Souza, Roberts.
Referee – D Gerrard (Aberdeen)

HIS TESTIMONIAL MATCH

15th September 1952 *Easter Road, Edinburgh* 28,000
Hibernian 7 (Reilly 3, Turnbull 2, Ormond, Smith)
Manchester United 3 (Rowley 2, Pearson)
Hibernian: McCracken; Govan, Howie, Gallacher, Paterson, Combe, Smith, Johnstone, Reilly, Turnbull, Ormond.
Manchester United: Wood; McNulty, Aston, Carey, Chilton, Gibson, Scott, Downey, Rowley, Pearson, Berry.
Referee – J Mowat (Rutherglen)

SFL INTERNATIONAL

8th October 1952 *Celtic Park, Glasgow* 10,000
Scottish Football League 5 (Reilly 4, Steel)
League of Ireland 1 (O'Callaghan)
SFL: Fred Martin (Aberdeen); Jock Govan (Hibernian), Sammy Cox (Rangers), Bobby Evans (Celtic), Jimmy Davidson (Partick Thistle), David Laing (Hearts), Gordon Smith (Hibernian), Bobby Johnstone (Hibernian), Lawrie Reilly (Hibernian), Billy Steel (Dundee), Willie Ormond (Hibernian).
LOI: Keogh; Cusack, Fuliam, Coad, Daly, Sweeney, Cunningham, Tracey, Glynn, Lipper, O'Callaghan.
Referee – R Phillips

MATCH TO RAISE FUNDS FOR THE NATIONAL PLAYING FIELDS ASSOCIATION – THE SECOND HALF TELEVISED LIVE ON BBC TV.

22nd October 1952 *Highbury, London* 56,000
Arsenal 7 (Roper 5, Lishman 2)
Hibernian 1 (Reilly)
Arsenal: Kelsey; Wade, Forbes, Smith, Daniel, Mercer, Milton, Logie, Goring, Roper, Lishman.
Hibernian: Younger; Howie, Govan, Gallacher, Paterson, Combe, Smith, Johnstone, Reilly, Turnbull, Ormond.

300TH HIBERNIAN GOAL IN HIS 518TH GAME

27th December 1952 *Easter Road, Edinburgh* 20,000
Hibernian 3 (Smith, Reilly, Ormond)
Aberdeen 0

Hibernian: Tommy Younger; Willie Clark, Hugh Howie, Archie Buchanan, John Paterson, Bobby Combe, Gordon Smith, Bobby Johnstone, Lawrie Reilly, Eddie Turnbull, Willie Ormond.

Aberdeen: Fred Martin; Jimmy Mitchell, Davie Shaw, Tony Harris, Billy Smith, Jack Allister, Ian McNeil, Harry Yorston, Paddy Buckley, Archie Baird, Jack Hather.

17TH AND LAST OFFICIAL HAT-TRICK

21st February 1953 *Broomfield Park, Airdrie* 27,000
Airdrie 0
Hibernian 4 (Smith 3, Reilly)

Hibernian: Younger; Clark, Howie, Buchanan, Paterson, Combe, Smith, Johnstone, Reilly, Turnbull, Ormond.

Airdrie: Fraser; Fryde, Cross, Cairns, Rodger, Doherty, Brown, McMillan, Baird, Quinn, McCulloch.

Referee – G Faultless

CHALLENGE MATCH IN A NEUTRAL COUNTRY

15th April 1953 *Heysel Stadium, Brussels* 32,678
Austria Vienna 3 (E Melchoir 2, Stojaspal)
Hibernian 2 (Turnbull 2)

Austria Vienna: Ondrieska; D Melchoir, Kowanz, Fischer, Stotz, Schleger, E Melchoir, Kominek, Pichler, Stojaspal, Auredrik.

Hibernian: Younger; Govan, Howie, Buchanan, Paterson, Ward, Smith, Combe, Anderson, Turnbull, Ormond.

CORONATION CUP FINAL

20th May 1953 *Hampden Park, Glasgow* 117,000
Hibernian 0
Celtic 2 (Walsh, Mochan)

Hibernian: Younger; Govan, Paterson, Buchanan, Howie, Combe, Smith, Johnstone, Reilly, Turnbull, Ormond.

Celtic: Bonnar; Haughney, Rollo, Evans, Stein, McPhail, Collins, Walsh, Mochan, Peacock, Fernie.

Referee – H Phillips (Motherwell)

HIBERNIAN'S OPENING GAME OF THE RIVADAVIA CORRÊA MEYER TOURNAMENT

7th June 1953 *Estádio do Maracanã, Rio de Janeiro* 33,671
Vasco Da Gama 3 (Maneca, Alvinho)
Hibernian 3 (Turnbull, Reilly 2)

Vasco da Gama: Osvaldo; Augusto, Belini, Eli, Mirim, Jorge, Sabara, Maneca, Genuino, Ipojucan, (Alvinho) Chico.

Hibernian: Younger; Govan, Howie, Buchanan, Paterson, Combe, Smith, Johnstone, Reilly, Turnbull, Ormond.

Referee – Mario Viana (Brazil)

2ND GAME OF THE TOURNAMENT

13th June 1953 *Estádio do Maracanã, Rio de Janeiro* 18,000
Botafogo 3
Hibernian 1 (Reilly)

Hibernian: Younger; Govan, Howie, Buchanan, Paterson, Combe, Smith, Johnstone, Reilly, Turnbull, Ormond.

Referee – Erik Westman

3RD AND FINAL GAME FOR HIBERNIAN IN THE TOURNAMENT

20th June 1953 *Estádio do Maracanã, Rio de Janeiro* 37,950
Fluminense 3
Hibernian 0
Hibernian: Younger; Govan, Paterson, Buchanan, Howie, Ward, (Anderson), Smith, Johnstone, Reilly, Combe, Ormond.

BENEFIT GAME FOR MANCHESTER UNITED TRAINER, TOM CURRY

30th September 1953 *Old Trafford, Manchester* 46,000
Manchester United 2 (Taylor, Aston)
Hibernian 2 (Reilly 2)
Manchester United: Wood; Foulkes, Byrne, Carey, Jones, Cockburn, Webster, Aston, Blanchflower, Taylor, Macshane.
Hibernian: Younger; MacFarlane, Paterson, Ward, Howie, Combe, Smith, Johnstone, Reilly, Buchanan, Ormond.

BROKE THE TIBIA BONE IN HIS RIGHT LEG

19th December 1953 *Easter Road, Edinburgh* 20,000
Hibernian 5 (Smith 2, Reilly, Turnbull 2)
Raith Rovers 0
Hibernian: Hamilton; Howie, Paterson, Buchanan, Ward, Combe, Smith, Johnstone, Reilly, Turnbull, Ormond.

FIRST FLOODLIT MATCH AT EASTER ROAD

18th October 1954 *Easter Road, Edinburgh* 25,000
Hibernian 0
Heart of Midlothian 2 (Tulloch, Whittle)
Hibernian: Younger; Higgins, MacFarlane, Ward, Paterson, Combe, Smith, Turnbull, Buchanan, Preston, Ormond.
Heart of Midlothian: Duff; Parker, Adie, Mackay, Gougan, Cumming, Souness, Blackwood, Whittle, Tulloch, Urquhart.
Referee – J Mowat

'FAMOUS FIVE' FINAL MATCH TOGETHER

29th January 1955 *Easter Road, Edinburgh* 15,000
Hibernian 2 (Reilly, Ormond)
Clyde 3 (Ring 2, Buchanan)
Hibernian: Miller; Ward, Paterson, Grant, Plenderleith, Preston, Smith, Johnstone, Reilly, Turnbull, Ormond.
Clyde: Hewkins; Murphy, Haddock, Granville, Anderson, Laing, Divers, Robertson, Buchanan, Brown, Ring.

600TH APPEARANCE FOR HIBERNIAN

12th February 1955 *Rugby Park, Kilmarnock* 19,059
Kilmarnock 0
Hibernian 3 (Reilly 3)
Hibernian: Younger; MacFarlane, Paterson, Grant, Plenderleith, Preston, Smith, Johnstone, Reilly, Combe, Ormond.

SFL INTERNATIONAL

16th March 1955 — *Hampden Park, Glasgow* — 29,834

Scottish Football League 3 (Collins, Haddock, og)

English Football League 2 (Evans, Bentley)

SFL: George Niven (Rangers); Jimmy Mitchell (Aberdeen), Harry Haddock (Clyde), Bobby Evans (Celtic), Danny Malloy (Dundee), John Cumming (Hearts), Gordon Smith (Hibernian), Alfie Conn (Hearts), Paddy Buckley (Aberdeen), Jimmy Wardhaugh (Hearts), Bobby Collins (Celtic).

EFL: Mathews; Foulkes, Mansell, Armstrong, Marston, Edwards, Hooper, Atyeo, Bentley, Evans, Bluntstone.

Referee – J Mowat

INTERNATIONAL

4th May 1955 — *Hampden Park, Glasgow* — 20,858

Scotland 3 (Gemmell, Liddell, Reilly)

Portugal 0

Scotland: Tommy Younger (Hibernian); Alex Parker (Falkirk), Harry Haddock (Clyde), Bobby Evans (Celtic), George Young (Rangers), John Cumming (Hearts), Gordon Smith (Hibernian), Archie Robertson (Clyde), Lawrie Reilly (Hibernian), Tommy Gemmell (St Mirren), Billy Liddell (Liverpool).

Portugal: Gomes; Caldeira, Carvaldo, Caido, Passos, Graca, Aguas, Matateu, Coluna, Travacos, Martins.

Referee – D Gardeazabal (Spain)

INTERNATIONAL

15th May 1955 — *Partizan Stadion, Belgrade* — 20,000

Yugoslavia 2 (Veselinovic, Vukas)

Scotland 2 (Reilly, Smith)

Yugoslavia: Beara; Belin, Zekovic, Cajkovck, Svarka, Boskov, Veselinovic, Milutinovic, Bobek, Vukas, Zebec.

Scotland: Tommy Younger (Hibernian); Alex Parker (Falkirk), Harry Haddock (Clyde), Bobby Evans (Celtic), George Young (Rangers), John Cumming (Hearts), Gordon Smith (Hibernian), Bobby Collins (Celtic), Lawrie Reilly (Hibernian), Tommy Gemmell (St Mirren), Billy Liddell (Liverpool).

Referee – V Orlandini (Italy)

SCOTLAND CAPTAIN (INTERNATIONAL)

19th May 1955 — *Prater Stadion, Vienna* — 65,000

Austria 1 (Docherty og)

Scotland 4 (Robertson, Smith, Liddell, Reilly)

Austria: Schmied; Halla, Roeckl, Barschandt, Hanappi, Ocwirk, Rofbauer, Wagner, Brousek, Probst, Shieger.

Scotland: Tommy Younger (Hibernian); Alex Parker (Falkirk); Andy Kerr (Partick Thistle), Tommy Docherty (Preston North End), Bobby Evans (Celtic), Doug Cowie (Dundee), Gordon Smith (Hibernian), Bobby Collins (Celtic), Lawrie Reilly (Hibernian), Archie Robertson (Clyde), Billy Liddell (Liverpool).

Referee – Dr G Bernardi (Italy)

SCOTLAND CAPTAIN (INTERNATIONAL)

29th May 1955 — *Nepstadion, Budapest* — 102,000

Hungary 3 (Hidegkuti, Kocsis, Feneyvesi)

Scotland 1 (Smith)

Hungary: Danka; Buzanszky, Lantos, Bozsik, Barhide, Szojka, Sandor, Kocsis, Hidegkuti, Puskas, Feneyvesi.
Subs: Farago (Danka) and Palotas (Sandor)

Scotland: Tommy Younger (Hibernian); Andy Kerr (Partick Thistle), Harry Haddock (Clyde), Tommy Docherty (Preston North End), Bobby Evans (Celtic), Doug Cowie (Dundee), Gordon Smith (Hibernian), Bobby Collins (Celtic), Lawrie Reilly (Hibernian), Archie Robertson (Clyde), Billy Liddell (Liverpool).

Referee – F Seipelt (Austria)

SFL INTERNATIONAL

7th September 1955 *Ibrox Park, Glasgow* 33,500
Scottish Football League 3 (Hubbard, Reilly, Smith)
Irish Football League 0

SFL: Tommy Younger (Hibernian); Alex Parker (Falkirk), Harry Haddock (Clyde), Bobby Evans (Celtic), George Young (Rangers), John Cumming (Hearts), Gordon Smith (Hibernian), Bobby Collins (Celtic), Lawrie Reilly (Hibernian), Bobby Wishart (Aberdeen), Johnny Hubbard (Rangers).

IFL: Russell; Keith, Davis, Neil, McCavan, Lawlor, Lawry, Nixon, Coyle, Dickson, Weatherup.

Referee – J Mowat

EUROPEAN CUP 1955/56: FIRST-ROUND (FIRST-LEG)

14th September 1955 *Georg Melches Stadion, Essen* 5,000
Rot-Weiss Essen 0
Hibernian 4 (Turnbull 2, Reilly, Ormond)

Rot Weiss Essen: Herkenrath; Jaenisch, Sastrau, Hoechling, Wewers, Roettger, Roemtig, Vorderbaumen, Abromeit, Sauer, Steffens.

Hibernian: Younger; Higgins, Paterson, Thompson, Plenderleith, Preston, Smith, Turnbull, Reilly, Combe, Ormond.

Referee – M Bronkhorst (Holland)

FLOODLIT CHALLENGE MATCH

19th September 1955 *Easter Road, Edinburgh* 23,569
Hibernian 5 (Ormond, Smith 2, Reilly, Turnbull)
Manchester United 0

Hibernian: Younger; Higgins, Paterson, Thomson, Plenderleith, Preston, Smith, Turnbull, Reilly, Combe, Ormond.

Manchester United: Wood; Foulkes, Byrne, Whitefoot, Jones, Goodwin, Webster, Blanchflower, Taylor, Violett, Berry.

Referee – J Mowat (Rutherglen)

SFL INTERNATIONAL

21st September 1955 *Dalymount Park, Dublin* 16,756
League of Ireland 2 (Gibbons, Fitzgerald)
Scottish Football League **4** (Wishart, Reilly, Collins 2)

LOI: Lowry; Noonan, Crawford, Hale, Keogh, Nolan, D Fitzgerald, J Fitzgerald, Gibbons, Coad, Toby.

SFL: Tommy Younger (Hibernian); Alex Parker (Falkirk), Harry Haddock (Clyde), Bobby Evans (Celtic), George Young (Rangers), Archie Glen (Aberdeen), Gordon Smith (Hibernian), Bobby Collins (Celtic), Lawrie Reilly (Hibernian), Bobby Wishart (Aberdeen), Johnny Hubbard (Rangers).

Referee – W Waldren

INTERNATIONAL

8th October 1955 *Windsor Park, Belfast* 58,000
Northern Ireland 2 (D Blanchflower, Bingham)
Scotland 1 (Reilly)

Northern Ireland: Uprichard; Graham, Cunningham, D Blanchflower, McCavana, Peacock, Bingham, J Blanchflower, Coyle, McIlroy, McParland.

Scotland: Tommy Younger (Hibernian); Alex Parker (Falkirk), Joe McDonald (Sunderland), Bobby Evans (Celtic), George Young (Rangers), Archie Glen (Aberdeen), Gordon Smith (Hibernian), Bobby Collins (Celtic), Lawrie Reilly (Hibernian), Bobby Johnstone (Manchester City), Billy Liddell (Liverpool).

Referee – J Kelly (Chorley)

SFL INTERNATIONAL

26th October 1955 *Hillsborough, Sheffield* 37,778
English Football League 4 (Turner, Lofthouse 2, Finney)
Scottish Football League 2 (Smith, Collins)

EFL: Williams; Hall, Byrne, McGarry, Wright, Dickinson, Finney, Turner, Lofthouse, Haynes, Hogg.

SFL: Tommy Younger (Hibernian); Alex Parker (Falkirk), Andy Kerr (Partick Thistle), Bobby Evans (Celtic), Willie Telfer (St Mirren), Archie Glen (Aberdeen), Gordon Smith (Hibernian), Bobby Collins (Celtic), Lawrie Reilly (Hibernian), Jimmy Wardhaugh (Hearts), Johnny Hubbard (Rangers).

Referee – S Seymour

INTERNATIONAL

9th November 1955 *Hampden Park, Glasgow* 53,887
Scotland 2 (Johnstone 2)
Wales 0

Scotland: Tommy Younger (Hibernian); Alex Parker (Falkirk), Joe McDonald (Sunderland), Bobby Evans (Celtic), George Young (Rangers), Doug Cowie (Dundee), Gordon Smith (Hibernian), Bobby Johnstone (Manchester City), Lawrie Reilly (Hibernian), Bobby Collins, (Celtic), John Henderson (Portsmouth)

Wales: Kelsey; Williams, Sherwood, M Charles, J Charles, Paul, Tapscott, Kinsey, Ford, Allchurch, Jones.

Referee – R Leafe (Nottingham)

EUROPEAN CUP 1955/56: QUARTER-FINAL (FIRST-LEG)

23rd November 1955 *Firhill, Glasgow* 21,962
FC Djurgården 1 (Eklund)
Hibernian 3 (Combe, Mulkerrin, Turnbull)

FC Djurgården: Arvidsson; Forsberg, Gustafsson, Holmstrom, Olsson, Parling, Anderson, Grybb, Eriksson, Eklund, Sandberg.

Hibernian: Younger; MacFarlane, Paterson, Thompson, Plenderleith, Preston, Smith, Combe, Mulkerrin, Turnbull, Ormond.

Referee – A Ellis (England)

EUROPEAN CUP 1955/56: QUARTER-FINAL (SECOND-LEG)

28th November 1955 *Easter Road, Edinburgh* 31,460
Hibernian 1 (Turnbull pen)
FC Djurgården 0

Hibernian: Younger; MacFarlane, Paterson, Thomson, Plenderleith, Preston, Smith, Combe, Mulkerrin, Turnbull, Ormond.

FC Djurgården: Arvidsson; Forsberg, Gutafsson, Edlud, Olsson, Parling, Andersson, Tvilling, Eriksson, Eklund, Sandberg.

Referee – A Ellis (England)

FINAL SFL INTERNATIONAL

30th November 1955 *Idraetsparken, Kobenhavn* 16,000
Danish Football Combination 0
Scottish Football League 4 (Conn 2, Hubbard, Smith)

SFL: Tommy Younger (Hibernian); Alex Parker (Falkirk), Harry Haddock (Clyde), Bobby Evans (Celtic), George Young (Rangers), Archie Glen (Aberdeen), Gordon Smith (Hibernian), Bobby Collins (Celtic), Alfie Conn (Hearts), Jimmy Wardhaugh (Hearts), Johnny Hubbard (Rangers)

THIS GAME IS IN THE RECORD BOOKS AS THE FIRST SCOTTISH CUP-TIE TO BE PLAYED UNDER FLOODLIGHTS

8th February 1956 *Easter Road, Edinburgh* 26,024
Hibernian 1 (Turnbull)
Raith Rovers 1 (McEwan)

Hibernian: Younger; MacFarlane, Paterson, Grant, Plenderleith, Preston, Smith, Combe, Reilly, Turnbull, Mulkerrin.

Raith Rovers: Stewart; Polland, McClure, Young, McNaught, Leigh, McEwan, Bain, Copland, Kelly, McMillan.

Referee – E Youngson (Aberdeen)

CAPTAINS A SCOTLAND TEAM FOR THE 3RD AND FINAL TIME

12th March 1956 *Ibrox Park, Glasgow* 60,000
Scottish Select XI 2 (Reilly, Collins)
Anglo/South African XI 1 (Hubbard)

Scottish Select XI: Younger (Hibernian); Parker (Falkirk), Rae, (Falkirk), Evans (Celtic), Malloy (Cardiff City), Glen (Aberdeen), Smith (Hibernian), McMillan (Airdrie), Reilly (Hibernian), Collins (Celtic), Mitchell (Newcastle United).

Anglo/South African XI: Rudham (Liverpool); O'Linn (Charlton Athletic), Hewie (Charlton Athletic), Purdon (Charlton Athletic), Neilson (Bury), Chamberlain (Charlton Athletic), Davies (Luton Town), Leary (Charlton Athletic), Kitchenbrand (Rangers) Foreman (Brighton and Hove Albion), Hubbard (Rangers).

Referee – J Mowat (Rutherglen)

EUROPEAN CUP 1955/56: SEMI-FINAL (FIRST-LEG)

4th April 1956 *Parc de Princes, Paris* 33,486
Stade de Reims 2 (Leblond, Bliard)
Hibernian 0

Stade de Reims: Jacquet; Zimmy, Giruado, Siatka, Jonquet, Cicci, Hidalgo, Glovacki, Kopa, Leblond, Bliard.

Hibernian: Younger; MacFarlane, Paterson, Thompson, Grant, Buchanan, Smith, Turnbull, Reilly, Combe, Ormond

INTERNATIONAL

14th April 1956 *Hampden Park, Glasgow* 132,817
Scotland 1 (Legatt)
England 1 (Haynes)

Scotland: Tommy Younger (Hibernian); Alex Parker (Falkirk), John Hewie (Charlton), Bobby Evans (Celtic), George Young (Rangers), Archie Glen (Aberdeen), Graham Leggat (Aberdeen), Bobby Johnstone (Manchester City), Lawrie Reilly (Hibernian), Ian McMillan (Airdrie), Gordon Smith (Hibernian).

England: Reg Mathews (Coventry City); Jeff Hall (Birmingham City), Roger Byrne (Manchester United), Jim Dickinson (Portsmouth), Billy Wright (Wolverhampton Wanderers), Duncan Edwards (Manchester United), Tom Finney (Preston North End), Tommy Taylor (Manchester United), Nat Lofthouse (Bolton Wanderers), Johnny Haynes (Fulham), Billy Perry (Blackpool).

Referee – L Callaghan (Wales)

EUROPEAN CUP 1955/56: SEMI-FINAL (SECOND-LEG)

18th April 1956 *Easter Road, Edinburgh* 44,941
Hibernian 0
Stade de Reims 1 (Glovacki)

Hibernian: Tommy Younger; Willie MacFarlane, Jack Paterson, Archie Buchanan, John Grant, Bobby Combe, Gordon Smith, Eddie Turnbull, Lawrie Reilly, Jimmy Thompson, Willie Ormond.

Stade de Reims: René-Jean Jacquet; Simon Zimny, Raoul Giraudo, Robert Siatka, Robert Jonquet, Michel Leblond, Michel Hidalgo, Léon Glovacki, Raymond Kopa, René Bliard, Jean Templin.

Referee – A Sensi (Spain)

WORLD CUP QUALIFIER

8th May 1957 *Hampden Park, Glasgow* 88,873

Scotland 4 (Mudie 3, Hewie pen)

Spain 2 (Kubala, Suarez)

Scotland: Tommy Younger (Liverpool); Eric Caldow (Rangers), John Hewie (Charlton Athletic), Ian McColl (Rangers), George Young (Rangers), Tommy Docherty (Preston North End), Gordon Smith (Hibernian), Bobby Collins (Celtic), Jackie Mudie (Blackpool), Sammy Baird (Rangers), Tommy Ring (Clyde).

Spain: Antonio Ramallets (Barcelona); Fernando Olivella (Barcelona), Marcleino Vaquero Campanan (Sevilla), Jesus Garay (Athletic Bilbao), Martin Verges (Barcelona), Jose Maria Zarraga (Real Madrid), Miguel Gonzalez (Athletico Madrid), Ladislao Kubala (Barcelona), Alfredo Di Stéfano (Real Madrid), Luis Suarez (Barcelona), Francisco Gento (Real Madrid).

Referee – A Dusch (West Germany)

WORLD CUP QUALIFIER

19th May 1957 *St Jacob's Park, Basle* 48,000

Switzerland 1 (Vonlanthen)

Scotland 2 (Mudie, Collins)

Switzerland: Eugene Parlier; Willy Kernen, Harry Koch, Andre Grobety, Iva Frosio, Heinz Schneiter, Charles Antenen, Eugen Meier, Roger Vonlanthen, Robert Ballaman, Ferdinando Riva.

Scotland: Tommy Younger (Liverpool); Eric Caldow (Rangers), John Hewie (Charlton Athletic), Ian McColl (Rangers), George Young (Rangers), Tommy Docherty (Preston North End), Gordon Smith (Hibernian), Bobby Collins (Celtic), Jackie Mudie (Blackpool), Sammy Baird (Rangers), Tommy Ring (Clyde).

Referee – F Seipelt (Austria)

WORLD CUP QUALIFIER AND HIS LAST INTERNATIONAL MATCH

26th May 1957 *Estadio Santigo Bernabéu, Madrid* 90,000

Spain 4 (Mateos, Kubala, Basora 2)

Scotland 1 (Smith)

Spain: Antonio Ramallets (Barcelona); Juan C Quinoces (Valencia), Jesus Garay (Athletic Bilbao), Juan Segarra (Barcelona), Martin Verges (Barcelona), Enrique Gensana (Barcelona), Estanislao Basora (Barcelona), Ladislao Kubala (Barcelona), Alfredo Di Stéfano (Real Madrid), Enrique Mateos (Real Madrid), Francisco Gento (Real Madrid).

Scotland: Tommy Younger (Liverpool); Eric Caldow (Rangers), John Hewie (Charlton Athletic), Dave Mackay (Heart of Midlothian), Bobby Evans (Celtic), Tommy Docherty (Preston North End), Gordon Smith (Hibernian), Bobby Collins (Celtic), Jackie Mudie (Blackpool), Sammy Baird (Rangers), Tommy Ring (Clyde).

Referee – R Leafe (England)

FIRST FLOODLIT MATCH AT TYNECASTLE PARK

7th October 1957 *Tynecastle Park, Edinburgh* 27,000

Heart of Midlothian 2 (Crawford, Wardhaugh)

Hibernian 4 (Preston 3, Baker)

Heart of Midlothian: Marshall; Kirk, Lindores, Mackay, Glidden, Cumming, Young, Murray, Bauld, Wardhaugh, Crawford.

Hibernian: Leslie; Muir, MacFarlane, Turnbull, Paterson, Nichol, Smith, Preston, Baker, Harrower, Ormond.

SUFFERED ANKLE-SHATTERING INJURY FOLLOWING CLASH WITH AIRDRIE DEFENDER

16th November 1957 *Broomfield Park, Airdrie* 8,000
Airdrie 1 (Reid)
Hibernian 4 (Turnbull, Baker, Ormond 2)
Airdrie: Wallace; Miller, Shanks, McPhail, Quigley, Quinn, Reid, Price, Cowen, Sharkey, Duncan.
Hibernian: Leslie; Grant, Muir, Turnbull, Paterson, Baxter, Smith, Harrower, Baker, Preston, Ormond.
Referee – F Crossley

RETURNS TO PLAY – TOO SOON

1st January 1958 *Easter Road, Edinburgh* 49,245
Hibernian 0
Heart of Midlothian 2 (Young, Mackay)
Hibernian: Leslie; Grant, Muir, Turnbull, Paterson, Baxter, Smith, Harrower, Baker, Reilly, Ormond.
Heart of Midlothian: Marshall; Kirk, Thomson, Mackay, Milne, Bowman, Blackwood, Murray, Young, Wardhaugh, Crawford.

HIS FINAL GOAL FOR HIBERNIAN AT EASTER ROAD – DIRECT FROM A CORNER-KICK

18th January 1958 *Easter Road, Edinburgh* 12,000
Hibernian 3 (Baker, MacLeod, Smith)
Falkirk 3 (Moran, McCole, O'Hara)
Hibernian: Leslie; Grant, Muir, Turnbull, Paterson, Baxter, Smith, Frye, Baker, Slavin, MacLeod.

HIS ONE AND ONLY APPEARANCE FOR THE HIBERNIAN RESERVE TEAM, AFTER BEING INJURED FOR 10 MONTHS

1st November 1958 *Easter Road, Edinburgh* 5,100
Hibernian reserves 2 (Thompson, McCalman)
Rangers reserves 2 (Duncan 2)
Hibernian: Wren; Boyle, McCelland, Turnbull, McCalman, Slavin, Smith, Buchanan, Christie, Thompson, Fox.
Rangers: Ritchie; Neil, Liddle, Miller, Paterson, Baird, Duncan, Hogg, Murray, Wilson, Hubbard.
Referee: – W. Mullan (Cardenden)

MAKES HIS LONG AWAITED FIRST-TEAM RETURN

8th November 1958 *Easter Road, Edinburgh* 14,789
Hibernian 4 (Baker 3, Allison)
Third Lanark 4 (Craig, McInnes, Dick, Gray)
Hibernian: Leslie; Grant, McClelland, Baxter, Plenderleith, Hughes, Smith, Allison, Baker, Fox, McLeod.
Third Lanark: Ramage; Caldwell, Brown, Kelly, Lewis, Slingsby, W Craig, R Craig, Dick, Gray, McInnes.
Referee – R Davidson (Airdrie)

LAWRIE REILLY'S TESTIMONIAL MATCH

15th December 1958 *Easter Road, Edinburgh* 6,785
Hibernian 9 (Baker 2, Smith 2, Ormond 2, Turnbull, Fox, McClelland)
International Select 3 (Johnstone 2, Liddell)
Hibernian: Leslie; Young, McClelland, Turnbull, Paterson, Preston, Smith, Fox, Baker, Gibson, Ormond.
International Select: Farm; Grant, McNaught, Docherty, McColl, Peacock, McKenzie, Fernie, Mudie, Johnstone, Liddell.
Referee – J Bissett (Edinburgh)

LAST EVER GAME FOR HIBERNIAN AGAINST HEART OF MIDLOTHIAN

1st January 1959 *Tynecastle Park, Edinburgh* 35,000
Heart of Midlothian 1 (Young)
Hibernian 3 (Fox, Ormond 2)

Heart of Midlothian: Marshall; Kirk, Thomson, Bowman, Milne, Cumming, Paton, Murray, Young, Bauld, Crawford.

Hibernian: Leslie; Grant, McClelland, Turnbull, Plenderleith, Preston, Smith, Fox, Baker, Gibson, Ormond.

364TH AND LAST GOAL FOR HIBERNIAN

31st January 1959 *Starks Park, Kircaldy* 19,000
Raith Rovers 1 (McEwan)
Hibernian 1 (Smith)

Hibernian: Leslie; Grant, McLelland, Turnbull, Plenderleith, Preston, Smith, Fox, Baker, Gibson, Ormond.

LAST HOME GAME FOR HIBERNIAN

28th February 1959 *Easter Road, Edinburgh* 27,300
Hibernian 4 (Aitken 2, Ormond 2)
Partick Thistle 1 (Smith)

Hibernian: Wren; Grant, McClelland, Turnbull, Plenderleith, Preston, Smith, Aitken, Fox, Gibson, Ormond.

Partick Thistle: Ledgerwood; Hogan, Donlevy, Mathers, Davidson, Wright, McKenzie, Thomson, Smith, McParland, Ewing.

LAST EVER GAME FOR HIBERNIAN AND SCOTTISH CUP QUARTER-FINAL

14th March 1959 *Cathkin Park, Glasgow* 18,000
Third Lanark 2 (D Hilley 2)
Hibernian 1 (Ormond)

Third Lanark: Ramage; Caldwell, Brown, Kelly, McCallum, Robb, D Hilley, R Craig, Dick, Gray, McInnes.

Hibernian: Leslie; Grant, McClelland, Turnbull, Plenderleith, Preston, Smith, Fox, Baker, Gibson, Ormond

Referee – R Davidson

SCORING DEBUT FOR HEART OF MIDLOTHIAN

18th August 1959 *Tynecastle Park, Edinburgh* 12,886
Heart of Midlothian Reserves 4 (Walker 3, Smith)
Dundee Reserves 2 (Gilzean 2)

Hearts Reserves: Brown; Ferguson, J Mackintosh, Higgins, Clark, Orphan, Smith, Walker, Dunsmore, Cunningham, W Mackintosh.

Dundee Reserves: R Morrison; Reid, S Morrison, Ryden, Macmillan, Stewart, Penman, Bonthrone, Adamson, Gilzean, Jardine.

FIRST TEAM DEBUT FOR HEART OF MIDLOTHIAN IN THE SCOTTISH LEAGUE CUP

22nd August 1959 *Tynecastle Park, Edinburgh* 35,671
Heart of Midlothian 2 (McFadzean, Young)
Kilmarnock 0

Heart of Midlothian: Marshall; Kirk, Thomson, Murray, Milne, Cumming, Smith, Young, Bauld, McFadzean, Hamilton.

Kilmarnock: Brown; Watson, Cook, Stewart, Dougan, O'Connor, Copeland, McInally, McBride, Henaughan, Black.

Referee – J Barclay (Kircaldy)

INITIAL GOAL FOR HEARTS' FIRST TEAM

26th August 1959 *Pittodrie, Aberdeen* 31,000
Aberdeen 1 (Mulhall)
Heart of Midlothian 4 (Bauld 2, Blackwood, Smith)

Aberdeen: Ogston; Caldwell, Hogg, Brownlee, Clunie, Glen, Ewen, Baird, Davidson, Wishart, Mulhall.

Heart of Midlothian: Marshall; Kirk, Thomson, Bowman, Milne, Cumming, Smith, Murray, Bauld, Blackwood, Hamilton.

Referee – T Wharton

HOME LEAGUE DEBUT FOR HEART OF MIDLOTHIAN

5th September 1959 *Tynecastle Park, Edinburgh* 40,000
Heart of Midlothian 2 (Murray 2)
Hibernian 2 (Baker2)

Heart of Midlothian: Gordon Marshall; Bobby Kirk, George Thomson, Andy Bowman, Jimmy Milne, John Cumming, Gordon Smith, Jimmy Murray, Willie Bauld, Bobby Blackwood, Johnny Hamilton.

Hibernian: Willie Wilson; John Grant, Joe McLelland, John Young, John Plenderleith, Pat Hughes, James Scott, John Frye, Joe Baker, Andy Aitken, Johnny McLeod.

SCOTTISH LEAGUE CUP FINAL 1959

24th October 1959 *Hampden Park, Glasgow* 57,994
Heart of Midlothian 2 (Hamilton, Young)
Third Lanark 1 (Grey)

Heart of Midlothian: Marshall; Kirk, Thomson, Bowman, Cumming, Higgins, Smith, Crawford, Young, Blackwood, Hamilton.

Third Lanark: Robertson; Lewis, Brown, Reilly, McCallum, Cunningham, McInnes, Craig, D Hilley, Gray, I Hilley.

Referee – T Wharton

NEW YEAR'S DAY DERBY GAME

1st January 1960 *Easter Road, Edinburgh* 54,000
Hibernian 1 (Johnstone)
Heart of Midlothian 5 (Young 3, Plenderleith og, Smith)

Hibernian: Jackie Wren, John Grant, Joe McClelland, John Young, John Plenderleith, John Baxter, Johnny McLeod, Bobby Johnstone, Joe Baker, Tommy Preston, Willie Ormond.

Heart of Midlothian: Gordon Marshall; Bobby Kirk, George Thomson, John Cumming, Jimmy Milne, Andy Bowman, Gordon Smith, Alex Young, Willie Bauld, Bobby Blackwood, Johnny Hamilton.

HEARTS – CHAMPIONS OF SCOTLAND

16th April 1960 *Love Street, Paisley* 32,000
St Mirren 4 (Bryceland, Gemmell 2, Baker)
Heart of Midlothian 4 (Young 2, Crawford, Bauld)

St Mirren: Walker, Wilson, Campbell, Doonan, Tierney, Thomson, Rodger, Bryceland, Baker, Gemmell, Miller.

Heart of Midlothian: Marshall; Kirk, Thomson, Cumming, Milne, Higgins, Smith, Young, Bauld, McFadzean, Crawford.

TOUR GAME

1st June 1960 *Wrigley Stadium,Los Angeles* 10,500
Manchester United 0
Heart of Midlothian 4 (Thomson pen, Bauld 2, Crawford)

Manchester United: Gregg; Foulkes, Carolan, Setter, Cope, Giles, Quixall, Violett, Brennan, Pearson, Charlton.

Heart of Midlothian: Marshall; Kirk, Thomson, Murray, Milne, Bowman, Smith, Blackwood, Bauld, Crawford, Hamilton.

TOUR GAME AND 'BATTLE OF THE CHAMPIONS'

9th June 1960 *Varsity Stadium, Toronto* 15,020
Heart of Midlothian 1 (Bauld)
Burnley 2 (Pilkington 2)
Heart of Midlothian: Marshall; Kirk, Lough, Thomson, Milne, Bowman, Smith, Blackwood, Bauld, Crawford, Hamilton.
Burnley: Blacklaw; Angus, Elder, Adamson, Cummings, Miller, Meredith, McIlroy, Pointer, Robson, Pilkington.

EUROPEAN CUP 1960/61: FIRST-ROUND (FIRST-LEG)

29th September 1960 *Tynecastle Park, Edinburgh* 45,000
Heart of Midlothian 1 (Young)
SL Benfica 2 (Aguas, Augusto)
Heart of Midlothian: Gordon Marshall; Bobby Kirk, George Thomson, John Cumming, Jimmy Milne, Andy Bowman, Alex Young, Jimmy Murray, Willie Bauld, Bobby Blackwood, Gordon Smith.
SL Benfica: Pereira; João, Cruz, Saraivo, Germano, Neto, Augusto, Santana, Águas, Coluna, Cavém.
Referee – N Lequesne (France)

EUROPEAN CUP 1960/61: FIRST-ROUND (SECOND-LEG)

5th October 1960 *Stadio do Luz, Lisbon* 30,122
SL Benfica 3 (Águas 2, Augusto)
Heart of Midlothian 0
SL Benfica: Pereira; Angelo, João, Germano, Artur, Neto, Augusto, Santana, Águas, Coluna, Cavém.
Heart of Midlothian: Gordon Marshall; Bobby Kirk, George Thomson, John Cumming, Jimmy Milne, Andy Bowman, Gordon Smith, Jimmy Murray, Alec Young, Bobby Blackwood, Ian Crawford.

LAST GAME FOR HEART OF MIDLOTHIAN

8th April 1961 *Tynecastle Park, Edinburgh* 15,000
Heart of Midlothian 1 (Cumming pen)
Third Lanark 0
Heart of Midlothian: Gordon Marshall; Bobby Kirk, Davie Holt, Jimmy Murray, John Cumming, Billy Higgins, Bobby Ross, John Docherty, Gordon Smith, Alan Finlay, David Johnston.

SCORES ON HIS DUNDEE DEBUT – TOUR OF ICELAND

6th July 1961 *Laugardalur Stadium, Reykjavik* 4,000
KR Reykjavik 1
Dundee 3 (Smith, Penman, Waddell)
Dundee: Liney; Hamilton, Brown, Seith, Ure, Wishart, Smith, Penman, Waddell, Cousin, Robertson.

FIRST GAME FOR DUNDEE IN SCOTLAND

19th August 1961 *Cathkin Park, Glasgow* 12,000
Third Lanark 3 (Harley 2, Wishart og)
Dundee 2 (Smith, Gilzean)
Third Lanark: Robertson; McGilvray, Lewis, Reilly, McCormack, Robb, Goodfellow, Hilley, Harley, Grey, McInnes.
Dundee: Liney; Hamilton, Cox, Seith, Ure, Wishart, Smith, Penman, Gilzean, Cousin, Robertson.
Referee – J Holburn (Edinburgh)

LEAGUE DEBUT FOR DUNDEE

23rd August 1961 *Brockville Park, Falkirk* 7,000
Falkirk 1 (Wyles)
Dundee 3 (Smith, Cousin, Wishart)
Falkirk: Whigham; Rae, Hunter, McCarry, Milne, McIntosh, Wyles, Murray, Lambie, Reid, Ormond.
Dundee: Liney; Hamilton, Cox, Seith, Ure, Wishart, Smith, Penman, Gilzean, Cousin, Robertson.
Referee – A McKenzie (Coatbridge)

HOME LEAGUE DEBUT FOR DUNDEE

9th September 1961 *Dens Park, Dundee* 20,000
Dundee 4 (Penman, Smith, Briggs og, Robertson)
Dundee United 1 (Gillespie)
Dundee: Liney; Hamilton, Cox, Smith, Ure, Stuart, Smith, Penman, Gilzean, Cousin, Robertson.
Dundee United: Ugolini; Graham, Briggs, Neilson, Smith, Fraser, Carlyle, Gillespie, Mochan, Irvine, McDonald.
Referee – J Stewart (Paisley)

VITAL LEAGUE MATCH IN TERMS OF DUNDEE'S SUCCESSFUL SEASON

11th November 1961 *Ibrox Park, Glasgow* 38,000
Rangers 1 (Brand)
Dundee 5 (Gilzean 4, Penman)
Rangers: Ritchie; Shearer, Caldow, Davis, Paterson, Baxter, Scott, McMillan, Christie, Brand, Wilson.
Dundee: Liney; Hamilton, Cox, Seith, Ure, Wishart, Smith, Penman, Cousin, Gilzean, Robertson.
Referee – R Rodger (Stonehouse)

ANOTHER VITAL LEAGUE MATCH

18th November 1961 *Dens Park, Dundee* 15,000
Dundee 5 (Gilzean 2, Wishart, Seith, Smith)
Raith Rovers 4 (Leigh, Clinton, Lourie, Adamson)
Dundee: Liney; Hamilton, Cox, Seith, Ure, Wishart, Smith, Penman, Cousin, Gilzean, Robertson.
Raith Rovers: Cunningham; Wilson, Mochan, Stein, Forsyth, Leigh, Lourie, Adamson, Clinton, Watson.
Referee – E Cowan (Glasgow)

LEAGUE MATCH

25th November 1961 *Easter Road, Edinburgh* 16,000
Hibernian 1 (Stevenson)
Dundee 3 (Gilzean, Penman, Smith)
Hibernian: Simpson; Grant, McLelland, Preston, Easton, Baxter, Fraser, Stevenson, Baker, Kinloch, McLeod.
Dundee: Liney; Hamilton, Cox, Seith, Ure, Wishart, Smith, Penman, Cousin, Gilzean, Robertson.
Referee – W Syme (Glasgow)

LEAGUE MATCH – PLAYED HOURS AFTER A CAR CRASH

13th January 1962 *Tynecastle Park, Edinburgh* 26,000
Heart of Midlothian 0
Dundee 2 (Cousin, Gilzean)
Heart of Midlothian: Marshall; Kirk, Holt, Ferguson, Polland, Cumming, Paton, Elliot, Wallace, Gordon, Hamilton.
Dundee: Liney; Hamilton, Cox, Seith, Ure, Wishart, Smith, Penman, Cousin, Gilzean, Robertson.
Referee – J Barclay (Kircaldy)

LEAGUE MATCH – DUNDEE GO 20 GAMES UNDEFEATED IN ALL COMPETITIONS

24th January 1962 *Dens Park, Dundee* 16,000
Dundee 2 (Gilzean, Penman)
St Johnstone 1 (McVittie)
Dundee: Liney; Hamilton, Cox, Seith, Ure, Wishart, Smith, Penman, Cousin, Gilzean, Robertson.
St Johnstone: Taylor; McFadyen, Lachlan, Little, J Ferguson, Donlevy, McIntyre, Townsend, A Ferguson, McVittie, Townsend.
Referee – J Barclay (Kircaldy)

FINAL LEAGUE GAME AT DENS PARK FOR 1961/62 SEASON

25th April 1962 *Dens Park, Dundee* 20,000
Dundee 2 (Cousin, Penman)
St Mirren 0
Dundee: Liney; Hamilton, Cox, Seith, Ure, Wishart, Smith, Penman, Cousin, Gilzean, Robertson.
St Mirren: Brown; Doonan, Wilson, Stuart, Clunie, McTavish, Henderson, McLean, Beck, Fernie, Millar.
Referee – W Syme (Glasgow)

FINAL LEAGUE GAME FOR 1961/62 SEASON DUNDEE; CHAMPIONS OF SCOTLAND!

28th April 1962 *Muirton Park, Perth* 26,500
St Johnstone 0
Dundee 3 (Gilzean 2, Penman)
St Johnstone: Taylor; McFayden, Lachlan, Little, J Ferguson, Donlevy, McIntyre, Townsend, McVittie, A Ferguson, Thomson.
Dundee: Liney; Hamilton, Cox, Seith, Ure, Wishart, Smith, Penman, Cousin, Gilzean, Robertson.
Referee – E Cowan (Glasgow)

EUROPEAN CUP 1962/63: FIRST-ROUND (FIRST-LEG)

5th September 1962 *Dens Park, Dundee* 23,821
Dundee 8 (Hemmersbach og, Wishart, Robertson, Gilzean 3, Smith, Penman)
FC Köln 1 (Hamilton og)
Dundee: Slater; Hamilton, Cox, Seith, Ure, Wishart, Smith, Penman, Cousin, Gilzean, Robertson.
FC Köln: Ewart; Regh, Sturm, Hemmersbach, Weilden, Benthaus, Thielen, Schafer, Mueller,Habig, Harnig.
Referee – K Jorggensen (Denmark)

EUROPEAN CUP 1962/63: FIRST-ROUND (SECOND-LEG)

26th September 1962 *Müngersdorfer Stadion, Köln* 37,998
FC Köln 4 (Ure og, Habig, Mueller, Schafer.)
Dundee 0
FC Köln: Schumachar; Polt, Regh, Schleninger, Weilden, Benthais, Thielen, Habig, Mueller, Schafer, Harnig.
Dundee: Slater; Hamilton, Cox, Seith, Ure, Wishart, Smith, Penman, Cousin, Gilzean, Robertson.
Referee – A Poulsen (Denmark)

EUROPEAN CUP 1962/63: SECOND-ROUND (FIRST-LEG)

24th October 1962 *Estádio José Alvalade, Lisbon* 45,000
Sporting Clube de Portugal 1 (Geo)
Dundee 0
Sporting Clube de Portugal: Carvalho; Carlos, Hilario, Perides, Lucio, Julio, Hugo, Osvaldo, Mascarenhas, Geo, Morais.
Dundee: Slater; Hamilton, Cox, Seith, Ure, Wishart, Smith, Penman, Cousin, Gilzean, Houston.
Referee – M Faucheau (France)

EUROPEAN CUP 1962/63: SECOND-ROUND (SECOND–LEG)

31st October 1962 *Dens Park, Dundee* 32,956
Dundee 4 (Gilzean 3, Cousin)
Sporting Clube de Portugal 1 (Figuerido)
Dundee: Slater; Hamilton, Cox, Seith, Ure, Wishart, Smith, Penman, Cousin, Gilzean, Robertson.
Sporting Clube de Portugal: Carvalho; Lino, Hilario, Carlos, Lucio, Julio, Figuerido, Osvaldo, Mascarenhas, Geo, Morais.
Referee – E Olsen (Sweden)

SCOTTISH LEAGUE MATCH – DUNDEE'S ALL TIME RECORD SCORE

1st December 1962 *Dens Park, Dundee* 12,000
Dundee 10 (Gilzean 7, Penman, Ryden, Houston)
Queen of the South 2 (Murphy 2)
Dundee: Slater; Hamilton, Cox, Ryden, Ure, Wishart, Smith, Penman, Cousin, Gilzean, Houston.
Queen of the South: Farm; Morrison, Kerr, Irving, Rug, Murphy, Hannigan, Martin, Frye, Anderson, Murray.
Referee – A Crossman (Edinburgh)

EUROPEAN CUP 1962/63: QUARTER-FINALS (FIRST-LEG)

6th March 1963 *Heysel Stadion, Brussells* 64,703
RSC Anderlecht 1 (Lippens)
Dundee 4 (Gilzean 2, Cousin, Smith)
RSC Anderlecht: Fazekas; Heylens, Cornelius, Hanon, Vebiest, Lippens, Janssens, Jurion, Stockman, Van Himst, Puis.
Dundee: Slater; Hamilton, Cox, Seith, Ure, Wishart, Smith, Penman, Cousin, Gilzean, Robertson.
Referee – M Dienst (Switzerland)

EUROPEAN CUP 1962/63: QUARTER–FINALS (SECOND-LEG)

13th March 1963 *Dens Park, Dundee* 38,232
Dundee 2 (Cousin, Smith)
RSC Anderlecht 1 (Stockman)
Dundee: Slater; Hamilton, Cox, Seith, Ure, Wishart, Smith, Penman, Cousin, Gilzean, Robertson.
RSC Anderlecht: Trappeniers; Heylens, Cornelius, Hanon, Verbiest, Lippens, Janssens, Jurion, Stockman, Van Himst, Puis.
Referee – M Dienst (Switzerland)

SCOTTISH CUP 1963: QUARTER-FINAL REPLAY

3rd April 1963 *Ibrox Park, Glasgow* 82,000
Rangers 3 (Hamilton og, Brand 2)
Dundee 2 (Gilzean 2)
Rangers: Ritchie; Shearer, Caldow, Greig, McKinnon, Baxter, Henderson, McLean, Millar, Brand, Wilson.
Dundee: Slater; Hamilton, Cox, Seith, Ure, Wishart, Smith, Penman, Cousin, Gilzean, Robertson.
Referee – J Barclay (Kircaldy)

EUROPEAN CUP 1962/63: SEMI-FINAL (FIRST–LEG)

24th April 1963 *San Siro, Milan* 77,993
AC Milan 5 (Sani, Mora 2, Barison 2)
Dundee 1 (Cousin)
AC Milan: Ghezzi; David, Trebbi, Benitez, Maldini, Trapattoni, Mora, Sani, Altafini, Rivera, Barison.
Dundee: Slater; Hamilton, Stuart, Seith, Ure, Wishart, Smith, Penman, Cousin, Gilzean, Houston.
Referee – V Caballero (Spain)

EUROPEAN CUP 1962/63: SEMI-FINAL (SECOND-LEG)

1st May 1963 *Dens Park, Dundee* 35,169
Dundee 1 (Gilzean)
AC Milan 0
Dundee: Slater; Hamilton, Stuart, Seith, Ure, Wishart, Smith, Penman, Cousin, Gilzean, Houston.
AC Milan: Ghezzi; David, Trebbi, Benitez, Maldini, Mora, Trapattoni, Pivatelli, Altafini, Rivera, Barison.
Referee – L Van Nufell (Belgium)

LAST APPEARANCE AT EASTER ROAD

19th October 1963 *Easter Road, Edinburgh* 11,071
Hibernian 0
Dundee 4 (Gilzean 4)
Hibernian: Simpson; Grant, McClelland, Preston, Easton, Baxter, Scott, Quinn, Baker, Stanton, Stevenson.
Dundee: Slater; Hamilton, Cox, Seith, Ryden, Stuart, Smith, Cousin, Waddell, Gilzean, Robertson.
Referee – H Phillips (Wishaw)

LAST GAME FOR DUNDEE

1st January 1964 *Dens Park, Dundee* 15,000
Dundee 1 (Gilzean)
Aberdeen 4 (Winchester 2, Cooke, Graham)
Dundee: Slater; Hamilton, Cox, Seith, Ryden, Stuart, Smith, Cousin, Cameron, Gilzean, Robertson.
Aberdeen: Ogston; Shewan, Hogg, Burns, Anderson, Smith, Kerrigan, Cooke, Graham, Winchester, Hume.

ONLY APPEARANCE FOR GREENOCK MORTON

18th February 1964 *Cappielow, Greenock* 3,000
Greenock Morton 2 (Smith, McTurk)
Queen of the South 0
Morton: Millar; Boyd, Mallon, McGugan, Kiernan, Strachan, Smith, Campbell, Caven, (McTurk), McGraw, Adamson.
Queen of the South: Ball; Morrison, Kerr, Irvine, Plenderleith, Currie, Hannigan, Elliot, Rodger, Law, Byrne.

FIRST APPEARANCE FOR DRUMCONDRA IN THE FAI CUP (QUARTER-FINALS)

6th March 1964 *Tolka Park, Dublin* 8,000
Drumcondra 1 (Lynch)
Drogheda 0
Drumcondra: Darcy; Whelan, Girvan, Rice, McGrath, Brennan, Smith, Crowzer, Lynch, Morrisey, Ryan.
Drogheda: O'Brien; Bailey, Nesbitt, Byrne, Plaice, Dowling, Emerson, Redmond, McCaffrey, McElroy, McGrath.
Referee – W O'Neill (Dublin)

LAST EVER REGISTERED FOOTBALL MATCH.

19th April 1964 *Powderhall Stadium, Edinburgh* 2,148
All Stars XI 9 (Smith 4)
Showbiz XI 10
All Stars XI: Jimmy Brown (Kilmarnock); Bobby Parker (Hearts and Scotland), Jimmy McColl (Queen's Park), Tommy Gallacher (Dundee and Scottish League), Willie Woodburn (Rangers and Scotland), John Paterson (Hibernian), Gordon Smith (Hibernian, Hearts, Dundee and Scotland), Jimmy Wardhaugh (Hearts, Dunfermline and Scotland), Harry Toff (Mystery deputy for Lawrie Reilly, who was ill), Vic Rickis (Millwall), Haynes (Edinburgh University).
Showbiz XI: Jess Conrad; Old Bailey (Archie Sinclair), Calum Kennedy, Raymond Boyd, Sammy Short, Dixie Ingram, Joe (Jock Weir) Brady, Douglas Cameron, Larry Taylor, Glen Daly, Don Charles.
Referee – Bob Delworth